Luminos is the Open Access monograph publishing program from UC Press. Luminos provides a framework for preserving and reinvigorating monograph publishing for the future and increases the reach and visibility of important scholarly work. Titles published in the UC Press Luminos model are published with the same high standards for selection, peer review, production, and marketing as those in our traditional program. www.luminosoa.org

The Sovereign Poison

The Sovereign Poison

Glyphosate, Poisoncraft, and Regulatory Politics

Tom Widger

UNIVERSITY OF CALIFORNIA PRESS

University of California Press
Oakland, California

© 2026 by Tom Widger

This work is licensed under a Creative Commons CC BY-NC-ND license.
To view a copy of the license, visit https://creativecommons.org/licenses.

All other rights reserved.

Suggested citation: Widger, T. *The Sovereign Poison: Glyphosate, Poisoncraft, and Regulatory Politics*. Oakland: University of California Press, 2026. DOI: https://doi.org/10.1525/luminos.266

Library of Congress Cataloging-in-Publication Data

Names: Widger, Tom author
Title: The sovereign poison : glyphosate, poisoncraft, and regulatory politics / Tom Widger.
Description: Oakland, California : University of California Press, [2026] | Includes bibliographical references and index.
Identifiers: LCCN 2025040257 (print) | LCCN 2025040258 (ebook) | ISBN 9780520426368 (cloth) | ISBN 9780520302396 (paperback) | ISBN 9780520972476 (ebook)
Subjects: LCSH: Glyphosate—Government policy—European Union countries | Glyphosate—Government policy—Sri Lanka | Poisons—Political aspects—European Union countries | Poisons—Political aspects—SriLanka | Pesticides—Government policy
Classification: LCC SB952.G58 W534 2026 (print) | LCC SB952.G58 (ebook)

LC record available at https://lccn.loc.gov/2025040257
LC ebook record available at https://lccn.loc.gov/2025040258

GPSR Authorized Representative: Easy Access System Europe, Mustamäe tee 50, 10621 Tallinn, Estonia, gpsr.requests@easproject.com

35 34 33 32 31 30 29 28 27 26
10 9 8 7 6 5 4 3 2 1

publication supported by a grant from
The Community Foundation for Greater New Haven
as part of the *Urban Haven Project*

CONTENTS

List of Illustrations ix
Preface: The Gifts of Poisons xi

Introduction: Glyphosate, the Sovereign Poison 1

PART I. POISONCRAFT: AN ANTHROPOLOGICAL HISTORY
OF A FIELD OF PRACTICE

1. Poisoncraft: Value and Power in the Noxious and the Good 21
2. The Worlds of European and South Asian Poisoncraft 36
Summary of Part I: The Crafts of Poison 52

PART II. GLYPHOSATE AND THE POISONCRAFT OF
EUROPEAN UNIFICATION

3. Poison and Deceit: Glyphosate and Europe's Polycrisis 57
4. Glyphosate, Bureaucratic Science, and the Idea of Europe 66
5. Regulatory Review and Sovereign Ignorance 80
6. Science and Solidarity for the 500 Million 98
Summary of Part II: Crafting Europe Through Poison Control 110

PART III. THE POISONCRAFT OF SRI LANKA'S POSTWAR RECOVERY

7. Kidney Disease and the Glyphosate Question 115
8. The Poisoned Isle 130

9. In Search of Compound X	155
10. The Presidents' Purificatory Work	170
11. Lions and Sharks: Agribusiness Resistance to the Glyphosate Ban	187
Summary of Part III: The Poisonous Gas of Communal Identity	198
Conclusion: The Cauldron of Poisoncraft	201
Acknowledgments	207
Glossary	209
Bibliography	211
Index	235

ILLUSTRATIONS

FIGURE

1. EFSA's depiction of hazard and risk   73

MAPS

1. Risk Distribution of CKDu in Sri Lanka   132
2. Sri Lanka's Cultural Triangle   133
3. The Mahaweli Development and Irrigation Project   135
4. Areas of Sri Lanka Contested During the Civil War   136
5. Average Levels of Fluoride in Groundwater   137
6. The "Eelam Border"   141

Preface

The Gifts of Poisons

The origin of this book lies in a conversation with Tharindi Udalagama, a friend then working at the University of Colombo, Sri Lanka, sometime in 2013. I was writing the final chapters of my first book, *Suicide in Sri Lanka*. Tharindi was in the process of planning an application for doctoral funding to carry out fieldwork on gender and social suffering in a rural community in the island. I was also carrying out new research on the role of charity and philanthropy in poverty reduction and development processes in Sri Lanka. The fact that these different projects shared a strong common theme—*pesticides*—struck us both as significant and interesting.

Over the course of the twentieth century and into the twenty-first, pesticides had significant impacts on human and environmental health and well-being in Sri Lanka. My doctoral work explored how the widespread availability of pesticides from the 1970s on had transformed an often-nonlethal practice of self-poisoning as a means of expressing and mediating relational disputes into a highly lethal one, by the 1990s driving the national suicide rate to among the highest in the world. My new research on charity was tracking how an emerging epidemic of chronic kidney disease in Sri Lanka's agricultural heartlands, possibly linked with pesticide exposure, was generating new forms of philanthropic focus and activity in the island. And Tharindi's interest was in how those same farming communities had experienced significant social and health challenges since their founding in the 1970s, passing through waves of malarial outbreak, civil war, suicide, and now kidney disease.

As we listed the many ways in which pesticides had brought misfortune to the country, it was a news story that Tharindi had recently read that stuck with me after our conversation. The report had described how producers of the local illicit liquor, the potent and sometimes highly toxic *kasippu*, were known to suspend a bottle of pesticide above the brew during fermentation, believing the drink would absorb something of the essence of the chemical and make it "hotter" (i.e., of greater alcoholic strength). Occasionally the bottle would accidentally spill or fall into the vat, contaminating the kasippu with poison. Rather than waste a batch, kasippu producers might risk selling the liquor anyway, leading to poisoning and even death for unsuspecting customers.

Now, as it happens, the low-income farmers who regularly consume kasippu are also those most at risk of suicide and kidney disease. At the same time, those farmers' livelihoods depend heavily on the use of pesticides (in Sinhala, *thel behet*, "medicine oil") for crop protection. In common with the agrarian precariat the world over, the Sri Lankan farmers that Tharindi and I were discussing were confronted with the everyday paradox that pesticides represent—of simultaneous health, economic, and social reward and ruin. Inspired by the story, I later argued that kasippu fermentation techniques could be understood as a locally grounded practice through which farmers took control of pesticides' slippery status as *ambivalent objects*—things they could afford neither to live with nor to live without (Widger 2014, 2018).

Those ideas subsequently found their way into an application for a Wellcome Trust Society and Ethics Fellowship, which I submitted in 2014. My plan for the "Agrochemical Lives" research project was to develop a "pesticide's-eye view" of the paradox they represent, tracking how politics and ethics change across their life course, from points of production in European industry settings to points of use in the Sri Lankan rice fields, via international and national regulatory bodies. The project would follow paraquat, a highly toxic herbicide the Sri Lankan government had recently banned due to its common use as a suicide method, from the Swiss offices of pesticide giant Syngenta, which produced paraquat, to rural communities, where farmers, confronted with suicide and kidney disease among other concerns, were searching for alternatives to its use. I took up the fellowship at Durham University later that year, happily coinciding with Tharindi's arrival as a PhD student, following the success of her funding application.

Yet, as my fellowship mentor, Bob Simpson (2006), once argued, "You don't do fieldwork, fieldwork does you," and my best-laid plans rapidly transformed as developments in pesticide regulation in Europe and Sri Lanka quickly overtook me. The book that I have eventually come to write is simultaneously much narrower and far more ambitious than I had imagined. In no small way, ethnography involves a process of what Simpson (2020) has more recently referred to as "peripheral vision." Anthropologists develop their insights not through direct observation of the world but through that which they catch in the corner of the eye—the unanticipated, the unplanned, and very often the serendipitous happenings in and of things as they take place around them. My conversation with

Tharindi was one such moment. Three others stand out as being important in the fermentation phase of the present work.

The first took place during a grant development workshop led by toxicologist Michael Eddleston at the University of Edinburgh in 2014. I was presenting my ideas for the "Agrochemical Lives" project and the inherently interesting notion—or at least, so it appeared to me—that pesticides are intrinsically paradoxical. At that time, I had never heard of the Greek *pharmakon*, or remedy-poison (I owe my Durham colleague Andrew Russell for the introduction, which came later), but something that Michael said during the day proved difficult to shake off. Michael was a direct intellectual descendent of Paracelsus, founder of modern toxicology. Paracelsus's contribution to knowledge was summed up in the five little words he is best known for—"the dose makes the poison"—and, as I show later in this book, they can be found lurking at the center of nearly all pesticide controversies. Yet for Michael, what I had found intellectually stimulating was quite mundane: pesticides are only paradoxical so long as you don't calculate the point at which safe exposure becomes dangerous exposure. Insofar as *any* substance can be poisonous when encountered in quantities large enough, pesticides are no more interesting than everyday things like water or salt. This is something toxicologists learn on the first day of their training.

Once it became clear that for toxicologists the paradox of pesticides was entirely obvious, it became an even more enticing anthropological problem. As one of my earliest teachers in anthropology, Maurice Bloch (1998), famously argued, what appears to simply "go without saying" is better understood as the surface of a much deeper and more profound tacit knowledge that rarely breaks into conscious thought but is, for that very reason, fundamental. It was then that I realized my ethnographic study of pesticide lives would need to engage centrally with the questions, what *is* toxicology, and what *is* poison? Furthermore, the Paracelsian tradition that Michael represented was only half the story, because when my research took me to Sri Lanka, I would also encounter Ayurvedic and other local traditions of toxicology for which those questions would produce very different answers.

The second moment that transformed the project was the arrival of an email from another Durham colleague, the human geographer Sarah Atkinson, in which she shared a recently published monograph of the International Agency for Research on Cancer (IARC). This was the document in which the World Health Organization (WHO) had announced its decision to classify glyphosate, the world's most-used herbicide, a Group 2A carcinogen—"probably" cancer-causing in humans (IARC 2015). The verdict set the pesticide and environmental worlds alight. In Europe, the report set in motion a protracted process of glyphosate reauthorization, while in Sri Lanka it added pressure to calls for a glyphosate ban following publication of a separate report linking the pesticide to kidney disease (Jayasumana et al. 2014). That both developments were occurring simultaneously in Europe and Sri Lanka offered an opportunity too good to pass up, so my attention shifted entirely from paraquat to glyphosate.

Regulatory action regarding glyphosate in Europe and Sri Lanka was also happening in real time with significant political changes in those places. When my fieldwork got fully under way in summer 2015, glyphosate's regulatory politics seemed to mirror national and international politics, each increasingly an extension of the other. Arguments taking place over glyphosate regulation in Europe could be understood as just one battle in a wider war about fundamental questions of European supranational sovereignty—which by 2016 led to the UK's vote to end its membership in the European Union (EU). Glyphosate became one more "poison" seemingly threatening European cohesion, alongside migrants and refugees, financial crisis, and resurgent nationalism. In Sri Lanka, the debate over glyphosate had already become deeply embroiled in a presidential election campaign and searching questions about the role of ethnic and religious minorities in a newly unified Sri Lanka following the end of civil war in 2009—questions that too were being debated in the language of poison.

The third moment helped reveal and carry forward the theoretical implications of the earlier moments. It was during a conversation in 2016 with another Sri Lankan colleague, my then research assistant (and later doctoral student), Upul Wickramasinghe, that I began to think more carefully about the relationships between glyphosate, toxicology, and Sri Lankan and European sovereignties, particularly how they were being expressed in and through rhetorics of poison. Upul introduced me to the work of early modern Sinhala poet Alagiyavanna Mukaveti, whom Upul had read during his O Levels. Most Sri Lankan schoolchildren can recite one verse of Alagiyavanna's *Subhāṣitaya* (Well-Spoken Words), which warns against the "poison" of bad people. It's a simple verse and a straightforward metaphor, yet as I show in part 1, when read in the context of Portuguese colonial conquest and Catholic missionizing in which Alagiyavanna was writing, it offers a powerful illustration of what I call *poisoncraft*—the use of poisons in all their material and metaphorical potential to think, to communicate, to act, to live, and to die. Thanks to Upul and Alagiyavanna, the historical correspondence of crises in pesticide regulation and sovereign identity that appeared coincidental in Sri Lanka and Europe began to take on more definitive, and defining, forms.

I say more about the comparative underpinning of this book in the introduction. Clearly, the EU and Sri Lanka are very different kinds of political and bureaucratic entities. However, what caught my attention as my fieldwork progressed was a similarity in emerging political debates in both places. Poisons became *sovereign* in both senses of the word: as objects with properties that seemed to transcend the specific localities in which I and others have studied them and hence could be understood as sovereign unto themselves; and as objects that are involved in the exercise, analysis, contestation, and subversion of sovereign power. The exercise of power through the control of literal and metaphorical poisons through poison-craft became the field of regulatory politics that I set out to describe in this book. The book you are reading thus has its origins in a series of fortuitous remarks and lessons about toxicology—the gifts of poison, if you will—made by friends and colleagues that set off a program of research drawing from social anthropology, science and technology studies, and the history of toxicology.

Introduction

Glyphosate, the Sovereign Poison

On March 20, 2015, the IARC, an arm of the WHO, designated glyphosate, the world's most-used herbicide, a Group 2A carcinogen—"probably cancer-causing." First developed and marketed by Monsanto as Roundup, glyphosate was thus propelled into news headlines around the world, escalating a range of anti-glyphosate movements that had already been taking place at local and national levels. Many of those movements used body burden and biomonitoring techniques to test for glyphosate residues in breast milk, blood, urine, hair, food, water, and soil, consistently showing its presence across a vast array of contexts. One study found that 45 percent of topsoil from a sample of eleven EU countries contained glyphosate traces (V. Silva et al. 2018). Another showed that 60 percent of all bread sold in the UK contained glyphosate (PAN 2013). A particularly well-known study showed that fourteen brands of German beer also contained trace levels of glyphosate (Copley 2016)—sparking heated debates over how this compared with the presence of another, highly toxic, chemical in the same product, alcohol.

During the run-up to a European Parliament debate on glyphosate safety in 2016, the European Green Party invited parliamentarians to test their urine for the chemical. The results suggested that, on average, participants had 1.7 micrograms/liter of glyphosate in their urine—seventeen times higher than the European drinking water norm of 0.1 microgram/liter (Green Party 2016). The Green Party argued the findings showed how "omnipresent this suspected carcinogenic substance is in our lives. No matter your age, sex, or lifestyle, everyone is exposed to this substance. Glyphosate is literally everywhere—in our environment, our food, our beer, our wine and also in our bodies" (Green Party 2016). Responding to growing public concern about the presence of glyphosate in the diet and the environment, Green and left-wing parliamentarians would then pass motions calling for the European Commission to ban glyphosate until its safety had been proven.

Tasked with deciding glyphosate's fate, the European Food Safety Authority (EFSA) found itself at the center of a scandal as its scientific procedures came under scrutiny and accusations of industry interference in its safety review processes flew. Unable to reach consensus on the evidence for glyphosate's cancer-causing properties but with EU agricultural competitiveness indelibly tied to the chemical, the European Commission granted a series of emergency approvals until late 2023, when it finally decided to approve glyphosate for a further ten years. Taking place during a decade of turmoil beginning with the Greek economic bail-out and the Syrian migration crisis and ending in the UK's vote to leave the EU, the case would reverberate at the highest levels of the European establishment. The EU's president, Jean-Claude Juncker, would warn how the seventy-year project of pursuing "ever closer union" was being threatened by poisonous divisions—stemming from money, from migrants, and even from molecules like glyphosate (Juncker 2016).

Meanwhile, on June 11, 2015, the South Asian island nation of Sri Lanka became the first country in the world to issue a total ban on the import, sale, and use of glyphosate-based herbicides. The decision had little to do with the IARC ruling but was a reaction to growing concerns that glyphosate was responsible for an epidemic of chronic kidney disease of unknown etiology (CKDu) affecting agricultural communities. In March 2012, a study cofunded by the WHO and the Sri Lankan National Science Foundation had found traces of glyphosate and other pesticides in two-thirds of CKDu patients' urine. Then, in February 2014, a professor of pharmacology at Rajarata University, Channa Jayasumana, published a hypothesis suggesting glyphosate was binding with heavy metals in domestic well water to form nephrotoxic "glyphosate-metal complexes" (Jayasumana et al. 2014).

For the newly elected Sri Lankan president, Maithripala Sirisena, the 2015 glyphosate ban was a flagship move in his Vasa Visa Nathi Ratak (Toxin-Free Nation) program—the objective of which was to promote "a wholesome agriculture, a healthy population." Accompanying literature stressed the negative health and environmental consequences of Sri Lanka's Green Revolution and the overriding presence of agrochemicals in bodies and landscapes. "Our nation has been poisoned," the government declared. Yet in the face of strong opposition from scientific and agricultural constituencies, who called into question Jayasumana's evidence, the government struggled to defend the ban. For a while, questions over glyphosate's regulatory fate—and pesticide control more broadly—played a central role in national politics, even helping bring about the downfall of three presidents. When the island experienced catastrophic inflation and the near-collapse of food systems after the government halted the import of all agrochemicals in April 2021, the government lifted the glyphosate ban.

In Europe and Sri Lanka, struggles over the regulation of glyphosate were simultaneously struggles over national identity, unity, and calls for chemical sovereignty. European and Sri Lankan legislators found themselves unable to enact glyphosate bans despite growing public calls for action because they were hamstrung by scientific uncertainty, concerns over the impact on agriculture and food security, and strong resistance from industry. As the debate became ever more toxic, it would come to embody for many the limits of sovereign power in Europe's free market and Sri Lanka's marginal position in the global economy. Taking place during a decade of resurgent civic, religious, and ethno-nationalisms in Europe and an increasingly militant Buddhist nationalism in Sri Lanka, debates over glyphosate toxicity would feed from and feed into discourses of social and political toxicity more widely.

By telling those stories together, this book explores the relationships between poison and politics in the modern world. It was no coincidence, I argue, that glyphosate regulation became such a controversial and public matter in Europe and Sri Lanka *when* it did and *how* it did. Both contexts were experiencing political, environmental, and health crises that had at their center fundamental questions of national and ethnic belonging. In each a concern with poison was crucial in the narrative construction of the dangers facing citizens and collectives, with glyphosate taking on the role of a chief antagonist in both locations. Those constructions drew in turn from schools of intellectual and practical knowledge about the dangers of poison in material, metaphorical, and rhetorical forms—ranging from the most recent toxicology of pesticides to some of the oldest examples of toxicology in Eurasian traditions. Linking the poison knowledge of the Ancients and the Moderns in those debates was a long-running concern with poison as an index of value and with poison control as an expression of power.

To help tell this story, I introduce and develop the concept of poisoncraft—the field of cultural ideas and practices spanning poison folklore and professional toxicology, the *mythos* and *logos* of poison. The word *poisoncraft* is a deliberate nod to the many traditions of witchcraft around the world that have noticed the power that lies within poison and the practice of statecraft pursued for the creation and defense of political territories. The ability to acquire and master the crafts of poison, I argue, has always been an important means by which people gain, negotiate, and express power, from the domain of intimate sociality within domestic and kin groups to the rule of populations. In an age of spiraling chemical exposures, when one of the chief responsibilities demanded of modern governments is the effective governance and regulation of toxic dangers, the importance of poisoncraft to achieving chemical sovereignty—understood here as a nation's and citizen's right to determine their exposures—moves to the fore. Thus, I show why a theory of power and governance requires an understanding of poisoncraft—and this holds if we are talking about the governance of persons by and for themselves, the governance of populations by and for others, or the governance of pesticides like glyphosate. To that end, I historicize the contemporary politics of pesticide regulation by showing its relationship to long-held ideas of how persons and their relations and values are made in a world of poisonous dangers. This book includes two case studies of attempts to ban glyphosate in Europe and Sri Lanka during the 2010s and uses those case studies as material to think more expansively about the nature and role of poisons and poison control in social and political life. If poisoncraft encompasses the whole range of ways that poisons feature in modern life, here I am primarily concerned with poisoncraft as it is expressed in the regulatory politics of glyphosate and the professional practice of specialists in poisoncraft—the scientists who test glyphosate's hazards and risks, the bureaucrats who define glyphosate's harms, the politicians and activists who debate glyphosate bans, and the agrochemical companies who seek to evade or influence regulatory control.

GLYPHOSATE: THE UNFORMED OBJECT

Thinking glyphosate historically seems necessary at this time of emergent climate emergency. Ten thousand years of Holocene history, during which human beings were subject to geologic processes, has in a very short period (since the age of European colonialism and the dawn of the Industrial Revolution in Britain) ended with human beings becoming a planetary force. In the Chemical Anthropocene, synthetic molecules have become present in huge quantities in the atmosphere, land, and oceans, contributing to climate change and driving extinction processes (Bernhardt et al. 2017). Biomonitoring research has shown how no part of the globe is free from agricultural, industrial, and domestic chemical synthetics: atmospheric winds and ocean currents have carried chemical waste to the remotest corners of the world and the deepest sea trenches. All creatures born today already carry a cocktail of chemicals in their blood, the contaminants having crossed from parent to offspring during gestation. Among thousands of omnipresent others, glyphosate, the world's most widely used herbicide, is *everywhere*—the anxieties it provokes about total pollution of the planet a product of its own commercial success.

Yet if glyphosate is everywhere, it is simultaneously *nowhere*—evidence of its harms too easily called into question by the inherent uncertainties of environmental science. Anthropologist Vincanne Adams (2023) has called the confusion of contradictory yet often seemingly accurate evidence about glyphosate a "swirl"— a disorientating flock of facts that emerge from the molecule's own history as a chelating agent first and an herbicide second. Scientists, regulators, activists, and farmers all approach glyphosate from different directions, according to whether they are interested in its chemical potentials, its use as a weed killer, its presence in food systems, and its spillage, leaching, and drifting into environments. From this, glyphosate gains multiple possible identities, each one scientifically, medically, and bureaucratically different from the other. Crucially, this means that we cannot take materials like glyphosate as "entities . . . retroactively transhistorical, fixed for all time" (Murphy 2013). They do not lie dormant in the world awaiting discovery but come into being through the coalescence of historically situated modes and ways of acting and thinking.

For anthropologist Anna L. Tsing (2015, 13), the question is "how do gatherings"—focal points within assemblages of human and other-than-human life—"become 'happenings,' that is, *greater than the sum of their parts*?" (emphasis added). Chemical compounds formed by two or more molecules are also *greater than* the sum of their individual elements. Glyphosate, the chemical formula for which is $C_3H_8NO_5P$, is *greater than* carbon (C), hydrogen (H), hobelium (NO), and phosphorous (P), none of which alone or in other combinations offers the same pesticidal properties. The name glyphosate itself is derived from—and *greater than*—the chemical compound of *gly*cine and a *phos*phon*ate* that forms one stage in the creation of $C_3H_8NO_5P$. Glyphosate-based herbicides—that is, the final formulations found for sale on shop shelves, of which there are more than 750 currently on the market, each serving unique applicatory demands and market niches—include glyphosate *plus* a range of adjuvants and are thus *greater than* $C_3H_8NO_5P$ alone.

The industrial-chemical complex that produces, markets, and sells these 750 different formulations—as well as the diverse agricultural customers that buy them; the governments that regulate, restrict, and ban them; and the lobby groups that argue for and against them—are when taken together an "assemblage" (Werner et al. 2022) *greater than* any single producer, farmer, country, or organization, either individually or in unison. Even fleeting combinations of glyphosate's forms create compounds that have social and political presence. For those who engage with glyphosate, for example, as producers, sprayers, regulators, activists, and academics, the herbicide acquires meaning and purpose. Glyphosate yields passionate responses in those who would seek its restriction or continued availability. In this book, I aim for an ethnographically and historically grounded exploration of glyphosate and the traditions of toxicological knowledge available to understand it. Thus, the book is a study of glyphosate as a molecule deeply embedded in social, economic, and political debates of the time—debates that all seemed to lead back, in one way or another, to questions of sovereignty.

CHEMICAL SOVEREIGNTY

From the 1990s to 2008, the assumed inevitability of economic and political globalization, the deterritorialization of markets, and international regulatory harmonization shaped world politics. The order of sovereign nation-states, born in the rubble of World War II but immediately undermined by the parallel development of supranational and global organizations, treaties, and trade deals, would finally give way to a new empire of global capital (Hardt and Negri 2000). At least for those who benefited, in the global North and South alike, it was an Age of Optimism fueled by and fueling a promise of post-boom-and-bust capitalism and, in the Anglo-Saxon world, the managerial politics of Bill Clinton and Tony Blair. Its zenith was the Gulf War, which saw the creation of a corporate-oligarchic state (Kapferer 2005a) in the form of the Iraqi Coalition Provisional Authority that, as a supposedly "transitional government," implemented a program of radical privatization, becoming the clearest example of how capital would drive the new imperial expansion.

The subprime mortgage crisis of 2008 in the United States would cause a global economic meltdown that brought to a halt that Age of Optimism and gave rise to an Age of Toxicity. In response to a new economic precarity, the rise of populist political movements and leaders from across the political spectrum all around the world but exemplified in the election of self-styled authoritarian "strongmen" in Brazil, China, Hungary, India, Russia, Sri Lanka, and the United States, as well as the United Kingdom's vote to the leave the European Union in 2016, signaled a resurgence in the ideology of the nation as the primary unit of political and economic affairs. It was indeed sovereignty, and the demand to "take back control" that became the rallying cry further linking those events. In the popular imagination, all around the world today, sovereignty pertains to a time of independent states comprised of a "people as one" (Lefort 1986)—nations held together by commonalities of language, religion, culture, tradition, and a rejection of multiculturalism and diversity, inclusion, and equality managers.

This theory of the nation-state originally emerged during the seventeenth century in the "Westphalian" origins of international law wherein states were understood to hold exclusive sovereignty over their territory (Ong 2006) and the power of the sovereign authority "to kill, punish, and discipline with impunity" within its borders (Hansen and Stepputat 2006, 295). Yet even then, the world as it was bore little resemblance to the Westphalian idea(l), with colonial powers in part justifying their conquest of other territories precisely because they did not resemble sovereign objects as they understood them (Bonilla 2017). In a reflection of the spirit of the Age of Optimism, the 1990s witnessed the birth of a doctrine of "humanitarian warfare" with interventions in Serbia, Sierra Leone, and Afghanistan, culminating in the invasion of Iraq. In each case, Westphalian sovereignty was expressly ignored when making a case for just war and when creating new states in the aftermath of war.

The truth is that no modern state maps onto the idea(l) of an independent, bounded territory, nor could it ever do. Anthropologists Aihwa Ong (2006) and Franck Billé (2020) have argued respectively for "graduated" and "voluminous" concepts of sovereignty to capture the realities of complex constructions and claims of contemporary states. They include the contested territories of nations like northeastern Sri Lanka during its civil war, the states within states created by international development programs, China's "belt and road" network linking East Asia to South America, and the EU's multilevel structure. What those examples suggest is a post-ontological sovereignty akin to the post-ontological object I described above. This is a sovereignty based on a "tentative and always emergent form of authority" (Hansen and Stepputat 2006, 297) over physical and conceptual territories that are subject to the effects of ongoing revision and reformation in response to local and global pressures.

Scholarship in this area has shown how alongside economic and cultural globalization and a deterritorialization of sovereign power there has been a corresponding localization and reterritorialization of sovereign identity (Deleuze and Guattari 2004a, 2004b; Hardt and Negri 2000; Kapferer 2005a, 2005b). Put another way, as national borders became increasingly irrelevant in economic matters, for some they became increasingly important in matters of local and national belonging (Geschiere 2009). Eschewing approaches to sovereignty that center the right to kill as the primary defining feature of sovereign power, anthropologists Rebecca Bryant and Madeline Reeves (2021, 3) have asked whether "sovereignty may be best understood as a concept mobilizing as-yet unfulfilled communal desires"—desires, for example, that might encompass the recovery of meaning in and for place. Their question, posed at the end of the Age of Optimism, draws together the sometimes breathless claims of global change made over the past decade with the more sober perspectives provided by ethnography. Attending to how normal people in everyday situations think and act with relation to sovereignty shows us how sovereignty is an ongoing project always in the process of creation, negotiation, revision, and reimagination.

Food systems often feature centrally in debates over the loss and reclaiming of sovereignty. Nowhere is the idea that people and place are intrinsically connected more clearly expressed than in movements for local food, slow food, and "food sovereignty." Those movements emerged from and gave form and voice to resistance to the industrialization and globalization of food systems, the holding of intellectual property rights over seeds, the creation of genetically modified plants, and the widespread use of agrochemicals (Edelman et al. 2014). At their core is the demand for farmers to have the right to decide what and how to grow and for consumers to have the right to decide what and how to eat. On one side, then, movements for food sovereignty have typically emerged from an understanding of sovereignty as self-determination over one's own body and one's own community. This is also the notion of the person as an individual who exists within a collective also understood as "one"—that is to say, the same notion found in right-wing populist movements—an often-uncomfortable pairing that features throughout this book.

Food sovereignty also aligns with what might be called demands for *chemical sovereignty*—the right of nations to control the flow of chemicals into their borders. In that construction, nations are conceptualized in similar terms to bodies—as entities in peril from poison attack. Until the first decade of the twenty-first century, pesticide production was largely contained within the Global North, which exported those chemicals to the Global South, which in turn exported food and fiber back to the Global North—a system of exchange referred to as a "circle of poison" (Galt 2008). Moreover, a global hierarchy existed between producing and consuming nations, with northern countries dominating regulatory structures and decision making. International organizations and treaties, including the Organisation for Economic Co-operation and Development (OECD) and the United Nations Environment Programme (UNEP) Stockholm and Rotterdam Conventions, emerged to regulate those exchanges, with northern countries better able to protect themselves from pesticidal harms than countries of the south.

Today such global inequalities remain but are more complex. While northern countries remain influential thanks to their dominance of branded molecules (such as Monsanto/Bayer's ownership of the Roundup trademark), the off-patent "generics" market is being powered from other parts of the world. China has become the world's biggest producer of generic molecules like glyphosate, closely followed by India. Efforts to reduce pesticide use in China are leading Chinese companies to place greater emphasis on export markets. Thus, global pesticide markets are transforming from a North-South-North "circle of poison" to one of zones of regional dominance and competition shaped by and shaping wider geopolitical relations (Berndt et al. 2025; Werner et al. 2022; Galt 2008). Calls for pesticide control at the levels of the local, national, and international trading blocs are often thwarted by the realities of global markets where chemical sovereignty is undermined by divergent regulatory standards between countries.

The emergence of new regimes of pesticide production, consumption, and control in a world where economic and political power is shifting provides the wider background for the anthropology of poisoncraft that I develop in this book. Thus far, I have written generally about the rise of sovereignty politics across the 2010s and the conceptualizations of bodies and borders that appear to give form and meaning to chemical sovereignty movements. But, of course, the world is rather more complex than that—and this is where the contribution of this book comes in. National and international structures and processes of pesticide regulation emerge from long-run ideas of what constitutes a poison, the body it threatens, and what protection from poison entails. Regulation—quite simply an effort to order relations of economic, social, and political life so they adhere to the values of those who call the shots—is thus very often a project that is fundamentally concerned with the shaping of body-poison relations at both the biological and political levels. What people think the benchmark of regularization should be thus reflects their own knowledge and assumptions about how the world is and how the world ought to be.

From this simple starting point, I argue we can think more comprehensively about the nature of and relations between poison and sovereignty in the modern world. Poison's polyvalence as a substance and idea that threatens biological bodies and the body politic both derives from and gives it considerable symbolic potency. As I begin to explore in the chapters in part 1, in this book I'm interested in asking: How does a poison's chemical, social, and political properties emerge from and shape each other? How are sovereign territories understood as being at threat from poison, be they the territories of sovereign or quasi-sovereign formations like postwar Sri Lanka and the supranational European Union? In what ways are the body politic and the bodies of citizens within those formations thus made?

GLYPHOSATE AS BOUNDARY OBJECT

As a poison moving between regulatory territories and traditions of social and political value, glyphosate is what scholars would call a "boundary object," in more ways than one. In the social sciences, the term describes things, concepts, or practices that serve as a point of connection between different social groups while allowing each group to maintain its own interpretation. The term was first introduced by sociologists Susan Leigh Star and James Griesemer (1989) in their study of scientific collaboration, where they described boundary objects as "both adaptable to different viewpoints and robust enough to maintain identity across them" (387). Geoffrey C. Bowker and Susan Leigh Star (1999) further developed the concept in their work on classification systems, arguing that boundary objects help structure and stabilize knowledge across different communities. Similarly, educational theorist Etienne Wenger (1998) explored their role in communities of practice, emphasizing how they bridge different social worlds by providing common ground for knowledge sharing.

Importantly, by creating opportunities for cross-community conversation, boundary objects play a role in generating boundaries themselves. Boundaries are not natural and never fixed, and neither are the positionalities of those who communicate across them; by working with(in) and across them, actors, objects, and boundaries themselves all gain substance and meaning. Thus, boundaries, objects, and actors are often in contention. This was clear in the case of glyphosate. As I have already mentioned, glyphosate is formed in moments of encounter between actors—scientists, regulators, activists, and so on—who work with the molecule in different ways. At the same time, boundaries of demarcation, for example, between corporate and academic science, international and national regulation, sovereign territory, and exposed and unexposed bodies, also come into being through the processes of debate, negotiation, controversy, and contestation that accompany glyphosate. When viewed from this perspective, glyphosate as a boundary object is the outcome of different kinds of scientific and political work—but equally glyphosate is put to work in the construction of different kinds of scientific and political boundaries.

In this book, I explore the boundary making that glyphosate became involved with in relation to the territorial and political boundaries of the European Union and the Sri Lankan nation-state and the bodies of citizens within those configurations. As I explore in part 1, vernacular traditions of poison knowledge coincided in contemporary agrochemical regulation to produce idea(l)s of pesticides and persons rooted in popular Westphalian concepts of the sovereign state, the sovereign body, and the sovereign poison. That is, where the desire to create a supranational sovereignty in and for Europe and the desire to establish the borders of a postwar, newly unified island of Sri Lanka emerged out of traditions of European and South Asian poisoncraft and found contemporary expression in efforts to control glyphosate. As a field of cultural ideas and practices about poison, what I call poisoncraft became a "vehicle ... through which polities ... [would] ... imagine their collective futures" (Jasanoff and Simmet 2017, 751) as they struggled to create and maintain borders around biological bodies and the body politic within and of the European Union and the Sri Lankan nation-state. In the next section, I excavate further the roots of this idea in two classic studies in the anthropology of toxicity.

THE TOXICOLOGIZATION OF SOVEREIGNTY CRISIS

The relationship between poison and sovereignty has been a theme commented on from some of the first anthropological engagements with industrial pollution. Although not stated in exactly those terms, research on the Bhopal and Chernobyl disasters, for example, highlighted how the toxicology of disaster became a chief method through which sovereign territories and identities could be stated and made afresh—that is, how *poison* crafted Indian and Ukrainian bodies. Kim Fortun (2001) showed how scientific, political, and legal work on Bhopal became significant in terms of India's self-positioning as a postcolonial nation emerging as a truly independent actor on the international stage. Nowhere was this more evident than in the debate about who should hold legal jurisdiction over the case, India or the United States. Developing a case against Union Carbide India Ltd would help ensure a voice for those directly affected by the disaster while highlighting India's ability to prosecute complex cases of corporate crime. However, developing a case against Union Carbide Corporation, headquartered in the United States, would hold the parent company to account but in so doing shift legal jurisdiction out of India to the United States. The final decision to try the case in an Indian court thus traded a potentially more far-reaching legal sanction against Union Carbide for a clearer expression of India's sovereignty on the global stage.

In the case of Chernobyl, Adriana Petryna (2002) has shown how the disaster became a crucial means through which the newly independent Ukrainian state could distinguish itself from the Soviet state and position itself vis-à-vis Western Europe. When the nuclear reactor failed in 1986, Ukraine was still five years from independence, which was only achieved in 1991. At that time, some 40 percent of the Ukrainian population received some kind of state welfare. The Soviet state tried its hardest to avoid recognizing the health effects of the radiation leak, for example, by setting the threshold for unhealthy exposure at a dose level that made it almost impossible for anyone to prove radiation sickness. After 1991, the Ukrainian state sought to establish its legitimacy by promising to improve and expand on the Soviet welfare system—principally by enhancing social protection packages for those who were affected by Chernobyl. For ordinary Ukrainians trying to survive in an increasingly difficult economy, the ability to claim "victim" status offered at least one way to keep at bay financial and social hardships. For Western European powers and the US, the move helped distinguish the newly formed post-Soviet state from the Soviet Union as a modern state committed to the rights of its citizens, even if the World Bank and the International Monetary Fund were deeply suspicious of the generous entitlements extended by the state.

Just as claiming legal jurisdiction over Bhopal became an important expression of Indian nationalism, so extending social protections to Chernobyl victims became an important expression of Ukrainian nationalism. Toxic disasters released poisons that damaged Indian and Ukrainian bodies that demanded purification just when the body politic was reforming internally and vis-à-vis their external relations. In both cases, then, toxic disasters provided the contexts and means through which the nation could escape or mark out an era "post-"—an era of "post-post-" colonialism in the case of globalizing India and an era of post-Soviet development in the case of Ukraine. In both cases too, toxicological methods and evidence became a frame through which crisis was understood and responses developed. By mapping exposures at the level of biological bodies within a body politic, popular languages of nationalism drew from toxicological languages, with everyday articulations of national crisis expressed in toxicological terms.

My analysis of European and Sri Lankan efforts to ban glyphosate extends those approaches to show how far the toxicologization of sovereignty narratives can be traced. For example, science historian Noemi Tousignant (2018) has shown how toxicology in Senegal helped give form to the postcolonial nation-state. Operating under conditions of severe resource shortage, the Senegalese toxicologists that Tousignant worked with used "fragments, hopes, and fictions" of toxicological evidence to generate a "landscape of exposure" (5) that was roughly coterminous with the postcolonial state. Their toxicology both identified and constructed a sovereign body in need of protection. In Europe and Sri Lanka, as I show, efforts to rid the body of contaminants have played with the polyvalence of poisons as literal and metaphorical markers of undesirable agents infiltrating the biological body and body politic and taken on a toxicologizing zeal. In both locations, this has been accomplished by establishing territorial thresholds over which incomers are not invited and exposure thresholds beyond which "small numbers" (Appadurai 2006) must not grow.

The double meaning of "threshold" at play in poison control—as a boundary demarcating the outside and inside of bodies and as a quantitative measure of dose toxicity—I shall argue, comprises a key component of the toxicologizing narratives of sovereignty politics as it has emerged over the past decade. During the 2010s, such concerns moved to the forefront of sovereignty debates in the European Union and Sri Lanka. In neither location did decisions over glyphosate emerge from uncontested scientific evidence and clear policy direction. Instead, they represented the most recent expressions of deep fissures in regulatory science and governance in European and South Asian settings that have long struggled with legacies of colonialism, imperialism, and nationalism.

European and Sri Lankan debates over glyphosate regulation became, at root, debates over how relationships between biological bodies and political bodies themselves were to be constructed and understood. In both contexts, too, pesticide control entered the same narrative domain as poison control in other registers, in particular, the health and social dangers presented by minority and migrant groups. In those ways, what I term poisoncraft became deeply embroiled in matters of sovereign governance—a toxicological statecraft, in other words. At its core was a concern with management of sociopolitical compounds and separations—the bringing together of people as one and the division of those who were not one. This book is thus an anthropological exploration of how pesticide regulation has come to be understood within the limited horizon of body-state relations and the effects of that horizon on the politics of glyphosate in Europe and Sri Lanka.

TAKING GLYPHOSATE SERIOUSLY

How should scholars write about contentious subjects, including those where some of the main characters might be, for whatever reason, unlikable? How should anthropologists write about pesticides, which cause such environmental devastation, and the pesticide industry that produces them, which seeks to disrupt efforts to regulate or ban them? While working on this book, I encountered many opinions about *how* I should write about glyphosate. Perhaps predictably, my interlocutors in industry feared I was out to get them. "Will you do a hatchet job on us?" I was asked, more than once. I was more surprised by some environmentalists who, on learning I was also talking with industry, refused to speak with me further. More surprising still was my fellow academic researchers accusing me of "two-sides-ism"—of giving space and time in my writing to industry and its arguments in some naive effort at "objectivity."

Anthropologists who study the environment seem especially prone to being told how they should write—and think—about difficult subjects. Tracey Heatherington (2010), who set out to document local resistance to external environmental projects in Sardinia, was chastised by her environmentalist participants who saw her efforts as a betrayal of the cause. "You cannot be an anthropologist and an environmentalist at the same time!," she was told (4). Likewise, Timothy Choy's (2011) efforts to understand the point of view of urban developers in Hong Kong saw him fall foul of the expectations of the community groups fighting against them. What Choy took as his commitment as an ethnographer to capture all sides of a story as a strategy for *avoiding* such accusations instead landed him squarely in controversy. Mark Anthony Falzon's (2020) desire to listen to and understand

Maltese bird hunters was similarly greeted with incredulity by environmentalists and acquaintances opposed to the sport: "My environmentalist friends resisted the idea that hunting might in some way be made sense of and rationalized. This was so even if the urge of understanding was rooted in anthropology. As they saw it, there were only two legitimate ways of writing about hunting: as folklore or as a primitive practice that had its roots in base urges and ignorance, and that by definition could not be rationalized" (47–48). In those examples, anthropologists sought to defend their work by highlighting their belief that indefensible practices can *be made sense of* if we take the time to listen to opposing views. The reason was not to *explain away* those practices but to *explain* them.

Similarly, my aim in this book is not to explain away the controversies surrounding glyphosate but to explain them—an effort that requires listening to and making sense of the views of European regulators, Monsanto toxicologists, and ultra-nationalist Buddhist scientists. I write within the ethnographic tradition that values *description* as an explanatory and theory-building activity—a case of "showing" through my research what glyphosate is all about and not "telling" readers what I think they ought to think (Candea and Yarrow 2024, 83). In that sense, I do not predetermine my ethnography by choosing to foreground *either* the good deeds of those resisting glyphosate *or* the misdeeds of those defending glyphosate, as if those were the only two possible kinds of anthropology open to me (see Hopkinson 2022). My aim, simply put, is to take glyphosate, and the debates it generates, "seriously."

Taking something "seriously" has become the hallmark of a recent recommitment in anthropology to understanding the world through the concepts of our interlocutors. Following growing interest among anthropologists in the ideas of critical theorists and poststructuralist philosophers, from the 1980s it had become typical for them to explain apparently unexplainable beliefs and practices as a symptom of something else—usually as resistance to inequality, exclusion, and oppression within global capitalism (what anthropologist Shelly Ortner [2016] called "dark anthropology"). The persistence of witchcraft in rapidly modernizing southern Africa, for instance, would be explained as a reaction to the ravages of capitalist transformation. Such an approach, while generative, also risked relegating micro sociocultural practices to the mere epiphenomena of macro political-economic structures, relations, and processes. Two critiques, initially cast in opposition to each other but essentially making the same point, would emerge in response. The first, as part of a wider "ontological turn" (Holbraad and Pedersen 2017) in the discipline, argued that anthropologists should take interlocutors' insistence on the reality of witches literally, to be explained in and through their own terms and not as a symptom of something else, for example, "neoliberalism." The second, as part of a call for a (re)turn to "ethnographic theory" (da Col and Graeber 2011), would stress the importance of paying attention to local concepts and resisting the urge to translate them into whatever fashionable concepts happened to be circulating in anthropology at that point (for a fuller critical engagement with Ortner's thesis, see Robbins et al. 2023).

Taking glyphosate seriously similarly means paying attention to glyphosate's sociocultural properties as a poison. Thus this book is not an exposé of industry misdemeanors, regulatory capitulation, and power relations, although such themes do run throughout. Rather, the book is a sociocultural account of glyphosate and the history of ideas that shape its regulation. My story engages with the history and anthropology of Indo-European toxicologies, understood here not simply as sciences of poison, but as approaches to understanding poison in multiple forms (biological, metaphorical) across multiple registers (scientific, medical, political, etc.). In *The Eurasian Miracle*, anthropologist Jack Goody (2010) argued that since the Bronze Age (ca. 2500–700 BCE) "Western" and "Eastern" societies have been involved in a process of economic, social, and political alternation—a swinging back and forth of centers of gravity and influence, resulting in a dynamic exchange and development of knowledge and ideas across multiple cultural domains. Poison knowledge offers a striking example. We can trace the development of foundational concepts, including the character of poison and the poisoner, from the early Indian texts of Sushruta (ca. 600 BCE) through the later Greek and Arabic writings of Galen (ca. 200 CE) and Ibn Washiyya (ca. 900 CE) up to the Paracelsian and post-Paracelsian toxicologies of modern times. As I describe in chapter 1, David Arnold's *Toxic Histories* (2016) offers a striking account of how that long fascination with poison was pressed into service for political domination in the modern era. As I trace glyphosate's regulatory ups and downs, I also pay attention to how the long history of poison has left its mark on modern toxicology. I thus ask how the past has shaped contemporary understandings of what makes a poison and trace the legacy of what I argue has been a long-running consensus on the ways that Indo-European societies have theorized poisons.

SCOPE AND PLAN OF THE BOOK

Writing an anthropology of glyphosate means drawing together two fields of scholarship that I see as deeply complementary yet have rarely been brought into conversation. The first is research on *toxicity* in the social sciences and humanities, and the second is the social anthropology of *poison*. In part 1, I trace relationships that link the stories I tell about glyphosate in the contemporary era to much older stories about how poison has come to offer a powerful material-semiotic frame for understanding and being in the world. Chapter 1 explores how the emergence of the world religions during the Eurasian Axial Age gave rise to a core duality that persists in the world today: the division between the pure gift and the pure commodity and the poisonous danger that lies in the unreciprocated gift. I argue that this poisoncraft was powerful because it helped regulate social and moral life, including the fundaments of sociality, intimacy, and relationality. I show how the recent fascination with *toxicity*—from toxic chemicals to toxic assets to toxic masculinity—can be productively tied to far older forms of political reasoning and control with and through and for poisoncraft. In chapter 2, I progress to the early modern period and the appearance of modern allopathic and Ayurvedic toxicology in political discourse. Focusing on two personages, a Swiss German alchemist and a Sinhala poet, I locate the origins of contemporary poisoncraft in the theories of bodies and nations that emerged, in unison with toxicology, at that time.

Parts 2 and 3 apply to two case studies of glyphosate regulation the ideas I developed in part 1. Taken together, the case studies show how debates over poison control exposed fundamental assumptions and problems in how the EU and Sri Lanka as sovereign entities, and how citizens' bodies within those entities, were constructed and actioned in regulatory terms. In each location, efforts at bordering Europe and Sri Lanka as physical and sovereign territories were also efforts at coming to terms with glyphosate's status as a boundary object in scientific, medical, and environmental debate. As an extension of the European toxicological body that I explored in chapter 2, I show how glyphosate regulation in Europe turned on an understanding of a "closed" biological body within the "open" borders of the single market, while in Sri Lanka regulation turned on an "open" Sinhala body within a nation "closed" off from minority and foreign bodies. It followed that in the EU the challenge that glyphosate regulation presented was how to prevent the flow of poison at the level of biological bodies so that political borders of the nation-state could remain open—with the aim of creating an open supranational European state. In Sri Lanka, the problem was reversed: how to establish and harden the borders of the national island territory so as to control the flow of poisons for the protection of bodies conceptualized as open. In both locations, however, the relationship between the body and the polity was not pregiven but in active and open contestation and construction. Simply put, *Europe was a polity in search of a body, while Sri Lanka was a body in search of a polity, and in both cases glyphosate helped those searches progress.*

The chapters in part 2 explore the challenges this foundational regulatory principle presented in Europe, where glyphosate jeopardized the unification project. In chapter 3, I discuss glyphosate in relation to the tension that has long existed between the "Two Europes" of the regulatory imagination—of a Europe in harmonious union and a Europe of cooperating but sovereign nations. During the 2010s, glyphosate would become a poison within the European body politic that threatened EU solidarity. In chapter 4, I show how the European regulatory architecture and the division of regulatory labor between European authorities and Member States reflected and reinforced a "molecular bureaucracy" (Hepler-Smith 2019) that turned on an ontological distinction between hazard and risk and the active molecule (glyphosate) and the formulated product (Roundup). While this gave form and function to the EU body, it also struggled to reconcile inherent limitations within that construct. Chapter 5 turns to the science behind the IARC's decision to classify glyphosate a possible carcinogen and the industry's application for glyphosate reapproval in the EU. Exploring this through an analysis of regulatory science writing and review, I show how the European body gained a voice in the pages of the glyphosate Renewal Assessment Report, although it was never clear who, the European authorities or industry itself, was speaking. Finally, in chapter 6, I pay close attention to a special committee established by the European Parliament to investigate the reasons that the EFSA had disagreed with the IARC's conclusion on glyphosate carcinogenicity. I show how the committee was a spectacle of effusive European solidarity, providing a remedy to glyphosate's poison.

Part 3 explores Sri Lanka's troubles with glyphosate in the context of postwar nation building and reconciliation, where glyphosate similarly jeopardized unification. Chapter 7 introduces the epidemic of chronic kidney disease of uncertain etiology (CKDu) to which the glyphosate question became firmly attached. I also introduce the three primary research groups directing CKDu science at this time, which advanced single-factorial and multifactorial hypotheses of CKDu causation, within which glyphosate played, for one group, a major role, and, for two groups, no role at all. Chapter 8 shows how CKDu research splintered in two directions, one asking "where to look" and the other asking "when to look" for the source of the poison. Chapter 9 investigates the Jayasumana hypothesis that led the government to ban glyphosate in 2015 and the development of a nationalist toxicology that underpinned it. In chapter 10, I show how glyphosate became a motivating factor in presidential politics and the role of the president in purifying the newly formed postwar nation. Finally, in chapter 11, I account for how Monsanto's efforts to reverse the glyphosate ban internationalized the debate while giving further force and effect to Sri Lankan demands for chemical sovereignty.

Although written as a book to be read from start to finish, readers can pick and mix according to interest if they so wish. Part 1 is aimed primarily at a more specialist anthropological readership. Those seeking to understand how glyphosate controversies unfurled in Europe and Sri Lanka can skip ahead to part 2 or part 3. I include a short glossary of theoretical terms and abbreviations at the end of the book.

THE POINT(S) OF COMPARISON

The European Union and Sri Lanka are not obvious objects for comparison. In size, scale, history, purpose, and operation, they differ so markedly that there would seem little common ground to do so. But many anthropologists abandoned formal comparison long ago—precisely because, as I showed with respect to molecules and sovereignties, objects evade bounding and hence the classification required for comparative evaluation (Candea 2019; Gingrich and Fox 2002). Yet anthropology remains an inescapably comparative enterprise, in the sense that all ethnographic writing juxtaposes either different ethnographic objects or the ethnographer's experience with the experience of those being studied (Candea 2019). A third form of comparison emerges from what Richard G. Fox (2002, 167) has called studies of "historical transformation"—a method that "aims to understand the interplay of (historical) event and (cultural) structure that leads to variant outcomes." The method is not concerned with the search for general laws of history but "divergent historical processes" that have roots in similar social, political, and economic formations.

This book is comparative in Fox's sense. My inspirations were Sidney Mintz's *Sweetness and Power* (1985), Bruce Kapferer's *Legends of People, Myths of State* (1988), and David Graeber's *Debt: The First 5,000 Years* (2011). By following the transformations of sugar, nationalism, and debt and their roles in world historical processes, they showed how ethnographic materials collected in and of the present link with wider and deeper meanings and practices that emanate from a narrow range of related sources. To those approaches I add a speculative dimension. I agree with the Sanskrit scholar Sheldon I. Pollock (2006, 35) when he argues that "a historical reconstruction of past practices, if considered apart from their potential to affect future practices, is an empty enterprise, however obscure the linkage may be between knowledge, especially knowledge of the past, and practices, especially practices yet to come." I take Pollock's commitment to a future-oriented, speculative historiography as an invitation to practice a reverse *speculative historical ethnography* that links cultural forms over millennia via chains of implicit and explicit signification. Those chains transcend the gulfs of time and space that exist between historical and ethnographic materials that if taken at face value might deter such efforts at all.

What might be called the *speculative comparison* achieved by placing the EU and Sri Lanka side by side is, it turns out, especially productive. It is precisely because they formed such different units that the similarities observed took on significance. It is because glyphosate managed to work its way into political discourse in both that its munificence as a source of meaning and a platform for expression became so apparent. There are two points to the comparisons I make. The first is, after the old anthropological adage, "to make the strange familiar, and the familiar strange." What in the stories I tell might be familiar or strange I leave for you, my readers, to judge, as our positionalities likely differ. However, I certainly want to avoid giving any impression that the problems I report with EU pesticide regulation should be taken as grounds for a more general attack on the European project itself. Likewise, the conflation of glyphosate regulation with an ultra-extreme Buddhist nationalism should not be taken as a wider criticism of Sri Lanka's efforts to protect human and environmental health through pesticide control, which have in the main been incredibly successful. Connecting both are, as I alluded to above, similar efforts to form relations between a concept of the body and a concept of the (supranational) state. Poisons become poisons when they encounter a body to injure; regulation becomes regulation when it has a body to protect. The EU's lifelong search for a "European body" to represent (Shore 2013) and Sri Lanka's postcolonial search for a nation capable of encompassing its ethnic and religious diversity (Kapferer 1988) provide the framework for a comparative analysis of glyphosate control as a form of poisoncraft in pursuit of both.

Second, linking the three parts of this book are threads emanating from multiple points of comparison. They include the shared experiences, opportunities, and challenges generated by glyphosate itself—inter alia, questions of value and power (chs. 1, 2, 6, and 10); pesticide regulation as humanitarian commitment (chs. 3 and 7); configurations of authority, bureaucracy, and risk (chs. 4 and 10); the politics of science writing, review, and publication (chs. 5, 9, and 11); corporate maleficence (chs. 3 and 11); contested science and the problem of consensus (chs. 4, 5, and 10); and the embodiment of glyphosate hazard in the construction of persons (chs. 2, 4, 6, 8, and 11). Each of those subjects could have formed chapters had I written this book in a different way. As it was, the story depends so much on a careful explanation of the specificities of the European and Sri Lankan examples that the case study format was best aligned with my goals. Nevertheless, readers should bear those and other interconnections in mind.

PART I

Poisoncraft

An Anthropological History of a Field of Practice

1

Poisoncraft

Value and Power in the Noxious and the Good

During the first decades of the twenty-first century, everything became toxic. In 2008, toxic assets obliterated global markets. Toxic masculinity sparked the #MeToo movement. Toxic trolls took over the internet. Toxic chemicals saturated our food, products, and air. As anxieties mounted about cumulative exposures from diet, the environment, and social media, a wellness industry promoting detox products, routines, and lifestyle choices would emerge. In 2018, the *Oxford English Dictionary* announced *toxic* its word of the year—chosen, the OED said, because it offered "an intoxicating descriptor for the . . . most talked about topics." It was fitting that the third decade should begin with a pandemic that saw the world locked down, with billions forced to stay at home to help prevent the spread of a deadly pathogen.

What connects the toxic harms of bad debts, violent masculinity, and chemical and viral exposures? Why and how did a discourse of toxicity come to frame them? And how were those toxic discourses related to efforts to ban glyphosate? In this chapter, I argue they all resonated with, and gave explicit form to, deep-seated anxieties in contemporary societies about the invasion and transformation of bodies, persons, and states by noxious agents. In so doing, I approach toxicity in all its material and semiotic potential—a move that leads me away from the word *toxic* and toward the word *poison*. I then go on to narrate a story of poison's social life in Eurasian ethics of exchange, commensality, gender, and anxiety. Through this, I develop an anthropological history of *poisoncraft*—a term that in its fullest sense refers to the ways people think and act with poison across multiple aspects of their lives. Poisoncraft encompasses vernacular and formalized traditions of toxicological knowledge and practice, from science and medicine to witchcraft and magic, as well as the everyday poison lore we all need to navigate a world of toxic dangers.

A key feature of poisoncraft, I shall argue, is how it provides a language and set of tools for understanding and expressing social values and sovereign power. In this book, I focus mostly on the poisoncraft of contemporary regimes of agrochemical governance, regulation, and bureaucratic management, and its emergence from early modern medical, political, philosophical, and artistic expressions in Northwest Europe and South Asia. Thus, the chapter seeks to answer two questions: (1) How does thinking with poison open new avenues for the analysis of toxicants? (2) How does a concept of poisoncraft help us to understand values and power?

THE TOXIC SPECTACULAR AND THE ORDINARY POISON

The term "toxic" appeared in English during the mid-seventeenth century, derived from the medieval Latin *toxicus*, indicating something poisoned or imbued with poison. It is from "toxic" that we derive "toxicant," which means a synthetic poison, as distinct from "toxin," a natural poison. As science scholar Max Liboiron (2017) has argued, to muddle toxicant and toxin is to obscure that difference. Toxin registers plant and animal life that can harm through sting or bite—an evolved defense mechanism for which antidotes are often available. Toxicant registers the industrial-chemical complex that underpins global capitalism and drives environmental devastation on a scale far beyond anything seen before. I understand the spiraling discourse of material and metaphorical threats posed by the synthetic toxicants of industrial modernity as a toxic acceleration of social and political discourse—a rush of events and ideas that captured the popular imagination, inspired by and inspiring an overt toxicologization of societal concerns and agendas. Toxic acceleration is thus one part of the Great Acceleration of the Anthropocene (Steffen et al. 2015)—the rapid upticks in chemical production and pollution that began with the Industrial Revolution. It is also part of key political movements, two prime examples being the events and debates surrounding the UK's vote to the leave the European Union and Donald Trump's "Make America Great Again" campaign, each driven by "accelerationist" thinkers who believed that pushing capitalism's contradictions to their limits would bring down the liberal cosmopolitan order and create a new era of ethnonationalism in its place (Noys 2014).

Toxic acceleration is thus a feature of a world in which many things—scientific and technological development, social and political change, environmental and climate change, and even history itself—seems to be moving faster, to be overheating, to have become *runaway* (Eriksen 2016). Such talk of a "runaway world" is not new; it was used by social theorist Anthony Giddens (1999) to describe globalization and before that by anthropologist Edmund Leach (1968) to describe modernization (both, incidentally, in the BBC Reith Lectures, delivered thirty years apart). That provenance too is illustrative, signaling an anxious turn across Euro-American societies during the second half of the twentieth century that things were getting out of control—that sources of comfort and security were always teetering on the edge of disaster. Theorists of late modernity argued the resulting ontological insecurity of this anxious turn was experienced in ambivalence, a loss of cultural and personal moorings in place and time (Smart 1999). As scientific and technological advances equipped modern societies with the power to destroy the Earth many times over, so with the onward march of progress came a mounting and inevitable peril. Modernity itself represented an existential paradox. Toxic disasters—paradigmatically the explosions at Bhopal (India) in 1984 and Chernobyl (Ukraine) in 1986—were the price to be paid for a comfortable life and for many people represented an inherent contradiction of the contemporary world.

The word *toxic* implies a rush of events and ideas that take the form of a spectacle—literally, the flash and the bang of industrial disasters. But toxicants far more routinely inhabit the level of the everyday, the unremarkable, and the often unremarked. Toxicity seeps imperceptibly into environments, communities, and bodies, only rising to the level of individual or collective awareness after some time—if it becomes known at all. Doubts about the existence, source, and effect of exposure prevents or limits possibilities for remedy (Cram 2016; Dumit 2006; Goldstein 2014; Murphy 2006). To live with toxicity is to live with uncertainty, itself a toxic state of being (Auyero and Swistun 2009). The ordinariness of the toxic signals the presence of something else at work in the play of meanings the word evokes. In his book *Writing for an Endangered World* (2003), Lawrence Buell argued that an emerging "toxic anxiety" found in contemporary literature reflected the public's growing fears of the chemical hazards of modern life but also what he called "deeper-rooted habits of thought and expression" (30). For Buell, toxic anxiety hinted at the presence of longer-run fears of the noxious in social life. A decade earlier, sociologist Ulrich Beck (1992) had also argued that people's understanding of chemical risks represented a continuity of fears of malevolent agents and forces. Dangers of the "risk society," Beck suggested, were "bringing about a kind of new 'shadow kingdom', comparable to the realm of the gods and demons in antiquity" (72). While for both Beck and Buell there was no simple line to be drawn between the terrors of the shadow kingdom and the toxic harms of modern life, neither was there no line to be drawn at all. Toxic acceleration did not herald a break from past understandings of the noxious but involved the persistence and often escalation of long-run ideas about poisonous perils.

To help think between fears past and anxieties present, I find it helpful to dispense with the word *toxic*, with its ultimately limited connotations of industrial capitalism and modern synthetics, and embrace instead the historically and socially expansive word *poison*. Poison, like something toxic, is a substance that harms and an index of the negative. In the hands of murderers, conspirators, or the witch, throughout history poison has enjoyed a sinister reputation—as a silent agent threatening the integrity of bodies, kingdoms, states, and empires (Arnold 2016; Burney 2006). Yet, unlike toxicity, which carries wholly negative connotations, poison is simultaneously a substance that helps and an index of the positive. In the hands of the healer, the champion, and the aesthetic, poison becomes auspicious—whether in the form of a medicine, a means of proving one's strength, or a way of gaining insight into the world beyond sight (Schulke 2017). Across societies, cultures, and languages, poison has provided a lexicon for talking about relations of sociality, value, and power. The point I want to stress is that if toxicity became a driver of and motif for a world of acceleration, it did not cause a rupture from the poisonous past.

A focus on poison allows anthropologists to tell stories that cohabit the world alongside the industrial-chemical complex. From research on botany, pharmacology, and the use of psychotropics in ritual through Evans-Pritchard's (1976) classic account of the Azande "poison oracle" as a divinatory material to the many ways they have speculated on the poisonous nature of social and political relationships, anthropologists have developed theory from detailed studies of poison in material and ideal forms. The extent of the ethnographic record on poison is extraordinary. The Human Relations Area Files, a digital anthropology archive hosted at Yale University, contains over 6,100 mentions of poison from 320 cultures around the world.[1] ("Toxic," by contrast, has only 295 mentions.) Despite this, there has never been a serious effort to develop an anthropological approach to this ubiquitous topic. The remainder of this chapter explores just a little of what anthropologists have had to say about poison, with attention to where it has been used as a means of regulation. Focusing on the poisons that arise between persons in contexts of economic exchange and social and domestic intimacy, I show how the varied and multiple crafts of poison—poisoncraft—have frequently played a central role in the ways in which persons, bodies, and relations are comprised and understood.

ORIGIN STORIES

The story of poisoncraft that I would like to tell begins in that expanse of land and cultures spanning East Asia to Europe, some four thousand years ago. This is the story of a Eurasian history of ideas about the relationship between the noxious and the good that over two millennia came to produce theories of what comprises poisons, poisoners, and the poisoned body within an increasingly narrow frame, establishing lasting codes of moral and political conduct and the means to govern such conduct. At the beginning of this story, the practitioners of poisoncraft—healers, assassins, sorcerers, rulers—made very little distinction between poisons in their material, moral, magical, and metaphorical forms (Levey 1963,

---

1. The archive is not without its critics, who point out, for example, how it separates human social groups into seemingly homogeneous "cultures" and apply Anglophone and Western-centric definitions to Indigenous terms and concepts. Nevertheless, the project provides important and useful access to the ethnographic record of world societies.

1966; Rao 1968). Poisons included animal venoms and plant toxins as well as the immorality, cruelty, and ritual pollution that could be found in living things. Those who knew the (often-secret) arts of poison were thus masters of the whole range of forms in which poison could manifest, which they placed in rank order from the pure and good to the polluted and evil. Poisons and poisoners were also intrinsically ambiguous in both character and conduct—and difficult to detect and to stop. Poison was often gendered female, with poison a companion of dangerous feminine power (Arnold 2016). By the end of my story, the practitioners of poisoncraft—toxicologists, regulators, agrochemists—drew sharp lines between rational and irrational beliefs in poison. It was only very recently—from around the sixteenth century—that poisoncraft specialists began to draw strict lines between literal and metaphorical poisons, the natural and the cultural. The most basic assumption of modern toxicology would become the idea that quantitative measurement can distinguish, in objective and final terms, the hazardous from the safe.

Yet the history of poisons that the contemporary practitioners of poisoncraft have liked to tell, at least those in the biomedical tradition, is mostly concerned with a progress narrative. In introductory textbooks, medical toxicologists present themselves as the inheritors of the poison knowledge of the Ancients, but one that thanks to modern developments has become a rationalized and objective science. As Richard Lane and Jospeh Borzelleca, in *Hayes' Principles and Methods of Toxicology*, explain things, "It is more difficult to capture the breadth of the history of toxicology than any other single discipline because it undoubtedly began before recorded history, is found throughout recorded history, and is intertwined with so many important aspects of human life such as eating, healing and medicine, occupation, religion, folklore, murder, and suicide" (2008, 3). Toxicology's origins lay in a basic human appreciation of the dangers that reside inherent in things. For example, Patricia Frank and Alice Ottoboni (2011, 31) speculated on how knowledge of poisons must have been acquired through rudimentary observation and experimentation: "The fact that certain substances could cause acute illness or death was known to even the earliest human populations because it was so obvious—the cause-effect relationship was so direct. . . . The possibility that traces of arrow toxins might be present in the flesh apparently did not concern primitive hunters. Meat obtained in such a manner today would probably not be accepted by the public." The theory that "prehistoric people" acquired poison knowledge by observing cause and effect, yet apparently did not notice that meat killed with poison could be dangerously contaminated, is pure speculation—a somewhat lazy guess at what the world must have been like before modern toxicology arrived on the scene. In her study of purity and pollution taboos, anthropologist Mary Douglas (1966, 37) quipped that it would be a shame if Leviticus's famous dietary rules were nothing more than the pronouncements of a public health administrator—if there was nothing more to learn from ritual avoidance than how to deal with food in hot climates. How toxicologists write about their own history is similarly disappointing. I suggest there is more to say about modern toxicology than that it represents the pinnacle of progress in culinary hygiene.

In its most basic manifestation, the toxicologists are surely right when they say their science is simply a form of ordered knowledge about the harmful or helpful properties of materials and processes. Yet even when viewed in that way, modern toxicology necessarily involves a value judgment—"one person's food is another's poison," as the old saying goes. And in fact, modern toxicology is little more than an attempt to resolve that compelling and inescapable paradox—that there is nothing good in the world that does not also contain something rotten, and the very worst poisons carry the seed of a gift, a remedy for ill. The Greeks have a word for this, *pharmakon*, or remedy-poison, though the principle long predates that one expression. The principle of the pharmakon has frequently formed the basis and focus of poisoncraft in past and present times, wherever and whenever it has been found.

From ancient China to the Greco-Roman world, toxicology and pharmacology, for their practitioners the craft of applying poisons and remedies, were inseparable pursuits (Kaufman 1932; Gould-Martin 1978; Maskiell and Mayor 2001a, 2001b; Li 1960). Healers were by necessity experts in the treatment of poisons because their pharmacopia built from materials with inherent toxicity (Rao 1968; Sigerist 1961). A small number of foundational texts, several of which merely codified existing toxicological knowledge probably already millennia old, established the theoretical parameters and therapeutic recommendations that would persist in only slightly altered form through to the eighteenth century (Levey 1966). From the middle of the twentieth century, in the guise of allopathic toxicology, poisoncraft became the dominant science of the new world of chemical dangers. Yet it drew deeply from the medical and political history of the pharmakon, even as new assessments of toxic risk called for the development of complexity science that exceeded the simple dualism of the remedy-poison. That toxicology flourished as a discipline in the modern era indicates the extent to which governance of the contemporary world would come to require a specialist knowledge of poison. Throughout history, the act of distinguishing poison from remedy has fundamentally been an act of power—a way of dividing and classifying the world into, for example, "good" and "bad." But as I have also suggested, this is an act that is never settled: the good can be bad and the bad can be good, depending on circumstance.

GIFTS AND POISONS

Poison has always provided a powerful motif for one of the longest struggles of Eurasian societies—of sorting out the good from the bad, the light from the dark. From the dawn of the world religions between the eighth and third centuries BCE—a period philosopher Karl Jaspers (1953) called the Axial Age—across Persia, India,

China, the Levant, Greece, and Rome similar modes of reasoning about the human condition emerged (Goody 2010). Philosophers, sages, prophets, and spiritual radicals of all kinds—including Zoroaster, Confucius, Buddha, Mohammed, and Jesus—began pondering the universalities of human existence, including the nature, purpose, and goals of ethics and morality. They explored the foundations of what would become the entire history of Eurasian thought that still shapes the contours and limiting horizons of the modern world—the dualisms that would seem to structure and constrain the human mind and the realms of political, social, and economic possibility, among them egoism and altruism, profit and charity, and calculation and impulsiveness.

For anthropologist David Graeber (2011), this story only makes sense when coupled with the story of the invention of coinage and the possibility of impersonal market exchange. The Axial Age was a time of growing literacy and cross-border trade and population movement far beyond the scale of everyday human lives. People could begin to imagine and believe in large-scale, complex societies made up of thousands or even millions of people who they would obviously never know. Markets functioned precisely in this manner: they were simultaneously local and translocal, governed by rules and practices of buying and selling that existed and persisted across known and unknown time and space. As goods became commodities, people became disassociated from goods, and both became nodes in a lengthening chain of exchange the start and end points of which no single person had any direct knowledge or experience. It was to this issue that the Axial thinkers kept returning. What did the emergence of the market—the domain of impersonal people, things, and exchange—mean for society? Was there a corresponding form of personal exchange that could temper its antisocial predations?

The answer was that adjoining the material world of narrow self-interest was an expansive world of common human being, of the immaterial soul, and of enlightened disinterest. Aesthetic detachment, taken to its fullest in Buddhism but found to greater or lesser degrees in all the world religions, became the stated remedy for the vice of material attachment. "The ultimate effect," writes Graeber (2011, 249), "was a kind of ideal division of spheres of human activity that endures to this day: on the one hand the market, on the other, religion." Alongside the spread of the market and religion as twinned concepts, institutions, and modes of practice, then, was the spread of a wider set of ideas about the nature of people and the world that would fit into the foundational dualisms implied by the Axial religions. As Graeber points out, "Pure greed and pure generosity . . . [were] . . . complimentary concepts; neither could really be imagined without the other" (249). Those ideas would help regulate human behavior to temper the excesses of the market through a habituation of moral and ethical conduct (Parry 1986).

Poisoncraft offered the means by which the regularization of such moral concerns and principles could occur. In *Toxic Histories*, historian David Arnold (2016) reflects on the mobile nature of poisons and their forms of knowledge across the Eurasian world. For Arnold, poison exhibits a special quality, being at once highly universalized, thanks to its biochemical properties and effects on bodies, and highly localized, through how such effects would be felt, understood, and responded to within distinct knowledge traditions. Coupled with its own dualism, in the form of the remedy, poison provided Eurasian thinkers with a generalized language for reflecting on a universalizing human nature but one that also had meaning within particular worlds where poisons were encountered. Like the peoples and things with which poisons had traveled, Arnold suggests, "we could ... think of poison diasporas, in which toxic plants and minerals, poison practices and poison lore have migrated or been knowingly transferred from one region of the world to another, taking on a virtual universality of their own" (2).

The most influential set of ideas came from Indian toxicology (which itself would have been borrowed and developed from earlier sources). In India, poison was central to social life, playing a role in the historical and mythological narratives that shaped understandings of religion, politics, and persons. "The conceptualization of poison as a universal negative," Arnold writes, "a coruscating, life-destroying principle in dialectical opposition to the nectar of purity and virtue, coursed through Indian religious imagery and permeated idioms of the everyday" (2016, 20). The sixth century BCE Indian Ayurvedic text, the *Suśruta-saṃhitā*, about which I say more in the next chapter, was itself steeped in pharmakon thinking. The *Samhita*'s ostensible author, Suśruta, made clear that an acute poison could become an effective drug if properly administered and a valuable drug, if not administered properly, could become an acute poison (Bhishagratna 1911; Wujastyk 2001). From that text the idea traveled widely. Classical sources tell us how, for instance, Asclepius, son of Apollo, learned from the centaur Chiron the art of *pharmaka*—the proper use of substances that can heal or harm—and in so doing mastered the secrets of health that involved the extraction of good from noxious things (Sigerist 1961). Centuries later, Ibn al-Washiya's *Book of Poisons*, the eighth century CE foundational text of Arabic medicine, helped introduce the pharmakon to new audiences from Mesopotamia to East Asia, Scandinavia, and northern Europe (Levey 1966). Eventually, the idea ended up in the hands of a young alchemist in Reformation Germany, who, in seeking to solve the paradox of the pharmakon, invented modern toxicology—a story I also tell in the next chapter.

Nowhere was the logic of the pharmakon clearer than in the paradox represented by the gift. Across the Axial world, the ideology of the "pure" gift that asked for no return but that nevertheless obliged the receiver to repay or to pass on the gift became paradigmatic of the tensions that sprang from the demarcation of market and religion as zones of interested and disinterested action, as anthropologist Jonathan Parry (1986) has argued. As every anthropology undergraduate learns, even the gift given with no thought for reward places the receiver in an indebted and unequal position vis-à-vis the giver. For anthropologist Marcel Mauss, whose book *The Gift* ([1925] 1990) remains the foundational text on this topic, that apparent contradiction of the supposedly "free" gift was taken as a universal feature of the gift itself. Revealingly, Mauss used the example of the High Germanic languages to press home his point. He wrote that the "danger represented by . . . [the gift] . . . is doubtless nowhere better sensed than in the very ancient Germanic law and languages. This explains the double meaning of the word Gift in all these languages—on the one hand, a gift, on the other hand, a poison" (62–63).

Mauss's observation that certain European languages used the same word for gift as they did for poison has not received the attention it perhaps deserves. Mauss himself thought it was only of passing curiosity. He dismissed the value of considering the etymology of *gift* in the Latin and Greek *dosis* (lit., "dose of poison"), as "this etymology presumes that High and Low German dialects would have preserved a learned name for a thing in common use" (122). Mauss, however, did accept that both the Latin "and above all the Greek use of the word *dosis*" suggested that "with the Ancients too, there was an association of ideas and moral rules of the kind we have been describing" (122)—what anthropologist F. G. Bailey, in *Gifts and Poisons* (1971, 24), described as a recognition "that some exchanges are co-operative and others are competitive: *all* exchanges have the seeds of both these opposed things within them" (emphasis in original).

Sometimes the poison in the gift exists beyond metaphor and has substantive biochemical effects. Parry (1994) used the example of the Hindu religious gift of *dan* to demonstrate where a poisonous substance could flow between giver and receiver. In his study of Brahman priests in the city of Benares, who received dan in exchange for their funerary labors, Parry described how it "embodies something of the bio-moral substance of the donor—something nasty at that[,] . . . the blood and excrement of the donor, or merely his 'sins'" (133). The Brahman who received dan opened himself like a "'sewer' or 'drain' . . . through which the moral filth of his patrons is passed." It was thus essential that the Brahman pass the gift on—if not, then "the priest's intellect is enfeebled, his body gets blacker and blacker and his countenance loses its 'lustre' with every gift received. He is liable to contract leprosy and rot; to die" (124).

While the poison in the dan is not representative of the dangers that may lurk in Hindu gifts (or any other) (Copeman 2011; Gregory 1992; Osella and Osella 1996; Raheja 1988; Snodgrass 2001), there has remained among anthropologists a general agreement that "gifts wound" (Douglas 1990). Work on highly modern gifts, for example, blood and organ donation (Copeman; Konrad 2005), as well as examples of philanthropy and development aid that have promoted the use of agrochemicals in the Global South (Birn 2014), has made explicit reference to a gift's hazards. These may take the form of a poison that lies hidden in the gift, for example, contaminated blood or an organ rejected when the body's immune system treats it as an invasive presence (Ibrahim 2014), or a poison that constitutes the very nature of the gift itself, such as seed-pesticide packages donated to farmers that trap them in an agrochemical "treadmill" (Nicholls and Altieri 1997). Similarly, recent work on global capitalism and its responses to inequality, poverty, and environmental damage has engaged precisely with the question of how to deal with the pharmakon-like ambiguities, ambivalences, and uncertainties of development and global health interventions (Benson and Kirsch 2010; Dolan and Rajak 2016; Russell and Widger 2018).

One might object that the anthropological literature on gifts and poisons has emerged from a limited Maussian reading of the perils of exchange—that is, of the *inequalities* between the givers and receivers of gifts. While not altogether unfounded, I argue that it is more accurate to read Mauss himself as articulating a long-running concern within Eurasian societies about the regulative potential that lies in poison, as indeed his recalling of the poison knowledge of the Ancients would suggest. Expressed as sociability's *other*, poison's affordances lie precisely in its highly mobile and manipulable character as a moral and ethical signifier of relational inequality, hierarchy, and exploitation, *as well as* its signifier of virtue and the good. A gift may contain poison, while poison may contain a gift. Each contains the possibility of the other and as such remains inherently indeterminant and ambiguous. When viewed that way, gift-giving becomes an example of poisoncraft, understood as the art of manipulating poison's inherent potential to do right and wrong. Steeped in ambiguity and ambivalence, poison also provides a description for a world out of balance—one that, despite its wide variety of local expressions, has ensured people have remained fascinated with it. When one starts to look, it turns out the ethnographic record is replete with such examples, scattered and unconnected throughout the literature though they may be. In the next section, I introduce four examples and use them to piece together the outline of the basic concerns of poisoncraft that turns on problems of relational intimacy, gender, and fear.

VALUE AND POWER

My starting point, which happens to be outside the Eurasian world, is anthropologist Nancy Munn's (1986) study of shell gift exchange on the Papua New Guinea island of Gawa, part of the famous kula ring of the Trobriand Islands (Malinowski 1922). On Gawa, Munn explains, value was understood to emanate from activities related in some way to the gifting and receiving of shells. All such acts began with the gifting of food, which constructed and extended social relations into the wider network of islands that participated in shell exchange. The result was a value system premised on an idea of motion, with men's potential to exchange shells the result of their active mobility across the island world. As Gawan men's ability to attract and exchange shells of ever-increasing value grew, so their fame grew. Within Gawan society, however, importance was placed on the absolute equality of social relations. Thus, shell exchange and the precepts of social order pulled in contrasting directions—one toward a hierarchy based on value creation and fame through shell exchange, the other toward egalitarianism based on modest displays of one's "lightness" and ability to travel. Men whose fame outgrew the bounds of social acceptability would come to fear the jealousy and envy of others, which manifested in a fear of witches. Always unknown and unseen, witches were an ever present source of negative valuation in Gawan society. She (for witches represented feminine power) worked her dark magic by poisoning food, corrupting the ultimate source of men's value and fame—the origin of masculine power, in other words—which was his lightness and motion.

Fears over material success and the witch's poison exist in many other societies. Among the Dechen Tibetans, for example, concerns about parasitic others stealing one's wealth manifests as a fear of kin, neighbors, or visitors wielding *duk* (poison) (da Col 2012). Such fears turn on the giving and receiving of hospitality, which, like gifts, can be extracted and exploited for self-gain without thought for appropriate recognition or return. Both those who would offer and those who would accept hospitality are at risk of poisoning, depending on how they approach the relation, that is, with good or malevolent intent. One particularly threatening manifestation of poison fears is again the witch, who for the Dechen symbolize the negation of moral norms of hospitality. As in the Gawan case, the gendering of poison and the poisoner is also important in this example. Women, as the keepers of the hearth and domestic realm, figure as the provider of hospitality on which the male world of economic relations beyond the household turns, and hence women can become the source of disruption to it through poisonous feminine power (Diamond 1988).

In a similar formulation, Georgina Ramsay's (2016) ethnography among Congolese refugees seeking asylum in urban Uganda shows how women confront displacement insecurities through food insecurities, including fears that food may have been poisoned by neighbors. Congolese refugees live in camps alongside other displaced people from often very different social backgrounds, forcing them to negotiate complex daily interactions with other camp inmates. Relational and cultural distance manifests in what Ramsay terms disruption to "cosmological flow" wherein the taken-for-granted logics of their home social worlds no longer hold in the camp environment. Again, it is women, as primary caregivers and hence those who seek out and prepare food for meals, who in this case operate at the forefront of this disruption to daily life. In the context of refugee camps, however, fear of poison is not directed toward dangerous individuals per se but instead toward a generalized other. In Ramsay's ethnography, it is thus women who adopt responsibility for avoiding the poisons of camp life to protect themselves and their children and restore cosmological security.

Finally, Bambi Chapin's (2014) ethnography of childhood socialization in a Sri Lankan village explores how mothers imbue moral lessons through the imparting of poison fears. Culturally inappropriate emotions like jealousy, envy, and greed are indexed to poison. Children are taught to avoid desiring what their friends might have, for example a tasty treat, by warning them of *aes vaha* (eye poison), which can cause their friend to suffer a stomach-ache. In a similar fashion, envious talk can transfer "mouth poison" (*kata vaha*) to the subject of conversation, causing them harm. Through such warnings, children—especially girls—learn to regulate their own behavior and hence the flow of poisons across their kin and friendship groups. In my own work, I have explored how these moral injunctions can lead to acts of self-poisoning. When children fail to avoid displays of jealousy, envy, or greed, they may be scolded by parents or others, which can cause children to feel *lajja* (shame). A shaming accusation may then be countered by the child through the consumption of poison that not only harms the child but also rebounds on the one who scolded them, causing them to feel shame in return (Widger 2012, 2015a). Poison in the guise of envy or greed thus gives material form to poison in the guise of a toxic substance, and both give expression to, and mediate, relations of shame and counter-shame. It is this, I have argued, that has given rise to the extraordinarily high rates of (especially *female*) self-poisoning and poison suicides in Sri Lanka over the past five decades (Widger 2015b).

While I could go on, my point is not to provide a litany of examples of poison practice drawn from the ethnographic record but instead to highlight three common themes: (1) the relationship between poison and commensality (the sharing of food); (2) the gender of the poison (and the threat of and to femininity); and (3) the prevalence of poison anxieties as a response to social disturbance, dislocation, and change. Those themes indicate how poison is theorized by people in diverse societies as a uniquely gendered threat to sources of value and the ambivalent power held by those who have capacity to either disrupt or protect those sources— what might be glossed as the perils of intimacy (Geschiere 2013). Each of the four examples suggests how threats to the social order turns upon the management and control of feminine power, specifically *witchcraft*, understood as both the source of and the threat to sociality, as well as the threatening presence of the witch and the threatening presence of poison (which can often amount to the same thing) to the substance—food—that sustains sociality.

(1) Commensality and Poisoning

Anthropologists widely agree that the sharing of food lies at the heart of human sociality, through which kin and community become "one" (Mintz and Du Bois 2002). In a survey of commensality practices around the world, anthropologist Maurice Bloch (1999) argued that poison, a substance so easily concealed in food and drink, acts as the negative of social relations that can be formed by taking from the same pot. If, as Bloch suggested, kinship and commensality are "cosubstantiated"—an idea(l) of common kinship invites the sharing of food, and the sharing of food invites idea(l)s of common kinship—then to risk being poisoned by others is both an expression of a commitment to kinship and a risk that comes with being related to persons that one might not fully like or trust. Drawing from his research among the Zafimaniry of Madagascar, Bloch described how prior to attending a feast laid out by relatives or strangers, Zafimaniry take "protective medicines" to defend against poisoning. Indeed, to offer or to accept an invitation to share food is a test of group solidarity: "Will you dare to eat with me and become one?" (1999, 145). Ethnographies of commensality and its other—the rejection or poisoning of food—shows us how poison requires intimate relations to exist between people, and it is those same intimate relations that poison betrays by so doing (see also Manderson 1981; Harrell-Bond 1978; Stevens 2000). Poison thus exists as a pharmakon of relations, simultaneously affirming and denying sociality.

(2) The Gender of Poison

Throughout most of known history, the practice of homicide and suicide by poison, each a denial of sociality in its own right (Widger 2015c), has overwhelmingly been cast as a feminine practice. Often this has been explained away as women resorting to a "weapon of the weak" (M. de Alwis 2012)—for example, one of the few choices available to a wife seeking to escape a violent abusive husband (Burney 2006). The same kind of argument has been made for why women tend to choose a "soft" method of suicide like poison, which may or may not result in death, in contrast to the "hard" and deadlier methods of hanging, jumping, or shooting more typically favored by men (Jaworski 2014). More widely, the relationship between poison and powerlessness is often drawn in the numerous examples where behavioral patterns would seem to suggest such a linkage—slaves poisoning their masters; servants poisoning their employers; subjects poisoning their kings (Arnold 2016; Bryson 2013; Tropp 2002; Helfield 1995; Gillin 1934). Precisely for this reason, all the great works of toxicology of the ancient world were primarily concerned with the protection of the *male* sovereign from the *female* poisoner and with the insidious power of female poison, cast often as the witch, to threaten the (male) body politic (Banerjee 2000; Ostling 2013).

From the early twentieth century, however, the gender of the poisoner and the poison victim, as well as the relation between them, dramatically changed (Arnold 2016). With the rise of industrial society, pollutants manufactured by corporations (typically owned or led by men) poisoned populations often located far away from their headquarters—with women, children, and people of color now the victims (Cole and Foster 2001). Geographic and social distance replaced domestic and familial intimacy as the defining relation between the poisoner and the poisoned (even while toxicants themselves continued to be experienced at an intimate level) (Chen 2012); the bodies of the powerless replaced the bodies of the powerful as those in danger of poisoning. At this point, the body in danger, previously cast as male, was feminized, racialized, and often infantilized. Alongside this, a concept of the people as sovereign, manifest in a commitment to "public health," came to replace the close relationship that had previously existed between toxicology and the protection of the king as sovereign.

(3) Poison Anxieties

The transformative effects of modernity on the gender in and of the poison are significant. Nevertheless, they should not distract from the persistence of an underpinning logic. The figures of witches and mothers are, of course, also joined by a pharmakon-like dualism in their own right: witches are to poison as mothers are to remedy. Preindustrial and industrial societies have foregrounded one or the other, but in both cases at stake has been women's sexual and reproductive capacities—twisted and corrupted in the case of the witch, becoming twisted and corrupted by industrial poisons and their effects on reproductive health in the case of modern women. The paradigmatic example of the latter is found in the growing fears across modern societies of the effects of endocrine-disrupting chemicals on bodily health, causing pregnancy troubles and fetal deformities in women and falling sperm counts and gender-bending "feminization" of men (Langston 2010). Evidence for this is controversial (Shotwell 2016) but as such merely points to how the relationship between gender and poison remains as potent today as it has ever been. All this would seem a long way from the feasts of the Zafimaniry—until one remembers the toxicity of the global food system, which, from farmland drenched in pesticides to processed foods pumped with chemical additives, represents one of the main accelerators of such health crises and moral panics.

POISON'S TIMEFULNESS

This returns me to where I started, so here I will conclude. As I suggested at the beginning of this chapter, the rapidly growing interest in toxicity among anthropologists and other scholars has engaged with some elements of what a focus on poison might invite but far from all of it. What for Mauss was just an interesting historical correspondence between the words *gift* and *poison* can better be thought of as a material effect with "force" (Bennett 2004) in the Axial world. Insofar as the patterns of poison practice I have described have been found across diverse contexts, it is perhaps common to the point of near-ubiquity, at least in Axial societies where dualistic thinking, for example, about the poison and the remedy, has structured thought and practice. This thinking only grew in significance as the poisoncraft of the Ancients traveled to the Moderns and the logic of the market became the dominating frame for all social and political action. Poison provided the material medium for describing and explaining the paradoxes of that world premised on a strict duality of self-interest and altruism, and poisoncraft became the set of social and political practices available for their regulation. From the cosubstantiation of kin in food sharing practices to the "chemo-socialities" (Shapiro and Kirksey 2017) that join people and things in toxic environments, poisons have always been understood as a vital relation in the making up of persons, bodies, and collectives.

By adopting this view, I do not seek to assign to poison the status of a cultural universal that has persisted out of time. Instead, I think of poison as a material and an idea that is *timeful*. In his evocative history of the modern fascination with ancient trees, environmental historian Jared Farmer (2002) argues that *elderflora*, trees that are centuries or even millennia old, are revered not because they are timeless but because they have the capacity to evoke past times and the passage of time, linking fleeting human lives with ancient and deep pasts of human civilization and geologic time. What Farmer calls the "more-than-human" time of trees is, then, a *timefulness* that extends beyond the ticking of a tree's biological clock—many times slower and deeper than a human's clock—to encompass the polytemporality of elderflora that endure across times.

Similarly, I think of poison as enduring across times, forming relations between the present age of synthetic toxicities and the past age of natural toxins (many of which derive from trees, of course). In that sense, poisons are overflowing with timefulness, inspiring a mindfulness in those who think and act with poisons and a temporal disposition that exceeds the present. Poison is not a long-*standing* but a long-*running* concern of human being. I make this distinction because *standing* implies rigidity and stasis, while *running* implies flex and change. Poison is a long-running topic of human thought, discourse, and action—a constant source of threat and inspiration that continues to provide a ready and potent material and metaphor for living and understanding lives that must always seek to reconcile, in some way, the noxious and the good in all things, but one that always adapts to new times, new environments.

Fear of poison simultaneously negates and is created by the ambivalent intimacies of relations and inequalities of reciprocity within them. Toxicology is thus a form of knowledge that exists at once as a science on par with other formalized knowledges and an everyday poisoncraft that helps people understand the implications of relations they have entered. The poisoncraft that regulates the everyday involves the habitation of that world of danger in and through logics of the noxious and the good—a practice of valuing and creating value in and of the world that would also become part of statecraft. Poisoncraft would thus become the governance of social life through knowledge and manipulation of poisons—a craft that has often been controlled by, or for, those with the power to produce and control the flow of poison. After all, what are food hygiene certificates but a way of saying, "You can dare to eat with us"? And just as restaurants may be placed in rank order according to how much of a threat they pose to customers' health, so poison as an index of value is also an index of hierarchy—a subject I explore in the next chapter.

2

The Worlds of European and South Asian Poisoncraft

A well-established principle in the social sciences is that values index hierarchy. We tend to place higher value on those things that matter to us and lesser value on those things that don't. Hierarchy also therefore indexes value; things with an elevated status in society are more greatly valued than those with a lower status (Dumont 1970, [1980] 2013; Graeber 2001; Hickel and Haynes 2018). Through a study of European and South Asian traditions of medical toxicology—by which I mean simply forms of poisoncraft developed and applied for the treatment of ill health and disease—in this chapter I show how the governance of poison played a role in shaping the status and value of modern persons and things in two times and places, fifteenth-century Reformation Europe and sixteenth-century colonial Sri Lanka,[1] that have significance for my ethnographic studies in parts 2 and 3. I focus on two personalities, Philippus von Hohenheim (1493–1541), a Swiss German alchemist, and Alagiyavanna Mukaveti (1552–1625), a Sinhala Buddhist poet. Unknown to each other and with no good reason to offer a comparison of their lives and works save for each man's writings on poison—which even then were of entirely incomparable quantity and concern—their thought nevertheless helps us understand how European and South Asian traditions of poisoncraft provided a language and framework for leading a moral life during challenging times.

While I delve into the specificities of each case, keep in mind the generalities that were then shaping the world. As chains of material and cultural exchange grew ever longer and more complex, so ideas of what constituted society, morality, and power changed with them. It was a time when previous certainties—of the

---

1. I use the modern name "Sri Lanka" to refer to the island and "Sri Lankan" to describe its peoples rather than the Portuguese name for the island, "Ceilão."

nature of the divine, of royal authority, of human being, and of ethics and politics—were questioned and new ideas arose. Key within this was the emergence of new theories of difference and similarity—value, status, and hierarchy—between persons. Civil wars and wars between nations produced a wealth of thinking on the constitution of bodies and states and the nature of political subjects. In Europe, economic and religious change led to the rise of an egalitarian ideology premised on the notion of the person as an individual with legal rights and freedom to enter into a contract in a market of individuals. In South Asia, hierarchy, most obviously in the Hindu caste system and associated forms found in other religious and ethnic communities, persisted in the face of colonial conquest and absorption into proto-capitalist markets (Dumont 1970). Within that milieu of social, political, religious, and scientific transformation and continuity there arose two key questions, which I explore in this chapter: (1) What kind of social and political order could or should toxicology imagine, and (2) What kind of body did poison threaten? As will become evident, in Reformation Europe and colonial South Asia toxicological ideas and rule through poisoncraft fused with theological and political ideas to give new expression to such idea(l)s.

"ALL THINGS ARE POISON": TOXICOLOGY FOR A WARRING EUROPE

On an unknown day late in 1493, Philippus Aureolus Theophrastus Bombastus von Hohenheim was born. His father was a German chemist and physician, his mother a Swiss bondswoman in the abbey of the village in which he spent his first years of life. Initially educated by his father, clerics and nuns subsequently schooled the young Philippus. At the age of sixteen, he traveled to the University of Basel to study medicine and then moved to Vienna and finally the University of Ferrara in Italy from which he may have earned a doctorate in 1515 or 1516. In 1522, Philippus joined the Venetian service as a military surgeon, a posting that saw him travel between the many Venetian wars waged in Holland, Scandinavia, Prussia, Tartary, and the Near East. Later, as an itinerant physician and sometime journeyman miner, he wandered through Germany, France, Spain, Hungary, the Netherlands, Denmark, Sweden, Poland, and Russia.

Philippus's movements were not always by choice. He was famously difficult, arrogant, and rude—an infamous drunk prone to brawling whose antics forced him to decamp at regular intervals. Once established as a physician in Basel, Philippus took every opportunity to antagonize and reject the classical Galenic canons that were so essential to medical and scientific education at that time, especially what he called "untested theory" (Ball 2006, 36). The commitment of the age to introspection as the only pathway to knowledge was at odds with his belief that "the patients are your textbook, the sickbed is your study" (Ball 2006, 38). Philippus invited barber-surgeons, alchemists, apothecaries, and others traditionally not welcome in academic halls to speak—a move that saw him ejected from his post after less than a year. The English word *bombastic*, which means to be "marked by or given to speech or writing that is given exaggerated importance by artificial or empty means," is said to be derived from Philippus's middle name, Bombastus (*Merriam-Webster* online). He died at forty-nine, "misunderstood by the world, embittered and poor" (Deichmann et al. 1986, 207), following a tavern punch-up.

Readers may know the character I have been describing by his adopted name, Paracelsus, after the second-century Greek philosopher, Celsus. The grandeur of his name was entirely in keeping with his propensity for self-promotion, which during his life and after his death has led many to dismiss him as a fraud—and just as many others to embrace him as a visionary. I prefer to think of Paracelsus as a figure whose very life and character embodied the poisoncraft that he developed, which warned of the dangers of excess and safety of moderation, a philosophy he singularly failed to observe in himself. As Paracelsus once wrote, "I am different, let this not upset you" (Grandjean 2016, 127). "But people did get upset by Paracelsus," reports Philip Ball (2006, 1), one of Paracelsus's many biographers. "He upset doctors and priests, he upset town authorities, Renaissance kings and princes, Lutherans, humanists, merchants, apothecaries and theologians. He upset his friends and his assistants. He upset generations of chemists and physicians who lived under the grotesque, distorted shadow that he cast. They are all still getting over it."

After Paracelsus, the ancient arts of medicine would never be the same. Paracelsus spearheaded the emerging chemical philosophy of the fifteenth and sixteenth centuries, which ensured that rapidly evolving alchemical ideas persisted in mutual relationship with the biology and physics more traditionally seen as the driving forces of the Scientific Revolution (Debus 1977; Debus and Walton 1998). While the claims that Paracelsus set in motion the great disenchantment of the world by foregrounding observation and rationality may have been overstated (Webster 2002; Bennett 1997), his influence on modern constructions of the regulated self was profound (and no less enchanted for it). Philosophers and historians of science may have stressed the modern incomprehensibility of his ideas (Hacking 2002; Weeks 1997), but Paracelsus remains a figure of widespread interest among scientists, alchemists, and spiritualists to this day.

The Creation

Science historian Allen Debus (1977) was among the first to draw attention to the crucial role that Paracelsus and his followers played in shaping the development of modern scientific thought. As a forerunner to biochemistry and medical chemistry, Paracelsus argued that alchemy was the true medical science and that the direct observation of, and experimentation with, chemical processes would yield extraordinary results. For Paracelsus, "Primary observations in nature would lead directly to further observations in the chemical laboratory or to analogies based upon them" (Debus 1977, 55), through which could be grasped the macrocosmic and microcosmic processes affecting health. Paracelsus added an alchemical spin to the biblical story of Creation in his *Philosophia ad Athenieses*, published in 1564. There he speculated on the existence of a primal matter, the *mysterium magnum*, from which all other "mysteries" of Creation were formed (55). God was "likened . . . to a chemist who separates one thing from another": "First the elements were formed, then the firmament was separated from the fire. Further separations resulted in spirits and dreams (from the air); water plants, salts, and marine animals (from water); wood, stone, land, plants, and animals (from earth)" (56). If God was the alchemist of the macrocosm, then within man resided a host of lesser alchemists, the *archei*, or life-forces, responsible for regulating bodily health. Crucial to Paracelsus's thinking was the belief that "like treats like"—that measured exposure to the cause of illness itself offers a cure, what would come to be called *immunization*. This marked a transformation from Greek medicine that emphasized the therapeutic potential that lay in the administration of opposing forces—for example, the application of cold substances to counter heat in the body, or of sour foods to counter illness caused by sweet foods. For Paracelsus, illness was thus no longer defined by an understanding of the healthy body as comprising a balance of its internal substances but its *invasion by* physical matter whose origins lay external to the body.

Paracelsus's medical theory would give the body itself a distinctive new form, now defined *in opposition to* what lay outside the body and threatened to penetrate the body. He employed a language of poisoncraft when he described the work of the archei, which he believed "separated the useful from the nonuseful substances applied" to the body. The most important of the archei resided in the stomach, through which many external agents entered the body to upset the functioning of specific organs. He wrote, "A person eating meat, wherein both poison and nourishment are contained, deems everything good while he eats. For, the poison lies hidden among the good and there is nothing good among the poison. When thus the food, that is to say the meat, reaches the stomach, the alchemist is ready and eliminates what which is not conducive to the well-being of the body" (*Paramirum*, quoted in Debus 1977, 59).

The Dose and the Toxic Threshold

The most enduring of Paracelsus's ideas appeared in his *Carinthian Trilogy*, published in 1564. Written as an attempt to impress the Carinthian Diet, which had refused to give him shelter after an unsuccessful attempt to take up his ancestral estate in Switzerland (the locals reportedly wouldn't have him), *The Third Defense* of the *Trilogy* became Paracelsus's most famous work. Its main thrust was a defense of his decision to treat syphilis with mercury, a deadly poison. It developed the divine origins of poison, a substance gifted to man from God, one that was entirely appropriate to use in medical applications by those who had mastered the proper knowledge. For Paracelsus, God's creation was difficult or even impossible to understand but never without purpose. Even noxious things created the seeds of something good, for they were an expression of God's divine plan. Thus, Paracelsus stated, in the Germanic where the word for "poison" doubles as the word for "gift":

> Alle Dinge sind Gift, und nichts ist ohne Gift, allein die Dosis macht dass ein Ding kein Gift ist.
> (All things are poison, and nothing is without poison, the dosage alone makes it so a thing is not a poison.) (Cited in Deichmann et al. 1986, 212)

Often shortened simply to "the dose makes the poison," this brief sentence in *The Third Defense* is undoubtedly the best-known piece of writing to have emerged from the age of the chemical philosophers. What mattered to Paracelsus was the threshold level of exposure—the point at which the inherent threat of all things becomes activated and a danger to health. With this, Paracelsus established what philosopher Alexis Shotwell (2016, 103) has referred to as a "hinge proposition on which whole arguments, practices, and ways of understanding the world turn." As I describe below, the whole architecture of modern pesticide regulation now turns on the notion that "the dose makes the poison"—a notion repeated by the chemical industries as the first and the last line of defense against attacks on their products. More importantly for my purposes here, however, is the relationship that Paracelsus established between the knowledge to discern and manipulate poison and power. His medical toxicology was the craft of harnessing poison's properties for one's own ends. The knowledge and skill required to do so singled out the emerging class of modern medical toxicologists as holders of unique and divine powers—qualities that have resonated across the ages for all those who manipulate poisons. This is as true for pesticide companies today as it was for Paracelsus five centuries ago.

The Two Kingdoms

Paracelsus was not specific about what constituted a poison. For him, all things—not only drugs, medicines, or remedies, but people too—were poison. "He was thinking of a general phenomenon," argued Deichmann and colleagues (1986, 212). In this wider view, Paracelsus the alchemist retreated and Paracelsus the theologian moved to the foreground. His poisoncraft was never restricted to the treatment of physical disease but extended to guidance on the navigation of the values of life, contributing to the emergence of an ethic of the governance of the self that characterized the time of the Protestant Reformation.

Paracelsus was a contemporary of the German monk Martin Luther, with whom he has often been compared (Ball 2006). Paracelsus was not actually like Luther in many respects. While Luther preached temperance, Paracelsus drank and fought. However, both men went against the traditions of their respective fields and incurred the wrath of the religious and medical establishments. And despite their revolutionary zeal, both men, paradoxically, proffered a central message of moderation. Historian Andrew Weeks (1997, 14) has argued that "Paracelsus as well as Luther saw ubiquitous strife in the world: a mixture of the good with the poisonous in nature; or the struggle of the warring kingdoms of Satan and Christ." The puritanism found in Luther and the Protestant Reformation was crucial for Paracelsus's poisoncraft, just as Paracelsus's empiricism, his questioning of Galenic authority, and the resulting secularism of his worldview (Ball 2006) played a role in the development of Luther's Protestant ethic. If moderation became the means and ends of Protestant virtue, then Paracelsus's toxicological equivalent, which focused on the management of dose as a means for corporeal protection, meant that his science also offered the tools by which Lutheran moderation in social and spiritual could be measured, tested, and expressed.

Given Paracelsus's reputation for bombastic behavior, the extent of his legacy in this regard is perhaps even more surprising. Paracelsus's *Third Defense* was not simply a retort to critics of his medical prescriptions; so were his philosophical prescriptions and indeed his ethical conduct. When Paracelsus asked, "What is there that is not a poison?," he was including that which was in him—and is in all of us. His poisoncraft postulated a radical separation of poison from remedy, with the ambiguous pharmakon resolvable through precise measurement of dose. His work helped set in motion the great disenchantment of superstitious medical traditionalism that paved the way for medical modernity, which would also separate man from nature and the body from its environment.

A Poisoncraft of Relations

Paracelsus's poisoncraft had an impact on European social and political philosophy, both directly and indirectly. This was a time when philosophers were trying to reconcile their understandings of religion and science, man's place in nature, and the meaning and potential of joy and happiness. Ideas explored during this period would help to define the nature and extent of persons and nations. Two areas where his thought took hold were the developing fields of modern ethics and theories of sovereignty.

A Paracelsian theory of poison provided the seventeenth-century Dutch philosopher Baruch Spinoza (1632–77) with a conceptual frame for understanding the origin and effects of evil in the world. He thought that God was not a distinct being but was contained within the entirety of nature itself. How could evil exist in such a world if that was the case? His answer, simply put, was that evil was the disintegration of the relation between man and God. For Spinoza, minds and bodies were not separate entities but two distinct attributes of a single substance—God, which was also Nature. Spinoza's ethics sought to understand the forms of relation that existed between those attributes of minds and bodies (Deleuze 1998). Two possibilities existed, a "composition" of *compatible* minds and bodies that formed a "more powerful whole" and a "decomposition" of *incompatible* minds and bodies that destroyed each other. Spinoza argued that we experience the effect of composition and decomposition as "joy" and "sadness," respectively. From compatible relations was derived all that was good in the world, while from incompatible relations was derived all that was evil.

Spinoza most clearly expressed his thoughts in what philosopher Gilles Deleuze (1998, 43) called his "letters on evil." In these letters, Spinoza reinterpreted the biblical story of Adam and the poisoned apple, asking what God's words to Adam, "Thou shall not eat of the fruit . . .," meant. As Deleuze interpreted Spinoza, "The anxious, ignorant Adam understands these words as the expression of a prohibition. And yet, what do they refer to? To a fruit that, as such, will poison Adam if he eats it. This is an instance of an encounter between two bodies whose characteristic relations are not compatible: the fruit will act as a poison; that is, it will determine the parts of Adam's body" (22). That Spinoza was able to find an example of modification of bodies in poison is, of course, more than coincidental. Poison, when cast as a negative value, harms the body and corrupts its relations. According to Deleuze, Spinoza was "categorical on this point: all the phenomena that we group under the heading of Evil, illness, and death, are of this type: bad encounters, poisoning, intoxication, relational decomposition" (22).

In fact, Spinoza, who lived a century after Paracelsus and who cultivated many of the seeds of rationalism the alchemist had planted, drew from and shaped the new poisoncraft then emerging. Paracelsus's toxicology offered Spinoza a ready language for expressing ideas of good and evil that turned on a radical separation of poison from remedy. As Deleuze (1988) would characterize it: "The good is when a body directly compounds its relation with ours, and, with all or part of its power, increases ours. A food, for example. For us, the bad is when a body decomposes our body's relation, although it still combines with our parts, but in ways that do not correspond to our essence, as when a poison breaks down the blood" (22). The distinction that Deleuze drew between food and poison extended Paracelsus's reflection on the nature of digestion in his *Paramirum*, which I quoted above. For Paracelsus and for Deleuze, the comparison served to illustrate the possibility of extracting the good from the bad, so long as the encounter between bodies could be regulated—what amounted to an "ethics of body practice" (Keane 2002, 35).

If Paracelsian poisoncraft had an impact on Spinoza's relational ethics and how bodies would be theorised, it also had an impact on political thought and how political bodies would be theorised. Just when Paracelsus was crafting a skin-bound body as the proper object of medical concern, so political thinkers were imagining a territorially bordered nation as the proper object for governance and protection. Reflecting the principle of treating "like with like," immunity of the biological body and the body politic would be achieved by the absorption of the external threat to counter it. Paracelsus's poisoncraft would contribute to reshaping the contours and expression of political power in modern states. For example, historian Jonathan Harris (1998) showed how Paracelsus's thought had a direct influence on early modern political ideas. Thinkers would model the nation as a functioning body, which, much like the biological body, regulated itself though the balancing of healthy and unhealthy influences. Nations, like bodies, survived thanks to poisoncraft. In England, this poisoncraft was directed toward the growing Catholic threat to the Protestant order, culminating in the 1605 Guy Fawkes plot to blow up Parliament and assassinate King James I. The foiling of the plot was not just understood as a successful operation in counterespionage; it also fulfilled the regulative function of knowledge about poisons within the body politic. Exposure to such dangers strengthened the common good, and enemy infiltrators were to be understood as purgative poisons necessary for vaccination.

Building on Harris's work, political philosopher Roberto Esposito (2011, 122–27) has read Paracelsus's medical toxicology as a turning point in the historical development of the body-state metaphor more widely. At a time of intense warring between kingdoms, threats perceived to the body politic in European states shifted from causes that lay internal to the body (such as moral decay) to causes with an external origin (e.g., civil war and foreign invasion). For Esposito, the disciplinary logic of Paracelsianism, with its emphasis on the regulation of the body, could be understood as the origin of an immunitary principle at the core of modern governance: "Whether the danger that lies in wait is a disease threatening the individual body, a violent intrusion into the body politic, or a deviant message entering the body electronic, what remains constant is the place where the threat is located, always on the border between the inside and the outside, between the self and the other, the individual and the common. Someone or something penetrates a body—individual or collective—and alters it, transforms it, corrupts it" (2).

To summarize, Paracelsian poisoncraft both reflected and influenced wider theories of social and political governance. The coalescence of medicine, ethics, morality, and social and political theory that took place from the sixteenth to the nineteenth century gave form to a poisoncraft that had at its center an allegorical relationship between the biological body and the body politic. The regulation of both required a rational understanding of the dangers of poison, and the governance of poison was crucial for the maintenance of compatible relations that comprised bodies and states.

THE "WELL-SPOKEN WORDS": A POETRY OF POISON FOR PORTUGUESE COLONIALISM

Alagiyavanna Mukaveti's *Subhāṣitaya* (Well-Spoken Words) was a compendium of verse drawn from a much older pan-Indic tradition dating from the first century CE or earlier (Berkwitz 2013). The original *subhā-ṣitaya* (codes for ethical life) that had inspired Alagiyavanna's *Subhāṣitaya* were handed down orally and spread over vast distances, their first authors unknown (Sternbach 1974). Alagiyavanna's compendium collected one hundred of those verses, each offering moral and ethical guidance and warning of the importance of virtue and the dangers of wickedness in leading a good life. The thirty-ninth verse used a simple poison metaphor (Wickramasinghe, pers. comm., 2015):

> Poison is the fang of vicious serpents,
> Poison is the sting of mosquitoes and flies,
> Poison is the tail of scorpions,
> Still, the whole body of cruel miscreants is poison.

Although the verse is more than four hundred years old, little effort is required on the part of modern readers to understand how Alagiyavanna may have sought to use the relationship with poison to communicate moral principles and warnings. In serpents, mosquitoes, flies, and scorpions, poison may be harmful or deadly but is always limited. In no sense is the total animal itself poison, either in a biological or a moral sense. However, "cruel miscreants," Alagiyavanna warns us, are poison in totality—even though we know that no part of them (a fang, sting, or tail) can deliver a dangerous wound. Even today, the meaning of the verse and its core message—"the entire body of cruel miscreants is poison"—will seem obvious to many readers and carry implications that have not significantly changed across the millennia during which the verse (in its earlier Sanskrit forms) has been in existence. Educators in contemporary Sri Lanka have thus endorsed the *Subhāṣitaya* as "a noble handbook for a moral lifestyle [and] . . . a unique book of advisory poems which holds an eternal significance . . . [as] . . . a moral reference for people for a purified mind-set" (De Thabrew 2011, 1). Every schoolchild can repeat from memory the verse I have quoted.

I find the verse compelling for two reasons. The first is the relationship that Alagiyavanna drew between the natural venom of wild creatures and the poisonous characters of bad people. The second is the historical context in which Alagiyavanna was writing—a time of colonial violence and enforced social, religious, and political change. The verse illuminates two central features of an emerging poisoncraft in early modern Sri Lanka, the contexts and conditions within and under which poisons acted as arbiters of moral conduct and governance; and how those contexts and conditions mediated the relationship between poisons as literal and metaphorical matter, with poison offering a language for expressing and making sense of sovereign danger. I take those two issues in reverse order, beginning my deeper reading of Alagiyavanna's verse through Buddhist scholar Stephen C. Berkwitz's (2013) biographical history of the poet and then through a discussion of the founding text of Ayurvedic toxicology, the *Susruta-samhita*.

Colonialism, Sovereignty, and Poison Discourse

According to Berkwitz (2013), the *Subhāṣitaya* offered a critique of social and ethical life during a time of transition from Sitawaka to Portuguese rule of the coastal districts of Sri Lanka. Alagiyavanna's creative journey mirrored those changes, with political and religious transformation reflected on and in his work. Born in 1552 to an elite Buddhist Sinhala-speaking family, Alagiyavanna began his career as a poet in the royal court of King Rajasiṃha I (1544–93) of the Kingdom of Sitawaka (1521–94), in the south-central region of the island. Alagiyavanna produced five works across his lifetime, the first three during his attachment to the Rajasiṃha court, while he was still a practicing Buddhist. In those works, Alagiyavanna had borrowed from classical Sinhala verse, combining rich aesthetic descriptions with praise for the monarch and celebration of the Bodhisattva's life. Their message was a celebration of Buddhist sovereignty within the flourishing kingdom. Alagiyavanna wrote his final two works, including the *Subhāṣitaya*, in a rapidly changing social and political context. He produced the *Subhāṣitaya* itself just after the fall of Sitawaka to the Portuguese in 1593.

The style and message of the *Subhāṣitaya* reflected the changes through which Alagiyavanna had lived. The Portuguese had destroyed the kingdom and dozens of villages across the country. At the same time, Portuguese Catholic missionaries were converting many Buddhists to the new faith. Reflecting this, Berkwitz argues, the *Subhāṣitaya* departed from the classical style of Alagiyavanna's earlier works, written under the benefits of royal patronage and exalting the virtues of Buddhist kingship, and conveyed instead a sense of fear and despair about encroaching colonial rule. In so doing, Alagiyavanna's writing came to foreground "moral admonitions over aesthetically rich poetic embellishments" (2013, 140). Faced with the loss of his courtly appointment and uncertain role in a Portuguese future, Berkwitz tells us, he "[saw] little to celebrate at all in such a world." Alagiyavanna's poetry turned away from a celebration of life and its "beauties and marvels" to focus on questions of survival "in a setting in which things are not as they should be" (140). In particular, the *Subhāṣitaya* highlighted the "ignorance and immorality" that Alagiyavanna felt was becoming rampant in the world following Rajasiṃha's demise, juxtaposing "virtuous persons (*sudana*) and wicked persons (*dudana*), and suitable acts versus immoral ones" (140).

Alagiyavanna's aim was to explore the meaning of morality and to defend an interpretation of moral living in a context where such could not be embodied in the figure of a "just Buddhist king" (140). His concern was precisely to ask what form moral authority might take in the absence of a sovereign ruler when faced with a historical transformation to colonial disciplinary power. Crucially, the "timeless" *subhā-ṣitaya* offered a gateway to a transcendental morality that did not require manifestation in the physical person of a sovereign Buddhist ruler. The teachings he shared descended from the "Sanskrit cosmopolis" (Pollock 2006) and, although vernacularized through Alagiyavanna's interpretation, carried the authority and wisdom of the classical age. Berkwitz (2013, 140) thus argues that Alagiyavanna meant the *Subhāṣitaya* as an "effort to anchor moral conduct outside the traditional Sinhala [polity] ... within the seemingly irrefutable scope of pan-Indic common sense."

From Berkwitz's work I take the insight that Alagiyavanna's poetry offered a bridge between the classical Sinhala Buddhist age and a new era of Portuguese rule, which heralded a changing relationship between the self and society. Moreover, poison provided Alagiyavanna with a ready language to describe the dangers of wicked persons that, according to literary theory of the time, "could . . . generate particular sentiments and emotional responses in an audience, conditioning different ways of thinking and acting in the world" (Berkwitz 2013, 2). Alagiyavanna would have expected his readers to respond positively to the message contained in the image he portrayed, carrying its admonitions with them into a new world untethered from vernacular Buddhist sovereignty. In so doing, he drew from the authority and wisdom of a great tradition of toxicology belonging to Ayurveda, the "Science of Life."

The Suśruta-saṃhitā

Although credited to the Indian physician Suśruta, the *Suśruta-saṃhitā* (Compendium of Sushruta) was likely composed by several authors between ca. 600 BCE and ca. 500 CE. The *saṃhitā* contains six large sections, the fifth of which, the *Kalpasthāna* (Section on Procedures), was devoted to the treatment of poisons. Historian of Ayurveda, Dominik Wujastyk (2001), commented that one surprising feature of the *Kalpasthāna* was its lack of medical theory. For that reason, Wujastyk argued, the "overall sense is that we are here in contact with a particularly ancient set of medical traditions" (79)—traditions that emerged contemporaneously with the moral and ethical concerns of the *subhā-ṣitaya* corpus from which Alagiyavanna had drawn. My discussion here draws from Bhishagratna's (1911) edited English translation of the Sanskritic text, which remains a valuable reference.

All six sections of the *Suśruta-saṃhitā* were written as if gifted from Suśruta to the king of Kāśī (Varanasi). The *saṃhitā* was thus concerned with the dangers that poisons represent to the life of the king and the protection of his kingdom—a concern that shaped the poisoncraft to which it would give rise. For example, in the *Kalpasthāna* Suśruta explained the origins, means of detecting, and effects of poison, as well as the characteristics of a would-be poisoner, before ending with medical treatments for poisons of immobile and mobile kinds—that is, plants and other immobile or inanimate things, and animals. (This distinction, which differs from the modern distinction between natural and synthetic poisons, and only partially overlaps the English-language distinction between poison and venom, is worth noting, though a fuller discussion lies beyond the scope of this book.)

Throughout the work, Suśruta developed his toxicology from the ultimate origins of poison, which lay in tales of Hindu cosmogenesis. Suśruta explained how the demon Kaitabha sought to obstruct Brahmá from creating the world, causing him to become angry.

> It is stated that there was a devil named Kaitabha, who out of vanity, obstructed in various ways the work of Lord Brahma, when he was engaged in the creation of nature. For acts of Kaitabha God Brahma grew very angry. His wrath then became manifest and came down in a violent form from his mouth. It burnt the mighty devil to ashes. Even after the destruction of the demon, that wonderful and terrific glow

went on surprisingly, at the sight of which all the Gods were deeply depressed in sprits (*vishada*). The term *Visha* is so called on account of its filling the Gods with *vishada*. There upon, Brahma after having created all living beings cast the remaining wrath both into inanimate and animate creations. (Bishagratna 1911, 698–99)

Representing the cosmogenic origin of poison, Suśruta writes that "all the sharp and violent qualities are present in poison" (699). For that reason, poison is "considered as aggravating and . . . deranging all the Doshas of the body" (699).

In Ayurveda, good health depends on regulating the three humors (*doṣa*)—wind (*vāta*), bile (*pitta*), and phlegm (*kapha*)—and how they interact with the seven basic constituents of the body—chyle, blood, flesh, fat, bone, marrow, and semen. In healthy functioning, the body takes food into the stomach, where it is burned and transformed first into chyle and blood and up through the basic constituents until it converts into semen, the highest substance of the body. Poison interferes with this process. As Suśruta explains, "The Doshas aggravated and charged with poison forego [sic] their own specific functions. Hence poison can never be digested or assimilated in the system. It stops the power of inhaling. Expiration (exhalation of breath) becomes impossible owing to the internal passages having been choked by the deranged Kapha [phlegm]. Consequently a poisoned person drops down in an unconscious state even when life is still present within his body" (Bishagratna 1911, 699).

Suśruta's descriptions of the properties of poison establish how in the Sanskrit tradition the power and protection of the sovereign was a matter of identifying the noxious in the good. Suśruta portrayed a world of full of poison dangers and hence the need for a close relationship between physicians with expertise in poison and the sovereign to be protected. Medical precept and practice were oriented to defense of the realm. Toxicology served the sovereign, who was always in danger of being poisoned by threats hidden within his court.

Poisonous Beings

Like all metaphors, Alagiyavanna's verse compared unrelated objects to render a complex concept simple. The moral and ethical failings of people are often difficult to comprehend, but we can all grasp the dangers posed by venomous creatures. Philosopher Graham Harman (2018, 73) writes that through metaphor "we are able to experience a new entity that somehow combines [traits of the two objects in comparison]"—what he terms a "sui generis" object. The sui generis is a metaphor with chemical purchase. Chemical compounds are formed by two or more constituent chemicals that when combined lose their original identities and adopt a new identity greater than the sum of its parts. The lesson I draw from this is that the sui generis compound object envelops the world; it "encompasses" it (Dumont 1970). The metaphor's identity is derived from constituent parts and re-formed into something different and new. In this sense, metaphor is cannibalistic of the parts that make up its comparison, which are completely absorbed and overcome by the compound object. The power of the metaphor to communicate new meaning thus derives from the greater mass of the metaphor that represents a doubling of the two constituent parts on their own—the metaphorical image weighs heavier on the mind of its receiver than the parts do alone. This is also an outcome with chemical purchase, as a foundational principle of modern chemistry, and one that distinguishes it from premodern "parachemistries," is that two materials cannot be combined without raising their weight (Mukharji 2016)—a distinction I return to below.

At first approach, Alagiyavanna's four lines in the *Subhāṣitaya* suggest a feature of early modern Sinhala metaphor operating on similar principles. The correspondence he drew between the poison contained in animals and the poison embodied in persons was important for the metaphor to work on a basic level. Lines 1–3 cast shadows of creatures that gave form, meaning, and mass to the fourth line, which contains the metaphor. Alagiyavanna's verse construction thus primed his audience to experience the fourth line in a particular and vivid way. What did reference to serpents, insects, and scorpions achieve? Certainly, it was more than the sharing of simple zoological information. Alagiyavanna drew our attention to fangs, a proboscis, and stings—appendages with sharp and violent qualities. In so doing, he generated a terrifying compound entity using venomous ingredients—a human-animal kind replete with the deadly parts of serpents, flies, mosquitoes, and scorpions.

The significance of Alagiyavanna's metaphor might derive from what Harman (2018, 74) termed the "theatricality" of the hybrid creature spawned by the three preceding lines—what I have called its mass. Yet the *Subhāṣitaya* foregrounded ethics over aesthetics, and the pleasure of artistic engagement with poetic metaphor was reduced in favor of simpler forms that communicated everyday wisdom. By any measure, the thirty-ninth verse was far from being a superior work of art. So from where did it draw its symbolic weight?

The first source came from the wider cosmological order within which Alagiyavanna was writing. Correspondence between venomous creatures and poisonous people existed not just in a metaphorical key; importantly, each occupied lower places in the karmic universe and were typically surrounded by suspicions of sorcery and evil intent. Alagiyavanna was not only suggesting that cruel miscreants were more poisonous than even the most venomous creatures, but that they inhabit the same cosmic level.

The second source is the *returning* nature of the metaphor, which is also evident in the structure of the verse. Dark venomous creatures and poisonous people were and remain stock literary figures in Indo-European cultures. Yet, unlike most other metaphors, the shadow cast by the venom of animals was *cast upon* by the dark shadow of evil people. That is, the metaphor has not only returned across time, but it also returns upon itself: *the metaphor generates meaning from resources within itself.*

Poison's "sharp and violent qualities" found their way directly into the metaphorical meaning of poison, and the potency of that association found its way back to the meaning of poison as a material that could have such qualities. Put another way, poison's meaning is independent of the semiotic chains of which it is a part—meaning is prior to language, in other words. Serpents *are*, and in past lives *were*, cruel miscreants, and in their poison form, we can catch a glimpse of our future should we fail to observe moral codes.

In Alagiyavanna's verse, the aesthetics of venomous creatures and poisonous people draw from each other. The metaphorical line does not cannibalize the three preceding constituent lines but builds a relationship with them. A principle of *rasayana*, a major tradition of Indian chemistry with early Ayurvedic roots, is that the weight of two substances combined does not always double their respective weights (Mukharji 2016). The same principle holds for Alagiyavanna's metaphor, which emerges with a mass equal to the literal verses from which it was constituted.

Alagiyavanna's metaphor illuminated the hierarchical order of the Sinhala Buddhist (and wider South Asian) universe and the compound forms of multi-beings (Dumont 1970). Venomous creatures and poisonous people were intrinsically related, their substance and character enmeshed in flows that ignore body and species boundaries. Alagiyavanna's poison metaphor thus illuminated key principles of Ayurvedic toxicology. The first is the hierarchical ordering of things in the universe and the lowly position occupied by poisonous creatures. The second is the compound form of the poisonous being, made up of material and moral qualities of many other kinds. The task of Ayurveda is to purify the body, physically and spiritually, to achieve balance and good health.

From Alagiyavanna's verse through Suśruta's toxicology to the returning metaphor of poison within the karmic world of porous beings, poison existed as a highly mobile and deeply malleable concept, linking the origins of anger and evil in the world to personal conduct and the dangers of others. Within this world, poison represented a cosmic and political hierarchy in which the first concern of poisoncraft was protection of the sovereign against the flow of poison.

THE WOR(L)DS OF POISON

For at least two millennia, in Eurasian societies poison has been mobilized as an index of value and an expression of power. For much of that time, poison operated in a system that drew analogous and hierarchical relations between poisons and the materials and morals that made up and gave form and meaning to the cosmos. The remedy-poison was an unequal relation, with the remedy spiritually and socially proximate to exalted beings and poison a substance that worked as a signifier of, as well as being signified by, evil. The hierarchical value placed on poison represented the vast cosmological system, with poisons of the macrocosm analogous to poisons of the microcosm. In Paracelsus's Europe and Alagiyavanna's

South Asia, poison provided a material and metaphorical index for creating and expressing rank orders, be they concerned with moral and ethical conduct or the establishment of state borders and territories.

In Paracelsian and Ayurvedic medicine, ill-health and disease would be caused by disequilibrium between levels as well as an imbalance of substances external and internal to the body. Treatment was via the administration of an opposite (such as substituting cold for heat in Ayurveda) or similarity (such as treating syphilis with mercury in Paracelsianism). Thanks to the logic of relation, analogy also became a system of morality. Paracelsus and Alagiyavanna, incomparable in almost all respects, can be productively compared on this point. Each man was writing within an emerging political philosophy on the cusp of South Asian and European modernities. If the time of Paracelsus was defined by a closure of the body into a sovereign object that mirrored the closure of the territory into a sovereign state, the time of Alagiyavanna was defined by the persistence of an open body but now within a deterritorialized colonial state. Their poisoncraft had very similar origins—in humoral Galenic and Ayurvedic theories, respectively—but would lead to very different visions of the body and the body politic—closed in the one, open in the other—visions that remain central to the politics of poison control and pesticide regulation today.

In Europe, Paracelsian poisoncraft created an approach to poison that would become crucial to emerging philosophies of individuating politics and ethics. In Sri Lanka, the arrival of the Portuguese marked the beginnings of a transformation of political power from its embodiment in a Buddhist king to its expression through a colonial administration overseeing an outpost of empire. Sri Lanka would be colonized for the next 450 years, and the great tradition of Ayurvedic toxicology would not be tilted toward the construction of a territorially bounded sovereign entity until the twenty-first century, as I discuss in part 3. As such, the influence of Ayurvedic poisoncraft did not diminish, but its focus was redirected. With the king dead, responsibility lay with all good Buddhists to manage their own exposure to the corrupting influences of the world. Fear of poisonous others, with their sharp and violent qualities, was one powerful means of doing so.

The two poisoncrafts would also represent the transformation of poison in the one and its continuity in the other. From the time of Paracelsus on, poison in the European world, which remained a moral problem as much as it was a medical-material one, was nevertheless fundamentally knowable and graspable; quantification would distinguish the bad from the good. In the South Asian world, poison continued its lively existence, transgressing categorical boundaries and mobilizing social, political, and religious lives, even while Paracelsian toxicology gained a foothold in universities and among regulatory authorities. Precise dosing permitted the emerging poisoncrafts to differentiate between the poison and the not-poison. Thus, the demarcation that gave poisons a body reflected the demarcations that gave society and the nation a body. Paracelsian poisoncraft theorized a world of individuated poisons invading individuated bodies and political territories. Ayurvedic poisoncraft theorized a world of extended poisons flowing between extended bodies and territories, with borders rendered opaque by colonial and postcolonial processes.

Finally, Alagiyavanna's poison metaphor provides a frame for thinking more widely about the meaning of poison. What I have been describing has been otherwise called "material semiotics"—how the physicality of "stuff" gives form to its meanings. Mary Douglas (1970) wrote about how many societies draw "natural symbols" of and for society from the body, the substance of which lends itself to telling understandable stories of the makeup and functioning of the social world. More recently, anthropologist Kath Weston (2013) has drawn attention to the "meta-materiality" of blood, the visceral physicality of which forces attention to and reckoning with the world in specific kinds of ways. Weston argues that the use of blood metaphors (e.g., lifeblood, circulation, liquidity) to describe economy and finance, as well as to describe crisis, collapse, and responses to them (cardiac arrest, transfusion), does more than naturalize what are cultural phenomena. Instead, she draws attention to how the "literal uses of blood" in anti-austerity protests and the selling of blood as an economic strategy to cope with precarity have meaning precisely because of finance's bloodlike qualities and blood's commodity value. As Weston (2013, S37) suggests, "Meta-materiality goes beyond metaphor to enlist the material, beyond the material to figure substance through metaphor, analogy, and whatever other historically situated heuristic devices people find available."

Understood as a *returning* metaphor—a metaphor that draws meaning from resources within itself and that returns across time and space—poison invites a fuller extension of meta-materiality. The lore of gifts and poisons that arose alongside the emergence of interested and disinterested exchange, the poison perils of female intimacy, sexuality, and power that arose alongside patriarchy, and the toxicologies that arose in conjunction with sovereign power are instances of poison's meta-materiality finding new opportunities for expression. Yet in each instance, too, poison's metaphorical meaning is never wholly reinvented; it never surrenders to history to become just an expression of whatever social, political, or economic conditions are ruling at the time. Poison's materiality returns repeatedly to give form and force to those conditions. Put another way, poison needs to be "taken seriously" as a historical material and not reduced to an epiphenomenon of human language and thought.

SUMMARY OF PART I

The Crafts of Poison

MY AIM IN PART 1 has been to introduce and develop a concept of poisoncraft as a field of cultural ideas about and practices with poisons in their multiple forms. From the poisons of gifts and commodities, witchcraft and magic, and intimate, domestic, and communal relations to the alchemical, allopathic, and Ayurvedic toxicologies, an understanding of and ability to work with poisons has, across societies, often been important to how people understand themselves, others, and the world around them. Understood as a specific form of governance, poisoncraft is an engagement with the uncertain, the ambivalent, the ambiguous, and the unruly that permeates social and political life. Poisoncraft is the negotiation of the indeterminant and of alterity—the always spinning pharmakon where the question of whether the poison is a remedy or the remedy is a poison is always and can only ever remain unanswered. The power of poisoncraft derives from an ability to harness and control ambiguity, bending poison's corrosive potential to one's own will.

Poison's material semiosis, which emerges from and returns upon itself, is one of the primary examples of what across societies is a deeply recognized and meaningfully productive phenomenon—that is, how the conditions of one are indelibly tied to the conditions of the other. Through such exchanges are derived an understanding of self and others in the world. Persons, relations, and social formations all derive their form from the same logical operations as from those we derive the formations of poison. Poison's power is not, however, a chemical biopower, even if sovereign power has always defined itself in relation to the management of poison as a means of ensuring life *and* death. Neither is poison's power an expression of hegemonic control over the meaning and potentiality of the noxious and the good, even if, again, sovereign power has always made good use of that ability. Rather, as evidenced by the many ways in which poison has existed as a cultural idea and practice, poison's power derives from its ambiguity as an expression of domination *and* subversion.

Poison is an uncertain and contested power, one that always and forever contained its own alter, the remedy. For while the sovereign's power is claimed and demonstrated through its control over and rule through poison, sovereignty is itself always in danger of succumbing to poison—tales of the *vish-kanya* standing as the most striking examples to have returned repeatedly across time. As we shall see in parts 2 and 3, the contemporary power wielded by the industrial-chemical complex over pesticide markets and agrochemical regulation is never absolute but always already undermined by the limits imposed by those products' properties. When pesticide companies invoke the *remedy* by defining their biocides as "plant protection products," they are invoking the *poison*, thereby opening themselves to a counterdiscourse that forces attention to negative value.

I understand Ayurvedic and allopathic poisoncrafts as ultimately the same kinds of efforts to control the intrinsic affordances of power that poison contains. Yet both descend from the same set of ideas concerning poison's duality and integral role in the constitution of persons, relations, and their relative valuations. Those who control poison control the means by which the noxious and the good in and of social life—what in many cases form the fundaments of hierarchical relations (between people, communities, and nations)—are understood and expressed. What I take from the history of poisoncraft is a reminder that at the very core of the modern industrial-chemical complex, that which comprises its very essence, is a material laden with mythos and logos—with the folk knowledge of poison and the canonical knowledge of toxicology. Together they comprise one part of a wider tradition I call poisoncraft. In the chapters that follow, I turn to recent struggles in pesticide regulation in the EU and Sri Lanka as case studies in contemporary poisoncraft.

PART II

Glyphosate and the Poisoncraft of European Unification

3

Poison and Deceit

Glyphosate and Europe's Polycrisis

Berlin, December 4, 2014. It is exactly thirty years since a methyl isocyanate gas leak from Union Carbide's pesticide factory in Bhopal, India, killed thousands and poisoned tens of thousands more. It is ten years since two American comedians, the Yes Men, played a prank on Union Carbide's current owner, Dow Chemical, by appearing on BBC News to announce the company would take full responsibility for the disaster and pay extensive damages to victims—wiping $2 billion off Dow's share value (CNN 2004). It is three months before IARC lights a fire under the pesticide industry by labeling glyphosate a probable carcinogen. I am sitting in a function room in a five-star Berlin hotel surrounded by representatives of the pesticide industry—all participants in a two-day breakout panel on pesticide business futures. Several dozen delegates are in attendance, representing mostly European offices of the (then) Big Six pesticide companies—BASF, Bayer AG, Dupont, Dow Chemical, Monsanto, and Syngenta—and smaller firms involved in R&D, regulatory support, and the formulation of off-patent (generic) molecules for global markets. As people involved in the production, selling, and use of plant protection products, they are practitioners of poisoncraft at the cutting edge of the agrochemical industry.

Over the two days of the panel, I will hear nothing of the Bhopal disaster or the financial cost of what some might call admitting liability for the event. Rather, I will listen to a succession of presentations by leaders of their fields in pesticide chemistry, crop protection, and agribusiness about the challenges the industry faces from European regulatory intervention. Speakers will overwhelmingly construe those challenges as the result of the public's "misplaced" worries over the toxicity of pesticides and politicians' "pandering" to public opinion, leading to an increasingly difficult legal and oversight environment. During coffee breaks, I will discuss with delegates the impacts of this on developing "new chemistry"—for example, the discovery and development of new molecules with biocidal properties—that they will claim is being stifled by lack of investment, competition, and innovation. As companies direct their research capacities ever more toward proving the safety of "old chemistry"—the molecules underpinning existing product ranges—there is less and less space for exploratory science to occur. The result, I will hear it said many times over, will be higher chemical loads as pests develop resistance to widely used molecules and new pesticides stall in development, leading to an increased reliance on older and often more toxic chemicals, increased food costs, and increased risks of food insecurity. During a Q&A session, one industry executive labeled this the result of a "public shitstorm" steeped in antiscience rhetoric. "If this goes on," she added, nothing less than the "the total collapse of world trade" would be a possibility—"*Where will it end?!*" was her exasperated plea. "With *glyphosate!*" came the answer from the chair, in an only half-joking tone.

By December 2014, industry insiders had still expected European regulators to give the molecule a clean bill of health. But the possibility that the IARC might classify glyphosate as a carcinogen was beginning to cause alarm, and Monsanto was already deeply involved in work to disrupt and discredit any such conclusion. The conference was also alive with discussion of what an IARC ruling against glyphosate would mean for the EU's pending judgment on glyphosate reapproval. Discussions on and off the podium by industry professionals revolved around the stringency of European regulation compared with those found in other territories. For example, during his presentation on risk management, a senior manager for one of the Big Six pesticide companies used David Vogel's *Politics of Precaution* (2012)—a history of twentieth-century American and European chemical regulation—to develop a criticism of EU "heavy-handedness." He spoke about how in the United States obtaining product approval was becoming increasingly simple, while in the EU the opposite was true. Turning to metaphor, the speaker likened US regulations to a "Gordian knot" and EU regulations to the "sword of Damocles." "Gordian knot" refers to what appears to be an intractable problem (an impossible knot) but that by *cheating* can be solved (or undone) quite easily. "Sword of Damocles," on the other hand, describes an imminent and ever present peril that can only be avoided by chance. Here was a remarkably open acknowledgment that US regulators were susceptible to "persuasion," while their EU counterparts were "closed to dialogue," as the speaker put it. As one delegate would tell me later, "In the US system they plan it [pesticide registration] out for you—what you need to submit, how to pass assessment. In the EU system, we guess what they want, and then they tell us what they really wanted after we get rejected." This difference, and what industry would view as the almost existential challenge posed by EU regulations, became something I would hear about often as I continued my research in the worlds of European poisoncraft.

Strasbourg, September 16, 2016. Jean-Claude Juncker, president of the European Union, opens his State of the Union address to the European Parliament with a stark warning: "Our European Union is, at least in part, in an existential crisis" (European Commission Directorate-General for Communication and Juncker 2016, 6). Three months after the United Kingdom's vote to leave the EU and against a decade of social, economic, and political turmoil, from the financial crisis of 2008 to the Syrian refugee crisis of 2015, Juncker reflects on the many challenges related to what he described as "not enough Europe in this Union . . . [and] . . . not enough Union in this Union" (6). Toward the end of his address, Juncker also describes the controversy that had surrounded Europe's decision to reapprove glyphosate herbicides and lamented the fact the European Commission (EC) had been required to intervene in disputes between the regulatory agencies and the European Parliament. This had led to a confusion between the separation of "technical" and "political" processes, he says, which should define the proper workings of the EU (20). In fact, glyphosate had brought to the surface a deeper democratic deficit and jeopardized the EU's legitimacy.

> It is not right that when EU countries cannot decide among themselves whether or not to ban the use of glyphosate in herbicides, the Commission is forced by Parliament and Council to take a decision. So we will change those rules—because that is not democracy. The Commission has to take responsibility by being political, and not technocratic. A political Commission is one that listens to the European Parliament, listens to all Member States, and listens to the people. (44)

In EU parlance, the glyphosate controversy represented a failure of "comitology"—the processes by which Member States via the European Parliament reach agreement on matters of law and regulation. More than that, however, glyphosate was just one calamity among a series of others that had struck to the core of Europe over the past decade.

Across a number of speeches delivered during that time, Juncker would return to the idea that the Union was facing a "polycrisis" (Juncker 2016). "Our various challenges," he suggested during an address to businesses in Greece, "from the security threats in our neighbourhood and at home, to the refugee crisis, and to the UK referendum—have not only arrived at the same time. They also feed each other, creating a sense of doubt and uncertainty in the minds of our people" (Juncker 2016). At the forefront of Juncker's mind was the sentiment of anti-Europeanism and growing nationalism that had started with the financial crisis in 2008, escalated in response to EU-imposed Greek austerity packages from 2010 and the influx of migrants beginning in 2015, and culminated in the Brexit vote of 2016. By the time of his State of the Union address in 2018, Juncker had married this with a language of poisoncraft: "To love Europe, is to love its nations. To love your country is to love Europe. Patriotism is a virtue. Unchecked nationalism is riddled with both *poison and deceit*" (European Commission Directorate-General for Communication and Juncker 2018, 8; emphasis added).

Juncker's remedy for the poisonous tide sweeping Europe was fitting. As he told the audience during his 2016 State of the Union address:

> Solidarity is the glue that keeps our Union together. The word *solidarity* appears 16 times in the Treaties which all our Member States agreed and ratified. There is impressive solidarity when it comes to jointly applying European sanctions when Russia violates international law. The euro is an expression of solidarity. Our development policy is a strong external sign of solidarity. And when it comes to managing the refugee crisis, we have started to see solidarity. I am convinced much more solidarity is needed. But I also know that solidarity must be given voluntarily. It must come from the heart. It cannot be forced. (European CommissionDirectorate-General for Communication and Juncker 2016, 16)

I read Juncker's solution of the humanitarian gift (expressed in volunteerism and solidarity) as one born from the long history of Paracelsian poisoncraft. His words show how governance of, in, and for European *union*—the forming of compatible relations in Spinozan terms—had become a project of poison control. This included the regulation of the civil space of European solidarity through citizen action and the regulation of pesticides like glyphosate that undermined European decision-making procedures and risked poisoning European bodies. Over the next few years, as Europe's struggles to reach agreement on whether glyphosate posed an unacceptable risk to human and environmental health, fears that the controversy was magnifying the poison of nationalism and threatening efforts to cultivate solidarity loomed large in the EU's proceedings.

In the chapters that follow, I explore the relationship between glyphosate and the project of European union through the words and actions of specialists of poisoncraft in regulatory agencies, industry, civil society, and academia. I ask how glyphosate had become such a lively topic for debating the future of Europe and how answers given to the problems that glyphosate posed can be understood as examples of poisoncraft. As European regulators often pointed out, only a few years earlier they had been celebrated as "world leading" by environmental groups for banning neonicotinoid insecticides, which studies had linked with bee colony collapse. Yet now, using the same assessment processes, critics of glyphosate accused the EU of having failed to follow "scientific methods," of being susceptible to industry "pressure," and of putting economic considerations, in particular, the protection of agriculture and the European market, before human and environmental health (Gillam 2017). Their expertise as practitioners of poisoncraft for the regulation of pesticide markets had been seriously questioned. My interlocutors in regulatory agencies and industry alike could only conclude the attacks they were coming under were less about glyphosate than what the chemical represented—namely, Monsanto defending its genetically modified "Roundup Ready" crops. Meanwhile, right-wing parliamentarians accused those leading the investigations, who not coincidentally happened to be predominantly left-wing and Green Members of the European Parliament (MEPs), of cynically exploiting fears over glyphosate to win votes in upcoming European elections.

Extending beyond those arguments, however, glyphosate risked corrupting and corroding European solidarity. Glyphosate's status as a boundary object (see introduction) helped generate the terrain for dispute as groups that were fundamentally in opposition—the pro- and anti-glyphosate lobbies—came into conflict over fundamental questions concerning the EU's right to establish a regulatory boundary around itself and to define and defend regulatory science that could be used in defense of European bodies. As I describe below, the European project has long been described by its founders and champions as a collection of individual nation-states becoming *sui generis* through the solidifying bonds of commonality and friendship. In that sense, the project of European unification has always been a project of poisoncraft. In this first chapter in part 2, I contextualize the glyphosate case in the history of pesticide regulation in Europe and situate pesticide regulation itself within the European project.

A POLITY IN SEARCH OF A BODY

London, July 7, 2016. Partway through a corporate training session on EU pesticide regulation, the facilitator displays an image of a curvaceous Marilyn Monroe as a means of illustrating problems with the system. Her body, in silhouette, has the qualities of a mirage, which in fact is the point. EU regulations, we are told, with their supposedly equal emphasis on protecting the competitiveness of European agriculture as well as health and the environment, have the power to allure. But that promise evaporates in the context of the EU's commitment to the precautionary principle, which prioritizes hazard assessment and makes impossible meaningful risk management. Like an oasis that appears in the desert before lost travelers, EU regulations have duped farmers and agribusinesses into thinking their livelihoods are being protected when they have been sacrificed in response to imaginary dangers. Like the mirage of Monroe's body, the European body, the trainer was saying, is a chimera—albeit one with very real implications for trade. At least from that one industry professional's point of view, Europe had a body—one whose solidity made it difficult for pesticide businesses to enter.

This construct of industry seeking to enter a rigidly bounded and regulated space speaks to the core principles of Paracelsian poisoncraft. Nevertheless, a fundamental challenge facing the European Union has always been the absence of a body to represent and to protect: there is no "European people" to whom to be held accountable and from whom legitimacy can be drawn. In Europe, poisoncraft is not simply used for the protection of the European body, but its active creation. That Europe has been built as a polity without a body has been an issue long debated. "Western democracy," anthropologist Chris Shore (2013, 20) has argued, "based on the Roussonian [sic] principle of the 'general will' and the sovereign people, 'requires both empowered representative institutions and a body politic to represent.'" Thus, both champions and critics of the European project have pointed to the lack of a body—and the absence of shared origins, common identity, united purpose, and legitimate cause to concentrate sovereign power in European institutions—as the fundamental reason to question the European Union's survival. In other words, there is little that holds the European body together. Europe's troubles with glyphosate revealed the political *and* scientific implications of this absence.

As work to build Europe has gathered pace over the past seventy years, politicians and bureaucrats have always worried about problems of legitimacy, authority, and accountability in, of, and for the union. The project of European integration began in 1951 with the creation of the European Coal and Steel Community (ECSC)—an explicit effort to prevent future war on the continent. Originally intended to encourage economic cooperation in specific areas, over the intervening decades European cooperation came to emphasize greater levels of legal, political, social, and cultural integration—the Common Market, the European Economic Community (EEC), the European Communities (EC), and, currently, the European Union. Over that time, Europe's architects assumed that greater economic cooperation within the European single market would lead automatically to greater social and political identification and integration—what the 1992 Maastricht Treaty called "ever-closer union"—and eventually a federal state (Shore 2013, 18). In EU parlance, the goal has been for regulatory "harmonization" across Member States to ensure the smooth functioning of the single market. In 1986, the EU sought to enshrine the "four freedoms"—free movement of goods, persons, services, and capital—as the cornerstone of what would define citizenship in the Union.

To help this process along, Europe came to acquire a flag, an anthem, an annual "Europe Day," and, in 2002, nineteen Member States adopted the euro as their currency. With those initiatives, the EU deployed the symbolic and institutional trappings commonly associated with *nation*-states to signify the existence of one *supranational* state (Shore 2013, 18). More controversially, in 2019, the EU created the position High Representative of the Union for Foreign Affairs and Security Policy—more commonly referred to as EU foreign minister—and has continued to urge the creation of a European army (currently Member States commit resources to a Common Security and Defense force). Both initiatives have proven particularly unpopular with hesitant integrationists and strident anti-European voices alike, for the very fact that they work to define the borders of the European body on the world stage. If the EU foreign minister represents "Europe" at gatherings of nation-states and international institutions, the army would adopt responsibility for defense of the European realm—and European bodies—back home and the furtherance of its interests overseas.

It is against this backdrop that the significance of poisoncraft through pesticide control for "ever-closer union" comes into view. Bubbling beneath Juncker's State of the Union address was a statement of intent directly illustrative of this challenge: "Nationalism is riddled with both poison and deceit," he declared (European Commission Directorate-General for Communication and Juncker 2018, 8). Fears that a literal poison was damaging an already (and always) uncertain political body arose just at the time that fears that glyphosate was damaging citizens' bodies arose. Indeed, Juncker's audience would not need to work hard to conjure up the associations he was developing. Rooted in the well-worn historical associations between poisons and bodies I charted in part 1, chemical regulation would provide the EU with a channel for taking on the defense of the European realm and European bodies and thereby fostering common identity by defining the form and meaning of those very entities. What I wish to argue, very simply, is that poison control became one of the chief arenas within which attempts to create "ever-closer union" has taken place, with the glyphosate case being the most recent and most challenging example.

GLYPHOSATE IN EUROPE

First introduced to Europe as an agrochemical during the 1970s, glyphosate came up for routine regulatory renewal in 2013. But faced with an application dossier containing thousands of studies and struggling to meet that deadline, the European Parliament granted the regulatory agency, the European Food Safety Authority, an additional three years to report. In 2015, just as the EFSA was getting ready to publish its verdict, the WHO's IARC released its own conclusion that glyphosate was a probable carcinogen. EU pesticide approval is premised on the precautionary principle with a commitment to cancer prevention at its core. Any evidence that glyphosate could be carcinogenic would be reason enough to ban the molecule outright. Parliament thus asked the EFSA to consider the implications of the IARC classification, and, as glyphosate's license was about to expire, it granted emergency approval for another five years. By 2021, with still no agreement between European agencies and Parliament reached, the European Commission granted glyphosate a one-year extension to 2022. In 2022, the Commission was forced to grant a further one-year extension. And in 2023, with still no clear verdict in hand and much to the dismay of environmental groups, glyphosate received a full ten-year reapproval.

Paralyzed by an inability to reach consensus on glyphosate for almost a decade, European regulators came under intense public and political scrutiny. In 2017, a motion to "ban glyphosate and protect people and the environment from toxic pesticides" became the first petition to receive over one million signatures in the new European Citizens' Initiative. This meant the issue received a public hearing in the European Parliament and a written response from the European Commission, which "concluded that there are neither scientific nor legal grounds to justify a ban of glyphosate, and [it would] not make a legislative proposal to that effect" (European Commission 2017). In the face of increasing pressure, industry and environmentalists alike demanded clarity, and farmers' representatives argued that uncertainties about the future of glyphosate was causing them harm. Companies told me that the rules should be loosened, environmentalists argued that they should be tightened, and regulators insisted that they were about right. In a system geared to "objective" oversight, regulators thus told me, being criticized simultaneously by industry and environmentalists had proven they were favoring neither.

Europe's struggles over glyphosate forced a lengthy consideration of how EU regulatory agencies and processes worked, including how well they reflected the workings of the chemical world. This involved several years of critical scrutiny of regulatory policies and procedures by the European Parliament and the European Commission, as well as by civil society, journalists, academics, and other nongovernmental groups—all of which produced a hefty pile of paperwork I refer to as the EU glyphosate archive. Between 2016 and 2018, four reviews of EU pesticide approval processes took place that had special relevance for how the controversy would come to be defined and understood, each giving shape to the European body being crafted.

- May 2016, a workshop on glyphosate hosted by the European Parliament's Committee on Environment, Public Health, and Food Safety (ENVI committee) (European Parliament 2016);
- June 2016, an "explanatory note on glyphosate" issued by the European Commission's Group of Chief Scientific Advisors (the "Scientific Advice Mechanism," SAM) (European Commission, Group of Chief Scientific Advisors 2016);
- February 2018, a special committee of the European Parliament on the EU's authorization procedure for pesticides (PEST Committee 2018b);
- November 2016–October 2018, a comprehensive evaluation of the EU legislation on plant protection products and pesticide residues as part of the European Commission's regulatory fitness and performance (REFIT) review.

The first three reviews involved efforts to understand the divergent conclusions on glyphosate carcinogenicity reached by the IARC and EFSA, and, in the case of the PEST committee, to restore a sense of public trust in EU processes. While the scope of the ENVI committee and the SAM note were highly limited and focused on the different methodologies employed by the different agencies, the remit of the PEST committee was wide-ranging and examined pesticide approval in the round. In contrast, the REFIT review took place as part of the Commission's "Better Regulation" agenda, which aims to reduce bureaucratic load and complexity and thus is not concerned only with glyphosate. Importantly, however, both the ENVI committee and the SAM note would become important reference points for the work of the PEST committee, including how it understood its scope and remit. Conversely, the REFIT review established its scope and remit via a separate process of stakeholder consultation that took place before the review of pesticide approval and safety processes.

The bulk of my research involved detailed reading of the comprehensive archive produced by the PEST committee: written submissions from hundreds of EU and national agencies, industry bodies, academics, and other experts; verbatim transcripts of committee hearings; and site visit reports. Chaired by Eric Andrieu, a member of the French Socialist Party in the European Parliament since 2012, the PEST committee had thirty members representing all political groups in the European Parliament. Its task, as mandated by the Parliament, was to evaluate the regulatory procedure for authorizing pesticides in the EU, the independence of bureaucrats from industry, the transparency of decision making and the means available, and the roles of stakeholders involved in the process, including the EFSA, the EU, and Member States. The committee held its first meeting on March 12, 2018, and had nine months to report. During that time, the committee heard from thirty organizations in eight public meetings. Those panelists also submitted answers in writing to around 650 questions prior to the public meetings. The committee conducted three fact-finding missions, including to the offices of the IARC and EFSA. On December 6, 2018, the PEST committee adopted "with an overwhelming majority" its final forty-seven-page report containing findings and recommendations (PEST Committee 2018b, 20).

As my research progressed, it became increasingly clear that the EU glyphosate archive not only offered insight into the debates and controversies that glyphosate spawned, but had also become a key element of the process by which ideas of what "Europe" was, is, or should or could be were generated and put into action by different groups. Thus, in my research the glyphosate archive became an object of study as much as it contained materials to study. Questions of the archive's representation and legitimacy dogged the arguments being constructed against glyphosate reapproval, as different traditions and expectations of regulatory oversight, scientific review, and commitments to European solidarity clashed. It was in those encounters that conflicts over the definition and meaning of glyphosate understood as a *poison for Europe* arose, extending far beyond narrow questions of glyphosate safety to encompass fundamental questions of European identity and belonging as a project of poisoncraft. Chapters 4 and 5 can be read as instances in which glyphosate jeopardized EU sovereignty and threatened to undermine the European project. Chapter 6 shows how the PEST committee itself became a key means through which commitment to the EU could be reaffirmed and reestablished, ridding the European body of the poison that glyphosate had spread. Taken together, the glyphosate archive can be read as a material expression of European poisoncraft and as a treasure trove of insights into the workings of poisoncraft within European regulatory and bureaucratic procedures.

4

Glyphosate, Bureaucratic Science, and the Idea of Europe

Everyone had a view on why Europe had failed to reach agreement on glyphosate. The herbicide's champions argued that the science showing carcinogenicity was flawed, while the herbicide's critics argued that industry had undermined EFSA's assessment. For the European regulatory agencies themselves, the question was why its processes, which they never stopped believing and arguing were the most stringent in the world, had been so widely misunderstood. How had others not grasped what fell within EFSA's scientific remit and what did not? As soon as the difficulties coming to agreement on glyphosate gained wider public attention, EU agencies had sought to portray its causes in the distinction drawn between the assessment of hazard and risk, nonspecialists' misunderstanding of what those assessments entailed, and how responsibility for those assessments lay with different organizations. I read the debates that tumbled out as examples of poisoncraft as it was being put to work in EU regulatory and bureaucratic procedures. On the one side were the paper regulations that enshrined EU governance, and on the other side was the practice of regulation and the complexities that arose when those rules, derived from Paracelsian poisoncraft, were applied. Joining both were efforts to define and control poisons that risked the European body.

As anthropologists Laura Bear and Nayanika Mathur (2015, 19) have recently noted, "Bureaucratic spaces are a central site for the forging of the personhood." However, they can also be spaces for the construction of collective commitment and belonging. Thus, I ask, in what ways did the regulatory bureaucracy around glyphosate help forge a sense of shared belonging and purpose in Europe's multilevel union? How did practices of European regulatory poisoncraft around glyphosate give rise to a sense of Europeanness? And what might this tell us about the nature of poisoncraft itself?

This chapter addresses those questions by exploring three challenges that arose in response to glyphosate governance. The first involved regulatory approaches to the chemical world, which has traditionally sought to make a strict division between a chemical's "intrinsic" hazards and its "extrinsic" risks. The second was the political and bureaucratic structure of the EU itself, which differentiated between the European level and the Member State level. The third was the centrality of human carcinogenicity, at the expense of other human and other-than-human conditions. As I show, in moments of encounter between regulatory law and its bureaucratic enactment, forms and meanings of the molecule glyphosate, the citizen's body, and the European body came into being.

FORTRESS EUROPE

The phrase "Fortress Europe" has a long history. During World War II, both the Allied Forces and Germans spoke of a "Fortress Europe" when referring to Nazi-occupied territories. More recently, pro- and antimigration groups have spoken of "Fortress Europe" when referring to the policy and material infrastructures meant to resist and repel the inward movement of people along Europe's eastern and southern borders. From the pesticide industry's point of view, "Fortress Europe" might also pertain to the EU's regulation of pesticides in the single market. In fact, Europe's commitment to the four freedoms among Member States relies on a solid border around its edges. If Europe has a body, it is Paracelsian in construction: closed to those from without but open to those from within. All contemporary European regulation can be traced to this fundamental principle and objective: to keep the body open internally by reducing barriers to movement and harmonizing standards of production, exchange, and consumption. This has translated into friction between efforts to protect EU agricultural competitiveness on the one side and efforts to protect human health on the other.

The EU's approach to pesticide regulation emerged from a long history of scientific and regulatory practice and debate. Across the Euro-American world, governmental regulation emerged from the late nineteenth century in the form of ad hoc responses to specific cases of human or environmental poisoning and pollution. From the 1960s, governments adopted a more proactive role that saw the creation of dedicated agencies for public health and environmental protection. Recognition that chemicals paid little attention to national borders also saw emerging international agencies establish their own health and environmental organizations at this time (Boudia and Jas 2016; Davis 2014). Since then, regulatory structures and regulatory toxicology developed together in important ways (Boudia and Jas 2016; Jasanoff 1995). The response-mode approach that characterized the early twentieth century was premised on the Paracelsian dose-response model of chemical harm. Regulatory interventions mostly responded to cases of mass acute poisoning—events both highly visible and with a clear "culprit" poison to blame (Davis 2014).

As toxicological knowledge developed there was also growing understanding and awareness of the effects of low-dose exposures, particularly to radioactive, carcinogenic, and endocrine-disrupting materials, which flouted Paracelsian rules (Vogel 2008). Unable to classify exposures as straightforwardly dangerous or safe, from the 1960s the question became, What makes a *socially or politically acceptable* level of risk? (Boudia and Jas 2016). Chemical regulation was no longer a scientific matter but fundamentally a social and political matter. Responsibility for chemical regulation was sharply divided between professional risk assessors who conducted safety studies and risk managers—elected representatives—who established parameters of tolerable and intolerable exposure on behalf of the public. Science historian Evan Hepler-Smith (2019) has termed the codevelopment of regulation and toxicology "molecular bureaucracy." He showed how the early response mode that focused on "culprit" poisons established a lasting assumption that the molecule—the "active ingredient" in a formulated product, for example, glyphosate—was the proper object of regulatory attention. Since then, the focus of regulation as well as the focus of industrial and environmentalist concern have been the molecule understood as sovereign. Risk assessors read across classes of molecules to make regulatory decisions about whole groups of chemical formulations, without needing to pay attention to their complex interactions and synergistic effects in real-world applications and settings. The result was a disembedding of chemicals from their places and contexts of use and a rationalization and abstraction of how chemicals interacted with bodies and environments, also abstracted as individual units removed from the relations that constituted them (Murphy 2017).

The whole world of chemical risk, regulation, and activism turned on a "moleculeism" that privileged one way of seeing the material over possible others (Hepler-Smith 2019). This benefited the chemical industry in three ways. First, the number of molecules that *should* be studied and regulated was so vast that the number of molecules that *could* be dealt with became tiny by comparison. Second, the apparent complexity of the chemical world would become a reason *not* to challenge the molecular orthodoxy. Third, the distinction made between a pesticide's active molecule and its product formulation elevated molecular investigation as the primary purpose of regulation. This in turn relegated to an afterthought the study of formulations and, crucially, their many, often-untested, ingredients, as well as any possible synergistic effects. The result was what Alessandra Arcuri and Yogi Hale Hendlin (2019) have called a "politics of separation." A double-layered "quarantine" emerged between those with the power to both govern and protect themselves from toxic exposures and the ability to obfuscate evidence for synergistic chemical harms by insisting on the primacy of the molecule and the proper object of regulatory scrutiny. I read the recent history of regulation as a story of how the Paracelsian poisoncraft that formed in early modern Europe would gain new form and expression in contemporary regulatory and bureaucratic structures. What Hepler-Smith calls molecular bureaucracy was none other than the

Paracelsian principle of identifying and separating the poisonous dose expressed in the new language of "active molecules." In so doing, molecular bureaucracy established a bridge to the past across which the deep history of poison's mythos and logos would travel to the present. When applied in legal frameworks, that history would in turn shape European regulations.

REGULATIONS 91/414 AND 1107/2009

Prior to 1986, risk regulation in Europe remained the responsibility of national governments. The Single European Act of that year transferred responsibility to the EU. In relation to pesticides, the EU would enshrine foundational principles of poisoncraft in two key pieces of legislation: European Council Directive 91/414/EEC, which established the current framework for pesticide approval processes in the bloc; and Regulation (EC) No. 1107/2009, which outlined the health, environmental, and economic objectives of pesticide regulation in the EU. Regulations 91/414/EEC and 1107/2009 thus established frameworks for the governance of poison within the EU with the objectives of establishing compatible relations between organs of the European body—the EU-level institutions, the Member States, the common market, the Schengen area (the twenty-nine European countries that have abolished border controls, allowing for the free movement for people within the zone), and the EU citizen.

Introduced in 1991, Directive 91/414/EEC determined that pesticide approval should take place at two levels, the European Community (what would become the European Union) and the Member States (MS). Two EU institutions, the European Chemicals Agency (ECHA) and the European Food Safety Authority (EFSA), came to hold responsibility for assessing the hazard and risk of active molecules, respectively. They reported to the European Parliament, which acted as the risk manager. Following this, the Member States, working in groups established according to geographic zones, would evaluate and approve individual product formulations for use at the national level. As I show below, this approach to pesticide regulation, which on the one hand separated responsibilities for hazard and risk assessment between two different agencies and on the other hand separated responsibilities for the molecule and the formulation between the supranational and national levels, became a defining characteristic and a key point of debate during reviews of the glyphosate issue.

Much of the glyphosate controversy would revolve around the meaning and application of Regulation (EC) No. 1107/2009. Introduced in 2009, 1107/2009 extended the previous legislation in two key areas. First, it established three principles that would determine pesticide regulation: (1) protection of human health; (2) protection of the environment; and (3) protection of the single market and competitiveness of European agriculture by "improving the functioning of the internal market through the harmonisation of the rules on . . . plant protection products" (PEST Committee 2018a, 16). As might be anticipated, the commitment to protecting human health and the environment was widely seen to conflict with the commitment to protecting the single market through regulatory harmonization. Second, 1107/2009 committed the EU to the precautionary principle and a focus on carcinogenicity when assessing pesticide hazard. As Article 4, Annex 2, Point 3.6.3. of 1107/2009 states, "An active substance, safener or synergist shall only be approved, if, on the basis of the assessment of carcinogenicity testing carried out . . . it is not or has not been classified . . . as carcinogen 1A or 1B (European Parliament and Council of the European Union 2009).

The EU's classification Category 1B holds regulatory equivalence with the IARC's classification Group 2A, which is "limited evidence of carcinogenicity in humans and sufficient evidence of carcinogenicity in experimental animals" (IARC 2019). As such, an IARC Category 2A ruling would in principle risk triggering the precautionary element of Regulation 1107/2009, resulting in the withdrawal of the chemical in question. In practice, however, the EU has often appeared reluctant to trigger the precautionary principle when faced with evidence of carcinogenicity, and the policy has generated considerable confusion and uncertainty among policy makers and the public alike (Arcuri and Hendlin 2019). In the case of glyphosate, the IARC's classification of the molecule as a 2A carcinogen *did* prompt the European Parliament to order EFSA to reassess the molecule considering that decision. However, EFSA disagreed with the IARC's conclusion and did not classify glyphosate a category 2B carcinogen—paving the way for the controversies that would then ensue.

Taken together, Directive 91/414/EEC and Regulation (EC) No. 11/07/2009 established a hierarchy of political, economic, and environmental priorities and relations that materialized Paracelsian poisoncraft in regulatory form. First, they further entrenched the distinction between hazard and risk by institutionalizing them within ECHA and EFSA. Second, they further entrenched the distinction between the active molecule and the formulated product by making them the separate regulatory responsibility of EU and Member State level review. *How* those distinctions were entrenched (and then put into practice) is what makes the European case so interesting. The regulatory division of labor for hazards, risks, molecules, and formulations, each of which lay with different agencies at international, supranational, and national levels, placed a bureaucratic distance between them that further naturalized their compartmentalization. The glyphosate controversy would draw attention not only to those separations and hierarchies but also to their economic and social contingencies, placing commitments to protecting human health squarely at odds with commitments to protecting EU farming. The regulatory object of concern was the sovereign poison and the biological body and how the relationship between them should be managed at the level of the European supranational state. At its root, the problem glyphosate posed was this:

how to prevent the flow of poisons at the level of biological bodies so political borders within Europe could remain open.

RISK'S RELATIONS

The challenge of translating Paracelsian poisoncraft into a regulatory framework for Europe proved crucial to how the glyphosate case unfolded. From the outset, virtually everyone involved in EU debates over glyphosate acknowledged that the divergent conclusions reached by the IARC and EFSA could be traced to their distinct mandated areas of scientific concern and methodological approaches. Those differences were systematic rather than accidental. First, IARC investigated hazard, while EFSA investigated risk. Second, IARC examined formulated products containing dozens of ingredients acting together—any of which could be carcinogenic individually or in combination—while EFSA studied only the active molecule, enabling it to isolate glyphosate's specific cancer risk. Third, IARC considered only publicly available safety studies, whereas EFSA also incorporated industry studies (a difference explored at length in the next chapter). And fourth, IARC and EFSA employed different statistical tests to assess the probable association between glyphosate exposure and cancer (European Commission, Group of Chief Scientific Advisors 2016). Taken together, these mandates meant IARC and EFSA approached pesticide safety research with fundamentally different starting points and endpoints. This divergence reflected their distinct concepts of where in the world poison lay (intrinsically or extrinsically) and correspondingly different constructions of poisoncraft.

Hazard Versus Risk

The primary area of contention centered on how each organization understood hazard and risk. IARC (2019) describes its purpose as "[seeking] to identify agents that are cancer hazards, meaning they pose the potential for the exposure to cause cancer. However, the classification does not indicate the level of risk associated with a given level or circumstance of exposure." Meanwhile, EFSA (2023) defines hazard simply as "something that has the potential to harm you" and risk as "the likelihood of a hazard causing harm." This seemingly straightforward separation establishes hazard as an intrinsic property and risk as an extrinsic quality of things in the world. The distinction emerged from an actuarial model of risk management developed during the late nineteenth and early twentieth centuries (Aven 2016), and it now permeates the poisoncraft of pesticide regulation. Avoiding the social and cultural dimensions of risk that would later define social scientific approaches (Boholm 2003), the actuarial model classifies the world according to statistical likelihood of harm coupled with cost-benefit analysis of intervention to reduce potential harm.

From this narrow economistic perspective, risk becomes simply a harm that can be controlled and reduced by managing exposure to the underlying hazard itself; for example, a poison may be deadly in theory but dangerous in practice only if ingested. The actuarial model contains an implicit theory of necessary relations between hazard and risk, commonly expressed in the formula *risk = hazard + exposure*. A poison must encounter others in the world before its latent hazard becomes a risk to others. As figure 1 illustrates, a solitary shark in the ocean poses no risk to us unless we enter the water with it.

This relational theory of risk carries intentional reassurance. Few would be foolish enough to swim with sharks, and extending that philosophy to the chemical world, we would be equally foolish to ignore pesticide safety warnings. "Glyphosate is safe when used as directed," is the industry's common refrain. Risk assessment thus assumes exposure will never be absolute and will always remain controlled. Whether through direct spray, drift, or food residues, absorption under normal conditions will stay below toxic thresholds of parts per billion, keeping hazard latent. This represents nothing but the Paracelsian principle that "the dose makes the poison," repackaged in actuarial language and returned to the chemical industry as risk management. Industry accordingly finds affinity with this formula and often retranslates it back into familiar Paracelsian terms, creating a "looping effect" (Hacking 1995) where risk language returns as poisoncraft language, which returns as risk language.

Evidence of this looping effect abounded during EU reviews of pesticide approval processes. European agencies repeatedly invoked the Paracelsian principle when describing and defending their hazard and risk assessment approaches. During the 2016 meeting of the Committee on the Environment, Climate and Food Safety (ENVI)—the first public meeting on the glyphosate question—agency representatives carefully highlighted the strength of their developed system (European Parliament 2016). They explained how the division of regulatory labor between IARC and EFSA enabled a comprehensive approach to hazard and risk assessment, arguing that the "overall framework . . . [was the most] . . . comprehensive and unique worldwide" (12).

However, the discussions that followed revealed how such responsibility distributions created problems for the EU. The ENVI committee cochair, MEP Alojz Peterle (who would later play a central role in the PEST committee), remarked how the "different results by IARC and EFSA have left many citizens concerned. The different methods employed [of assessing hazard and risk] have led to a clash between the agencies" (European Parliament 2016, 9). He painted a picture of continental confusion and uncertainty that was contaminating both glyphosate science and politics. "Newspapers are full of articles with contrasting messages," Peterle cautioned, "and debates in the European Parliament have created a polarising atmosphere. Politics can become scientised, and science politicised" (9).

FIGURE 1. EFSA's depiction of hazard and risk illustrates the danger of entering into close relations with sharks while swimming. (EFSA 2016)

The same debates occupied the 2018 PEST committee. Ettore Capri, an ecotoxicologist from the Università Cattolica del Sacro Cuore in Italy, argued that the contrasting agency conclusions resulted precisely from their different perspectives on hazard and risk. "The IARC assessment was simply considering if there was enough evidence to show the glyphosate posed cancer-causing hazard . . . and the study duly found that it did," he suggested (PEST Committee 2018a, 648). In contrast, Capri noted, the "EFSA conclusions specifically consider[ed] the risk of glyphosate being harmful based on actual use as a PPP and exposure—ie: they follow[ed] the fundamental maxim of toxicology 'the dose makes the poison'" (648).

Industry groups, otherwise among Paracelsian poisoncraft's strongest champions, criticized IARC and EFSA on similar grounds. The European Crop Protection Authority (ECPA), for example, took IARC to task for its focus on hazard. "If the IARC classification was to be used as a starting point for the regulatory system in Europe," ECPA argued with notable sarcasm, "then arguably those who used IARC as the basis of the argument to ban glyphosate should also be arguing to ban charcuterie and wine" (PEST Committee 2018a, 134). While such industry retorts often appear to willfully miss the point (consumers can choose to avoid meat and wine, but glyphosate is literally everywhere), what ultimately mattered more to ECPA was glyphosate's chemical and environmental relations.

Risk's Relations

The separation of hazard from risk, enshrined in the regulatory division between IARC and EFSA, emerged from an understanding of object relations that appeared in seventeenth-century Europe, particularly Britain. As anthropologist Marilyn Strathern (2020) has shown, this understanding also generated a theory of relationality that underpinned thinking about connections between people, beginning with kinship and friendship and then encompassing the entire social order. Central to this understanding was a distinction between objects' intrinsic properties and their extrinsic qualities. Crucially, intrinsic properties possessed independent reality (belonging naturally to the object), while extrinsic qualities emerged only through an object's relations (taken from the world). This theory, when applied to toxicology, ultimately produced the hazard/risk demarcation.

The theory that hazard equals intrinsic property and risk equals extrinsic quality represents a simple relational model, yet remains one of today's most important ideas. The identification and classification of intrinsic hazard and extrinsic risk forms the foundation of the modern world's entire health and safety infrastructure and underpins the multibillion-dollar risk management industry. Many readers will have completed health and safety training that operationalizes this model. It also constitutes, I argue, one of the most significant channels through which key elements of Paracelsian poisoncraft have entered the popular imagination, helping create an understanding of the world and its dangers in terms descending from Paracelsian thought.

Nevertheless, the Anglophone origins of the distinction between intrinsic properties and relational qualities have posed problems for safety regulators. At the meeting of the PEST committee, for example, EFSA cited challenges it faced when communicating the difference between intrinsic hazard and relational risk to a European public speaking diverse languages. As EFSA noted in a written response to the PEST committee, "The meanings (or even existence) of the terms 'hazard' and 'risk' are not the same in all languages" (PEST Committee 2018a, 271). For EFSA, the solution to the problem it faced when communicating risk was practical: how to develop new and better ways to communicate basic risk assessment principles, beginning with the calculation *risk = hazard + exposure*, to a public not only reluctant to engage, but sometimes unable to comprehend because of language differences.

This contentious point is crucial for understanding poisoncraft in contemporary European pesticide regulation. As a mode of governing social life through poison, Paracelsian poisoncraft centers on the construct of an individuated molecule with intrinsic properties and extrinsic relations. The responsibility of risk assessment is to account for extrinsic relations only. During the 2018 PEST committee meeting, for example, the ECPA pointed to what it called the often-overlooked difference between glyphosate molecules. "By nature," ECPA explained to the PEST committee, "glyphosate . . . is a strong acid but is never used in commercial products as such. Glyphosate is always formulated as a salt" (PEST Committee 2018a, 137)—in which form glyphosate has a much lower acute toxicity profile. This mattered, ECPA argued, because formulating glyphosate as a salt "neutralizes the acidic and hazardous properties and eliminates the need for classification of the active substance [as a hazard]" (137).

What I want to highlight is how ECPA's argument drew from a theory of chemical relations that complicated the notion that glyphosate possessed intrinsic properties as such. As a molecule, glyphosate was already suspended in webs of relations that chemists had spun, even before being formulated with other chemicals that together made the products ending up on shop shelves. Formulation merely extended those relations to a wider set of molecules, from which glyphosate's risk profile would then be generated. From ECPA's perspective, meaningful safety assessment of glyphosate could only involve consideration of relational risks, never a pre-relational molecule resting in its "natural" state, which is what IARC had considered. Professor Capri reached the same conclusion: "What's important is not to confuse hazards with risks, because the classification you referred to [i.e. glyphosate's hazardous properties], which is perfectly right, in reality refers to an intrinsic property of substances"—not the chemical as it actually exists in the world (ibid., p. 210).

To summarise, their respective epistemological commitments to hazard and risk assessment, and between intrinsic properties and extrinsic qualities, separated IARC and EFSA. IARC was interested in glyphosate in splendid isolation, while EFSA was interested in glyphosate in the world. To be sure, EFSA was not committed to fully exploring glyphosate in all its relational potential; EFSA was not conducting the kind of relational analysis explored by critical theorists in this field (Murphy 2017; Hepler-Smith 2019; Arcuri and Hendlin 2019; Hendlin et al. 2020)—but neither was it, as a risk assessment organization, retreating into the molecule to establish harms based on intrinsic properties. Simply put, EFSA, as a risk assessor operating within the relational tradition that regulatory poisoncraft has developed within, could not envision how glyphosate's intrinsic poison could be understood as having force and effect in the world without prioritising the molecule itself.

The Molecule Versus the Formulation / the European Union Versus the Member States

The confusion arising from IARC's and EFSA's divergent glyphosate conclusions exemplifies how different theories of chemical relations manifest in regulatory poisoncraft. Throughout the PEST committee's proceedings, many of its contributors pointed to organizational challenges facing EU pesticide approval because of this separation. The clearest expression was the regulatory division of labor between the EU and its twenty-seven Member States, with the EU responsible for assessing active molecules' risk and Member States responsible for assessing formulations' risk. Given the task's sheer scale, Member States organized into three regional zones with ostensibly similar environmental conditions bearing on how pesticides would behave once released: a northern zone encompassing Scandinavia, a central zone including Germany and eastern countries, and a southern zone including France and southwestern and southeastern countries. National regulators in those countries would then divide responsibility for reviewing safety studies submitted by producers of dozens and potentially hundreds of different pesticide products containing the active molecule they wished to sell. In glyphosate's case, for example, approximately 750 different products contain the molecule, each requiring Member State approval.

For the EU, the zonal system would promote efficiency and avoid duplication while enhancing harmonization and cooperation. By introducing a system that standardized regulatory procedure and mutual recognition of "national competencies," the free movement of pesticide products and food and fiber carrying pesticide residues within Europe was guaranteed. When the PEST committee questioned the regulatory division of labor with EFSA, the latter responded by highlighting what it termed "scientific and practical" reasons for doing so: "Separation of assessments for both the active ingredient and the Plant Protection Product is both scientifically and practically justified. Indeed it is necessary to assess the properties of an active substance as a first step before using the outcome of that process to feed into the assessment of each plant protection product" (PEST Committee 2018a, 211). EFSA's response adhered to the relational nature of the chemical world that Paracelsian poisoncraft had established. The most important ingredient, the active molecule, should undergo assessment first; thereafter the derivative pesticide product would be reviewed. However, in doing so, EFSA signaled the relational nature of the political world that poisoncraft had also established, which from EFSA's perspective corresponded neatly with the chemical world's relations. EFSA, as the organization with leading authority in poisoncraft, should judge the active molecule's risk first, removed from its formulated relations. Thereafter Member States, working together, would judge the formulated product, glyphosate-based herbicides.

Many national regulators agreed with this division, also resorting to what they deemed strong scientific and practical reasons. When asked why national regulators should not become more active in assessing formulations, for example, the Belgian regulator's head took an especially strong position on the active molecule's primacy: "We take the view, which is also stated at European level, that only the active substance is stable. Only the active substance will eventually end up in the human body" (PEST Committee 2018c, 133). This represented a remarkable application of Paracelsian thinking by any measure, apparently dismissing not only the regulatory significance but also the toxicological fate of chemical adjuvants comprising the formulated product, which do, via spray, drift, or residue, end up in the human body.

Not all national governments agreed, however. Regulation (EC) No. 1107/2009 permits Member States to make independent decisions on active molecules the EU has approved. In most cases, Member States simply accept the EU's decision and allow it within their borders. In a few cases, though, they disagree and take action to ban a molecule. Perhaps unsurprisingly, glyphosate became one of those cases. Several countries, including Belgium, France, Germany, and the Netherlands, banned glyphosate for home garden and/or public space use. Meanwhile, Austria and Luxembourg both attempted but failed to ban glyphosate outright. In December 2020, French President Emmanuel Macron announced his government would pay farmers to stop using glyphosate when an earlier effort to ban the chemical for agricultural use had failed. In all cases, the realities of farming without glyphosate were the limiting factor. While banning the molecule for domestic or municipal uses was relatively straightforward, farmers across Europe resisted calls to abandon glyphosate—even when offered financial incentives.

The regulatory relations between active molecule and formulated product, and between EU and Member States, that 1107/2009 brought into being reflected and reinforced thinking about the chemical world's nature and structure. The EU's assumption was that organizing pesticide approval processes this way would bring national markets into harmonization. However, some Member States' attempts at regulatory divergence showed how difficult it was for individual countries to swim against the European tide. With their national agricultural sectors deeply reliant on the molecule, they could not afford to make independent decisions. But this signaled most clearly how poisoncraft would shape the bureaucratic construction of both biological and political bodies in the EU. Governance of, by, and for poison was integral to the very construction of agreements between EU and national authorities.

THE POISONCRAFT OF TOXIC BUREAUCRACY

In this chapter, I have explored the bureaucracy of European pesticide regulation. As I have shown, pesticide risk management structures and processes all have at their core a concern with the definition and management of poison. The Paracelsian roots of regulatory orthodoxy in Europe dictated that what counts as a poison is the active molecule in pesticide formulations, and its poisonous qualities are themselves only activated when they form relations with others in the world. This relation of the poison world was reflected in the relation of the political world, with each reinforcing the other: as the principal organization the EFSA would handle the active ingredient, in turn strengthening the notion that the active ingredient is the principal poison. As EU institutions took on responsibility for protecting the European public from poison, sovereign power flowed to them. It was those institutions that would define the scope and borders of the political and biological bodies needing protection, and those same institutions would then commit themselves to realizing the European project of cohesion by making possible the free movement of goods and people free from poison.

This productive relationship between regulatory bureaucracy and regulatory toxicology was not, however, coincidental. Anthropologists, after sociologist Max Weber and philosopher Michel Foucault, have generally agreed that bureaucracy is "politics by other means"—the pursuit of utopian goals (Bernstein and Mertz 2011). One of the most common themes in the study of bureaucracy has thus been how institutions and their governance processes operate through the pursuit of cold rationalism and the imposition of coercive rules to render subjects powerless—what Weber famously called the "iron cage" (Bernstein and Mertz 2011). In this sense, anthropological approaches to bureaucracy have tended to echo and reinforce popular understandings that view its procedures and rules as a "violent simplification" (Gupta 2012). The regulatory bureaucracy of glyphosate (and other chemicals) might be understood in similar terms—as indeed much research on chemicals has done, both directly and indirectly.

Here, though, I wish to pursue a different line of inquiry. For anthropologist David Graeber (2015, 183), the persisting attachment of people in modern societies to bureaucracy suggests another way of thinking about such relationships. Despite their protestations otherwise, Graeber argues, people value bureaucracy precisely because it imposes rules on a world that would otherwise be in chaos. It is this notion, of bureaucracy generating order from chaos, that I apply to the glyphosate case. Even from what little I have related about it so far—and much more is to come—readers will have grasped a sense of how much confusion seemed to surround the chemical, what anthropologist Vincanne Adams (2022), writing about the US context, has called a "swirl." The rules of poisoncraft that the EU has put in place to control chemicals are an effort to take hold of the swirl and impose some kind of order on it. The way the EU has tried to do so has been to replicate, in the chemical world, the order of the EU world. This is not to explain away what the EU is (or isn't) doing regarding glyphosate regulation but rather to spotlight the notion of *order*.

Bureaucrats attempt to generate order in a world that would otherwise be in chaos. Chaos is precisely understood as the absence or negation of bureaucratic rules, that is, a world without systems of classification, routinization, and regulation. Poison is a corrosive, divisive, and unsettling force—a force that carries within itself those exact same connotations of danger and disorder that would comprise a world without bureaucracy. As I argued in part 1, poisoncraft has origins in the opposed worlds of rationalism and magic. As a project of rationalism, poisoncraft is concerned with weights and measures—Paracelsus's dose management. As a project of magic, poisoncraft is concerned with harnessing poison's ambivalent powers for good or ill. As Graeber has argued, the magical world is a world without bureaucracy—a world that is simultaneously alluring and unsettling. At least in Euro-American traditions but perhaps everywhere that bureaucracy has become established, poison's material semiosis has lent itself to becoming the antithesis of a world of cold rationalism—a means of escaping Weber's iron cage, in other words.

We do not only need to turn to the magical world to imagine the poisons of a world without bureaucracy. Bureaucracy's *others*, for example, governance by the sovereign's whim, the disorder of adhocracy (Elizabeth Cullen Dunn 2012), or even the shadow world of a deep state, are each implicitly or explicitly understood to represent a toxic threat to the well-being of citizens and nations. In such cases, it is the absence of bureaucracy, or the quasi-bureaucratic structures of a secret government within a government, that accounts for the spread of poisons in the pursuit of sinister ends. One of the most common tropes of conspiratorial thinking is the deployment of an invisible poison to an unknowing population, the remedy for which is usually an accountable bureaucratic machine staffed by public servants working for the common good. In those examples, "good" bureaucrats—typically, bureaucrats who do not overreach and who support the ideals and goals of libertarians and populists—do the work of ridding the body politic of noxious contaminations.

As the standard-bearers of order, then, bureaucrats *are* specialists in poisoncraft. Their mission is precisely to take up the fight against the disorder and danger of a world of ungoverned poisons, with governance understood as a remedy for the ills of the world. The craft of bureaucracy is also poisoncraft—just as poisoncraft is also the bureaucracy of poison. Almost all areas of the modern economy turn on the creation, exchange, and disposal of poisons as products and by-products. The task of all governments is to plan for and control those poisons. Likewise, the task of crafting a European body politic through the development and implementation of bureaucratic procedure is fundamentally a project of poisoncraft. In the next chapter, I explore how principles of poisoncraft were put into action in risk assessment and regulatory science writing.

5

Regulatory Review and Sovereign Ignorance

How will the text seek to convince? By means of other texts produced in the laboratory and "produced" here as evidence.
—BRUNO LATOUR AND PAOLO FABBRI, "THE RHETORIC OF SCIENCE"

Whoever writes the first draft, sets the tone.
—DR. CHRISTOPHER PORTIER, WEBINAR, MAY 2022

During a webinar hosted by the NGO Corporate Europe Observatory in May 2022, Dr. Christopher Portier, a strong critic of the EFSA's glyphosate risk assessment, drew attention to what he considered fatal flaws in European regulatory authorship. Portier was seeking to explain how the IARC and the EFSA had come to different conclusions on glyphosate's carcinogenic risk. For Portier, a significant problem lay not only in who did or should conduct safety studies (industry, regulators, or independent third parties), but how their findings appeared in regulatory reviews of the literature and decisions being made from those reviews. In his presentation, Portier highlighted different traditions of scientific authorship that fed into regulatory processes, from the subject experts who wrote for law courts to the academic literature that the IARC had consulted to the involvement of industry in writing their own studies for regulatory review: "Whoever writes the first draft, sets the tone. In the case of the courts of law, the scientists who are defending their position write everything, and they have to sign something to the effect that they have written everything. In IARC, the working group, the scientists themselves write the original draft of the entire document. For EFSA and ECHA, industry writes the first document, and they set the tone. And from there, it's all downhill."

A cancer expert who at the time I met him was "semiretired," Portier had spent the later stages of his career directing US scientific and regulatory agencies, including the US National Toxicology Program, before contributing to the

IARC's glyphosate assessment in 2015. He then became an expert witness for the case law firms were building against glyphosate, including the team that first challenged Monsanto over cancer risk in the United States, and a regular contributor to European Parliament reviews of pesticide approval processes. He published detailed analyses of what he considered the EFSA's failings around glyphosate (Portier et al. 2016; Portier and Clausing 2018; Portier 2020) but also complained the European agencies had failed to take his contributions seriously. As became clear throughout the numerous testimonies he gave to glyphosate hearings in Europe and the United States, his experiences first working inside those agencies and then as an outside advocate for change had helped Portier develop a finely tuned understanding of how processes of regulatory authorship gave structure and meaning to the scientific arguments being brought for or against glyphosate. Allowing industry to adopt the role of author of safety studies determined quite simply how the evidence on glyphosate was eventually going to be read.

Thus far, I have been reading regulatory documents for what they can tell us about the EU's approach to glyphosate. In this chapter, I pay attention to the regulatory lives of the documents themselves—the traditions of authorship and readership that gave them form on the page and would determine how and by whom they would be read. Anthropologists have shown how bureaucratic documents and styles of bureaucratic writing are not simply outputs of governmental and state practices, but fundamentally constitutive of those practices. For example, Akhil Gupta (2012) argues that bureaucratic writing gives form to sovereign decree; it is where, perhaps more than anywhere else, governance is enacted and takes effect at the everyday level. As Matthew Hull (2012, 253) has also observed, "Documents are not simply instruments of bureaucratic organizations, but rather are constitutive of bureaucratic rules, ideologies, knowledge, practices, subjectivities, objects, outcomes, and even the organizations themselves." They "help generate larger-scale forms of sociality . . . as vehicles of imagination" of and for states (260).

I continue my exploration of poisoncraft by showing how as a practice of regularizing the world of unruly poisons, regulatory science writing wavered between the worlds of knowledge and ignorance, order and chaos. As artifacts that produced and gave legitimacy to poisoncraft, bureaucratic documents played a significant role in the construction of what was to be known—and not known—about glyphosate. I examine how and by whom the "scientific literature" had been authored and how and why that mattered to those who read it. I place "scientific literature" in quotation marks precisely to highlight how what was defined and read as the scientific literature was rarely straightforward. European regulation is based on an "industry pays" rule: the applicant for molecule authorization must provide the safety studies the regulator requires to assess toxic hazard and risk. While many consider the financial burden falling on industry the right and proper way to manage this process, significant problems arise in terms of how applicants' preferential outcomes may end up reflected in the research submitted. Industry studies are typically conducted in-house or contracted to private laboratories. In both cases, significant conflicts of interest exist to prove the safety of a molecule. However, even ostensibly "independent" studies conducted by academic researchers, those who are (in theory) not in the pay of industry, have sometimes been heavily influenced by, or completely authored by, pesticide companies. One of the biggest scandals to emerge from the Monsanto Papers was evidence of industry toxicologists writing or editing draft sections of articles that were favorable to glyphosate but later published under the names of ostensibly independent researchers (Gillam 2021b).

The fallout from the Monsanto Papers continued to be felt during the EU's debates over glyphosate, but here I focus on the EU's revised Renewal Assessment Report (RAR) on glyphosate that the EFSA published in response to the IARC report. To some of its readers at least, the RAR appeared to plagiarize the industry's own (inevitably favorable) interpretation of the safety studies conducted on glyphosate, on which basis the EFSA had not found glyphosate carcinogenic. While the RAR's authors argued they had followed correct regulatory procedure, the accusation cut to the core of how different expectations of and for scientific authorship and the production of knowledge and ignorance came together in approval processes. This included questions over how regulatory devices like Good Laboratory Practice (GLP) and the Klimisch score—intended to harmonize and build trust in regulatory science—could or should be used and how evidence produced using standardized guidelines for safety assessment differed from evidence produced by hypothesis-driven science. This chapter thus traces two key problems that emerged during the period of this study: (1) How was glyphosate constructed as a problem of regulatory science *writing*? (2) How was Europe imagined, projected, and contested through practices of regulatory scientific authorship, readership, and criticism about glyphosate? In answering those questions, the chapter shows how European sovereignty was claimed and expressed in and through the right and ability to make pronouncements on glyphosate as a poison—pronouncements that emerged from sovereign control of ignorance as much as control of knowledge.

REPORTING REGULATORY SCIENCE

During the summer of 2019, an addition to my office space appeared: the mass of paperwork produced by and in response to the EU's assessment of glyphosate. Among the piles of reports published by specialists in poisoncraft across the public, private, and charity sectors—the EFSA and the ECHA, the PEST and other parliamentary committees, environmental NGOs, academics, and industry—sat the pièce de résistance, all 4,322 pages of the *Final Addendum to the Renewal Assessment Report*, published in October 2015 (BfR 2015). Produced in response to the European Parliament's request that the EFSA reexamine the chemical in light of the IARC's findings, this was the revised and extended edition of the original Renewal Assessment Report on glyphosate, published two years earlier.

The RAR is where the Rapporteur Member State (RMS)—the "national competency" tasked by the EFSA to review the application dossier—assesses the "completeness and quality" of safety studies against international guidelines and concludes whether the results of each submitted study should be accepted or rejected. The RAR subsequently feeds into the work of the EFSA's risk assessment panel, where a conclusion on the hazardous potential of a molecule is reached. In this case, the European Glyphosate Taskforce (GTF), a consortium of twenty-four glyphosate-producing companies led by Monsanto, had made the original renewal application. Germany's Federal Institute for Risk Assessment (BfR) had been responsible for conducting the 2013 assessment as well as the 2015 reassessment following the Parliament's intervention and compiling the revised RAR.

As the first stage in the EU's molecule (re)authorization process, the RAR would "set the tone," as Portier put it, of the hazard and risk assessment to come. Not only did the RAR inform the EFSA's risk assessment panel that would make an ultimate recommendation on whether to approve or reject glyphosate, but it also sought to demonstrate the careful analytical work that had gone into that decision. In that sense, the RAR "sought to convince" (Latour and Fabbri 2000) through a set of representational techniques that demonstrated "rigor" and "objectivity." The RAR was deliberative in how it described the exhaustive search for and review of relevant studies the BfR undertook, as well as how the BfR considered those studies against international guidelines. From this view, the practice of poisoncraft involved in the authoring and reviewing of glyphosate safety studies was one of the most important ways in which glyphosate hazard and safety would come into being through practices of paper inscription and presentation.

At more than four thousand pages, the document comprised a revised and expanded version of the original RAR published in 2013. The RAR provided introductory, technical, and summary information on glyphosate and regulatory recommendations concerning the risks of glyphosate for human, animal, and environmental health and summaries of individual safety studies, including the conclusion stating that the evidence did not suggest that glyphosate was genotoxic or carcinogenic. In addition, the RAR contained two sections responding specifically to the IARC report, one of them an assessment of the studies the IARC had used. The BfR indicated the presence of revised and new additions to the original RAR using a color-coded schema, with yellow indicating changes made following peer review in January 2015 and green indicating changes following peer review in March 2015. Finally, large parts of the RAR included blacked-out text, indicating where closed proprietary studies had been reviewed.

Test Guidelines

The EU's regulation on the registration, evaluation, authorization, and restriction of chemicals (REACH) defines the scope and contents of the RAR, including a requirement that industry studies should be conducted according to the OECD's GLP test guidelines and that academic studies should be assessed for validity against the Klimisch score. GLP guidelines are supposed to ensure the "completeness" and "quality" of industry studies, while the Klimisch score provides a measure of the "reliability, relevance, and adequacy of data" in third-party studies, using GLP as the de facto baseline (Klimisch et al. 1997).

The OECD introduced GLP guidelines in 1978 with the intention of building "trust and confidence" in regulatory studies by harmonizing methods of testing and data analysis across the industry. Successful regulatory review requires a weight of evidence approach, which is to say, what counts as evidence never lies with just one study but the same finding repeated across dozens if not hundreds of studies. As the ECHA tells applicants, "As a general principle, the more information you provide, the stronger your weight of evidence is" (European Chemicals Agency 2011). To be confident that findings *are* the same, regulators need to know the many different studies they have looked at have been conducted in the same way and that their findings have been reported in the same way. Thus, among other things, GLP establishes the parameters of studies by determining the test material to be used, the animal specimens to be exposed, the dose regimes and patterns of exposure, the methods of quantification and statistical analysis, and the reporting templates.

Meanwhile, regulators have come to judge the completeness and quality of academic studies in large part according to the degree to which they approximate, and hence can be compared with, GLP studies. To assess this, the EU favors applying the Klimisch score, which provides a standardized framework for assessing the regulatory value of academic studies. The score was published in the journal *Regulatory Toxicology and Pharmacology* in 1997 by Klimisch, Andreae, and Tillmann (1997), all employees of the chemical company BASF but writing on behalf of an advisory committee on chemical regulation of the German government. It applies criteria for evaluating *reliability, relevance,* and *adequacy* based, among other things, on the extent to which methods used and data collected are appropriate for the hazard identification or risk characterization (the toxicological endpoints) sought,[1] the way methods and results are described to give evidence of the clarity and plausibility of the findings, and how evidence on different endpoints is judged according to the weight of evidence found. However, because academic studies rarely meet such criteria, they often fall short of the Klimisch assessment and regulators reject them from their review.

While GLP has become the international standard for regulatory science, critics have argued that the guidelines are not a neutral reflection of the best scientific methods available at the time. Rather, they are heavily contingent on a series of negotiations over several decades between the OECD, industry, and regulatory

---

1. A toxic endpoint is the result of a study conducted to determine the hazardous properties of a substance. Toxic endpoints can be acute or chronic and include different forms of injury or fatal outcomes.

authorities that have come to construct what counts as the best scientific methods according to specific interests and concerns. Those concerns have tended to reflect industry and regulatory priorities and reporting styles that enable the creation of a weight of evidence through harmonization and exclusion of outlier studies. Similarly, efforts to retroactively harmonize academic studies with GLP guidelines have been criticized for downgrading the scientific status of academic studies (Kase et al. 2016). Writing in the journal *Environmental Research*, a consortium of environmental organizations argued how this process has artificially elevated the status of GLP studies over non-GLP studies and has "created a de facto total ban of academia's diverse and sensitive toxicity tests from most risk assessment" (Buonsante et al. 2014, 139).

Thus, the authors of GLP studies produce research that adheres, at least in principle, to OECD guidelines. In that sense, GLP studies are authored as bureaucratic documents suitable for regulatory science purposes, and their assumed readers are the toxicological and other disciplinary specialists employed by regulatory authorities. In contrast, academic authors may not write for regulators, but they do write for audiences—principally other academics working in their field. What champions of academic studies over GLP studies have tended to miss, however, are the efforts to achieve standardization and harmonization at work in academic studies themselves. As sociologist Lawrence Busch (2000, 280) has noted, "Only by maintaining scientific and technical standards in the laboratory can experiments be made to appear universal in character"—and hence appeal to those audiences. When appropriated for regulatory purposes, their users must first convert academic studies into a form suitable for bureaucratic readership, which is achieved by their retroactive standardization with and evaluation against GLP requirements.

Much of the debate on glyphosate has thus focused on the relative value of GLP guideline studies versus academic non-guideline studies as mechanisms for establishing trust in regulatory processes. While the benefits of GLP came under sustained questioning from EFSA's critics, industry questioned the benefits of academic studies. Although I met no one working in regulatory contexts who thought that industry studies without government oversight would be "unbiased" (at best, and "downright duplicitous" at worst), many argued that the existence of GLP ensured they would be fair and reliable even if industry itself was not. Conversely, those same people agreed that academic researchers are less likely to be biased, but because they did not follow standardized protocols, their studies were rarely comparable with one another or with industry studies. At stake were thus the relative merits that industry and academic authors did or ought to have. Regulatory guidelines did not simply bestow relative weightings to those merits, but helped create and cultivate them as a matter of regulatory concern.

Speaking before the PEST committee, the OECD's head of the Environment, Health and Safety Division, Bob Diderich, described the strengths and weaknesses of GLP and academic studies in precisely such terms. For Diderich, however, the two kinds of studies were better thought of as complementary rather than contradictory or in conflict. As Diderich put things:

> The advantages of [non-GLP studies] done by research laboratories are that they may ... advance the science. They may look at things that have not been standardised yet, so they may find issues that you maybe wouldn't find with standard methods. The disadvantage is the issue of reproducibility. One advantage of the standardisation of test methods is that they have proved to be reproducible across multiple laboratories, which research laboratories would not necessarily have done. (PEST Committee 2018c, 33)

The EFSA's executive director, Bernhard Url, agreed: "We are not saying that GLP certification is a label for quality. You can find high-quality GLP studies, you can find low quality GLP studies, you can find high-quality non-GLP studies and the other way round" (PEST Committee 2018c, 67).

Critics of GLP, meanwhile, have argued that the guidelines favor industry by limiting the design and hence the possible results of a study. Adhering to the guidelines limits scientific creativity in the conceptualization and conduct of studies that could help produce findings not observed before. In crucial ways GLP predetermines the results of tests, and because industry played a role in deciding what GLP tests should include, results usually come out in industry's favor. As Portier argued:

> Regulatory studies are generally limited to specific dosing regimens, specific strains and specific species and seeing no positive responses in these studies does not guarantee safety. Non-regulatory studies are more flexible, using different strains, different species and different dosing regimens that may be more indicative of the likely response to be seen in humans. (PEST Committee 2018a, 272)

Others pointed to the lack of regulatory bite contained in GLP. In the view of Helmut Burtscher-Schaden, director of the environmental organization Global 2000, the GLP system was not properly monitored, and GLP-accredited laboratories may not be adhering to the regulations (PEST Committee 2018c, 16).

Finally, the historical preference given to GLP studies over academic studies and the continued ways in which regulatory discourse differentiated between guideline and non-guideline studies meant academic studies continued to have lesser significance in regulatory decisions. Academic studies lacked the merits that made guideline studies reliable—namely, the guidelines that implied a known method had been followed and the study would be reproducible. For the OECD's Bob Diderich, regulators struggled with how to make sense of unusual results produced by non-guideline studies: "If results are slightly out of the ordinary—risk assessors may have the problem that they do not know how to use them, because reproducibility has not been established" (PEST Committee 2018c, 103).

Through those debates, what counted as "the scientific literature" and the relative merits of guideline and non-guideline studies were deployed for rhetorical purposes to win or defeat arguments. Supporters and detractors alike thus converged on an understanding of "the literature" that juxtaposed the two possible traditions by which knowledge about glyphosate could be made and what kinds of ignorance could be tolerated. One of those traded standardization and harmonization for discovery; the other traded discovery for standardization and harmonization. What is striking is that everyone accepted, albeit to different degrees, that this trade-off produced ignorance of some form. For the defenders of guideline studies, this was ignorance of what unrestricted scientific investigation might uncover. For the advocates of academic studies, it was ignorance of whether the findings from one or a handful of studies were truly replicable and reliable. Both forms of ignorance were nevertheless an inevitable and acceptable price to pay for trusting what knowledge guidelines and academic studies then produced. To trust was to accept ignorance. To accept ignorance was to trust.

Trusting Ignorance and the Sovereign Exception

The workings of contemporary governance and bureaucracy rely on trust—a social bond premised on a mutual recognition of one's knowledge, experience, and expertise vis-à-vis others, which can be affirmed through commitments to standards, transparency, and audit. However, as social scientists have shown, the very need for standards and audit *itself* produces the conditions for mistrust. Rather than being characterized as an absence of trust, mistrust, anthropologists have argued, can be better thought of as generative of new forms and relations (Strathern 2000; Carey 2018). In the regulatory context, as I have shown, knowledge produces mistrust, which in turn produces knowledge; ignorance produces trust, which in turn produces ignorance. Social scientists have long been interested in this form of "cultivated ignorance" (Proctor 1995), showing how both knowledge and ignorance of chemical harms (for example) emerges from strategic decisions about what counts as knowledge, how knowledge should be sought, and how the pursuit of certain forms of knowledge should be prioritized over other forms of knowledge (Benson and Kirsch 2010a, 2010b; Fortun 2010; Singer and Baer 2009). Translated into my language of poisoncraft, efforts to manage knowledge and ignorance can be understood as efforts to manage order and chaos.

However, most of the scholarship on ignorance has been produced in the context of North American, typically US, organizations, scandals, and debates, which has witnessed dramatic deregulation. In Europe, where a very different political and regulatory culture has emerged, there has been much less attention. But the presence of stronger government regulation in Europe did not prevent or solve the problems of strategic ignorance and uncertainty that have been so well documented in the United States; it merely relocated spheres of power and action from the private sector to the public sector. The US government has always aided and abetted US industry, of course, but in Europe the difference was that governments retained a stronger influence over the market mechanisms that in the US drove deregulation. Moreover, as degrees of regulatory harmonization strengthened, these traveled downward and outward from the emerging supranational body of the EU to the level of Member States. If in the United States private actors would shape the form and content of knowledge and ignorance, in Europe state actors would continue to monopolize them—even if, most of the time, it would often still be for the benefit of industry rather than the public.

Approaching the construction of knowledge and ignorance as processes being shaped by different, often competing public and private agendas between the national and international levels requires a reconceptualization of the adage that knowledge equals power. It also provides us with one of the most striking insights into the bureaucratic workings of European poisoncraft. To explore this, I take up sociologist Linsey McGoey's (2007) use of the philosopher Friedrich Nietzsche's concept of the will to ignorance as a form of power. Rather than assume that a will to knowledge was people's prime motivation, Nietzsche believed that the majority embraced and reveled in ignorance—enjoying what one might call the benefits of an unexamined life. The significance of this was precisely the limits and value of knowledge as a necessary or desirable precursor for action in the world. For Nietzsche, ignorance was not only the more general condition under which most human action took place but also the means to living a simple life, which was the desire of most people. Nietzsche's will to ignorance thus broke apart the causal relationship between knowledge and power long before Foucault had even proposed the absolute significance of their attachment. And, as I have already indicated, if the will to ignorance meant an ability to lead a quiet life, the will to knowledge meant a rather busy and confusing one. In the knowledge economies of the twentieth and twenty-first centuries, the phrase "ignorance is bliss" would come to indicate a happy if passive acceptance of unknowing.

Yet, as contemporary research on agnotology and ignorance has shown, there is little easy or simple about it. Maintaining ignorance, for example, of chemical harms in the face of ever-growing mountains of evidence, requires a special dedication among a dedicated community industry professionals and sympathetic others—even if the political class and wider public are apparently happy to ignore the visceral experiences of environmental breakdown happening all around them. Thus, it is important to ask: Who labors *for* ignorance and who revels *in* ignorance? McGoey's research demonstrated how the UK's pharmaceuticals regulator avoided culpability for failing to consider evidence of suicide risk caused by antidepressant medications, simply by stressing its own ignorance of such evidence. She showed how what she called a "bureaucratic will to ignorance" allowed the regulator to protect itself against claims of regulatory failure and oversight. As she concluded, "One must dispel the automatic equivalence of knowledge as power and realize that in cultivating a purposeful ignorance—in refusing to admit even that one harbours a secret—one often wields the most strength" (McGoey 2007, 221).

Ignorance, it is commonly suggested, is no defense in the eyes of the law. Whether true or not, that legal presumption has power when the defendant itself makes and implements the law. Extending McGoey's argument, the sovereign exception to law enjoyed by the UK's pharmaceuticals regulator as a *state agency* allowed for protection against its own ignorance of the law—something that distinguishes, in a fundamental way, sovereign from corporate constructions of ignorance. It is not just the sovereign production of knowledge and ignorance, but the *sovereign monopolization of ignorance* that interests me here. Test guidelines of European pesticide regulation clearly demarcated areas that fell within its remit and those that did not. This included what kind of knowledge about glyphosate was valid and meaningful and by extension what kind of knowledge was not. It also included the regulator's ability not just to be ignorant of other kinds of knowledge about glyphosate, but to claim a monopolization on ignorance about glyphosate. Understood as a right and an ability to pronounce on the poison status of glyphosate, the sovereign monopolization of ignorance is thus one of the clearest articulations of EU poisoncraft. The EU's sovereign power was an expression of its unique right to make a pronouncement on poison, and it was expressed in the act of making that pronouncement. From the bureaucratic point of view, ignorance can be key to the creation and maintenance of order—by ridding the public body of the poison of mistrust. Nowhere was this more evident than in the BfR's reading of industry studies.

REGULATORY REVIEW AS PERFORMATIVE POISONCRAFT

In Bruno Latour and Paolo Fabbri's (2000) framing, "texts produced in the laboratory" give science its convincing authority and trust. For many who would become involved in the glyphosate debate, however, this trust was missing from the regulatory science they were reading, which was always several authors removed from the laboratory. While the companies applying for glyphosate reapproval had supplied the EU with original safety studies, they had also provided their own summaries of those studies—and it was those summaries the authors of the RAR had reproduced in the document. It was not just that this process risked admitting reproduction error and bias into the RAR. The identity of the several authors who had been involved along the way was also missing. While the purpose of devices like GLP and the Klimisch score was precisely to mitigate against the absence of the traditional scientific author, for those already suspicious of industry authorship, or the ability or willingness of the EFSA to evade industry influence, those checks and balances were far from adequate.

"Matters of Fact" and "Matters of Opinion"

Glyphosate's supporters often celebrate the number of safety studies to which the molecule has been subject, which for them provides a clear weight of evidence in their favor. Monsanto's head of research and development, for example, argued,

"Glyphosate is one of the most studied molecules that has ever been introduced into the agricultural marketplace. Time and time again it's been shown to have a tremendous safety record" (Sfiligoj 2019). Thus, the GTF has sought to convince through the repeated demonstration of glyphosate's safety. Importantly, of course, glyphosate only became the most studied molecule in the world thanks to its market dominance. The EU's REACH regulation and the regulatory trust devices of GLP and Klimisch worked to simultaneously produce the number of glyphosate studies *and* define those studies' acceptable modes of authorship and readership. Regulation required the applicant to produce the hundreds of studies over years providing evidence for glyphosate toxicology across myriad toxicological endpoints. That in turn required the harmonization of method and presentation across studies as an administrative necessity if authorities were to be able to read them all. Finally, harmonization "enframe[d] and categorise[d] the world" (Gupta 2012, 154) according to the requirements of standardization, comparison, and portability.

More significantly, I also read the mass of studies in the literal sense—as an effort to overburden the regulator with the sheer weight of evidence. The BfR did not underplay the extent of the task involved in the assessment process. Andreas Hensel, BfR president, stressed this point when appearing before the PEST Committee: "Our risk assessment report . . . is . . . four and a half thousand pages—I hope that you have read it all. It has taken a lot of work to complete" (PEST Committee 2018c, 9). Faced with a veritable mountain of research to review, the BfR sought to make the process manageable by including only short summaries of studies in the RAR. As the BfR (2015, 13) explained, we were "not able to report the original studies in detail and an alternative approach was taken instead." The BfR described its approach as involving a reproduction of the "study descriptions and assessments *as provided by the GTF*" (13; emphasis mine) in the RAR itself—essentially, a summary of the summaries the GTF had already written and supplied as part of its application dossier. The BfR had then removed "redundant parts (such as the so-called 'executive summaries')" and created new data tables. Furthermore, "obvious errors were corrected" (13). Following this, the BfR added a comment of varying length and detail on the validity and significance of each study summary. Through this procedure, the BfR was able to distill the mass of information it had received into standardized and comparable units of evidence.

One of the most important ways the relationship between knowledge and ignorance played out was where the GTF and the BfR made concluding statements on each of the studies reviewed. Those statements were clearly identifiable in the text by the format of headings used to distinguish them from surrounding text—the GTF's comments included under a section titled "**Conclusion by the Notifiers**," always in boldface, and the BfR's response directly beneath it, under "*RMS Comments*," always in italics. In total, the document contained some 320 examples of each statement—640 in all. The relation between the GTF and the BfR was thus precisely defined and formulaic, with the GTF stating a study's conclusion as a "matter of fact" and the BfR expressing an opinion. The GTF almost always wrote its conclusions in the form of an uncontroversial outcome of a reliable study that should pass into the realm of established knowledge about glyphosate. Conclusions were rarely more than a sentence or two long and chose to report one or two key findings. Written with the absolute minimum of elaboration and always, as conventional for scientific writing, in the passive voice, what stood out from GTF's conclusions was their immutable nature. BfR comments, on the other hand, displayed greater variety. They ranged from the briefest agreements with the GTF's conclusions to lengthier critical reviews. The shortest replies commented on the reliability of the study, then repeated a key conclusion the GTF might also have highlighted. The BfR's longest comments drew attention to, among other things, the strengths or weaknesses of a study, whether or not it had received support from comparative studies, and/or noted errors of reproduction or interpretation by the GTF.

I include here four examples taken from the RAR that illustrate the range of ways the BfR read and commented on studies. The first example includes the briefest of conclusions and comments: the GTF (the "Notifiers") concluded from the study that glyphosate was non-genotoxic, with the RMS validating the reliability of the study and adding a qualifier to the GTF's conclusion that the study found genotoxicity only at very high levels of exposure (BfR 2015, 840).

Conclusion by the Notifiers
The test material glyphosate was non-genotoxic.

RMS comments:
The study is considered acceptable. Glyphosate proved non-genotoxic. Cytotoxicity was confined to very high concentrations.

The second example illustrates the BfR's role as a critical reviewer in greater clarity. The BfR highlights problems with the GTF's (and/or the study's original authors) writing, where and how the study reproduces previous research, and how existing literature plugs gaps in the study's approach or findings (BfR 2015, 523; edited for length).

Conclusion by the Notifiers
After oral administration of glyphosate (HR001) at least about 25 % are absorbed. Absorption was similar in both sexes. About 75 % and 25 % of the parent compound are excreted via faeces and urine, respectively. There was no indication of accumulation of glyphosate.

RMS comments:
The study is considered acceptable. As in some other studies of this section, it is not clear if the animals were fasted before sacrifice but this will not have affected the outcome of the study. The results confirmed previous knowledge. . . . The identity of the second minor component in faeces (beside AMPA) should have been elucidated. . . .

> *Unfortunately, no experimental group receiving multiple treatment was included in this study. Thus, final proof for the absence of an accumulating potential cannot be taken from the results of this study alone. However, such investigations have been performed by other researchers (XXXXX 1996 (TOX2000-1979); XXXXX 1992 (TOX9300343); XXXXXXXXX 1988 (TOX9552356)) giving sufficient information on this endpoint.* (Authors' names elided in original.)

In the third example, the BfR comments how crucial evidence missing from those studies could be taken from work performed by others. It draws attention to important findings about bone residues that the GTF had not commented on (BfR 2015, 552).

> **Conclusion by the Notifiers**
> Orally dosed glyphosate acid was excreted rapidly and predominantly in the faeces. 48 hours after dosing the greatest intensity of radiolabelling was in the bone and intestinal tract plus contents.
>
> *RMS comments:*
> *The study is considered supplementary despite its good quality. However, the number of animals of one sex and timepoint is too low for definitive conclusions. All the parameters examined (i.e., excretion and distribution) had been addressed in other studies before. This previous knowledge was confirmed. Oral absorption was generally low but showed a remarkable interindividual variability.*

Finally, in the fourth example, the full extent of the BfR's role as peer reviewer is evidenced in its outright rejection of the study. Note that the BfR not only highlights the weight of evidence that shows glyphosate toxicity in this test but also stresses that "a single study cannot contravene or even outweigh all this data coming from a number of (independent) laboratories." The BfR also takes aim at public criticism that they had ignored those independent studies—"even though this was suggested by a comment that was provided in the public consultation" (BfR 2015, 876; edited for length, highlighting in original to indicate revised text by the BfR).

> **Conclusion by the Notifiers**
> The test material glyphosate technical was non-genotoxic.
>
> *RMS comments:*
> *The study is considered not acceptable since it was seriously flawed (see below) and because the dose levels were much too low for any meaningful conclusion with regard to micronucleus formation, in particular when application by the oral route is taken into consideration. In the original report, some justification is given, based on a range-finding test suggesting effects at rather low dose levels. In fact, two animals that were administered 2000 mg/kg bw, died on day 3 after having shown ataxia and prostration before. The same observations were made in 3 animals which received an oral dose of 320 mg/kg bw. They all died on day 2. . . . A single study cannot contravene or even outweigh all this data coming from a number of (independent) laboratories even though this was suggested by a comment that was provided in the public consultation.*

The examples demonstrate how the GTF and the BfR, by adopting different roles of author and reviewer in the evaluation process, entered into dialogue as specialists in poisoncraft. The GTF wrote the study summaries and conclusions with the result of producing limited and precise "statements of fact" on glyphosate (Latour and Woolgar 1986). In response, the BfR read the GTF's conclusions and added comments of varying degrees of agreement or disagreement and in some cases also commented on feedback received from public consultation. While the GTF's clipped style worked to suggest that nothing more could be said on a study's findings, the BfR's lengthier responses, often introducing equivocation or uncertainty, combined statements of fact with statements of opinion. Importantly, however, the BfR did not always support those statements by citing the available literature but referred to what one assumes should be taken instead as common or established knowledge about a particular area of toxicology.

The routinized exchanges between GTF and BfR enshrined in the RAR established the BfR as a "competent authority" on the reading and judgment of the authorization submission. It was precisely the *un*clipped style of the BfR—and its more informal modes of writing—that gave the BfR both competence and authority, in so doing giving *voice* to the sovereign European body. The BfR did not have to justify its position on a study, one way or the other, because of the implied existence of a wider and deeper pool of knowledge and expertise that it signaled in the style of readership and authorship that it adopted. When the BfR found reason to question the reliability or significance of a study it did so, just as when it found reason to reject the conclusions of a study. Whether or not the BfR did so consistently or as often as it should have done is not the only question here. Also of interest is how the BfR entered a performative dialogue with the GTF's writings. The BfR read and wrote in the manner of a senior reviewer, passing judgment on whatever the GTF had offered up. What the statuses and processes of author and reader attached to the RAR as a literary device had established was a literal hierarchy between the BfR and the GTF. While the textual exchanges between the BfR and GTF would suggest a natural authority of one over the other—and hence give the entire document similar authority—thanks to the relative merits of the ignorance produced by guideline compared to non-guideline studies, it was, in fact, the GTF that benefited from the review process. As Portier commented, "whoever writes the first draft, sets the tone," and by being the one responsible for summarizing the studies, the GTF had in each case been able to frame the narrative.

The Plagiarism Controversy

As a material expression of regulatory harmonization, the RAR embodied a particular form of authorship that required in turn a particular approach to readership among its various audiences. This was especially clear in how readers of the RAR interpreted the method by which the BfR reported and commented on the GTF's review of third-party studies. Widely understood as an act of flagrant plagiarism, the controversy first surfaced in 2015 and then came to detain the PEST committee throughout 2018. At the heart of the case was the discovery, first brought to light by *The Guardian* (Neslen 2017), that the BfR had "copy-pasted" the GTF's summaries and conclusions of safety studies, including, most controversially, rationales for accepting industry studies that showed low carcinogenic risk and rejecting academic studies—including those relied on by IARC for its evaluation—that showed high carcinogenic risk. Critics argued that responsibility lay with the BfR to conduct a truly independent assessment of studies, which would necessarily involve writing new summaries and conclusions—not simply relying on those supplied by the GTF. The BfR and its defenders countered that their role was only to agree or disagree with the summaries the GTF had submitted; the absence of original authorship had no bearing on how well it had accomplished that task.

The plagiarism allegations had placed the BfR as well as the EFSA in the full glare of the international news media. Both organizations made repeated public statements denying any wrongdoing, and their directors had received thousands of expressions of concern from members of the public, including some death threats. The controversy also featured during the PEST committee meeting, with the BfR's president, Andreas Hensel, coming under heavy criticism. How those who had been critical of the BfR's handling of the study summaries expressed their concern helps reveal the different expectations at work around regulatory science writing. Swedish MEP Jytte Guteland was unequivocal in her view that the RAR had been heavily plagiarized, and that revelation had severely undermined her trust in the EU's ability to protect citizens' health. Moreover, even though the regulators had been caught in the act, their refusal to accept responsibility was equally damning.

> EFSA was caught with its trousers down—you must excuse my directness; I come from Sweden; I may be too direct, but that was how I saw it: you were caught with your trousers down. Yet it does not feel as if the authority is in the act of pulling its trousers back up: rather, what we see before us is a smokescreen. So I am not happy; I do not feel either happy or safe. (PEST Committee 2018c, 79)

The case would rapidly spiral into a heated and very public spat over what constituted plagiarism in the context of regulatory review, where the identity and meaning of an "author" of a text differed from those in the academic world. Stefan Weber, a "professional plagiarism hunter," and Helmut Burtscher-Schaden, director of Global 2000, would publish a fifty-nine-page report that examined, in detail, areas of the RAR highlighted by plagiarism software to contain elements copied from industry studies (Weber and Burtscher-Schaden 2019). They found that in the chapters dealing with non-guideline studies, the BfR had copied 50 percent of the content from GTF evaluations. This included "each of the 58 so-called Klimisch evaluations of published studies . . . copy pasted from the application for approval and presented as the assessments of the authorities" (7). Consequently,

Weber and Burtscher-Schaden alleged, "the authority failed to classify even a single published study on glyphosate and/or its commercial formulations as relevant or reliable. This also applies to the epidemiological studies on non-Hodgkin lymphoma, which, according to the IARC experts, raise suspicions that glyphosate causes cancer in humans" (7).

The Sovereign Adhocracy

In a critical take on why bureaucracies are not as all-powerful as they, and their detractors, might claim or fear them to be, anthropologist Elisabeth C. Dunn (2012, 2) argues instead for thinking about bureaucracy as a "form of power that creates chaos and vulnerability as much as it creates order"—what she calls "adhocracy." Dunn suggests that behind bureaucracy's rational veneer is a "process based as much on guesswork, rules of thumb, and 'satisficing'" (2)—an ad hoc approach to rule, in other words. For Christopher Portier, too, the whole process around glyphosate approval would come to resemble an adhocracy. As he explained during an interview, he found serious fault with the review methods adopted, accusing the regulatory agencies (European and others) for the "selective" application of their own standards and rules. The plagiarism controversy went beyond a mere matter of the BfR not showing its workings to encompass how different approaches to authorship could create a positive narrative on the science of a molecule. Rather than reaching their own conclusions on glyphosate, Portier accused the agencies of conspiring to produce evidence that would put glyphosate in the most favorable light. As he told me during an interview:

> When I looked at the EPA risk assessment, I saw exactly the same problems as EFSA, and then I found out that they had actually worked together. And then I found out, they were actually communicating. And then I found out that EPA was giving EFSA incorrect advice on some of the studies. Then I read Australia's risk assessment, and it was equally bad with the same problems [as EFSA's and EPA's]. Canada's risk assessment equally had the same problems. New Zealand had the only decent risk assessment. They didn't make the same stupid mistakes.

The most critical failing, Portier told me, had been the agencies' decision to include the results of historical control studies that suggested the evidence for glyphosate carcinogenicity in animal tests was statistically insignificant—i.e. the association had arisen because of random chance rather than exposure to glyphosate. Portier highlighted how the guidelines of major international and national agencies *all* stressed historical controls should not be used in that way, yet only the IARC had followed its own rules; the other agencies had simply chosen to ignore the rules. Becoming increasingly agitated as he spoke, Portier lambasted those agencies for their selective handling of findings that should have led to a glyphosate ban. Importantly, however, Portier did not accuse the regulatory agencies of acting to purposefully favor industry. Rather, he saw the problem as stemming from a lack of expertise within the regulatory agencies themselves. "Most of the reviews are done by toxicologists who don't have a lot of training in epidemiology," he told me, and hence do not understand inclusion and exclusion criteria for the different studies they examine and the different statistical tests they use. Instead, regulators fall back on what Portier called "toxicology's rules of thumb"—the workarounds required to summarize and make sense of a mass of data on a molecule like glyphosate that they are being asked to contend with. Allowed by the sovereign's exception, the regulatory agencies' own ignorance of epidemiology meant glyphosate would pass regulatory review thanks to an ad hoc application of the rules.

WRITING EUROPE THROUGH GLYPHOSATE TOXICOLOGY

Michel Foucault (1979) once asked, "What is an author?" His question was posed as a response to a running debate in philosophy about the significance of the figure of the author in the interpretation and meaning of a text. Foucault challenged the conventional understanding of authors as singular creative geniuses who served as the ultimate source of their work's meaning and interpretation. He observed that literary creation has transformed from simply conveying an author's personal thoughts to becoming a complex system of linguistic symbols that operate independently. This transformation reflected a fundamental shift whereby texts gained autonomy from their creators, with meaning emerging more from the work's internal structure and language than from authorial intention. Whereas writers once viewed their craft as a path to eternal recognition and lasting influence, contemporary writing represented a deliberate erasure of the self, where authors willingly dissolved their personal identity to allow their works to exist as independent entities.

Science writing is one such place where the author is supposed to disappear and the text stand on its own status as a piece of writing produced using external protocols. Within the world of European bureaucratic science, however, it was the identity of the author as a European citizen writing on the behalf of the Union that was paramount. It was that vision of Europe as an author and adjudicator of glyphosate safety and risk assessment that threaded through the narratives of both supporters and critics of the EU's pesticide safety processes. Europe, as a collective body, was a specialist in poisoncraft that could work to keep the chaos of the unregulated world at bay. Writing the documents that drew conclusions on glyphosate's toxicity would give form and reason to the European project. It was in the production of knowledge and gaps in knowledge about glyphosate's dangers, and in the bureaucratic arts of "satisficing" and "adhocracy" in response to the knowns and unknowns of those dangers, that sovereign identity and power was expressed. In so doing, the RAR gave life to more than sovereign decree.

In writing about glyphosate, the European Union through the EFSA and the EFSA through the BfR gave a voice to the organizational body of the multilevel union. In the next and final chapter in part 2, I turn my attention to the parliamentary committee set up to restore public trust in EU pesticide approval processes.

6

Science and Solidarity for the 500 Million

The world has a solid structure: there is the Commission for applying things, scientists for making the remarks you have just made and we [legislators] are here to make the rules. . . . We will make progress collectively here . . . so that we can ensure that tomorrow things will improve for the 500 million European citizens.

—MEP ERIC ANDRIEU (PEST COMMITTEE 2018C, 118)

To investigate the glyphosate controversies, in 2018 the European Parliament launched a special committee, commonly referred to as the "PEST committee," to look at the EU's authorization procedure for pesticides. The committee was chaired by French MEP Eric Andrieu, who presided over a series of meetings during which dozens of representatives from industry, academia, and civil society. Andrieu made the remarks quoted above following an especially challenging set of discussions concerning the rigor of regulatory processes in Europe. A center-left MEP had expressed concerns that science "deliberately shuts its eyes" to negative evidence about the herbicide because it risked damaging European agricultural competitiveness. An academic scientist involved in glyphosate research had then sought to reassure the MEP that "there are a lot of things going on in science, including things which are actively scattered across Europe," which proved difficult questions *were* being asked. The exchange had followed a long session exploring the failings of EU regulatory processes, including the bureaucratic order and influence of the pesticide industry on glyphosate science. MEP Andrieu had a fondness for the rhetorical flourish, often opening and closing sessions—or, as in this case, seeking to resolve polarized arguments—through evocative references to the greater European good that the committee was ultimately supposed to serve. His comments on the "solid structure" of the world envisioned a Europe defined by a clarity of regulatory office and purpose in which the constituent parts—administrative, political, and scientific—worked in happy union.

In this chapter, I explore the rhetoric of science, democracy, and solidarity put into service by specialists in poisoncraft—EU parliamentarians, bureaucrats, and other representatives of the academic community and civil society—when discussing glyphosate regulation. After glyphosate had become a poison to European union, the PEST committee sought to identify a path for achieving *re*union by working out how science and democracy would complement each other and provide a remedy to the problems that had arisen. Through this, the PEST committee would embody the "solid structure" of the EU—a matter of strengthening the European body through a strengthening of European poisoncraft. After reading the committee's transcripts, I identified a series of illustrative exchanges between participants (along with more causal one-liners, asides, scoldings, and celebrations issued from the chair) that show how speakers used rhetorics of science and democracy to explore the meanings and potentials of and for solidarity within the EU. The exchanges, reproduced here so to capture the full flavor of the contributions, demonstrate the tension between attempts to create a solid European Union from a solidarity movement.

SOLIDARITY: A EUROPEAN OBSESSION

In chapter 3 I showed how for EU President Juncker, expressions of European solidarity would offer the antidote to the poison of disunification. As he recalled in his State of the Union address, solidarity had been a key concern of the European project since its very inception. The authors of Europe's earliest treaties centered solidarity as an aspirational value to be nurtured. The preamble to the "Treaty Establishing the European Coal and Steel Community Treaty," for example, stated that "Europe can be built only through real practical achievements which will first of all create real solidarity, and through the establishment of common bases for economic development" (ECSC, High Authority, 1951, 1). Commitments to solidarity also appeared in the Single European Act (1986), the Maastricht Treaty (1992), and the Treaty of Lisbon (2006). In the latter, the treaty's authors described solidarity as a value that would bind the citizens of individual Member States as well as all Europeans, transcending Member States (Sangiovanni 2013). An idea of European solidarity—which manifested in debates about Europe's past, present, and future as both a presence and an absence—has been seen in different ways as the cause of and the solution to the EU's problems over the decades (Lahusen and Grasso 2018).

The political concept of solidarity has historical roots in Marxism and is usually associated with the left. Beyond the EU treaties, in contemporary Europe solidarity has as much been an oppositional praxis *to* the EU rather than *for* the EU (Katsanidou et al. 2022; McDonough and Tsourdi 2012). During the 2010s, for example, the emergence of Greek "solidarian" movements in reaction to EU-enforced austerity programs became an example of how solidarity returned as a powerful political force at national level at exactly the moment solidarity at the EU level was seen to be waning (Rozakou 2017; Theodossopoulos 2016). Anthropologist Theodoros Rakopolous (2016, 143) noted how, in Greece, solidarity practices were "at once specific to crisis and austerity *and* an issue with a sociocultural history of [their] own" (emphasis in original). Rakopolous suggests that solidarity emerged as a "bridge concept" connecting diverse sets of ethics and values of mutuality, assistance, charity, and humanitarianism with wider experiences of economic, political, and social turmoil, exclusion, and suffering. Thus, for Rakopolous, solidarity was not something that simply existed but had to be brought into being through responses to crisis that sought to link quotidian experience with collective endeavor. Approaching solidarity as an ethnographic concept can likewise help us understand how people make connections between subjectivity, practical action, and the forces that impinge on their lives. The point is not to compare collective action to an existing definition of solidarity and check whether it matches those criteria but to explore how collective action might encourage a concept of what people term "solidarity" to emerge at all. An ethnographic approach to solidarity at the EU level can take seriously the interplay between the historical textual commitments to solidarity found in the treaties and the everyday actions that EU representatives identified as practices of solidarity for them.

Residing at the core of the European discourses of solidarity is a theory of the Paracelsian sui generis—of a whole greater than the sum of its parts (see chapter 2). Europhiles conceptualize the project as one of individual nations becoming greater than the sum of their parts and of European citizenship as bestowing rights and freedoms that surpass those bestowed by national governments. Chief among them is the right to freedom of movement across national borders in mainland Europe that comprise the Schengen Area—a freedom of movement that manifests the Paracelsian commitment to unity in regulatory language. Thus, European solidarity turns on a tension between the bonds that make for solidarity at the national level, the bonds that make for solidarity at the EU level, and the difficulties that emerge from attempts to join or to reconcile those two forces through a conscious fluidity in terms of how national and European identities may be formed, expressed, and maintained. If this has meant the project of achieving European solidarity, much like the project of forming a European body, has always been unfulfilled (di Napoli and Russo 2018), then corrupting, corrosive influences that work against those projects are cast as poisons. Glyphosate was a potent material and symbolic threat to the foundational principles of the European project.

THE PEST COMMITTEE

It was in response to the poisonous danger glyphosate posed that the European Parliament established the PEST committee. Reading its proceedings and reports reveals how ideas of and commitments to Europe as a political and technocratic project played out in the debates that took place. The committee's chair, MEP Eric Andrieu, was himself a model of European collaboration and cohesion. A French politician of the Socialist Party and member of the European Parliament since 2012, throughout his time in Brussels Andrieu had sat on several parliamentary committees concerned with agriculture and the environment. Careful to stress the cooperative nature of the process and the involvement of PEST committee members in its design and functioning, Andrieu, in his opening remarks on how the hearings would operate, provides a window onto how the bureaucratic process would come into being. What they show is that Andrieu deemed the pursuit of science, democracy, and solidarity central to the very workings of the committee itself. At the core of his remarks were commitments to translation, transparency, commonality, inclusion, and collective responsibility. I reproduce an abridged, albeit still lengthy, example here.

> Ladies and gentlemen, I suggest that we commence our working committee. . . . Firstly, I would like to check that none of the members dispute the agenda. If there are no objections, I suggest that we adopt it. I do not see anyone speaking up and I would like to thank you very much. I would then like to inform you that interpreting is available in 16 languages.
> . . .
> [F]or the sake of transparency, from tomorrow, the written questions that we send to all of our guests and the responses that we receive from them before our committees will be on the Parliament website after our committees take place. This is again in the interests of providing the greatest level of transparency and information to everyone who follows our work, so that we can pursue a common pathway and move together towards an objective of improved protocols for authorising the placing on the market of certain molecules.
> . . .
> As we had decided with the coordinators, today we are going to welcome four speakers, who I will introduce to you shortly. The method remains the same, but I would like to clarify it. . . . We have collectively chosen the so-called ping pong method, i.e. a question, then an answer. I will be attentive, and I say this at the request of the groups, that a question is asked in the minute that you are allocated.
> . . .
> This process was decided upon collectively. It seems a very strict method, but I did not create it. We decided upon it. . . . I hope that the rules are clear. I am going to have to ensure that they are respected and I would like to thank you for your collective discipline, but I have no doubt of your understanding in this regard. That is the process. (PEST Committee 2018c, 3–4)

As was normal for parliamentary meetings of this kind, comprehensive translation was crucial to the functioning of the PEST committee, as was what Andrieu referred to as finding "a common pathway" for the purpose of "[moving] together towards an objective." As the committee's work progressed, Andrieu would often return to the principles of translation, transparency, commonality, inclusion, and collective responsibility that he saw as underpinning their efforts. Whenever discussions polarized on contentious issues, for example accusations that the regulators had ignored the IARC ruling or other crucial evidence, or the influence of industry on European politics, Andrieu would remind participants of their commitment to those principles. Likewise, when speakers or members of the audience deviated from the "ping pong" method or took up more than their allotted time, it was the process "decided upon collectively" that Andrieu evoked to restore discipline.

If the values and principles of the European project made up the very substance of the committee's proceedings, they were under constant scrutiny regarding how its members would deliver against them. Questions of how science, democracy, and solidarity served the greater good—the protection of the four freedoms and/or the protection of Europeans' health and environment—were assumed fundamental to the problem of glyphosate. Throughout the proceedings, participants referred to science and democracy in ways that were often contradictory—as words and ideas that had solid and shared meaning but also as words and ideas that indicated inherent instability and movement, concepts with rigidly defined meanings but also open-ended projects of improvement in the face of open-ended failure. Grappling with the meanings and possibilities for science and democracy, I argue, became an important way in which the question of European solidarity was also addressed.

Science

Anthropologists have long been interested in how and in what ways the boundaries that make up science, politics, and society broadly defined are generated and maintained. However, as Latour (1990, 145) once suggested, it is the "language that transports politics outside of science . . . [that we] . . . need to understand and explain"—language that, it should be emphasized, only becomes possible thanks to the wider relations within which actors are operating. While the hard and fast conventions demarcating "science" from "not science" (e.g., religion, magic, or irrationality) have their origins in the long history of scientific and political thought stemming from at least seventeenth-century England (Shapin and Schaffer 1985), what has changed over the decades that social scientists have been writing about science is an increasing recognition among scientists themselves that boundaries are historical and that science doesn't really observe the world "from nowhere." Scientists are socially and politically engaged; they may even have social science or humanities degrees. Despite this, the social science literature has tended to portray scientists as somewhat uncritically committed to outmoded beliefs in universal rationality and objectivity.

In the EU context, in part in response to problems like glyphosate, organizations like the EFSA have begun exploring approaches to what it terms "open science" and greater "democratic accountability"—two ideas that purposefully blur the boundaries between "science" and "not science." All those I spoke to at the EFSA were well aware that science was shaped by location; this was, for them, perfectly obvious when working in teams made up of people drawn from across Europe. If anthropologists' accounts of how scientists think about science have often been unflattering, what I hope to demonstrate here is how the scientists appearing before the PEST committee had a rather more sophisticated view of their practice. To be sure, for those I worked with, the concept and indeed value of and need for boundaries still existed. But how and why they existed and just how firm they were or could or should be became questions tied to the navigation and avoidance of conflict as much as they did any universal concept of science floating above the fray. They were not taken for granted, even if the ultimate end for many was to arrive at a place where they *could* take them for granted.

Throughout the PEST committee's proceedings, disputes brought forth by the glyphosate controversy meant the definition and meaning of "science" were to be stated and restated at every turn. "Science" helped determine what constituted the committee's remit or an acceptable line of questioning pushed by a participant. "Science" was a line of attack to take up, as well as a defensive position to adopt. Appeals to science were deployed to affirm one's own position, to discredit another's position, and, crucially, as a tactic to cool the heat of an argument. Equally, science was both timeless and something that progressed and evolved. Science provided epistemic security while also being something that could and indeed should be continuously improved, thereby introducing the notion that science was also compromised and contingent. When committee members and participants evoked "science," they evoked a shared identity as professionals with disagreements rooted in, but always resolvable by appeals to, a universal yet always highly malleable notion and practice. Although "science" was and could therefore be many things, what it was *not* was also clear—namely, "emotion" and "politics." As one speaker would simply affirm at the end of a long debate over precisely such matters, "science is science"—and with that apparently self-evident statement drew the conversation to a close.

For many of those who participated in the committee, science was thus both unimpeachable and in need of constant defending from conscious or unconscious bias, malign influence, or ulterior motive. One of the main areas of the committee's focus was science funding, with the paramount question being whether the industry-sponsored studies routinely used in regulatory decisions could ever be trustworthy. This question arose specifically in relation to the work of the BfR, which the EFSA had tasked with the glyphosate reassessment and had then been accused of plagiarizing industry studies in its final report. The following exchange took place between four committee participants: Andreas Hensel, BfR president; MEP Andrieu, committee chair; MEP Alojz Peterle, European People's Party (PPE); and Helmut Burtscher-Schaden, director of an environmental NGO. Hansel and other BfR representatives had been defending their glyphosate report for some time, both in and outside committee meetings. Under attack and on the defense during a prolonged session, Hensel was taken to task first by Andrieu for apparently dismissing the committee's concerns.

> **Hensel,** *BfR.* – The question is not whether the authorities that have worked like this up to now have been wrong to do so [i.e., use industry-funded studies], but the question now is why are there such great misgivings about their outputs? And there we encounter two worlds. The first is the world of science, which of course can, and also wants to arm itself with scientific arguments, because it is not political, and then [and this is the second world of politics] the question whose agenda do these decisions suit, or not. (PEST Committee 2018c, 17)
>
> **Andrieu,** *Chair.* – Excuse me, Mr Hensel. . . . This committee was created for a reason. It was not just for the pleasure of meeting or getting together, even though the friendliness between us is useful for our meetings. It is because there is a scientific controversy (whether you like it or not) and there are conflict of interest issues which are arising in the initiatives being taken, which are real, and we must work on improving the procedures. . . . [T]here is a collective effort [to improve matters] and, as you have said yourself, our shared task is to work together to improve mutual trust. (17–18)

Peterle questioned his references to science as a deflecting tactic.

> **Peterle,** *PPE.* – I am not impressed when one refers to science, as science on its own does not guarantee the truth. Science may be political, and politics is about what science wants to see or what it does not study. If it does not look in a particular direction, it will see nothing there. And if it is only interested in short-term effects, it will not be able to report on the long-term ones. (23)

Burtscher-Schaden spoke out in favor of a science committed to objectivity.

> **Burtscher-Schaden,** *Global 2000.* – I believe that science, if really done . . . objectively and transparently and according to scientific criteria[,] . . . can definitely be a benchmark that can offer good guidance for decision-making for political risk managers. (23)

Unchastised, Hensel finished with a defense against what he perceived to be the "cheap" lines of attack to which the committee had subjected him.

> **Hensel,** *BfR.* – I have to mull it over for a minute, since of course it's the best argument that counts in science. It's not always about who's doing it, it's the argument itself which counts. And if someone can draw on the wisdom of experience—forty years, thirty years, ten years, whatever—then that's the person who is best able to judge the scientific facts, and who is able to evaluate advances in knowledge due to publications or statistics. There are just people who are better and who are worse at it. It's the same as with hairdressers. (36–37)

I read the exchanges as illustrative of two separate views of science that would return throughout the committee's meetings. Hensel and Burtscher-Schaden, who were otherwise in disagreement over most things, expressed the first, which was that solid rules governed science. Andrieu and Peterle expressed the second, which was that science was simultaneously shaped by other forces *and* undergoing change—which for them also meant improvement—all the time. Throughout the committee's proceedings, the question of what lay inside or outside the remit of science led to disputes over if or how questions of the context in which science was conducted should be acknowledged. MEP Maria Noichl, a member of the center-left Socialists and Democrats Group, expressed concern that what she termed "European science" had become too narrow and too partial because it did not want to upset European economic development. She suspected pro-glyphosate groups had put pressure on regulators to approve a molecule that that science had shown to be dangerous.

> In Europe, science is not tasked with keeping the wheels turning, i.e. to keep the money flowing. So if science is more or less just grease for the wheels which drive commerce, then I'm thinking that that isn't the kind of science which I want for Europe. I want science which progresses naturally, and science should always be linked to curiosity and seeking out new things, and finding improvements—that's what science is to me. But if science—I'll say it again—lowers itself and knowingly only dares to take a narrow view so as not to shake up systems which have needed shaking up for a long. (117)

In this case, science was not "just science" but could and should be qualified as *European* science—a science of and for Europe as a social and political project, a science of and for solidarity and activism. For Noichl, it was precisely the absence of shared European values from regulatory science that had caused the loss of public trust in the glyphosate approval process.

Democracy

Like science, *democracy* was a word and an idea that came to mean and do different things during the committee meetings. With roots also in the seventeenth century and much like science, democracy pivoted between solidity and fluidity—an anchor for the world while also being something under constant attack and being at risk of falling foul of the antidemocratic predations of the world. As committee participants discussed glyphosate, questions about why and for whom they were working became paramount, helping steer scientific controversies toward resolution and consensus. As the chair would remark:

> The debates are rich and lively because the stakes are high. . . . These are all issues that are at the heart of our debates on which we must collectively and responsibly move forward so that tomorrow we can, indeed, have the guarantee that our 500 million Europeans can drink healthy, eat healthy and breathe healthy. (PEST Committee 2018c, 82)

"The 500" (or "our 500") became the rallying point—the one permanent truth against which always contested and contestable democratic decision making and accountability could be compared. From the committee's perspective, the question was always, "How we can best act in the interests of the greatest number in order to move forward together?" (150). MEP Andrieu would resort to familiar tropes of "strength from diversity" to help build legitimacy and purpose in the work of the committee and the EU thereafter. "The strength of democracy is nourished by the extent of our differences" (186), Andrieu would retort to MEP Pilar Ayuso, who had dismissed the arguments against glyphosate as ideological. "I believe that we must listen to each other and respect each other in our differing opinions. This is the basis on which majorities are arrived at and democracy functions," Andrieu added (186). Indeed, democracy had allowed debate and identified a role for science to help resolve the question of glyphosate once and for all.

> I believe that . . . at the EU level . . . we would gain a great deal . . . from working in synergy . . . to provide the political executive that we are with elements that would improve things in terms of unacceptability of risk. We will move forward because there is no absolute truth . . . to guarantee . . . the 500 million EU citizens that the food they eat, the air they breathe and the water they drink will not, in the future, contain any molecules that can damage their health. Because when it comes down to it, that is what concerns us collectively. (190)

At some point during the PEST committee's proceedings, however, questions had been raised about the EU's long-term commitment to pesticide regulation. Speculation had mounted that the EU, having been burned by controversies like glyphosate, was poised to delegate all responsibility for pesticide approval to the Member States. Committee members strongly reacted to the rumor, regarding it as anathema to the European project and the importance of the EU taking responsibility for poison control as a key element of its mission. The exchange below took place between MEP Michèle Rivasi, Green Party, and Vytenis Povilas Andriukaitis, European Commissioner for Health and Food Safety. For Rivasi, collective action on pesticides lay at the heart of what for him a *European* Union should be about, with Andriukaitis responding that he also wanted to see more "solidarity" at the European level.

> **Michèle Rivasi,** *Greens.* – I have heard that the Commission would be happy to leave everything relating to pesticides and GMOs to Member States. Could you confirm that there is a Commission proposal on this matter? Because, if this is the case, I cannot see why we are building Europe, because if there really is one sector where harmonisation is needed . . . it is pesticides. (90)

> **Vytenis Povilas Andriukaitis,** *EU Commissioner.* – Of course we want Europe, and I am very happy that you raised questions about Europe. We want to see more solidarity. (91)

Throughout the committee hearings, science and democracy would thus be presented as twin commitments, each reinforcing and fulfilling the other. *European* science and *European* democracy were what would help to give the European Union its solid structure. This was a position that the head of ECHA, Bjorn Hansen, during an interview with me a few years later, would also stress. Although he received criticism during the PEST committee and often adopted a stronger line on the definition and meaning of science in that context, Hansen expressed a more generous view of what science was and does when I spoke to him after the heat had cooled. For Hansen, Europe's cultural diversity created a context where science could produce different questions and different answers, so the EU agencies had to make space for compromise. Bernhard Url, head of the EFSA, made a similar point during my later interview with him too. For Url, the regulatory agencies' locations in Member States (EFSA in Parma, Italy; ECHA in Helsinki, Finland) and broad Member State representation via their international staff makeup meant they benefited from the diversity of approach and opinion only the EU could bring. As Hansen put it:

> The beauty about science is that science always has uncertainties, so it always gives the opportunity for anybody who wants to say anything to say something. Because you have a variation within which you can vary your arguments and still claim that it's true because it's scientific. So even though the Swedish scientist is generally much more green than the British scientist, I don't think that these scientists are politically influenced. I think it's simply, you know, countries have different cultures. . . . [T]he beauty of the Union is that you are forced to listen to all the other views and answer to them and work on a compromise.

Solidarity

EU Commissioner Andriukaitis's desire to "see more solidarity" provides a departure point for my discussion in this section. Andriukaitis had meant solidarity to overcome disagreements on European pesticide approval processes: solidarity was a necessary precondition of successful bureaucratic work. As MEP Andrieu's opening remarks made clear, "the world has a solid structure"—a solid structure made up from the work of EU professionals pulling together for a common cause, within the terms laid out in the treaties (such as they may have been interpreted). Throughout the committee hearings, collective expression was found not only in the physical gathering of the committee in session but also in the forms of affective life it helped bring into being. In his rebuttal to the BfR, Andrieu pointed out that "the pleasure of meeting . . . [and] the friendliness between us" were not reasons to evade difficult questions. Exchanges between participants, devoid of their expressive content when reproduced in the *Verbatim Reports* cited here, were often lively and sometimes heated. On occasion, participants quarreled, and the chair scolded them. But generally the tone was what can best be described as emotionally effusive but never to a level that reached affectation or false performativity. The dialogue I have shared illustrates how committee procedures turned on an effervescence of affect.

Anthropologists understand affect as an "intensity that variously energizes, contradicts, deconstructs, and overwhelms the narratives through which we live"

(White 2017, 178). During the PEST committee meeting, participants expressed their commitment to solidarian action by being *against* scientific and democratic intransience and inertia. An affective zeal *for* the work of the committee expressed at the level of discourse was what was needed to accomplish this. Showing solidarity with Europe and as Europeans was a matter of being *for* a movement of change and improvement in science and democracy and *against* the status quo that worked in favor of agribusiness interests. In fact, taking part in efforts to strengthen bureaucracy was also an expression of solidarity, creating a kind of solidarian bureaucracy within and for Europe. The "Brussels bureaucrat," in the popular imagination an archetypal faceless, nameless, gray-suited manager working in a gray building producing reams of unreadable gray literature, can nevertheless become a radical solidarian working against corporate malfeasance when mobilized by their sense of Europeanness.

And in fact, expressions of solidarian bureaucracy were commonplace during PEST committee meetings. Four examples provide further evidence of this commitment. First, MEP Younous Omarjee, a member of the Left Group in the Parliament, affirmed that as "representatives responsible for health and safety—these being public health issues—we [the committee] are right to ask these questions and then take the appropriate political action. It is up to us to take responsibility in the end" (PEST Committee 2018c, 70). Second, even though they frequently confronted difficult questioning, regulatory heads saw it as their ultimate responsibility to participate in the committee for the good of Europe. Bjorn Hansen, executive director of the ECHA, would thus remark that he was "proud to be able to fulfil my duty as Head of Agency and as a civil servant contributing to democracy in action—as you put it Chair—in clarifying issues in the case of glyphosate" (45). Third, following his own uncomfortable experience in front of the committee, EU Commissioner Andriukaitis told the members that he would "be more than happy to cooperate—collectively, once again, collectively—because I think here we are all like-minded friends" when it came to implementing the committee's recommendations. The fourth and final example, as seems fitting, comes from the committee chair, Eric Andrieu.

> Thank you all for your contributions and for taking part in this game of questions and answers. Thank you, and I hope that we will progress together to ensure that the report we are going to produce really serves the interests of health, and this is the main concern of 500 million European citizens, so that everything that happens tomorrow is even better than what is happening today. (40)

In chapter 3, I quoted EU President Jean-Claude Juncker's lament that glyphosate had threatened the necessary separation between risk assessors and risk managers—a separation premised on an understanding of science as science and politics as politics, and never should they meet. The specialists in poisoncraft—scientists, bureaucrats, and politicians—appearing before the PEST committee all expressed theories of the relation between science and politics that far exceeded this simple formula. To be sure, old boundary conventions still appeared. However, they did so less as a solid view of the world and more as a fluid definition expressed during a debate. Participants would refer to science as something that existed simultaneously outside and within history—as something generated from social and political concerns and as something that allowed the possibility of escaping such concerns. Yet it was, of course, never the PEST committee's task to adjudicate on the risk assessment of glyphosate itself; the committee did not and could not rule on whether regulation should be tightened. But through its work, the pitfalls and failings of science and democracy and their relations in and through solidarity would become apparent. The imperfect fit between regulatory structures and the makeup of the chemical world that I traced in chapter 4, as well as the nefarious influence of industry on regulatory science that I traced in chapter 5, would be overcome, at least, by the solid structure of the world offered by the EU and its solidarian bureaucrats.

SUMMARY OF PART II

Crafting Europe Through Poison Control

IN HER BOOK *DESIGNS ON NATURE* (2005), Sheila Jasanoff showed how the development of EU regulations on genetic modification during the late 1990s emerged alongside the deepening of EU commitments to closer union. The sciences of life—what can otherwise be termed the sciences of *remedy*—became incorporated into imaginaries of Europe as a collective of nations open to scientific progress *and* a sense of shared solidarity built around a commitment to progressive and ethical regulation. This was, as I described in Chapter 1, an Age of Optimism when rapid advances in gene science not only promised to transform society but also, through the public and political debates that followed, allow projects like European unification an opportunity to shine as countries came together over common ethical cause. Fast-forward three decades, however, and today it is the sciences of *poison* that feature in Europe's stories about itself. In an Age of Toxicity, poisoncraft has become a tool of European statecraft as it struggles to find common purpose in a time of economic and political crisis, nationalist division, and spiraling environmental concerns.

The chapters in part 2 explored how practices of poison gave a body to ideas of European cohesion and belonging—in the regulatory architecture of pesticide control, in the traditions of bureaucratic science writing and review, and in the committee hearings that would be held to assess those activities. Reading the practice and politics of risk regulation, assessment, and decision making not as dry managerial procedure but as examples of lively poisoncraft opens up new approaches to understanding contemporary power and governance in Europe. I argued that the EU's sovereign power is derived from and expressed in its regulatory activity, one of the most important instances of which is its power over which poisons can be admitted to and used in Europe. It was Europe's struggles with glyphosate that highlighted the continuing centrality of poison control, as a historical practice, to the European mission. It was a mission that, in turn, bore the hallmarks of the Paracelsian tradition.

For sociologist Émile Durkheim (1858–1917), society functioned like an organism whose constituent parts worked in unison to create something greater than themselves. Similarly, what Durkheim (1933) called "organic solidarity" arose from the workings of constituent but different parts; in complex societies, it was the interdependence of those parts that generated solidarity. The European Union itself is a project of practical structural functionalism, directly inspired by Durkheim's thinking. From its earliest days as a trading arrangement for steel and coal, the aim has been to create unity from fostered interdependence—organic solidarity, in other words. But just as with any organism, the introduction of a poison affects how it works. Here, then, is where Paracelsian poisoncraft comes in. Poison corrupts European relations, corroding the whole.

As a project of poisoncraft, Europe is not a biopolitical project in the manner of Esposito's (2011) *immunitas*. In that view, immunity of the political body is achieved by exposure to poison for the purpose of developing defenses against future attack. Conversely, Europe's relationship with poison is as ambiguous, indeterminant, and uncertain as poison itself. Affirmations of European solidarity would be achieved through a successful regulation if not repulsion of poison. It was from the ability to manipulate poison and turn its powers to European ends that claims to sovereign power derived—to turn poison to the task of forming compatible European relations or to avoid its corruptive effects on relations—not an ability to ingest and survive exposure to poison. And it was, of course, precisely on those grounds that Europe's failure to control glyphosate proved so troublesome. In part 3, I turn my attention to the relationship between pesticides, power, and poisoncraft in a very different setting: Sri Lanka.

PART III

The Poisoncraft of Sri Lanka's Postwar Recovery

7

Kidney Disease and the Glyphosate Question

"This forum is for the discussion of CKDu. Why are we spending so much time talking about glyphosate?" A contributor to an online forum, *CKDu and Sri Lanka*, hosted on the project management system Basecamp.com, asked this question after several days of heated exchange on the herbicide's possible role in an epidemic of chronic kidney disease of unknown etiology (CKDu) in Sri Lanka. The government's Coordinating Secretariat for Science, Technology, and Innovation (COSTI) had established the *CKDu and Sri Lanka* Basecamp forum a few years earlier to provide an interdisciplinary space for knowledge exchange and discussion on CKDu. COSTI's aim for the platform was to foster consensus on the likely cause or causes of CKDu that could then be used to direct policy interventions. Yet, as with other CKDu initiatives described in the following pages, the subject of glyphosate would come to dominate the discussions. During the five years that the COSTI platform was live, no other topic generated as much debate or saw so many members leave the forum in anger—or moderators expel members for breaking forum rules—as did glyphosate.

Why did glyphosate come to dominate the debate? In a close parallel with arguments then also taking place in the EU, the chemical had become a focus for a politics of division. For commentors across the political spectrum, glyphosate, and the arguments it engendered, embodied all that was wrong with Sri Lanka as a postwar nation seeking to reconcile and reunify after thirty years of bloody conflict at a moment in history when new threats—new poisons—to the national body were emerging. What had started life as an effort to build consensus across the CKDu research community more often ended in discord and disagreement as contributors proposed, and argued over, the many potential nephrotoxins in the environment that could cause the disease. None was debated as forcefully or as comprehensively as glyphosate. As Saroj Jayasinghe, a leading specialist, noted wearily on the forum's pages after yet another argument about the molecule, "Have we given a consensus statement . . . as to what could be the cause for CKDu or any likely solutions? Isn't it time that we develop a consensus statement for the public?"

Consensus is a scientific and political idea. As a scientific idea, it is assumed to come from the work of an epistemic community, "a network of professionals with recognised expertise and competence in a particular domain and an authoritative claim to policy-relevant knowledge in that domain or issue area" (Haas 1992, 3). The defining characteristic of an epistemic community is a commitment to consensus as both a process and an aim; that is, an epistemic community is one that, bar minor routine differences and disagreements, has agreed on its fundamental purpose and goals. As a political idea, Maja Horst and Alan Irwin (2010) argue, consensus emerges from institutional and national identities that uphold ideals of "open and inclusive dialogue" between many "stakeholders" who should have an equal say in the debate. From that perspective, consensus leads to the collective resolution of controversies as much for scientific as for societal reasons, putting people—and nations—at ease within themselves (Horst and Irwin 2010).

Having recently emerged from decades of war, Sri Lanka was not a nation at ease with itself. Old fears of separatist rebels had been replaced by new fears of internal threats that took the narrative form of poisons endangering the project of national unification. For the new Buddhist nationalist groups promoting those fears, Muslims and pesticides were the main threats. In this milieu of material-semiotic discord, the search for consensus on glyphosate's role in CKDu joined with the search for ways to protect the Sri Lankan body politic from toxic dangers. Both would require the attention of poisoncraft to resolve. Thus, debates over glyphosate cut to the core of fundamental questions concerning authority and legitimacy, politics and religion, agricultural transformation, and regulatory action and uncertainty in a nation seeking to recover from years of violence at a time when emerging extremist groups were seeking to agitate religious conflict.

In this part of the book, I develop my second case study of glyphosate regulation as an example of where poisoncraft and sovereignty claims have joined in contemporary scientific and political dispute. The case brings together a story of pesticide regulation and public health in a context where multiple stakeholders involved in kidney disease research were also asking questions about what kind of nation Sri Lanka was or wished to be. In fact, how they went about proving or disproving glyphosate's role in causing CKDu became one of the chief arenas within which competing communities of specialists in poisoncraft, including toxicologists, global health researchers, elected representatives from across the political spectrum, and a host of others, asked and answered those questions. In the remainder of this chapter, I introduce the agricultural and scientific landscapes within which kidney science and glyphosate science had come together. The first is the agricultural landscape where the CKDu epidemic is located, the

Mahaweli Development and Irrigation Project, and the second comprises the three research groups that were at the forefront of the debate over the relationship between CKDu and glyphosate.

SRI LANKA'S TOXIC ACCELERATION
The Mahaweli

At the time of its launch in the late 1960s, the Mahaweli Development and Irrigation Project (MDIP) was the largest hydroelectric and agricultural infrastructure development project in the world. Centred upon the country's longest river, the Mahaweli, the project's aims were to capture, store, and channel water to produce electricity and to water "under-utilized" lands across the climatic Dry Zone while also modernizing subsistence agriculture by introducing new seed varieties, fertilizers, and pesticides (Maddduma Bandara 1985). Indicating its scale and ambition, some 40 percent of the island's landmass would fall under Mahaweli development, with 700,000 people—more than 5 percent of the country's population—targeted for resettlement as colonist-farmers (Muggah 2008).

The Mahaweli project was the postcolonial undertaking of a colonial vision for Sri Lankan rural development premised on large-scale irrigation that had first been explored by the British almost a century before (Bandarage 1983). Inspired by their "discoveries" of the remains of ancient civilizations in the Dry Zone that vast networks of irrigation infrastructure had once supported, the British had initiated a series of infrastructural works that sought to rejuvenate remains of the old system. The results of their archaeological surveys had also suggested what they understood to be an ethnic, linguistic, and religious continuity between the old hydraulic civilizations of the island and the Sinhala-speaking Buddhists who comprised the majority community under British rule. It was thus members of the island's Sinhala Buddhist community that would come to benefit from agricultural development projects during the colonial and postcolonial periods, creating an indelible claim among Buddhist nationalists to their right to govern the island and their superiority over minority Tamil, Muslim, and Christian communities. The consequences of this were profound, with ethnic grievances created by the Mahaweli project helping foster Tamil demands for greater rights and eventually the emergence of Tamil separatist groups (Muggah 2008; Peebles 1990; J. Perera 1992; Woost 1999; Brow 1996). The most active of those, the Liberation Tigers of Tamil Eelam (LTTE), would demand the creation of a greater Tamil nation encompassing northern Sri Lanka and southern India.

The Mahaweli Master Plan (MMP) had envisaged a thirty-year timetable to complete building works and population relocation. Keen to maximize the economic and social returns of the project, in 1978 the incoming president, J. R. Jayawardene, "accelerated" the Mahaweli project to complete building works and relocations within just *six* years. This decision proved calamitous in several ways, including producing huge budgetary overruns and failure to provide social infrastructure and support for settled communities (Muggah 2008, 115). More than this, however, the newly named Accelerated Mahaweli Development Project (AMDP) sought to quicken the agricultural cycle itself. A key objective had been to create a third cultivation season between the two traditional seasons of Maha (late September to early March) and Yala (late May to early August). Important to accomplishing this would be the introduction of new technologies, including hybrid rice varieties that shortened growing time from 60 to 45 days, new chemical fertilizers and pesticides better suited to the hybrid varieties, and faster land clearance using herbicides.

With those goals in mind, the Accelerated Mahaweli project organized the functioning of the irrigation system around a 45-day calendar that matched the demands of these new seed and chemical inputs. Previously, farmers flooded their rice fields for three weeks to kill weeds, after which they plowed rotting matter back into the soil before planting rice. Under the new approach, farmers would use herbicides to kill weeds quickly and after just seven days conduct shallow plowing before planting. This would help the Accelerated Mahaweli save huge volumes of water and help farmers save several weeks—both of which were essential if the goal of creating a third season was to be achieved. Chemical herbicides were thus crucial for their accelerationist properties, enabling weed control at a pace that far outstripped manual methods (Widger and Wickramasinghe 2020).

Mahaweli planners were surprised to find farmers showing early enthusiasm for the adoption of "modern" methods of weed control to help them achieve this aim as they transitioned to a working time set by acceleration. Yet almost immediately, the government, too, found reason to ban molecules for their damaging environmental and health effects, including the use of pesticides as a method of suicide. Over the coming decades, efforts to achieve acceleration became conjoined with regulatory decisions that introduced friction and delay to the system. Regulators banned old chemicals and introduced replacement chemicals, each time draining the pool of available herbicides. At the time of the Accelerated Mahaweli's launch, some 95 percent of farmers reported using 2,4-D (2,4-dichlorophenoxyacetic acid) to control weeds. After 2,4-D was banned because of concern for its environmental impacts, paraquat took the market share.

Government regulators had initially approved glyphosate in 1984 as an alternative to 2,4-D and paraquat but only for use in the estate sector and railway sidings. Approval for use in agriculture, including rice and vegetable cultivation within the Accelerated Mahaweli, was not forthcoming until 1998—some years after paraquat had received similar approval. Initially, uptake of glyphosate in the agricultural sector was slow. With no GMOs approved for use in Sri Lanka, Monsanto was never able to promote the herbicide with its Roundup Ready seeds engineered to withstand the chemical—one of the primary drivers behind glyphosate dominance in other markets. Moreover, Monsanto retained ownership of the patent at that point and branded glyphosate products were significantly more expensive than the off-patent paraquat. When Monsanto's glyphosate patent expired in 2000, cheaper glyphosate-based herbicides produced by third-party companies flooded Sri Lanka, and the price dropped to parity with paraquat. Even then, however, glyphosate sales remained low.

The turning point came when the government banned paraquat in 2007. Over the next seven years, glyphosate, the last broad-spectrum herbicide for sale in Sri Lanka, would become deeply entangled in the functioning of the irrigation system. A thriving cottage industry sprang up around its distribution and sale, in the form of a network of small pesticide stores at field level that sold nothing but glyphosate-based herbicides. By 2015, the year glyphosate was banned, when rice farmers I worked with spoke about chemical weed control they rarely used the generic Sinhala term for pesticides, *thel behet* (lit., "medicine oil") but referred specifically to Roundup or glyphosate. Although its dominance of the herbicide market had never been inevitable, by 2015, glyphosate had become a key disciplinary agent of Mahaweli acceleration that farmers believed they could simply not live without.

The Mahaweli as Humanitarian Space

Generations of social researchers have cast Mahaweli acceleration as a "critical event" in Sri Lanka's modern history (Das 1995)—a policy decision and a landscape of agricultural modernization from, within, and through which socially and morally corruptive forces would be generated, accumulated, and spread outward, endangering the nation. The project captured precisely what social theorists have described as the *pathos* of contemporary capitalism—an effect and affect of living in a system calibrated for speed (Duclos et al. 2017; Rosa 2013; Shaviro 2015). Stories told about the Accelerated Mahaweli have played with "outbreak" narratives (Kelly et al. 2019)—an ever-replenishing source of health and social crises that established the Accelerated Mahaweli as a space in need of and primed for humanitarian intervention. Thus, since its launch, the Accelerated Mahaweli came to be associated with a range of health and social epidemics of alcoholism, domestic violence, child abuse, and suicide. The most recent has been CKDu.

Formally, CKDu is diagnosed "by exclusion," by establishing the *absence* of evidence of traditional causes of chronic kidney disease (CKD), such as diabetes, hypertension, or injury (Almaguer et al. 2014). CKDu is thus not a diagnosis as such but rather a "residual category" generated by diagnostic failure (Kierans and Padilla-Altamira 2021). CKDu's classificatory uncertainty has proven crucial to how the disease has come to be understood as an object of scientific research and health intervention. Like other occupational and environmental diseases for which causal identification can be difficult and perhaps even not possible (Senanayake 2020; Dumit 2006; Murphy 2006), efforts to build consensus have stumbled on fundamental questions of disease ontology, even before work identifying cause and cure can begin. In epidemiological terms, however, CKDu in Sri Lanka shares features with other outbreaks of CKDu around the world, including the Balkan states, Egypt, and Mesoamerica (Weaver et al. 2015). For example, affected communities tend to be in (tropical) lowlands, of lower socioeconomic status, and employed in agricultural and laboring jobs in which exposure to harsh working conditions and/or chemical pollutants is common (Weaver et al. 2015). In Sri Lanka, this similarity has created ongoing debate over whether CKDu is a uniquely Sri Lankan disease or a disease shared across countries—the answer to which leads to very different conclusions about disease etiology and social, cultural, and political significance.

Anthropological interest in CKDu began with Sherine Hamdy's (2008) work in Egypt, through which she drew attention to how narratives of failing kidneys wrapped around narratives of the failing Egyptian state, forming what she termed "political aetiologies" that accounted for both processes. Drawing from her research on CKDu in Mexico, anthropologist Ciara Kierans (2020) extended Hamdy's approach by referring to CKDu as a "worksite" around which different disciplines, agendas, and worldviews meet—in conflict as much as in collaboration—in their attempts to deal with uncertainty. Kierans showed how this work takes direction from the physical landscape with which the disease is associated—namely, the industrially polluted waters of Lake Chapala and its surrounds in the east of the country. For Kierans, CKDu's relationship with the "blasted landscapes" (Tsing 2015, 3) of the Chemical Anthropocene and the fraught nature of CKDu "worksites" shows how toxic landscapes are "not an unobtrusive background to everyday life" but exist "very visibly in the foreground" of people's efforts to live with and overcome the disease (Kierans 2020, 138).

In Sri Lanka, CKDu is of course closely associated with the Accelerated Mahaweli. Cultural geographer Nari Senanayake (2019) has pointed to a disjuncture between the "hypervisibility" of CKDu in Sri Lankan national discourse about the Mahaweli—which has become what Kierans (2020) might call a worksite—and its seeming invisibility in clinical encounter, where CKDu remains an uncertain diagnosis. Senanayake shows how physicians might overcome diagnostic uncertainty by basing their decisions on patients' residence in a supposed CKDu "hotspot" in Mahaweli communities. If in medical theory a diagnosis of CKDu is made by exclusion, in clinical practice diagnosis is often made by association with toxic landscapes. Thus, efforts to identify CKDu hotspots across Sri Lanka has led to a handful of communities being classified as "potentially diseased" (Senanayake 2019), making them sites of intensive scientific and humanitarian intervention (see Wickramasinghe 2023a, 2023b).

In this book, I extend anthropological approaches to CKDu by exploring how scientific and medical professionals' attempts to explain that the disease performed other kinds of work at the national and international levels. As specialists in poisoncraft, from the WHO through national and international researchers to regulators, policy makers, politicians, and agribusiness groups, tried to establish a clear definition of CKDu in medical terms, so the question became which aspects of the disease to highlight—its general or its particularistic characteristics. By asking this, I explore how debates over CKDu emerged as a central channel through which science and medicine would be pressed into service in the pursuit of nation-building aims. As a disease that required the attention of diverse practitioners of poisoncraft, CKDu created a battleground on which clashed visions of toxicology and of the nation that were fundamentally at odds with one another. Poisoncraft became a key mode of articulating, constructing, and contesting new forms and relations of similarity and difference in a new territorial-political space.

A Fear of Quickening Numbers

After anthropologist and historian Ann L. Stoler (2013, 11), I approach the Accelerated Mahaweli not only as a landscape but also as a timescape of "ruination"—what she calls the "different durations and moments of exposure to a range of violences and degradations." Paying attention to the temporalization of the Accelerated Mahaweli allows us to calibrate the tempo of CKDu against the tempo of chemicals like glyphosate used to achieve acceleration. Medical anthropologist Vinh-Kim Nguyen (2019), for instance, shows how ethnography can help reveal the vectors of viral epidemic spread. His examples, Ebola and HIV, are "fast" and "slow" moving respectively, evolving and reproducing at rates that reflect the material and social infrastructures of their human hosts. I refer to the coalescence of acceleratory chemicals and occupational and environmental conditions and experiences in the Accelerated Mahaweli as an example of *toxic acceleration* described in part 1—what for many groups came to be seen as a condition of lives lived at pace in hydrochemical infrastructure—which in turn helped construct and construe the Accelerate Mahaweli as a humanitarian space.

Fears over how far and how fast CKDu may have spread echo the tempo of toxic acceleration. The language around CKDu has often implied an environmental health disaster—what Sri Lankan science writer Nalaka Gunawardene (2012a) called a "humanitarian tragedy on a mass scale" that affected millions of people living in areas where CKDu had become "endemic." Scholars, activists, and public commentators have routinely described CKDu as the biggest health challenge the nation has ever faced—with the most terrifying estimates suggesting that upwards of one-third of the population, around 7 million people, might be destined to fall ill. Sarvodaya, Sri Lanka's largest civil society organization, also described CKDu as "Sri Lanka's #1 public health issue." "An estimated 13 people die from [CKDu] every day, with 20,000 current patients and a death toll of 400,000 since 1997," it reported. Other commentators have compared CKDu to the island's thirty-year civil war. For example, sociologist Asoka Bandarage (2013) reported, "As many as 400,000 people in Sri Lanka's north central region may be affected by the disease.

. . . Some 22,000 people have died from CKD over the past 2 decades in the NCP [North Central Province] with at least 5 or 6 out of 100 people there currently affected. . . . In other words, more people in the NCP have died from CKD than from the armed conflict in Sri Lanka."

In an announcement for a fund-raising event in support of CKDu charities, one of Sri Lanka's most prolific writers and activists on the disease, US-based Professor Sunil Wimalawansa, wrote in the Basecamp forum that CKDu was a "disaster that kills ~13 farmers, every day, destitute 13 families each day. At the current rates of deaths, unless [we] intervene . . . efficiently . . . and timely, this will soon surpass the deaths due to LTTE-terrorism!" The equation of the disease and civil war is rhetorically powerful. CKDu emerges as a humanitarian crisis of epic proportions, yet one that compared to war remained what Wimalawansa called a "silent killer . . . due to its lack of symptoms at disease onset, complex multifactorial etiology, social determinants, and a lack of research and international attention."

Despite this "avalanche of numbers" (Hacking 2015), it is surprisingly difficult to find any comprehensive figures for CKDu prevalence or deaths. The numbers I quoted above suggest vastly different rates. According to Sarvodaya, the number was 20,000 "current patients" and a "death toll" of 400,000. Bandarage, however, identified 400,000 "current patients" and 22,000 deaths. Little of the scientific literature produced on CKDu includes estimates of the national picture, and those that do are based on data drawn from the local level. Anthropologist Upul Wickramasinghe (2023b) showed how data being produced on one well-known CKDu hotspot counted cases of traditional CKD as CKDu, vastly overestimating the scale of the problem. Reflecting on the paucity of epidemiological data, the nephrologist credited with having first noticed CKDu, Tilak Abeysekera, suggested that scientific and environmental groups have routinely inflated the numbers. "Some writers to newspapers have claimed that the kidney disease is worse than the tsunami [which killed at least 30,000 people]. The two tragedies are not comparable, and many numbers being mentioned in the media are gross exaggerations," he argued in the Basecamp forum. Yet the sense of threat conveyed by breathless reporting on CKDu is entirely consistent with the material experience of lives led in an infrastructure geared for speed. Toxic acceleration generates numbers dizzying in their magnitude and malignance.

SPECIALISTS IN POISONCRAFT: THE CKDu RESEARCH COMMUNITY

Theorizing the Accelerated Mahaweli as a toxic acceleration has been at the heart of attempts to identify the cause of CKDu in what researchers cast as "man-made" and "natural" sources: agrochemicals and heavy metals. All the major hypotheses for CKDu have centered the role of the irrigation system, its quickening tempo, and the urgency to act in the face of a "spreading" epidemic and "spiraling" disease numbers in one way or another. The contributions to the CKDu debate of three university-based research groups shaped discourses of poisoncraft in Sri Lanka during the 2010s.[1] The groups were headquartered at three public universities, Rajarata, Peradeniya, and Colombo, each of which had strong connections with other academic institutions and NGOs in Sri Lanka and overseas, especially in the United Kingdom and the United States. I dub them the "Rajarata-Kelaniya group," the "Peradeniya group," and the "Colombo group."

The Rajarata-Kelaniya Group

The Rajarata-Kelaniya group was centered at Rajarata University in the NCP, established in 1996 as Sri Lanka's eleventh university. The group had strong support from present and past members of Kelaniya University, in the Western Province. Rajarata's location in the NCP helped ensure that health researchers from the university took a leading role in CKDu research from an early stage. The Rajarata-Kelaniya group became synonymous with Channa Jayasumana, a pharmacologist whose work on CKDu led to the glyphosate ban and who consequently became a well-known figure in international environmentalist and CKDu communities. Jayasumana studied medicine at Peradeniya University and commenced his doctoral research on CKDu at Kelaniya University, before transferring to Rajarata to take up a junior lectureship in 2008. He also visited California State University on a training fellowship, during which time he formed a collaboration with Sarath Gunatilake, a regular coauthor. Sisira Siribaddana, also at Rajarata, was another regular coauthor. Public figures linked with the group included Nalin de Silva, a figure of some controversy in the Sri Lankan scientific community for his work on "constructive relativism," which also provided a philosophical and political direction to the group (see chapter 9), and Ven. Athuraliye Rathana Thero, a Buddhist monk and chairman of the religious nationalist political party, the Jathika Hela Urumaya (JHU; National Heritage Party).

Jayasumana's earliest contribution to the CKDu debate was his theory of the "Eelam border" and LTTE bioterrorism, which attracted some attention during the early 2010s. However, he quickly abandoned that argument to develop agrochemical theories of CKDu etiology. I explore both at length in chapter 9. A concern running through all the work produced by Jayasumana and the wider Rajarata-Kelaniya group, however, has been a commitment to decolonizing Sri Lankan science and promoting a Buddhist epistemology, fostering what science journalist Nalaka Gunawardena has dubbed a "saffron-green" politics—a combination of environmentalism and Sinhala Buddhist nationalism. If environmentalists outside of Sri Lanka have celebrated Jayasumana's work on glyphosate

---

1. I focus on the three most active research groups in the glyphosate debate that also dominated national discussions of CKDu. Others were actively involved in CKDu research, though they kept well away from the glyphosate debate. The activities of those other groups are outside my focus here.

for challenging global agribusiness, within Sri Lanka his well-known links with nationalist movements and involvement with agitations against Muslim communities have encouraged others to treat him with caution.

The Peradeniya Group

Located in lush grounds on the outskirts of Kandy in the hill country, the University of Peradeniya, originally established in 1942 as the University of Ceylon, is Sri Lanka's second oldest university. Peradeniya is also Sri Lanka's most prestigious university, its status an expression of its age and origins and its distinction from "new" universities like Rajarata. Importantly, as the premier seat of learning in Sri Lanka, Peradeniya University is more closely associated with the scientific and medical establishment than places like Rajarata, with members of the Peradeniya group sitting on various national technical, medical, and scientific panels and boards, from which the Rajarata-Kelaniya group is largely and notably absent.

Unlike the Rajarata-Kelaniya group, no single figure, discipline, or political affiliation explicitly characterizes the Peradeniya group. The focal point is the Centre for Education, Research, and Training in Kidney Diseases (CERTKiD)—an interdisciplinary cluster that includes nephrologists, epidemiologists, and sociologists. However, among CERTKiD's more publicly active members have been Tilak Abeysekera, one nephrologist among a handful of others credited with first noticing the emergence of CKDu; Oliver Ileperuma, a specialist in inorganic chemistry; and the late Ranjit Mulleriyawa, an agronomist and community activist.

The Peradeniya group has promoted geologic hypotheses of CKDu, specifically, fluoride and hard water. Those hypotheses have emerged from earlier research by members of the Peradeniya group that had shown high levels of dental and bone fluorosis in Mahaweli communities (Dharmagunawardhane and Dissanayake 1993). Fluoride maps had also suggested a very close correspondence between the distribution of geologic fluoride in Sri Lanka and the distribution of CKDu (Chandrajith et al. 2012). While fluoride levels in the CKDu area may not by themselves be nephrotoxic, Oliver Ileperuma has claimed fluoride's interaction with other environmental chemicals renders them a risk to health. Ileperuma has argued that aluminium and lead residues from cheap cooking and water storage vessels may have formed with fluoride to create nephrotoxic aluminofluoride complexes (Ileperuma 2011).

The Peradeniya group's promotion of geologic poisons has placed it in direct confrontation with the Rajarata-Kelaniya group. Peradeniya academics and CERTKiD as an organization have led calls for the separation of science, politics, and religion so publicly unified by the Rajarata-Kelaniya group, and dismissed the role of glyphosate in causing CKDu. However, while the Rajarata-Kelaniya group's commitment to anticolonial science has helped it win support among nationalist parliamentarians and influence over the political narratives around glyphosate, the Peradeniya group has remained largely excluded from the levers of hard political power. Even so, the Peradeniya group has benefited from its associations with the scientific establishment. Peradeniya researchers received funding from a range of national and international sources, including the Sri Lankan National Science Foundation, the WHO, and China.

The Colombo Group

Established by the British colonial government in 1921 as an affiliate of the University of London, University College Colombo (UCC) is Sri Lanka's oldest university. UCC was predated by the Ceylon Medical School, established in 1870. The identity of the Colombo group is less distinct than that of the Peradeniya and Rajarata-Kelaniya groups. The Colombo group's work on CKDu spans the medical and arts faculties but lacks a single interdisciplinary structure—as well as a single culprit poison like glyphosate or fluoride—to pull different teams and projects together. However, because several Colombo researchers have been closely involved in government initiatives, its impact on CKDu politics and policy has been no less significant. Like the Peradeniya group, members of the Colombo group are also more closely involved with the institutions of the scientific and medical establishment and have a history of collaboration.

The most influential contributions have been produced by members of the Colombo medical faculty in support of a multifactorial, complex adaptive systems (CAS) approach to CKDu causation, especially approaches adopted by Saroj Jayasinghe, a professor of medicine. Internationally, the work of the Colombo group was foregrounded by, and has most in common with, the work of Sunil Wimalawansa and Shehani Wimalawansa (hereafter "the Wimalawansas"), who have been especially prolific. In fact, Jayasinghe (2014) had earlier championed pesticide etiology and only later adopted the multifactorial position advanced by the Wimalawansas. Jayasinghe and the Wimalawansas continue to differ, however, on the role played by pesticides. Neither dismisses them out of hand, but they disagree on the contribution of individual chemicals, for example, DDT (Wimalawansa 2018; Jayasinghe et al. 2019) and glyphosate (Wimalawansa 2014, 2015; Jayasinghe and Herath 2018). I refer to the guiding hypothesis of the Colombo group as one defined by a complex systems approach.

The Wimalawansas' many contributions to the study of CKDu, which they have renamed CKD-mfo (CKD of multifactorial origin; see below), offered the first attempt to grapple with this challenge. Their message has been nothing less than to highlight the need for comprehensive intervention targeting biological and social processes. The Wimalawansas have suggested that multiple water contaminants, including agrochemicals, fluoride, arsenic, petrochemicals, algae, salinity, iconicity, and ions, have synergistic effects that when combined with multiple health burdens (poverty, low birth weight, childhood malnutrition, poor diet in later life) and environmental factors (e.g., heat stress) cause kidney damage (Wimalawansa 2015). They have also highlighted the importance of the Accelerated Mahaweli in creating and compounding these effects (Wimalawansa and Wimalawansa 2015; Weeraratne and Wimalawansa 2015).

While also emphasizing a root relationship with water pollution, Saroj Jayasinghe has been interested in developing a CAS approach to CKDu research, which he criticizes as having been "dominated by Newtonian mechanistic thinking" (2011, 1; Jayasinghe and Zhu 2020). Jayasinghe identified four aspects of mechanistic thinking: reductionism, hierarchy, linearity, and boundedness. He argued that population health research has been dominated by approaches that assume "the whole system (or the macroscopic properties) can be understood by identifying, describing and analysing all its constituent parts (i.e. its microscopic components)" (Jayasinghe 2011, 1). This approach also relies on an assumption of hierarchy between macroscopic wholes and microscopic parts and the existence of linear processes that drive cause and effect between parts and wholes. Finally, mechanistic models are conceptualized as closed systems, operating on their own part-whole logics driven by internal feedback loops. In contrast, complex adaptive systems are characterized by "adaptation, lack of hierarchies, self-organisation, and emergence" (Jayasinghe 2011, 4). In place of hierarchical, linear relationships between parts and wholes, CAS are comprised of interacting subsystems across multiple ranges and dimensions. Jayasinghe thus also argues for an interdisciplinary approach to CKDu research that can grapple with complex processes.

"Ethical Plateaus" of Glyphosate-CKDu Research

The work of the three research groups features throughout part 3. As specialists in poisoncraft, their contributions to the glyphosate debate proved essential to how the herbicide came to be defined as a problem and regulated in Sri Lanka as a nation seeking to redefine itself after decades of war. The mechanistic toxicologies of the Rajarata-Kelaniya and Peradeniya groups took the form of strident criticisms and defenses of various culprit poisons, from terrorist bioweapons and arsenic and glyphosate to fluoride. Members from both groups engaged in lengthy public arguments, often accusing the other of being in the paid service of the (always described as foreign) environmental or agrochemical lobbies. In contrast, the Colombo group's focus on multifactorial, complex processes was strikingly more collaborative. Just as there was no single poison that if removed would cause the epidemic to subside, so Colombo group members avoided adopting entrenched positions and engaging in reductionist, combative argument. Importantly, the Colombo group's emphasis on complexity enabled affiliated researchers to act as mediators between the Rajarata-Kelaniya and Peradeniya groups. Figures associated with the Colombo group chaired most of the national consultations on CKDu that I attended during my fieldwork, a role entrusted to them precisely because of their seemingly neutral position between Rajarata-Kelaniya and Peradeniya.

Drawing from ethnography conducted in US toxicology labs, anthropologists Kim Fortun and Mike Fortun (2005) have argued that working within mechanistic and complexity frames leads toxicologists to develop different ethical commitments. For example, they found that mechanistic toxicologists tended to have more positive views of corporate partners, whereas complexity toxicologists were more critical. Among the reasons for this was the shared understanding by mechanistic toxicologists and industry actors of how exposure worked through linear pathways of single toxicants, which complexity toxicologists rejected. Borrowing from the philosophy of Deleuze and Guattari, Fortun and Fortun argued those understandings formed distinct "ethical plateaus" of toxicological practice.

Relations between the toxicological frames of the three research groups and their wider social and political commitments manifest in divergent visions of and commitments to Sri Lanka as a sovereign space. The single-factorial mechanistic models developed by the Rajarata-Kelaniya and Peradeniya groups lent themselves to constructs of contaminated bodies and territories that adhered to Westphalian idea(l)s of nationality, nationhood, and the nation-state. The multifactorial complexity models of the Colombo group lent themselves to constructs that adhered to idea(l)s that transcend the Westphalian vision. This was most pronounced within the Rajarata-Kelaniya group, where single-factorial exposures to bioweapons, arsenic, and glyphosate became crucial to their understanding of Sri Lanka as a Sinhala Buddhist territory under attack from conspiratorial agents, both foreign and domestic. It was no coincidence that it was a Colombo group member, Saroj Jayasinghe, who called for the scientific community to produce a consensus statement on CKDu. Jayasinghe had meant his rejection of "love for science" as an invitation to colleagues in the CKDu research community to develop a science of CKDu built solely on universal humanitarian principles. Instead, a group committed to Buddhist nationalism produced the most influential work. Across the chapters that follow, I explore how and why Jayasinghe's call remained unanswered.

WRITING WITHIN A POLITICALLY CHARGED SPACE

Anthropologists writing about Sri Lanka have long struggled with the challenge of how their ethnographies may be taken up and used by nationalist actors, with whose politics they may disagree. Writing during the civil war, Jonathan Spencer (1990) noted how an anthropological concept of culture had been deployed by Buddhist nationalists to argue their cause. Both nationalists and anthropologists, he suggested, depicted the island as a bounded space comprised of an internally coherent set of beliefs and identities. Meanwhile, some Buddhist nationalists would attack anthropology on the grounds that it was a colonial enterprise. For example, in *Anthropologizing Sri Lanka* (2001), political scientist Susanthna Goonathilake took aim at four foundational figures in Sri Lankan anthropology, two from the island and two from overseas, for their depictions that he argued served to undermine Sri Lanka's civilizational past and justify its subordination vis-à-vis the West. While numerous reviewers would point to the many factual inaccuracies and personal biases that peppered Goonathilake's argument (see Lynch 2002; Bass 2003; Guneratne 2004), the book was influential in Sri Lanka, where it was read by nationalist groups, including some of those associated with the Rajarata-Kelaniya group. Around a decade later, I would also come under criticism by members of that group who accused me (erroneously) of arguing that Buddhism was a cause of suicide in Sri Lanka. "Anthropologists should stay out of Sri Lanka," was their message.

Anthropology's difficult status in Sri Lanka—as well as my own slightly complicated relationship with some key figures in the CKDu research community—motivates me to issue a clarifying statement. As I explained in the introduction, my aim is to take glyphosate and the debates that it generates seriously—an ethnographic commitment that compels me to leave my own politics aside. To that end, I set out to document and explain the different theories that have been advanced for CKDu. My research thus leads me to discuss the work of scientists and others who some involved in CKDu research have labeled as "cranks," some of which is antagonistic if not dangerous for ethnic and religious minorities in the island. Their work advances entirely unfounded claims about the cause of CKDu in Tamil Tiger terrorism or the fall of Buddhist civilizations. At their core is a shared understanding that the Sinhala community is under attack. By repeating those theories, am I at risk of giving them legitimacy? Should I take a stand and call them out?

When faced with "crank" science, some scholars, like Naomi Oreskes (2010), have decided that they should. Having spent a career documenting the ways in which industry undermines research on the harms it produces, Oreskes has written convincingly about the responsibility of academics and others to defend science conducted with the spirit of free inquiry against science conducted with a particular position (e.g. corporate interests) in mind. Others have rejected her approach—also convincingly—because it can too quickly start drawing boundaries around what they would understand as science's changing and contested nature, as well as the fact that scientists are *always* working from a position. I discussed how similar debates would play out around notions of "European science" in part 2 and engage with those debates again in chapter 9, where I explore their complexities at a time when science's "post-truth" moment is playing out in a wider context of academic decolonization.

Here, though, let me be plain. At the time of writing in January 2025, the cause of CKDu remains unknown. There is no evidence that the Tamil Tigers or Muslim terrorists played any role in causing CKDu, and anyone familiar with either group would know they would have had neither the means nor the obvious intention of doing so. There is also no evidence that glyphosate causes CKDu, and the hypothesized glyphosate-metal compounds proposed by the Rajarata-Kelaniya group have never been found in water samples or the kidneys of CKDu patients. While absence of evidence is not evidence of absence, everything we currently know about CKDu suggests a complex etiology that may be impossible to associate with any single causal factor.

8

The Poisoned Isle

During the 2010s, Sri Lanka experienced a period of mounting and interconnected crises as it grappled with a complex web of challenges that seemed to mirror each other. Political power had become increasingly concentrated within a single ruling family, the Rajapaksa dynasty, while the economy faced mounting pressures from growing foreign debt, particularly to China. Democratic institutions came under strain as opposition voices were systematically suppressed. Social tensions escalated as Buddhist nationalist movements targeted Muslim minorities, creating communal divisions. Meanwhile, public awareness grew regarding the health consequences of environmental contamination, with chemical pollutants posing serious risks to human and environmental health. This convergence of political authoritarianism, economic vulnerability, social fragmentation, and environmental degradation created a sense that the nation itself was suffering from systemic illness—a toxic assault on the body politic that paralleled the toxic assault on biological bodies. This was a moment when Sri Lanka's various ailments seemed to reinforce and reflect one another, suggesting deeper underlying problems with the country's political, economic, and social foundations.

It was during this time that an image of the *island* of Sri Lanka itself came to feature as the terrain on which those challenges were unfolding. This was a view of a body politic that had only come into being in 2009, after the conclusion of the civil war. Public and political debate was increasingly grappling with the question of what that new sovereign object was or could become. As science historian Michelle Murphy (2006, 111) reminds us, "Perception is characterized by historically specific modes of paying attention." What modes of paying attention did Sri Lanka imagined as an island in environmental and health discourses require? The allegory of biological bodies and the body politic was evocative of the rhetorical work that nephrotoxins played in Sri Lanka during the first decades of the twenty-first century. As the poisoncraft of CKDu acquired a central role in an increasingly urgent debate, the kidney and the nation emerged as fleshy and ideological mirrors of the other. At the national level, poisons funneled into the waters of the island's rivers, canals, tanks, and wells. At the level of the body, water drawn from those sources funneled poisons into the kidneys of local people. This imagery captures the toxico-kinetics of absorption, distribution, and elimination that have been at work in Sri Lanka—first, of the nation and its system of watersheds, tanks, and rice fields that cascade from the hill country to the ocean; and second, the body and its renal system that processes the nation's poisons.

As I describe in this chapter, CKDu's toxico-kinetics inspired new approaches to understanding Sri Lankan geography, geology, history, and majority and minority bodies. Central to this was the relationship between health, environmental, and nationalist politics in the postwar era, in their conflation creating fertile grounds for poisoncraft to emerge as an overriding approach to postwar governance. CKDu became a biological marker of multiple threats to the reproduction of Sinhala Buddhist culture, and glyphosate regulation was a principal means of staking out the new borders of the postwar nation. Questions of national sovereignty and ethnoreligious identity asked by political groups manifest in two questions: *where to look* and especially *when to look* for the source of the nation's poisons.

WHERE TO LOOK

> *The National Atlas of Sri Lanka has seventy-three versions of the island—each template revealing one aspect only, one obsession: rainfall, winds, surface waters of lakes, rarer bodies of water locked deep within the earth. The old portraits show the produce and former kingdoms of the country; contemporary portraits show levels of wealth, poverty and literacy.*
> —MICHAEL ONDAATJE, *ANIL'S GHOST*

Disease epidemiology uses locational research techniques to produce heat maps that signal clusters of disease prevalence of greater or lower intensity. Heat maps have become ubiquitous in scientific and political work on CKDu, generating striking spatial representations of where in the island CKDu is located and inspiring divergent hypotheses related to geologic and historical features of the landscape. Map 1 shows CKDu epidemiology, with darker shades indicating higher rates (de Alwis and Panawala 2019), and highlights those areas' clustering in the North Central Province (NCP) of the island. The geographic focus in the NCP is significant for three reasons. First, the NCP was the historical wellspring of Sinhala Buddhist culture, the Cultural Triangle (map 2), centered on irrigated rice agriculture; second, it has been the site of rapid postcolonial agricultural and agrochemical development,

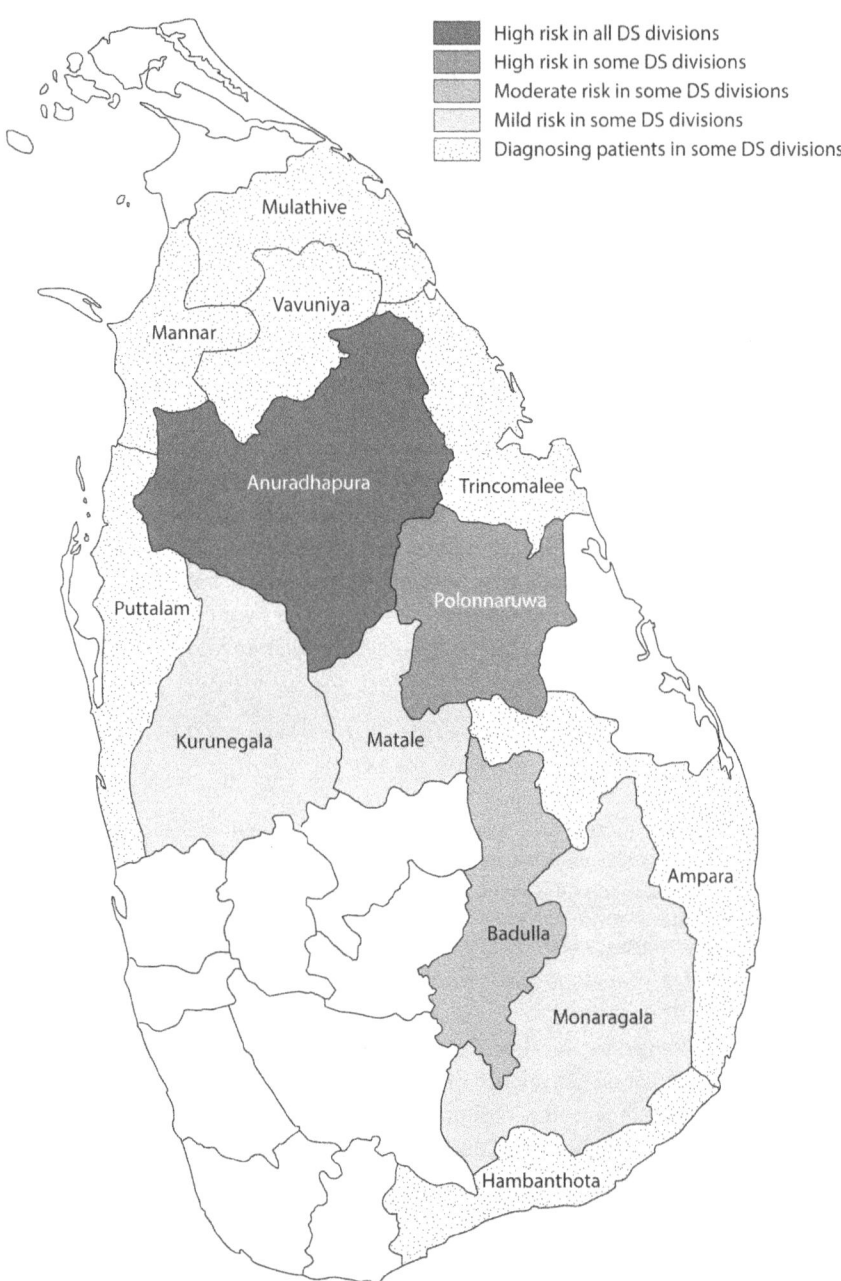

MAP 1. Risk distribution of CKDu according to Divisional Secretariat (DS) areas within districts of Sri Lanka. (Original data source: de Alwis and Panawala 2019, 84). Map by Bill Nelson.

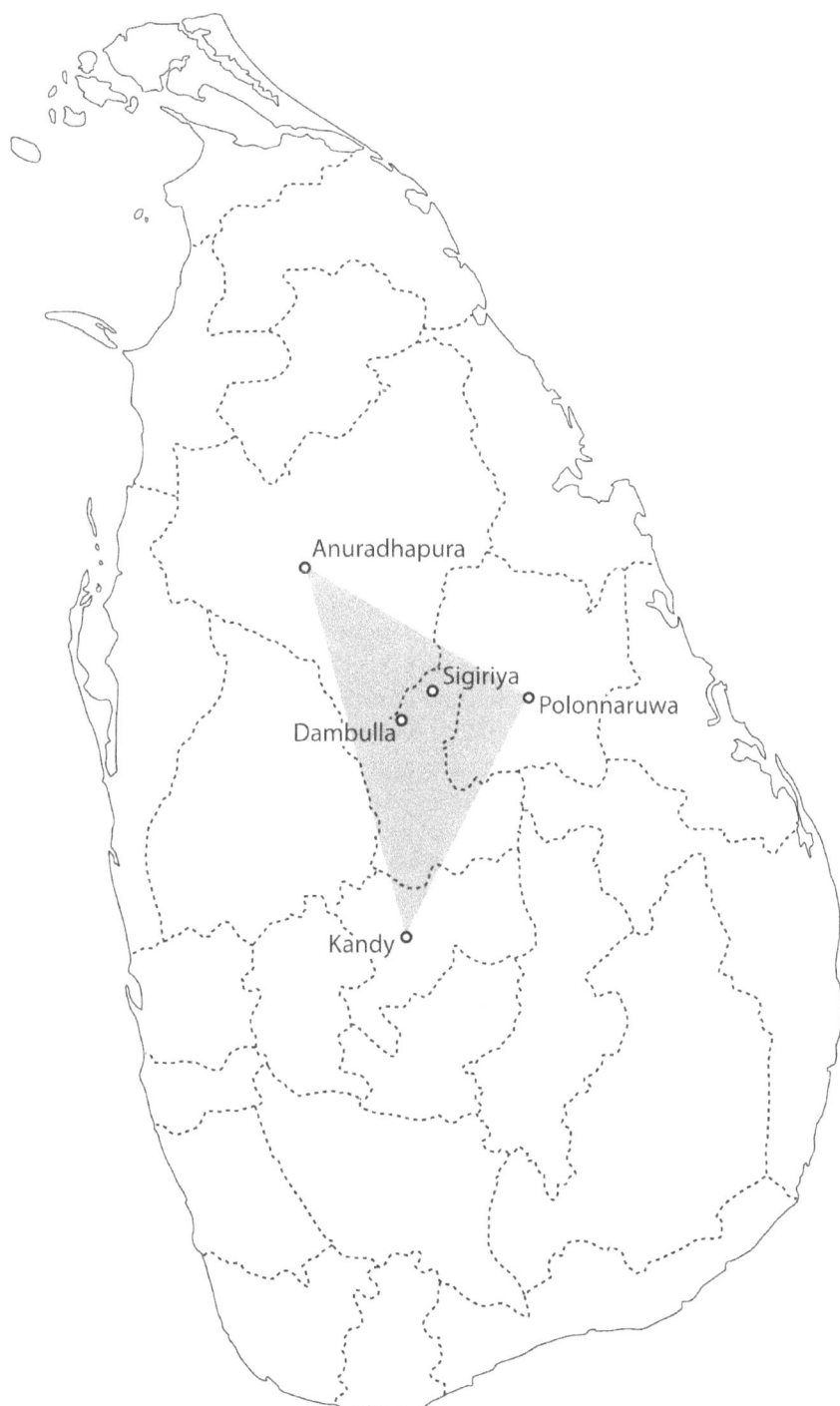

MAP 2. Sri Lanka's Cultural Triangle, formed of the ancient Sinhala Buddhist cities of Anuradhapura, Polonnaruwa, and Kandy. CKDu is epidemic in this region, although not exclusively so. (Map based on Goran tek-en, CC BY-SA 4.0, https://commons.wikimedia.org/w/index.php?curid=78521760.) Map by Bill Nelson.

the Accelerated Mahaweli (map 3); and third, it has always been troubled by poor quality groundwater, indicated by high levels of mineral deposits and water hardness (map 4). Moreover, CKDu's clustering in the NCP means the disease is found within a politically contested space—the frontlines of the civil war and zones of contention fought over by Tamil separatists and government forces (map 5). When the CKDu heat map is displayed alongside those four other maps representing other dangers lurking in the NCP, different versions of the CKDu story can be told, each a "template revealing one aspect only, one obsession" (Ondaatjee 2000, 35), of the Rajarata-Kelaniya, Peradeniya, and Colombo groups investigating the disease. In the toxicological imaginary of Buddhist nationalism, CKDu heat maps would come to represent danger lurking within and beneath the newly bounded nation.

A Critical Cartography of CKDu

Reading CKDu heat maps through the lens of critical cartography illuminates the political significance and significations of disease epidemiology. Cartography draws borders and boundaries around and through places and people that otherwise might not identify as such, as an expression of sovereign power. For political scientist Sankaran Krishna (1994, 504), "Cartography . . . [is] . . . nothing less than the social and political production of nationality itself." Nowhere have the effects of this been clearer than in the postcolonial world, where violence followed independence as new states struggled to generate common nationhood from an ill-fitting patchwork of other modalities of association. As historian Sujit Sivasundaram (2013) has shown, British colonial conquest and rule of Ceylon involved a dual process of "partitioning" the island from the Indian mainland and defining Ceylon as an "islanded" whole ringed with a continuous shoreline. This process of partitioning and islanding created new classifications of people, language, and space and was to prove essential in the development of a postcolonial nationhood that naturalized the relationship between Sinhala and Tamil languages and Sinhala and Tamil ethnicities and established Theravada Buddhism as the national religion.[1] The bounded nation became, in historical, mythological, and political terms, coterminous with the Sinhala Buddhist nation-state as defined along language, ethnicity, and religious lines (Spencer 2002; Kapferer 1988; Jeganathan and Ismail 1995; Daniel 1996; Spencer 2014).

The Sri Lankan civil war was in an important sense fought over the continuing work of partitioning and islanding that the British had started. Following independence in 1948, Sinhala-led governments enacted a series of policies that

---

1. Theravada Buddhism is the oldest surviving Buddhist school, predominant in Sri Lanka, Thailand, Myanmar, Laos, and Cambodia. It emphasizes individual liberation through the Eightfold Path, meditation, and ethical conduct. Unlike Mahayana Buddhism, which is found in China, Japan, Korea, Mongolia, Tibet, and Vietnam and emphasizes the bodhisattva ideal of aspiring toward full Buddhahood to help all beings achieve liberation, Theravada focuses on personal awakening as an arhat by eliminating suffering via wisdom, ethical discipline, and meditative practice.

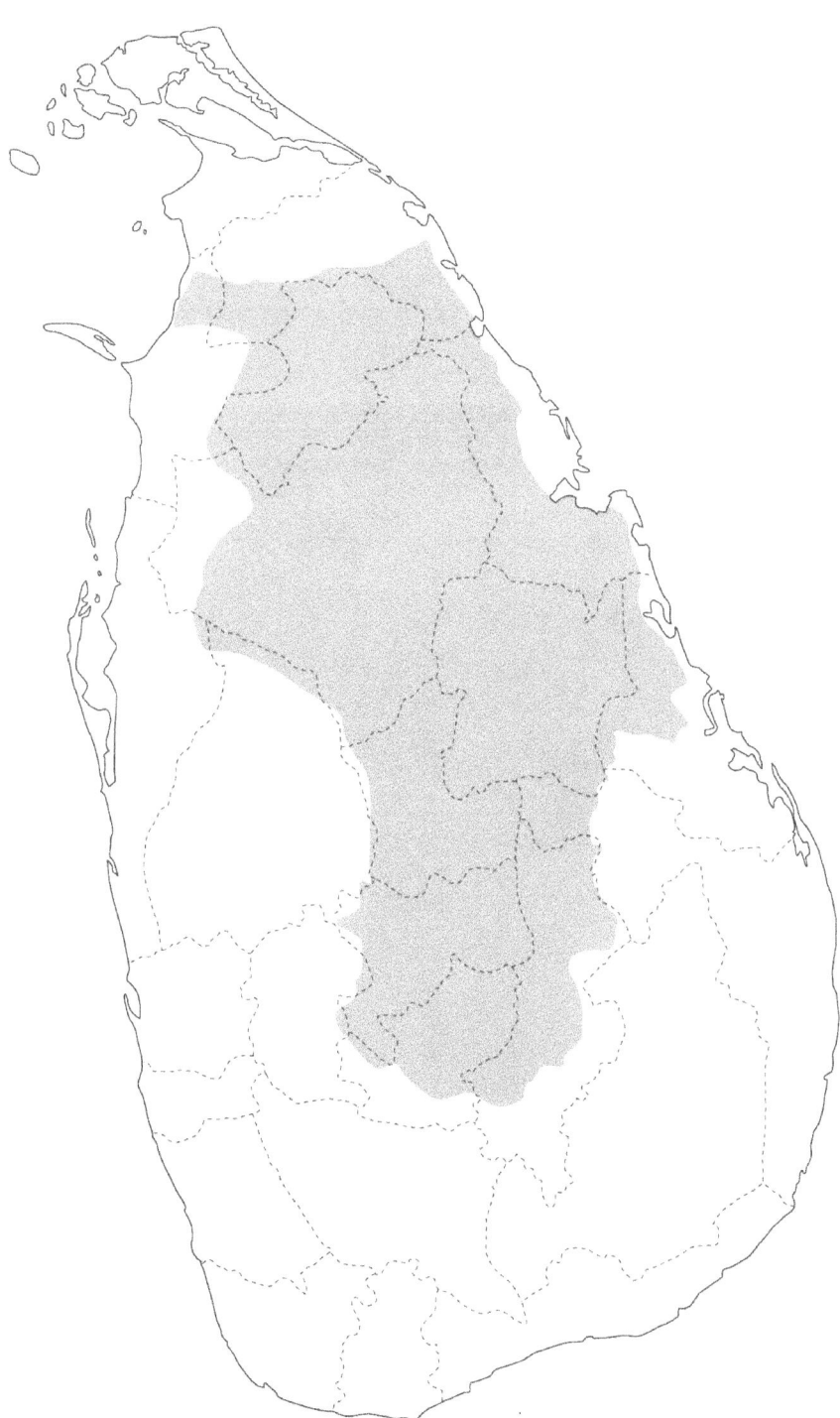

MAP 3. The Mahaweli Development and Irrigation Project, covering the North Central Province and beyond. CKDu is largely epidemic in this region. Map by Bill Nelson.

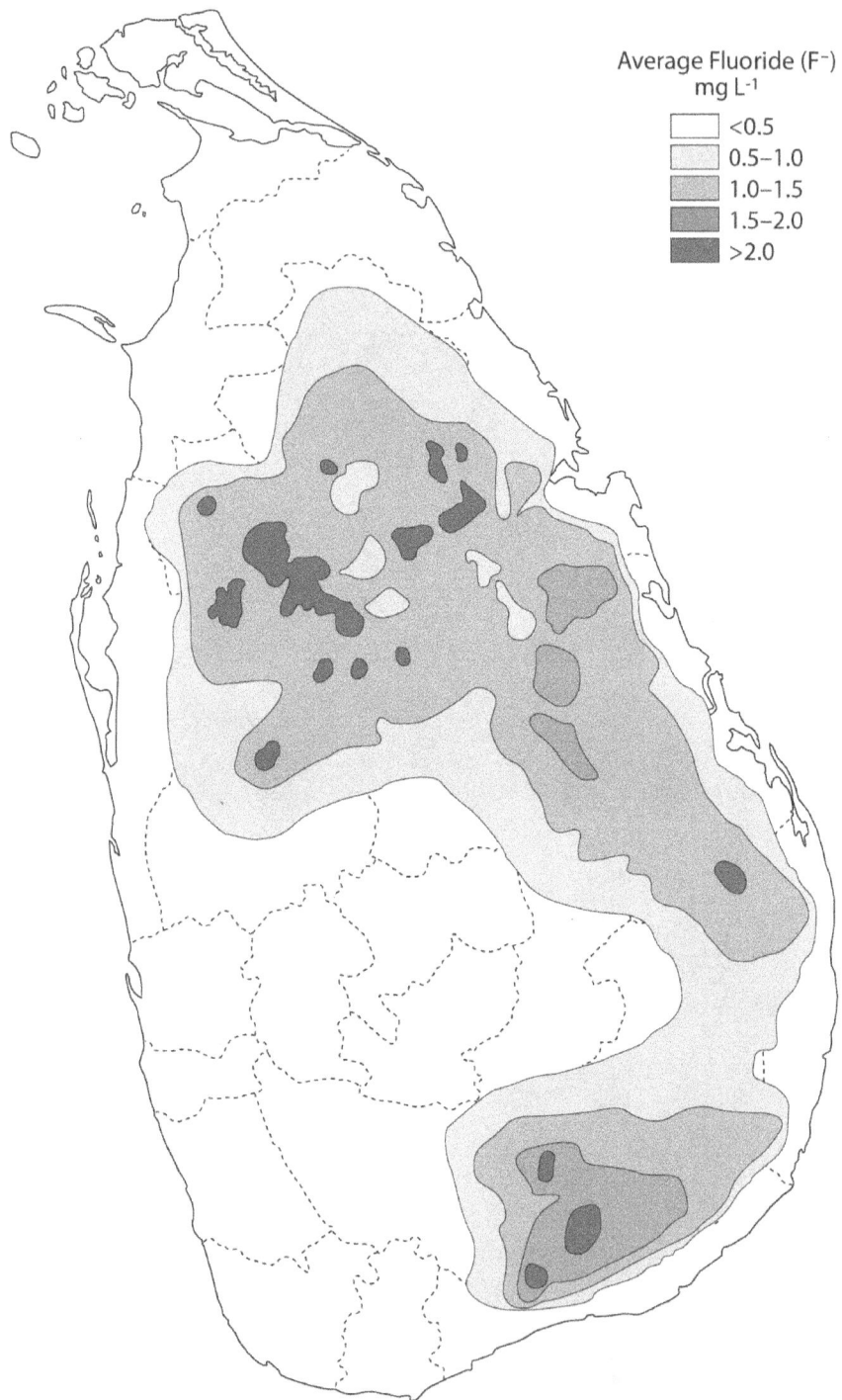

MAP 4. Average fluoride levels in groundwater, with the highest levels recorded in the CKDu epidemic region. Fluoride forms a key component of the Peradeniya group's work on CKDu. (Map based on Indika et al. 2022, CC-BY). Map by Bill Nelson.

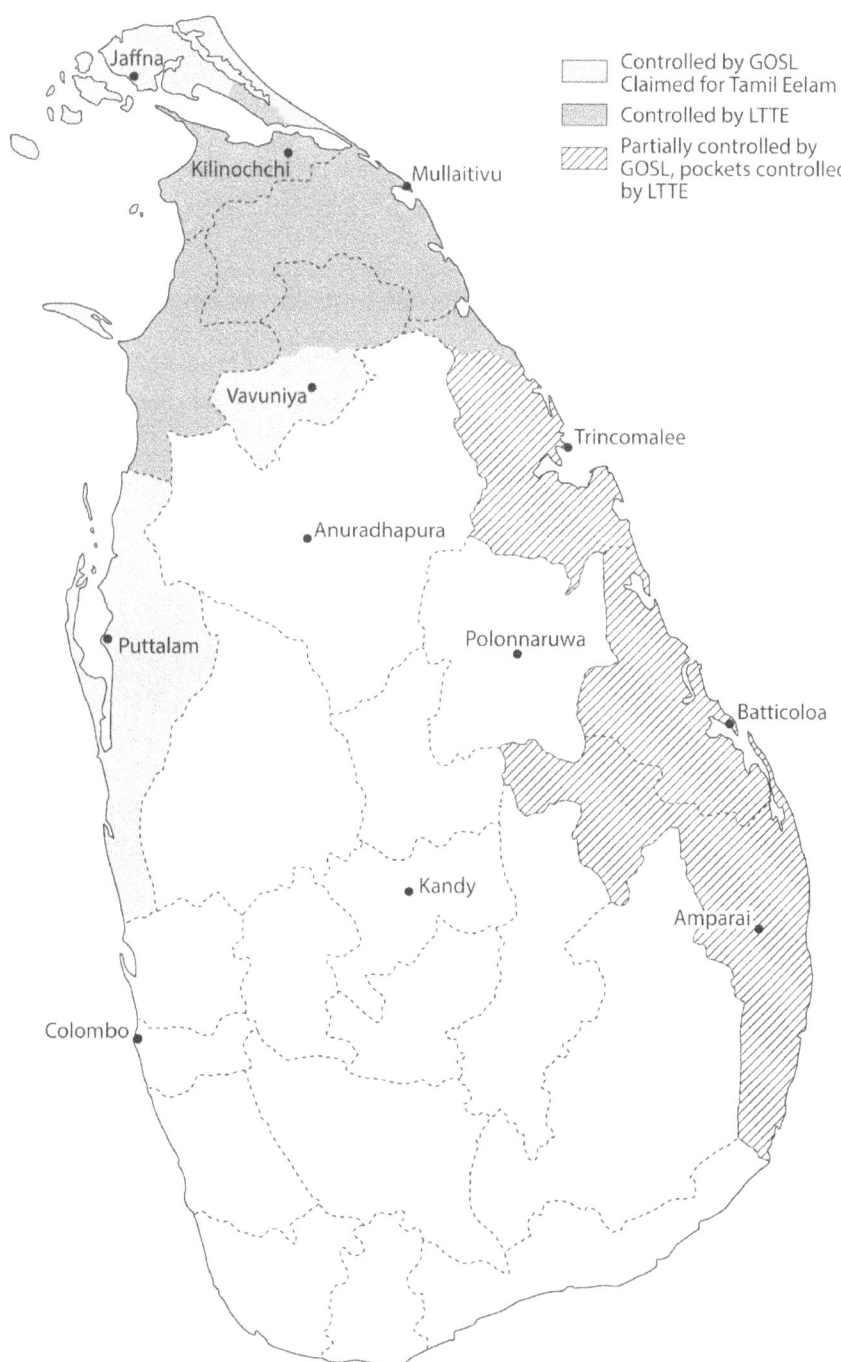

MAP 5. Areas controlled and contested by the Government of Sri Lanka (GOSL) and the Liberation Tigers of Tamil Eelam (LTTE) shifted over time, with this map showing the fullest extent of territorial disputes during the war. (Source: https://en.m.wikipedia.org/wiki/File:Extent_of_territorial_control_in_sri_lanka.png.) Map by Bill Nelson.

increasingly privileged Sinhala language and ethnicity in terms of access to and representation within state education, employment, and other benefits and made Buddhism the de facto national religion. In 1956, a surge in Sinhala nationalism led to the election of a leftist government on the promise of enacting a "Sinhala Only" language policy. Tensions between the majority Sinhala community and the minority Tamil community over the "national question"—that is, whether the island was home to multiple ethnicities claiming equal status and participation or instead home to a dominant Sinhala Buddhist community superior to all other groups (Krishna 1999; Tiruchelvam 2000; Wickramasinghe 2007; Kapferer 1988)—subsequently grew. Over the following decades, increasing discrimination against Tamils on all fronts—economic, educational, social, political, and linguistic—created the conditions for a radical Tamil nationalism premised on the demand for a greater Tamil homeland, "Tamil Eelam," which would join Tamils living in the north and east of Sri Lanka with Tamils living in southern India.

The threat posed by the Liberation Tigers of Tamil Eelam (LTTE), the militant group that emerged in the 1970s in pursuit of the Tamil superstate, which would eventually wage war against the Sri Lankan state, to the "islanding" project was thus fundamental. Anthropologist Bruce Kapferer (1988) developed a historical analysis of Sinhala nationalist discourse to demonstrate the ontological equivalences it draws between the sovereign state, the nation, and the body. Kapferer argued that in the nationalist imaginary, the triad played a role in, and featured as part of, the construction and defense of the other. "The state," Kapferer (1988, 7) suggested, "protectively encloses the nation of Sinhalese Buddhists, whose integrity as persons is dependent on this encompassment." In direct contravention of the nationalist imaginary, Tamil Eelam would undermine the protective ring that the Sinhala state would create around Sinhala bodies. However, Kapferer also argued that the threat flowed in the other direction. Attacks on Sinhala bodies were attacks on the Sinhala nation and the Sinhala state. It was precisely for this reason that demands for Tamil self-governance could never be tolerated and were met with such a violent response: they represented an existential challenge to the integrity of the Sinhala nation *and* Sinhala bodies.

Even while the Sinhala nationalist imaginary had envisaged a bounded nation with clearly demarcated ethnic and linguistic roots and hierarchies, a complex heterogeneous mix of origins, belongings, and claims and counterclaims to "indigeneity" was always the historical and social reality. The political maps that nationalists would seek to draw were incomplete and unstable objects, lacking internal and external coherence in space as well as time. As ethnic identities, the categories "Sinhala" and "Tamil" were the products of precolonial "nationalisms," colonial strategies of "divide and rule," and postcolonial state formation (Kemper 1991). What they lacked was any clear claim to indigeneity or authentic presence in the island. Tamil nationalists identified themselves as Jaffna Tamils and claimed deep ancestry on the peninsula, considering themselves quite distinct from the "Indian

Tamils" whom the British had imported to the island to work on the tea and rubber plantations in the central highlands. A third community of Tamil-speaking Muslims, whose origins involve a complex mix of mythico-historical claims, only further undermined the argument of the Tamil nationalists that the north and east of the island was rightfully theirs (McGilvray 2008).

Moreover, a modern history of large-scale internal and external migration threatened the idea of Sri Lanka as a nation defined as "the same people living in the same place" (Spencer 2003). Anthropologist Jonathan Spencer has argued this continuous movement of people rendered the construction of a national political identity based on a particular kind of people inhabiting a particular kind of place "impossible." As anthropologist E. Valentine Daniel (1996, 48) has also argued, after the settler colonies of the United States and Australia, Sri Lanka has the longest experience of colonialism among all modern nation-states: three and a half centuries between the arrival of the Portuguese in 1597 and the end of British rule in 1948. What made up the content of nationalist rhetoric and the modalities of nationalist political expression itself, beginning with the very notion of a nation-state, were in and of themselves not indigenous to Sri Lanka but imported during the colonial period and formally established on independence in 1948. If protagonists on both sides fought the ideological war in the name of claims to supposedly timeless origins, the weapons they deployed were highly modern (Moore 1993).

Following the collapse of the separatist state, the bounded nation became a possibility once again. Sinhala nationalists presented the end of war as "reunification"—a future created by returning the island to its imagined historical status as a single territorial space—a *shore-ringed nation*. Yet with the LTTE vanquished, new threats to the integrity of the shore-ringed nation quickly emerged: the CKDu epidemic, fears of Muslim terrorism, and the growing role of China in Sri Lanka's economy, politics, and society. Ostensibly unconnected phenomena, threats posed by CKDu and Muslim terrorists captured Sinhala Buddhist anxieties about corporeal integrity within a unified political territory whose "wholeness"— its "islandness"—was to be understood in direct contrast to the island's fragmented past. Conversely, the material risk to Sri Lankan sovereignty posed by Chinese investments in infrastructure and land reclamation projects received notably less attention from Buddhist nationalists even while China's presence undermined their very claims to the veracity of the shore-ringed nation. This apparent disinterest is revealing, because it highlights the contingent and shifting nature of the Sinhala nationalist cause.

It is against this background of island unification that poisoncraft became such an important part of postwar statecraft. To explore this, I tell a story of the four maps presented above—the four "obsessions" of agricultural development, water quality, cultural heritage, and the war's borderlands—that together narrate how epidemiological representations of CKDu have come to play a role in longer historical processes of Sri Lankan islanding. Placing the maps side by side reveals a complex entanglement of disease epidemiology, military and ancient history, and contemporary social and environmental development and change—all of which have informed, and recently been informed by, the work of the Rajarata-Kelaniya, Peradeniya, and Colombo research groups. In the sections that follow, I develop my analysis by narrating three themes that emerged from my study of the maps, including matters of nationalist belonging, reproduction, and historiography. Together, they engage with problems of *autochthony*—an indigeneity that grows from claims of "belonging to the soil" of place, even when soil is feared to have become poisonous.

Autochthonies

As with many stories told about postcolonial Sri Lanka, the story of CKDu is also a story of the civil war. One of the earliest theories of CKDu causation to gain the public's attention linked the disease with LTTE bioterrorism. In so doing, it encapsulated the territorial anxieties produced by those ongoing processes of partioning and islanding that the war involved. Widely credited to Channa Jayasumana, the pharmacologist whose work on glyphosate with the Rajarata-Kelaniya group would later come to dominate CKDu debates in Sri Lanka (see chapter 9), the bioterrorism hypothesis is no longer found today in published form. The premise of the bioterrorism hypothesis was that the military line separating the government-controlled south from the LTTE-controlled north and east, the so-called Eelam boundary, demarcated CKDu endemic and non-endemic areas (map 6). Proponents of the theory asked why CKDu was endemic only to the south of the boundary when all other environmental and social factors were equal on either side.

Akila Weerasekera (2008), a chemist then attached to California State University (an international outpost of the Rajarata-Kelaniya group), suggested that the LTTE could have used one of three possible agents to contaminate water—mycotoxins, depleted uranium, or genetically engineered biological weapons. After reviewing the history of chemical and biological warfare, Weerasekera concluded, "It is certainly a possibility that terrorists and their allies could use such weapons to systematically destroy the people residing in a certain area." Echoing widely held beliefs in the nationalist community that "foreign agents" provided ideological and material support to the LTTE and their struggle, he argued that "it is the responsibility of the [Sri Lankan government] to investigate the past activities of INGOs and NGOs in the CKD affected areas." Drawing similar conclusions, medical historian Kamalika Pieris (2016) also settled on the significance of the Eelam boundary as an explanation for CKDu. For Pieris, the agricultural communities of that region had become a target for the LTTE because of their own claim to farm those lands.

The bioterrorism hypothesis came to form one axis of an "enemy within" thesis that has dominated the allegorical imaginary of the shore-ringed nation. During

MAP 6. The "Eelam border," which runs immediately north and east of the CKDu epidemic region, along the frontlines of the civil war. Map by Bill Nelson.

the war, the LTTE posed an existential threat to the sovereign isle. Drawing from approaches in psychoanalysis, anthropologist Gananath Obeyesekere (1984) long ago argued that the Tamil threat was the manifestation of a deep-rooted Sinhala entitlement complex drawn from their mythic claim of being the guardians of Buddhism in its proper home, Sri Lanka. From the perspective of the majority Sinhala community, the nature of that threat was external, in the sense that the LTTE saw itself as belonging to an independent state joined with southern India. Those with interest in the war have often followed historian K. M. de Silva's (1998) definition of the conflict as one between a (Sinhala) ethnic majority with a minority complex and a (Tamil) ethnic minority with a majority complex. When the LTTE threat dissipated, a void opened in political discourse—one that CKDu and its legion of invisible poisons threatening the nation quickly filled. Sinhala nationalists' attention turned to threats internal to the shore-ringed nation, specifically, the other minority communities, particularly the Muslims. The triumphant Sinhala nationalist community sought to deal with those minorities on two fronts, colonization of provinces previously held by the LTTE on the one side and increased agitations against Muslims on the other side.

The Shore-Ringed Nation

> *Our water bodies from the smallest well and pond to the largest reservoirs and rivers have become vats of toxins unfit for human or animal consumption. That wondrous natural gift to the peoples of Sri Lanka, its large water resources, have now been mostly rendered dangerous for human use.*
> —PRESIDENT'S OFFICE 2015, 12

The CKDu threat owes its specific logics of endangerment to the new geopolitical territory of the shore-ringed nation. Nowhere has this been clearer than in the new water politics that has emerged in postwar Sri Lanka. The process of islanding has reoriented water politics, connecting up-country headwaters with the rice fields downstream and the ocean beyond. When the war ended, the ocean, previously the domain of fishing trawlers and the sea-going arm of the LTTE, the Sea Tigers, was reframed as a national resource and brought into the fold of environmental discourse previously focused on the interior. At first only small indications of this appeared. They included the "discovery" of blue whales off the southern coast, which the Sri Lankan Navy quickly developed as a tourist attraction, and a growing interest among fisher communities in long-distance, deep-sea trawling, accompanied by a new narrative of the fisher castes descending from some forgotten ocean-voyaging people (Stirrat, pers. comm. 2012; see also Radicati 2019). During the 2010s, against a background of growing global environmental awareness and activism around water pollution and management, the focus of Sri Lankan environmentalism similarly extended from a postcolonial concern with the protection and renewal of the hinterlands of paddy fields, forests, and national parks in the North Central Province (Jazeel 2013; Seneviratne 2000) to a new "global" concern with ocean conservation. Volunteer beach clean-up campaigns that became an increasingly common sight along the coast of Sri Lanka during the postwar years epitomized this reorientation.

The postwar years too witnessed a concerted effort to occupy LTTE-held areas of the north and east—militarily, culturally, and ethnically. Processes of purificatory "Sinhalization" and "Buddhification" took place. The Sri Lankan military displaced those who had been affected by the war to build army camps on seized lands, erected Buddhist temples on top of old Hindu shrines, and settled Sinhala families in areas occupied previously by Tamils and Muslims (Human Rights Watch 2018; Correspondent 2012; Seoighe 2017). Accompanying those moves was a program of building so-called victory monuments on LTTE shrines and cemeteries and key battlegrounds of the war, which would become centerpieces of "battlefield tourism" attracting tens of thousands of mostly Sinhala visitors every year (Bastin and de Silva 2018; Hyndman and Amarasingam 2014; Perera 2016). Among the most famous was the Victory Monument at Mullivaikal Lagoon on the northeast coast of the island, the scene of one of the most controversial battles in the last stages of the civil war. The monument opened in December 2009 and was described by the Sri Lankan Army as built "in memory of all those War Heroes who triumphed over evil and sacrificed their lives for the noblest of all noble causes" (Sri Lanka Army 2009).

Anthropologists Rohan Bastin and Premakumara de Silva (2018) draw attention to the ethno-mythical symbolism of the Mullivaikal monument. This included the association made between the four guardian lions placed at its corners and the Sinhala (People of the Lion) "sons of the soil" (*bhumiputra*)—the ordinary rural youth who rose up and joined the army to vanquish the Tamil threat. Bastin and de Silva argue that the reference evokes the story of the mythical first monarch of the world, Mahasammata, who also arose from among the people to establish the social order. The Sri Lankan Army itself emphasized the process of islanding the monument represents. According to a press release, "Four Lions at four corners of the memorial . . . immortalize the contribution of the War Heroes who came from all four directions to win the final battle. . . . The National flag on it demonstrates the sovereignty, independence and dignity of the nation" (Sri Lankan Army 2009).

More than this, the Mullivaikal monument contains strong environmental imagery. According to the Sri Lankan Army's press release, the water base represents "the blue ocean that surrounds the island" and the "natural granite boulders . . . [that] . . . depict the mother earth, replete with natural resources." Such references further "island" Sri Lanka as a shore-ringed nation not simply in the Indian Ocean but also in time, when the process of islanding that commenced in the ancient past has finally been realized in its fullest potential. The monument too presents water and soil not simply as the fundament from which the "sons of soil" emerged but also to which they shall return, now cleansed of impurities. The Mullivaikal monument thus symbolizes "reterritorialized" belonging through an explicitly autochthonous representation: a soldier emerging victorious from the native soil. It is a territory that requires management through poisoncraft.

Muslim Conspiracies and Buddhist (In)fertilities

While Sri Lanka's on- and offshore territories became subject to a new toxicologized discourse concerning poison threats to sovereign integrity, Sri Lankan bodies became subject to similar concerns. Throughout the period of my inquiry, growing fears of Muslim conspiracies to undermine Buddhist fertility emerged in Buddhist nationalists' discourses as a novel threat to the shore-ringed nation. The Muslim threat was of a different order from the Tamil threat. While the LTTE jeopardized the possibility of the island nation by dividing the land, Buddhist nationalists have argued that "Muslim terrorists" pose a more pernicious threat to the nation from within. Extremist Buddhist groups like the Bodu Bala Sena (BBS; Buddhist Power Force) and Sinhala Ravaya (Sinhalese Roar), as well as grassroots movements like the Sinha Le (Lion's Blood), have combined older nationalist rhetoric with inspiration drawn from anti-Muslim movements across northern Europe, the United States, and Southeast Asia (Zuhair 2016; Holt 2016; Imtiyaz and Mohamed-Saleem 2015). In those groups' Islamophobic discourse, Muslims have been accused of dominating private enterprise and accumulating wealth; having large families, driving a demographic shift in their favor; trying to convert Buddhists to Islam; and, via ISIS, planning to incorporate the island into an Islamic state (Stewart 2014; Ali 2013; Widger 2016; Zuhair 2016; Holt 2016; Imtiyaz and Mohamed-Saleem 2015).

Public discourse in Sri Lanka has always been rife with conspiracy theories concerning unseen threats to the nation. As anthropologist H. L. Seneviratne (2000, 226n) has argued, "Instances of this paranoia are extensive and varied," although the usual suspects include "the CIA, the United States in general, India, the Tamils, the Muslims, the Christians, [and] the World Bank." Seneviratne has suggested that conspiracy theories at the national level are expressions of "local and domestic paranoia expressed in the suspicion of magical and other harm that can emanate any moment from kinsmen, neighbours, fellow workers, and even friends" (2000, 226n; see also Widger 2015c, 142–51). While the fear of harm from unseen forces in village contexts may indeed give narrative form to fears of agents operating at the national level, the conspiracy theories involving Muslims that dominated postwar nationalist anxieties had quite different social and political significance.

During the 2010s, numerous theories arose about Muslims posing a danger within and to the national body via plots against Sinhala Buddhist reproductive biology. The BBS came to national attention in 2012 following a series of street protests directed against Muslim-owned clothing chains popular among Sri Lankan youth of all backgrounds, alleging the stores sold women's underwear laced with infertility poisons. Other examples followed. In 2017, a theory circulated on Facebook that a group of Muslims posing as doctors was going around injecting Sinhala people with sterilizing chemicals (it later transpired that the video evidence for the claim depicted Sinhala doctors testing people for the blood disease thalassemia). That same year, theories also circulated about an Indian-manufactured motorcycle seat contaminated with male sterilization chemicals. In 2018, a group of Sinhala youths attacked a restaurant in the town of Ampara after allegedly witnessing a Muslim worker poisoning food with sterilization pills. During the days following the ISIS-inspired suicide attacks on hotels and churches on Easter Sunday in 2019 that had seen retaliatory violence on Muslim communities, rumors began spreading about a new Islamist plot to poison drinking water—prompting a national information drive to quell fears and communal unrest.

The most notorious example of conspiratorial thinking involved allegations against a Muslim surgeon, Dr. Mohamed Shafi, in the gynecology and obstetrics department of Kurunegala Teaching Hospital, northeast of Colombo (Ulmer and Rajarathnam 2019). A month after the Easter Sunday attacks, a Sinhala nationalist newspaper carried a front-page story claiming a Muslim doctor working at the hospital had sterilized four thousand Buddhist women after performing cesarean deliveries. In a significant twist to the CKDu-glyphosate story, that same day Channa Jayasumana, a leading figure in the Rajarata-Kelaniya group, named Dr. Shafi as the chief suspect on his Facebook account. Two days later, police arrested and detained the doctor under antiterrorism laws after investigators subsequently "uncovered" ties with Muslim terrorist organizations. Following his arrest, more than six hundred women came forward to "lodge complaints" against Dr. Shafi. In a press conference, Jayasumana claimed that Dr. Shafi had sterilized the women by "pressing together" their fallopian tubes during the cesarean procedure.

Jayasumana's allegations drew angry responses in Sri Lanka and abroad, with critics claiming they were a transparent attempt on the part of Buddhist nationalists to stoke communal tensions following the Easter Sunday attacks. Vice president of the Muslim Council of Sri Lanka, Hilmy Ahmed, called the claims a "stage-managed" ploy by supporters of presidential hopeful Gotabaya Rajapaksa to exploit Buddhist fears about wider Muslim conspiracies ahead of the 2019 election. At that time, Jayasumana was campaigning on behalf of Rajapaksa's party, the Sri Lanka Podujana Peramuna, and by his own admission was using an anti-Muslim platform to win Sinhala Buddhist votes (Colombo Telegraph 2019). Unnamed sources also alleged that Jayasumana had been motivated in his campaign against Dr Shafi because of an argument he had with Shafi's wife, a nephrologist, "over kidney diseases" (Lanka News Web 2019). By July, however, the case against Dr. Shafi collapsed; a police investigation found no evidence to support the allegations against him (AFP Sri Lanka 2019).

Akin to cartographic anxieties, reproduction anxieties have been commonplace across South and Southeast Asian societies for some time. Majority Buddhist and Hindu communities in Sri Lanka, Myanmar, Thailand, and India, among others, have long held a fear that birthrates in their communities have been falling while those among the Muslim minority have been increasing (Simpson 2004; Pethe 1973; Jeffery and Jeffery 1997; Smith 2009). While the conspiracy theories I have related merely continued this tradition, Dr. Shafi's case also illuminates the close overlap between Sinhala Buddhist agitations against Muslims and the national debate on CKDu and glyphosate—an overlap exemplified by the leading role taken by Channa Jayasumana in both cases. To my knowledge, neither Jayasumana nor any other nationalist figure has attempted to link CKDu with Muslim plots against Sinhala Buddhist reproduction (although Jayasumana's early work did link the disease with the LTTE). Nevertheless, both crises have provided Jayasumana and other nationalists with potent material to develop and extend a nationalist toxicology. In the language of anthropologist Mary Douglas (1966), Buddhist nationalists have come to consider Muslims a minority community "out of place" in the shore-ringed nation. The conflation of ethno-religious pollutant with chemical poison in nationalist rhetoric is not arbitrary but serves to reinforce and extend the potency of the other. Within the newly bounded nation, danger lurks in the form of a Muslim pollutant plotting to bring about the downfall of the Sinhala Buddhist majority using reproductive poisons.

WHEN TO LOOK

Dredging Pasts

Often cited as the first published record of CKDu is a memorial oration delivered in 1993 by S. Ramachandran (1994) titled "Renal Diseases: Sri Lankan and Global Spectrum" (Dharmawardana 2016; Gooneratne et al. 2008; Wanigasuriya 2012). Ramachandran was a senior physician at the General Hospital in Colombo. Reporting observations he made between 1989 and 1993 while working in that post, Ramachandran identified five patients from 448 cases where the cause of the disease was unknown. The citation of his article in this way is perhaps a strange one, given that Ramachandran based his paper on data drawn from Colombo, far away from the epidemic region, and that he described the cases in question as acute and not chronic CKD. There is nothing in Ramachandran's address to suggest that the case histories he studied were CKDu.

Nevertheless, the significance of the Ramachandran oration in CKDu history has many defenders. Writing in support of the oration in the online *CKDu and Sri Lanka* Basecamp forum, one of Ramachandran's colleagues, Duminda, a consultant nephrologist, commented, "I know that many of these cases of unknown etiology were from NCP and probably early CKDu cases—because I worked with him [Ramachandran] in the eighties and was closely involved in collecting data." Similarly, in an article published in *The Island*, S. A. M. Kularatne (2015) described his tenure as a consultant physician at the General Hospital in Anuradhapura between 1994 and 1998: "In 1995, there were sporadic cases of CKD inviting my special attention. Then, I realized numbers of CKD were increasing by 1996. In early 1997, I carried out an audit on CKD related deaths in my male medical ward. The results astonished me as more than 100 patients have died in 1996 due to CKD in my ward alone. . . . CKDu would have emerged in the early 90s and was in full swing by 1996." Kularatne concluded with a stark warning: "Researchers need to think about what environmental changes had taken place in the Dry Zone from the early 90s by critical comparison to previous decades."

CKDu research necessarily involves an experiment in chronotopic travel—a journey across time and space in the hunt for causations that may be forgotten or unknown in medical or social history yet with legacies manifestly present in failing kidneys. The first recorded cases of the disease are widely reported to have dated from the early 1990s. If accurate, that pushes initial exposure or damaging harm back to the early 1980s or late 1970s (assuming the disease takes on average ten years to become symptomatic, as is generally thought). Those are dates with resonance in Sri Lanka, as they are associated with the Accelerated Mahaweli and more widely the turn from a planned to an "open" economy and escalation of civil war. Yet others have argued that the disease is thousands of years old, playing a hitherto unnoticed role in the fall of Sri Lanka's ancient civilizations. To prove their point, they have sought evidence in historical writings and the archaeology of population movement that might provide clues on water quality and the kidney health of those communities. Researchers dredge personal and institutional memories and historical archives and published medical papers for clues to poisons and deaths that might help to pinpoint "patient zero" and reveal CKDu's ultimate origins.

I use the word *dredge* with the specific intention of calling to mind an image of watery sediments that when searched may give up secrets about their nephrotoxic histories. The allusion is important, because two and a half millennia of complex irrigation have transformed Mahaweli hydrology, geography, and sociology, their toxic effects leaving lesions on kidney tissues and indices of human development and welfare. This history is far from an unbroken one, with events marking the rise and fall of civilizations and postcolonial civil war inscribing their own stories on bodies. *When to look* thus becomes a matter of reorienting the experience of chronic disease to recent and deep pasts, requiring historical sensibility as much as it does nephrotic or epidemiological sensibility. In one view, the hubris of chemical modernity poisoned a region watered by a postcolonial irrigation system in which "everybody lives downstream" (Gunawardene 2012b). In a second view, the poison has always lurked beneath the ground, laying waste to entire civilizations before lying dormant until disturbed once again by the arrival of colonist-farmers who had long forgotten why the lands they settled were absent of human life.

Chemical Hubris

Staff scientists at the Movement for Land and Agricultural Reform (MONLAR), an NGO that advocates for farmer rights and has campaigned against glyphosate, urged me when to look. For them it was impossible to separate CKDu from the history of the modern irrigation system and intensified farming practices, including the introduction of hybrid seed and chemical packages that made the Accelerated Mahaweli possible. They dated CKDu to specific events that took place during the second half of the twentieth century—events that represented calamities in the health of people and the nation. The first event was in 1961, the year the government inaugurated the Mahaweli project as part of a national drive to increase rice production and food security. The second was 1977, the year of wide-ranging market reforms that opened the economy to unregulated imports, including new agricultural technologies. The third was 2002, the year of a World Bank report that reoriented the Mahaweli project from an irrigation "development zone" to a "river basin management project," resulting in a further "liberalization" of paddy production.

MONLAR's suggestion about when to look linked CKDu with Sri Lanka's Green Revolution, the toxic legacies of Western colonialism that began the process of breaking traditional relationships between subsistence farmer and the land, and the consequences of chemically intensive industrialized agriculture today. Since its inception, the Accelerated Mahaweli had come to stand for the negative consequences of modernization that destroyed "traditional" means of rural livelihood (Morrison et al. 1979; Sarkar and Tambiah 1979; Gombrich and Obeyesekere 1988). In the popular imaginary, the Mahaweli districts became somewhere distanced or "over there," away from the urban centers of modern Sri Lanka (Widger 2012, 2015c)—a place of violence, disease, and death where the claims of Sinhala Buddhist autochthony came into conflict with the historical realities of legitimate Tamil and Muslim claims to belonging and a population of Sinhala colonists left to fend for itself.

Writing within this same tradition, Asoka Bandarage (2013), a political scientist, and sociologists de Silva, Albert, and Jayasekara (2017) have used structural violence theory to explain the relationship between CKDu and the Mahaweli. The crux of their argument is that the introduction of plantation agriculture and monocropping by the British during the nineteenth century and the chemically intensive approach of irrigated agriculture introduced by the Mahaweli program in the twentieth century disrupted a socially and environmentally balanced form of "traditional" agriculture. This in turn "introduced a more competitive and individualist approach to agriculture and social relations" (Bandarage 2013, 6) and created a large landless wage-labor class that was more exposed to productivity and price fluctuations, poverty, and poor health (de Silva et al. 2017). As de Silva and colleagues highlighted, "The wage laborers in these agricultural settlements have become the principal risk takers, working in waterlogged paddy fields, applying chemical fertilizer, spraying pesticides, and lacking access to water safe for drinking. The wage laborer engaged in a system of production beyond his control has become subject to all the pathogens of paddy production" (193). Likewise, Bandarage (2013, 7) argued that despite experiencing the detrimental health and environmental effects of agrochemicals, Sri Lankan farmers became "addicted" to pesticides: "They now have little confidence in themselves and in the organic, traditional agricultural methods of their ancestors. They have been made to believe that the new chemical-industrial approach represents progress and that chemical pesticides are indispensable for their survival." For Bandarage, the contemporary political economy of CKDu has emerged from an industrialized agriculture that has blinded its victims to their own complicity in perpetuating a system that is killing them. Bandarage's conclusion was both powerful and nostalgic (and powerfully nostalgic): "[The] Rajarata, home to the CKD tragedy, was the seat of the ancient hydraulic civilization and is still the 'rice bowl' of the island producing much of its staple food. However, now, CKD is decimating the bearers of the noble occupation who amid enormous hardship and suffering continue to till the land to feed the country" (5).

Popular historical narratives of the kind articulated by Bandarage position contemporary Sri Lanka as a "hydraulic" society. The close relationship between Sinhala identity and irrigated rice agriculture, the correspondence between water and Buddhist ritual practice, and the pride that Sri Lankans take in the beauty of the island's natural water heritage all work to establish the far-reaching significance of poisoned water as a specific sovereign threat. A key element in this paradox is thus the irrigation system itself. Rivers flowing from the central highlands toward the coast feed the cascade system that underpins the network of canals and channels that water fields across the Accelerated Mahaweli. Rains falling in the hills charge a system of small reservoirs (*wewa*) that irrigate individual paddy systems (*yaya*) in the dry plains. During a workshop on organic agriculture held in Colombo in 2016, one speaker made the case for chemical-free farming: "The whole country is poisoned by vegetable cultivation in the highlands. Over one hundred rivers start in the highlands and carry the poisons across the whole country." Another speaker referenced a "toxic sludge" that moves along river and canal beds and eventually finds its way onto rice fields and people's dinner plates. Under the cover of natural and cultural heritage, nephrotoxics travel freely across the island, contaminating the heartlands of Sinhala civilization. In political and public discourse, the imagery is often coupled with concerns that farmers will leave their farmlands, migrating to southern districts in search of clean water and good health for their children. If they did, then CKDu would have achieved what decades of civil war could not: the removal of Sinhala colonist-farmers from Mahaweli lands.

The distribution of nephrotoxic agents via the cascade system does not depend on the existence of a unified nation to function. However, it does require the idea(l) of the nation as a sovereign territory susceptible to new kinds of threat. Activist descriptions of emerging environmental challenge portray the nation in terms of chronic pollution flowing out from the center of the island to affect areas lying downstream. When viewed against the backdrop of decades of debate concerning how to unify a divided nation, it is compelling precisely because what people can refer to as "the whole island" now exists as a territorial and conceptual space that can be polluted, from inside out. A subtle but far-reaching shift has taken place in environmentalist concerns, wherein threats to the nation stem not from those separatist groups demanding territorial breakup but instead the viability of the territory at all. The "national question" becomes an environmental question about the very habitability of the shore-ringed nation—and one ultimately concerned with the problem of what kind of nation Sri Lanka is or wants to be. Looking for the causes of CKDu in the recent past leads to the seminal infrastructure project of the postcolonial era. Figuring so centrally in the nation's narrative since the 1970s, the Accelerated Mahaweli emerges as the most obvious culprit and one that has already been implicated in a string of public health crises since its launch.

History Repeating

Senarath, a senior manager who headed up glyphosate sales for the Sri Lankan pesticide company Lankem, also urged me when to look. He explained how recent debates among archaeologists and historians about why in 1017 CE the Anuradhapura kingdom had relocated its capital 100 kilometers southeast to Polonnaruwa had led some to argue that "the answer's in the water." Pick up any textbook on Sri Lankan history, and you will read that the Anuradhapura kingdom, which survived for 1,400 years (377 BCE–1017 CE), collapsed following a mix of internal and external pressures, in particular, repeated invasions from southern India (a historical echo of twentieth-century Sinhala nationalist fears of Tamil Eelam and "Indianization"). After the capture and death of the last Anuradhapura king in 1017, the invading Chola rulers shifted the capital 60 miles southeast to Polonnaruwa, where the new kingdom survived three hundred years, until 1310. It then shifted 90 miles southwest to Dambadeniya, far beyond the Rajarata, marking the final decline of the Sinhala Buddhist "Golden Age."

As archaeologist Jacquetta Hawkes (1967, 174) famously once observed, "Every age has the Stonehenge it deserves—or desires." She meant that theories concerning those great Bronze Age monoliths on England's Salisbury Plain have tended to reflect wider social currents and fascinations in society across the ages. Colonial and postcolonial archaeologists in Sri Lanka have similarly read the concerns of their own generation in the Rajarata ruins. For the British they provided historical evidence that the "unproductive" Dry Zone had once sustained complex civilizations and gave focus to their colonial agricultural development programs. In 1903, the governor of Ceylon, Sir Joseph West Ridgeway, commented, "We have testimony of the past that vast tracts of country at present almost entirely uninhabited at one time supported a teeming population, and I confidently assert that in the course of a few short decades, history will repeat itself and these extensive areas again come under cultivation" (1903, 56). Following independence, that same story became essential in the creation of the Mahaweli program and colonization of the Dry Zone by southern settlers. After the civil war, it did not take long for readings of the Rajarata ruins to reflect changing political priorities. Allusions to the geographic correspondence between CKDu and the Rajarata are common throughout the scientific, policy, and popular literature. An example from a 2012 report by a Colombo-based Rotarians club on its work combating CKDu illustrates what I mean: "Anuradhapura was a prosperous and then a hi-tech Kingdom. However, today there are more than 15,000 kidney affected patients *in and around the Kingdom* who need regular dialysis. It is believed this kidney failure is mainly due to a quality defect in the water found in the area" (Rotarians Colombo West 2012; emphasis added). The Rajarata has long provided an important imaginary for Sri Lankan development interventions being viewed as a place of both pride and shame. The juxtaposition of the Mahaweli districts as home to the Cultural Triangle—a region encompassing most of the island's UNESCO heritage sites between the three great cities of Anuradhapura, Polonnaruwa, and Sigiriya—and as a place of poverty and desperation provides further support to the imaginary of an island being poisoned from inside out, corrupting the very heart of the nation.

The emergence of CKDu as a disease endemic to the Rajarata has resulted in unexpected collaborations between archaeologists, epidemiologists, and agribusiness seeking to address this challenge. Glyphosate sales representative Senarath told me that recent discoveries made by Sri Lankan archaeologists about the real cause of Anuradhapura's and Polonnaruwa's downfalls questioned the textbook narrative of Chola invasions.

> Why did the kings only move 100 kilometers to the east if the problem was invasion from the north? We think it's because they knew the water in Anuradhapura was bad and tried to find somewhere with good water. They thought the water would be safe in Polonnaruwa but eventually noticed the same disease spreading and decided to abandon the North Central Province altogether. When you, the British colonials, arrived, you opened the area back up again. Forty years ago, when the Mahaweli project started, the area was repopulated, and so now the disease is spreading again.

While the identity of the poison remained unknown, Senarath told me that archaeologists had been able to make use of new CKDu research that had shown the extent of geologic fluoride in the region. It was thus very likely, he assured me, that the Rajarata kingdoms had fallen victim to fluoride poisoning: "Now we know the water has high concentrations of fluoride, we can say the health the ancient kingdoms was affected in the same way [as today] and the people decided to move."

Throughout my fieldwork, I encountered similar rereadings of Rajarata history as a reason to look beyond the temporal horizon of the Accelerated Mahaweli as the source of CKDu. For example, Diyon, a director of a competitor pesticide company, told me that once retreating Sinhala communities had abandoned their tanks, the stagnant waters became breeding grounds for nephrotoxic cyanobacteria. Leaching of those toxins contaminated neighboring sources of drinking water, eventually making the whole groundwater system at Anuradhapura unfit for human consumption. Following a brief move to Polonnaruwa to escape the encroaching poison, the people eventually moved southward. With the arrival of the Mahaweli colonies centuries later, the settlers unknowingly tapped the same polluted water sources.

The theory has also appeared in academic publications. In a paper exploring the spatial correspondence between CKDu and the Mahaweli, Colombo group scientists Stanley Weeraratne and Sunil J. Wimalawansa wrote:

> Peasants and rulers had no choice but to flee from region to region, first within the NCP, and then to central and southern regions of the country. . . . These historic facts raise a number of questions, including what is the real reason for the abandonment of this region centuries ago. It is not known if the migration was caused by a pandemic of malaria or if the region was badly affected with a different serious disease similar to [CKDu] or something else. It is not clear whether this is a sheer coincidence or history is repeating. (2015, 23)

Looking beyond the Accelerated Mahaweli as the cause of CKDu means dredging for any evidence of disease in historical records, both recent and distant. Reading ruins has become an exercise in and of toxicological desire—those with something to gain as well as something to lose notice in the past not just reflections of their own times but also an echo of a future anticipated, things as they could or should be. In Sri Lanka, the travel from present to past has also been accompanied by travel from past to present, as exemplified by Governor West's hope that colonization of the ancient irrigation system would see history repeating and Weeraratne and Wimalawansa's fear that it had.

Historical consciousness always plays an integral role in the rise of nationalist movements, and Sri Lankan historiography has been criticized for its nationalist teleology—a tale of rightful progress to Sinhala Buddhist hegemony, yet one that counterforces have continuously undermined. Histories written during the postcolonial era, when the conflict was escalating and full war eventually broke out, captured this by offering a version of the past perpetually under threat from South India—a projection from the present shaped by the dangers of LTTE separatism. In the CKDu era, revisionist histories have received a boon from CKDu research as much as theories of CKDu etiology have drawn inspiration from revisionist histories. Water poison has emerged as a third actor in the nation's narrative, as an insidious geotoxic force ultimately more devastating than the two opposing armies of the Rajarata and Chola kingdoms or the Sri Lankan Army and the LTTE. With the LTTE vanquished, the present threat of poisons within has emerged and has in turn been projected onto the past.

TOXICOLOGICAL ANXIETIES OF A POSTWAR NATION

In postwar Sri Lanka, questions of where to look and when to look for poison became a sovereign concern, a chronotopic project involving the identification of poisons within the body politic. CKDu came to hold special resonance in terms of how different constituencies—Sinhala nationalists, public health scientists, environmental activists, and agribusinesses—imagined the nation and its poison threats. Anthropologist Peter Geschiere (2009) has shown how as globalization has driven the deterritorialization of national identity, counterforces of localization have generated new claims of belonging that emerge from imaginaries of ground and soil—what he glosses as "autochthony." A central aspect of such reterritorializing processes has been what Geschiere calls an "obsession with having traitors on the 'inside' and the urgent need to unmask them" (131). In Sri Lanka, this has manifested in recurring fears of poisons within—from the infertility chemicals spread by Muslim terrorists to the cyanobacteria laying waste to ancient kingdoms and the geologic and microbial poisons welling up from deep underground—each reaping havoc on Sinhala Buddhist bodies, polities, and futures.

Extending Sankaran Krishna's (1994, 1999) work on cartographic anxiety from the level of sociopolitical relations to nonhuman processes, I argue that CKDu has made manifest new fears of sovereign threat encompassing infrastructural and subterranean poisons—what I call toxicological anxieties. Krishna's concern was to show how the act of representing "India" as a bounded nation-state in public culture, for example, through maps and schematics, media reports, and political rhetoric and campaign literature, was one inherently suspended in doubt. Such acts have involved the drawing of borders and territorial claims as to what lies inside and outside the national territory—a question that India has never settled with its neighbors and that remains something Hindu nationalist groups cannot take for granted. For Krishna (1994, 517), cartographic anxiety was to be understood as a postcolonial condition within a modernist frame—what he termed "an obsession to approximate a historical original that never existed, except as the telos of the narrative of modernity: a pure, unambiguous community called the homeland." Cartographic anxieties thus emerged from one-dimensional readings of a nation's threats, the surface plane of political maps. While cartographic anxieties remain powerful forces in Sri Lankan political culture, CKDu has highlighted the emergence of toxicological anxieties as maps depicting dangers to the nation have extended beyond the cultural-political to encompass the challenges posed by irrigation infrastructure, fluoride, and cyanobacteria. Asking *when to look* introduces the problem of deep time to nationalist temporality, and along with it forms of what feminist philosopher Elizabeth Grosz (2011) has called "geopower"—the geologic and "inhuman" forces bound up with ethnicity, gender, and class.

Sri Lanka falls within a geoclimatic zone that extends down the whole of the eastern coast of the Indian subcontinent, which by 2100 is projected to heat beyond a range that can sustain human life (Im et al. 2017). Simultaneously, subterranean arsenic and fluoride across Bangladesh, India, and Sri Lanka are responsible for what scientists have called "the largest mass poisoning in history" (Mori et al. 2018). Such "earth-shocks" (Liu et al. 2009) of the Chemical Anthropocene make redundant the basis of modernist territorial-nationalist claims within those zones without the possibility of terraforming that could reverse the effects of changing climate and environment. Responding to matters, materials, and materialities of varying historical and geologic depth, toxicological anxieties in Sri Lanka recall anthropologist Yael Navaro-Yashin's (2009, 4) understanding of affect as encompassing "the mark of the energy discharged upon them by dwellings and environments." As an "embroilment of inner and outerworlds" (Navaro-Yashin 2012, 24), toxicological anxieties echo their geologic, microbial, and agricultural sources and, ultimately, would thus require exploration of "the relations between the earth and its life forms . . . [that] . . . run underneath and through power relations" (Yusoff et al. 2012, 945). It was precisely in response to toxicological anxieties that politics and governance in and of the postwar period became dominated by poisoncraft. The (Sinhala) public would begin calling for protection from the poisons within, and the government would respond with a program of interventions aimed squarely at the purification of the island. Glyphosate arrived on the scene at precisely the right moment. In the next chapter, I explore the furor that would as a consequence encompass debates over glyphosate.

9

In Search of Compound X

In science, there is a God. That God does not appear nor is visualized in a simple manner. If you go deep into western science, we can see their God. This is a kind of cultural imperialism. At school and university level, we were taught about it. We tend to accept it as an objective reality. We leave behind our values. In the name of science, we have fallen in to a new belief. The ultimate result is the dilution of Sinhala Buddhist culture.

—CHANNA JAYASUMANA, QUOTED IN BANDARA, "SINHALESE CULTURE AND THERAVADA BUDDHISM"

Lead scientist of the Rajarata-Kelaniya group, Channa Jayasumana, spoke the words quoted above to a reporter in 2017. He was referring to what several researchers and theorists, from anthropologists and postcolonial science scholars to historians and philosophers of science, would also recognize: the ongoing relations of colonialism, cultural imperialism, and racism that shape ideologies, institutions, and practices of contemporary science. But Jayasumana's words also signal where the recent call for academic decolonization blurs into chauvinistic nationalism, where (in his eyes) the rise of a culturally hegemonic "western science" has displaced a previously hegemonic "Sinhala Buddhist culture." The problem as Jayasumana defined it was how this displacement had led the Sri Lankan scientific community to overlook or willfully ignore the role of glyphosate in causing CKDu, an etiology he championed and for which he became internationally known. His theories direct our attention to how poisoncraft in Sri Lanka drew from diverse sources to understand and engage with a world full of poisons that threatened the Sinhala Buddhist nation.

This chapter continues my investigation of the scientific work that led to the glyphosate ban through a closer examination of how toxicological theory and method allied with nationalist science and rhetoric. I explore how disagreements between the Rajarata-Kelaniya, Peradeniya, and Colombo research groups have unfurled around two core questions that I introduced in the previous chapter: Is CKDu caused by a single poison or multiple poisons and processes working synergistically; and do those poisons and/or processes derive from anthropogenic or natural sources? As an exploration of toxicological science and religion in postcolonial South Asia, the chapter thus approaches the debate over glyphosate as an example of where poisoncraft shapes the formation of nationalist projects.

CONSTRUCTIVE RELATIVISM

The philosophical and political underpinnings of the Rajarata-Kelaniya group lie in the work of polymath Nalin de Silva. His writings on Buddhist epistemology, what he called the "hegemony of western science," and efforts to link CKDu with arsenic poisoning provided the foundations for Jayasumana's later work on glyphosate. Born in 1944, Nalin de Silva is described in Wikipedia as a philosopher, a scientist, and a political analyst. He received his doctorate from Sussex University in theoretical physics in 1969, after which he held positions at several Sri Lankan universities. He was fired from his position at Colombo "for engaging in unlawful political activity within the campus" and was subsequently appointed to a chair in the Department of Mathematics at Kelaniya University, where he also held the position of dean of the Faculty of Science. In 2020, newly elected President Gotabaya Rajapaksa appointed de Silva ambassador to Myanmar. He died in 2024.

De Silva's work, which he "refused" to publish in peer-reviewed outlets, preferring Sinhala- and English-medium newspapers and his own website, explored questions of epistemology, ontology, and politics from an anticolonial perspective. Combining varieties of Marxism, philosophies of science, and Sinhala nationalism with his own approaches to Buddhist forms of knowledge, de Silva wrote about the failings of "western Christian Modernity (WCM)" (2011d), its destructive influence on the planet, and the negative forces polluting and degrading indigenous Sinhala Buddhist culture, including those emanating from minority communities. He saw his mission as one of developing and promoting Buddhist thought and practice as a radical alternative to WCM and the only route through which Sri Lanka could be free of its colonial (Western and Indian) influences.

Key to de Silva's philosophy was his approach to the Western scientific method, which he called "a set of damned lies (patapal boru)" (2013c). De Silva argued that Western science relies on a self-contradictory commitment to the inductive method and direct experience as the source of knowledge. His preferred example was Newton's explanation of gravity, which as a material force is simultaneously invisible to the human eye yet still accepted by scientists as an unquestionable fact. As de Silva (2013c) explained, "Western science is based on induction in order to formulate abstract generalized statements which cannot be observed though the scientists make a hue and cry on the so called experimental method." In its place, de Silva (2006) proposed an antimaterialist, anti-idealist philosophy he called *constructive relativism*. He distinguished constructive relativism from Indo-European materialist philosophies and various traditions of "Eastern" idealism to propose a third approach informed by Theravada Buddhism. His mission was to resurrect a "Sinhala Buddhist science" that had existed before the corrupting influences of Western colonialism and postcolonial supplication on Sinhala Buddhist thought: "I am a Sinhala Buddhist and I am proud to be so, even though the Sinhala Buddhists at present are very imitative and hypocrite [sic]. The Sinhala Buddhists have a proud record of protecting Theravada Buddhism and building a rich culture that enabled the people to live in harmony with nature" (de Silva 2013a).

According to de Silva, the defining features of the Sinhala Buddhist science underpinning his constructive relativism was knowledge acquired from the gods and "Buddha Prathyaksha"—a kind of "seeing." The concept of Prathyaksha or vision/the seeing eye is central to South Asian Buddhist traditions. "Throughout Buddhist literature," wrote historian David McMahan (2002, 2), "knowledge and vision are paired, often in the standard phrase 'the knowledge and vision (*jñāna-darśana*) of the Buddha.'" Vision not only penetrates misconception and misinformation to reach truth, but only those beings that are spiritually exulted have the capacity to see. Conversely, an inability to see or blindness is associated with "ignorance, darkness and even stupidity" (Simpson and Sariola 2012, 565).

Following Buddhist precept, de Silva (2006) argued that "the world an observer 'sees' is created by the observer due to 'avidya' of anicca, dukka and anatta which could be 'roughly translated' as ignorance of impermanence and soullessness." By this, de Silva meant our *avidya*, or misconception/misunderstanding, of the world is an inevitable consequence of the mind's inability to grasp the core Buddhist concepts of *anicca* (impermanence), *dukkha* (suffering), and *anatta* (non-self). Grasping all three concepts in their entirety is what leads to nirvana. For de Silva, however, the ability to see and thus to grasp knowledge of the world was a privilege only of Sinhala Buddhism, which as a community and culture "have acquired knowledge from the devas (Gods)" (2013a). In his view, the misconceptions and misunderstandings that limit human knowledge must derive from the imperfections of the human origins of knowledge and, in turn, the corruption of Sinhala Buddhist culture. De Silva argued that the "observer creates knowledge of the 'world', and hence the 'world' is relative to the sense organs, mind and the culture of the observer" (2006). Only higher beings, those on the path to nirvana, that is, the gods (*deviru*), have "correct sight" and can distinguish truth from falsity. Only they can grasp anicca, dukkha, and anatta—the stepping-stones to true knowledge.

For this reason, de Silva regarded consultation with deviru via *bhavana* (contemplation; spiritual cultivation of the self) an essential method of his constructive relativism. As De Silva explained, "Our group at Kelaniya consists of people who are interested in developing our own systems of knowledge and . . . our own theories (*ape pravada*) rather than simply importing ideas from the West." Experimentation with "ape pravada" led to what he termed "another source of knowledge, namely the . . . [gods] . . . who communicate knowledge when necessary to a lady who is known to us" (2011a). The "lady who is known to us" was Mrs. Priyantha Senanayake, a *maniyo* (pl. *maniyan*; a term de Silva translates as "divine medic," though it is more usually translated as "mother") whose consultation with Natha Deviyo, one of four guardian deities of Sri Lanka, proved instrumental in the Rajarata-Kelaniya group's work on CKDu.

De Silva's description of Mrs. Senanayake was distinctive of a Buddhism purified of what nationalists have rejected as "superstitious" elements borrowed from Hinduism that had grown in popularity since the late nineteenth century (Gombrich and Obeyesekere 1988). In the ethnographic literature, maniyan are often described as working-class women, frequently from abusive domestic contexts, for whom a career as a ritual specialist offers a route out of their situation (Obeyesekere 1981; Bastin 2002; Salgado 1997). Mrs. Senanayake, by contrast, was of a solidly professional background, holding degrees from international universities in molecular biology and wildlife management, and at the time of writing headed her own philanthropic foundation that promoted herbal remedies, including for CKDu. Clients seeking her "divine" medical advice have included several well-known figures in upperclass Sri Lankan circles, including government ministers and the principal of a leading private school. Stressing this distinction, de Silva (2011a) commented that Mrs. Senanayake "does not go into a trance or any such peculiar position . . . but communicates with the devivaru while she is in conversation with the others." She represented a wholly professionalised consultant of the deities whose presence in scientific seminars would be no less remarkable than that of any other kind of expert.

THE ARSENIC CONTROVERSY

De Silva was a controversial figure in Sri Lankan science. His typically bombastic intervention in the CKDu debate illuminated the extent of his influence on wider political discourse. Arsenic dominated disputes within the CKDu research community between 2011 and 2014 in much the same way that glyphosate dominated from 2014. In June 2011, Jayasumana, then a probationary lecturer in pharmacology at Rajarata, announced he had acquired kidney biopsies that demonstrated the presence of arsenic in CKDu fatalities. Jayasumana also claimed he had developed a "new methodology" (Fernando 2011) for tracing the origins of contamination in the mixing of arsenic-based pesticides with hard water to form the highly toxic compound calcium arsenate. Sri Lanka had banned its arsenic-based pesticides decades earlier in response to the suicide epidemic, but Jayasumana suggested that tests conducted on eight different products had demonstrated the continued presence of arsenic in pesticide imports. According to the *Sunday Observer*, "The research team says that the agro companies had violated the law by bringing arsenic based products into the country. They alleged false declarations have been made via laboratory test reports that were submitted for approval from the Pesticide Controller" (Fernando 2011). Jayasumana claimed his group's extensive analysis of dietary exposures had shown extraordinarily high levels of arsenic in food. "We found arsenic not only in rice grown in the area, but in vegetables, cucumbers, corn, and even the Kohomba (Margosa) trees in the area have it. It's everywhere," he said (Wamanan and de Alwis 2011).

De Silva credited the arsenic discovery to his own interventions. Before becoming involved in the CKDu issue, de Silva argued, the scientific and medical community had overlooked the seriousness of the epidemic. The disease "has been there for more than two decades but neither the public nor the so-called intellectuals nor the ... media nor politicians paid any attention to it until we came out with the arsenic issue in connection with the CKDu," he wrote (de Silva 2013b). De Silva explained how the arsenic hypothesis came about thanks to his consultations with Mrs. Senanayake. She helped the Rajarata-Kelaniya group transcend avidya (misconception/misunderstanding) thanks to her ability to consult with the Guardian Deities of the island:

> When Dr. Jayasumana informed me of the plight of the patients in Rajarata I was naturally disturbed and thought of a way to help these innocent people who supply the food including rice. By this time I had been cured of several diseases by what may be called divine medicine through Mrs. Priyantha Senanayake, who could communicate with a few whom she calls deivaru. Among them Natha Deviyan and Vipassaka Deviyan [two of four guardian deities who keep watch on the isle of Lanka] are the foremost in the sense that they are the most knowledgeable and also most spiritually advanced. I had no hesitation in directing Dr. Jayasumana to Mrs. Senanayake.
> ...
> When Dr. Jayasumana went to Mrs. Senanayake he was told by Natha Deviyan and Vipassaka Deviyan that the main cause of the CKDU was arsenic, the hard water and the particular soil called the "Kumburu Pasa" being the other two causes. What the Devivaru told was that the Kumburu Pasa has a tendency to retain arsenic which finally mixes with the Calcium and Magnesium salts found in hard water. The arsenic gets into the Calcium and Magnesium salts in a peculiar way making it almost undetectable in hard water. The hard water or kivul jalaya contributes to the spread of the CKDu and people who consume water from Vevas [reservoirs] that does not consist of much hard water are less likely to be victims of CKDU. (de Silva 2013b)

Although de Silva and Jayasumana had no reason to question the information that Mrs. Senanayake had provided, they realized that to convince the wider scientific community they must also prove the arsenic link using what de Silva termed "Western chemistry" (2013b). To that end, they enlisted the support of colleagues in the chemistry department at Kelaniya whose work also showed the presence of arsenic in imported pesticides and dietary sources. However, because "no one had ever previously demonstrated a link between arsenic and kidney disease," none of the existing tests available in the published literature could replicate what Natha Deviyo had told them (2013b). "Again the devivaru came to our rescue and suggested a particular method that could be adopted. Using this particular method, and using chemicals only, our group has been able to detect Arsenic (Arsenates) in the samples of hard water" (de Silva 2011c).

For de Silva, the arsenic discovery offered proof of constructive relativism. With Mrs. Senanayake's help, the Rajarata-Kelaniya group had accomplished in a matter of months what fellow scientists committed to "Western" methods had failed to do in years. Despite their achievements, de Silva complained, the wider scientific community fixated on the divine origin of the hypothesis and ignored their findings. "We did not go by the word of gods alone in announcing our results, though I had no reason not to believe what they told," he stated (de Silva 2013c). Although the history of European science is full of examples of notable personages embracing mysticism—famously, Copernicus, Galileo, Newton, Darwin, and Einstein—many in the Sri Lankan scientific community dismissed de Silva as a crackpot. On July 8, 2011, the Sri Lanka Association for the Advancement of Science (SLAAS) published an open letter in the English-language *Daily News* in which it argued de Silva's group was undermining science.

> The press has publicly identified as the leader of this group an individual, who despite holding a responsible position, professes a disdain for "Western" science. He has publicly claimed supernatural revelations . . . as the source of his group's information and even methods. While recognizing that many scientists are deeply religious, the SLAAS wishes to state categorically that superstition and the supernatural have no place in science, and that scientific results inspired by such sources are highly suspect because of a probable bias on the part of the investigator. (SLAAS 2011)

Offering a heady mix of pesticide conspiracy and Buddhist science, the Rajarata-Kelaniya group's arsenic claims quickly escalated into a national scandal. "When the [Rajarata-Kelaniya] group announced to the media that Arsenic is the main cause of Chronic Kidney Disease . . . all hell broke loose," wrote de Silva (2013c). A Sinhala nationalist development organization, the Swarna Hansa Foundation, organized protests outside the offices of the UN Food and Agriculture Organization (FAO) in Colombo, accusing it of importing dangerous pesticides to the island (Bandara 2012). The Rajarata-Kelaniya group itself came under fire for being involved in a conspiracy to undermine local agriculture. As news of the link between arsenic-contaminated rice and CKDu spread, worried consumers began switching to bread as their staple carbohydrate. In response, government figures implicated the group in a *paan thrasthavadya* (bread terrorism) movement that sought the destruction of traditional rice agriculture in the island. According to de Silva (2011c), "The [Agriculture] Minister stated that there was a conspiracy against cultivation of rice in this country, and appears to have implied that our group is discouraging the farmer by claiming that arsenic is present in pesticides."

He added, "The Minister of Agriculture should refrain from making such insinuations without finding out facts. We are not a group against cultivation of rice in this country."

To quell public fears, the Rice Research and Development Institute (RRDI), a government body, sought to prove that rice was safe to consume (Wamanan and de Alwis 2011). The RRDI claimed it had tested sixty samples of rice and had found arsenic traces in none of them. The Pesticide Registrar also investigated the Rajarata-Kelaniya group's accusations. The Registrar tested the same pesticide products that the Rajarata-Kelaniya group had tested, with mixed results. Of twenty-eight samples, three contained arsenic "but not to the levels . . . allege[d]" by the Rajarata-Kelaniya group (Wamanan and de Alwis 2011). Asked whether the presence of arsenic in those three pesticides posed a danger to health, the Registrar was noncommittal: "It is not possible for me to decide whether the levels of Arsenic detected are harmful for the human health and environment. To take such decisions there is a Pesticide Technical and Advisory Committee" (Wamanan and de Alwis 2011).

The response was to haunt the Pesticide Registrar, whom the Rajarata-Kelaniya group accused of stating that arsenic was not a poison. The president of the Government Medical Officers' Association (GMOA), a trade union with links to Rajarata group members, accused the Pesticide Registrar of "a Category One offence according to the Establishment Code." He further added that "President Rajapaksa has instructed the officials concerned to conduct an investigation into [the Registrar's] statement and take disciplinary action against him if he was found guilty" (Wijewardena 2014c). "Arsenic is a class one poison which had been used from the time of India's King Asoka and also to kill Napoleon Bonaparte," de Silva also responded (Fernando 2011). Writing in *The Island*, the Pesticide Registrar sought to defend his actions on glyphosate and draw attention to the panic the arsenic hypothesis had created.

> Our country depends on export of many agricultural products. Loose tongues and irresponsible reporting could lead to irrevocable repercussions in the export sector and thereby adversely affect the whole economy of Sri Lanka. One interested group has already termed this as As [arsenic] terrorism. Yet close scrutiny of the fact and media sensation created points at wheat flour terrorism or even Biological Warfare, in my opinion. (Wijesekara 2011)

Yet by the end of 2011, the Rajarata-Kelaniya group had withdrawn its claim that contaminated rice was causing CKDu. During an interview in 2013, a director at the Ministry of Health told me the group had come under pressure from the president himself to do so. My source accused the group of making statements that threatened the livelihoods of millions of small-scale food producers in the island and of causing unnecessary anxiety for the 21 million people who "ate rice at every meal." For this reason, the government had become fearful that the arsenic hypothesis posed a threat to not only civil order but also the very fabric of Sinhala Buddhist culture: "When the researchers came out with the arsenic claim, there was a huge outcry, and then they backtracked. They said, 'Well, no it's high, but it's not toxic.' I mean, come on! You are telling the public they are getting poisoned! You have to be careful when you come out with statements like that. You need to be pretty sure what you're saying. It affects the public, it affects the political situation."

The arsenic hypothesis was the first CKDu theory to gain national and even international attention. The Rajarata-Kelaniya group and especially Jayasumana rose to prominence as authorities on CKDu. Although the arsenic claim had proven difficult to defend on both empirical and political grounds, the fact that some of the group's claims about arsenic-contaminated pesticides had been vindicated by the government's own tests, together with evidence for the role of arsenic published by the WHO, meant that arsenic itself could not be ruled out. For Jayasumana, the idea given to him by Natha Deviyo would be one that he would subsequently develop further in his glyphosate hypothesis.

GLYPHOSATE-METAL COMPLEXES

On February 20, 2014, Jayasumana, Sarath Gunatilake (a medical scientist at California State University), and Mrs. Priyantha Senanayake (the divine medic) published "Glyphosate, Hard Water and Nephrotoxic Metals: Are They the Culprits Behind the Epidemic of Chronic Kidney Disease of Unknown Etiology in Sri Lanka?" as a hypothesis paper in the *International Journal of Environmental Research and Public Health* (Jayasumana et al. 2014). The authors' key claim was that "although glyphosate alone does not cause an epidemic of chronic kidney disease, it seems to have acquired the ability to destroy the renal tissues of thousands of farmers when it forms complexes with a localized geo environmental factor (hardness) and nephrotoxic metals" (2139). The crux of their argument lay in the strong correlation that multiple research teams had observed between CKDu and arsenic exposure. To that end, the authors suggested that "the totality of scientific evidence gathered so far has highlighted the fact that an unknown factor (Compound X) originating from agrochemicals, when combined with hardness/Ca/Mg can cause significant kidney damage; thus explaining many current observations including the unique geographical distribution of the disease" (2139).

A long-running challenge in attempts to develop causal hypotheses of CKDu had been explaining the specific geologic, geographic, historical, and sociological factors of the disease. Jayasumana, Gunatilake, and Senanayake proposed that the "expected properties of the chemical Compound 'X'" (2129) would need to fit historically within Sri Lanka's recently industrialized and liberalized agricultural and agrochemicals sector, ecologically within Sri Lanka's geo-hydro profile, and sociologically within the medical profile of CKDu. They argued Compound

X would need to exhibit several key characteristics, including (1) a history in the epidemic region dating back to the 1980s or 1990s; (2) an ability to form stable complexes with hard water; (3) an ability to deliver arsenic and nephrotoxic metals to the kidneys; and (4) an ability to evade detection using conventional analytical toxicological methods (2129). The only pesticide on the market that fit the profile was glyphosate.

Coming soon after the arsenic hypothesis and published by two of its key protagonists, the glyphosate hypothesis caused an immediate stir locally and internationally. When read against the backdrop of the troubles Jayasumana and Senanayake had encountered over the arsenic hypothesis, it seems clear that the herbicide offered a new route to develop the information provided by Natha Deviyo. Jayasumana called on the government to start legal proceedings against pesticide companies and demanded they pay compensation of US$1 million to each CKDu patient (Wijewardena 2014b). El Salvador, which was battling its own CKDu outbreak, sought to introduce a ban on glyphosate after reviewing Jayasumana's paper. Meanwhile, the pesticide industry mobilized to challenge the hypothesis (see chapter 11), and a flurry of rebuttals appeared in Sri Lankan newspapers, many authored by members of the Peradeniya group (I am not suggesting they were working with industry by doing so). Critics highlighted several of the hypothesis's weaknesses as they saw them, including its publication in a "rubbishy" (Waidya-natha 2018) journal named on the infamous *Beall's List of Predatory Journals and Publishers*,[1] the existence of the hypothesized "glyphosate-metal complexes" that opponents argued "broke the laws of chemistry," and the authorship credit given to "divine medic" Mrs. Senanayake. When challenged to confirm whether Natha Deviyo had been involved in the development of the hypothesis, Jayasumana was only happy to oblige. "Divine power was involved throughout the formulation of this hypothesis," he wrote in a newspaper article responding to his critics (Jayasumana 2014).

As with the arsenic hypothesis, the Rajarata-Kelaniya group only sought empirical evidence for their glyphosate claims because they assumed the mainstream scientific community would reject the supernatural inspiration. In later interviews, Jayasumana would develop Nalin de Silva's ideas about the cultural imperialism of Western science, which he claimed provided a cover for monotheist thinking at odds with his own Buddhist tradition that too was not to be conflated with other "indigenous" medicines recognized in Sri Lanka, including Ayurveda. For Jayasumana, the abilities of divine medics like Priyantha Senanayake exemplified the strength of the Buddhist alternative to Western science. Realizing that "western medicine has almost failed in the treatment of this chronic kidney disease" (Jayasumana, quoted in Bandara 2017), his team at Rajarata had begun to explore the

---

1. This is a database of "pay to publish" academic outlets that critics suggest lack peer review and can encourage academic fraud.

role of *veda mahaththaya* (village physicians) employing traditional *visha vedakama* (poison healing) treatments for CKDu. As with previous articulations of his scientific method, Jayasumana combined appeals to indigenous village and Buddhist teaching and practice. "Though I am a professor in western medicine, I have to accept the truth," he concluded (*Daily Mirror* 2018).

"CHEMICAL ARSENICS AND OTHER ARSENICS"

Navigating the nexus of science, religion, and politics at the core of CKDu can be a challenging task. Constructive relativism is both a reactionary philosophy that seeks to provide intellectual justification for Sinhala nationalism and an attempt to build theory from sources "local" to Sri Lankan experiences. It is a nationalist approach to the decolonization of scientific practice and science studies currently much favored by those typically on the intellectual left (Harding 2009) and an application of what anthropologist Nireka Weeratunge (2000) called the "root metaphors" of *harmony* and *nature* in global environmentalist discourse for specific nationalist purposes. Constructive relativism thus shares similarities with the scientific commitments of environmental nationalists the world over, which elevates antirationalist populism to the level of what historian Meera Nanda (2001, 2003) called "authentic indigenous knowledge," thereby giving a veneer of legitimacy to often reactionary and exclusivist views.

While scholars have paid considerable attention to questions of scientific nationalism and "archaic modernity" in India (Nanda 2001, 2003; Abraham 1996, 2006; Subramaniam 2000, 2019), much less has been paid to the situation in Sri Lanka—with recent engagement coming several decades "late" (Shanmugaratnam 2020). In both India and Sri Lanka, colonial and postcolonial histories have shaped the development of science and religion as modes of social, political, and environmental thought and practice, including the sense of "indigenous" sciences existing prior to Western science and the need to "decolonize" and "re-traditionalize" as a way of claiming (or reclaiming) those unique identities and their owed recognition in the world. As in India, Sinhala nationalists see "syncretic collaboration" (Subramaniam 2019, 8) between science and religion as vital to Sri Lanka's postcolonial development and ability to "live in harmony" with nature (Weeratunge 2000). Conversely, others regard the promotion of scientific rational thought as an urgent remedy to the poisonous effects of superstition on modern governance and the politicization of science.

However, despite historical, political, and religious similarities between those two places, arguments developed in relation to India cannot be straightforwardly applied to Sri Lanka. While Hindu nationalists have embraced idea(ls) of capitalism, Western science, and technology as elements of a modern, Hindu nation (Subramaniam 2000), in Sri Lanka recent forms of Sinhala nationalism have involved a very public rejection of science, at least as applied to agriculture. Furthermore, what some Sri Lankan commentators refer to as "Our Science" maintains an ambivalent relationship with Ayurvedic science, which is often coded as problematically "Indian." If Ayurveda is strongly associated with Hindu nationalism in India, the tradition sits uncomfortably in Sri Lanka precisely because of its engagement with an assumption of Vedic revivalism that marginalizes Sinhala Buddhism within a pan-Indic field of history and culture. As this chapter shows, the process of establishing an "authentic" Sinhala Buddhist science involves a process of "de-Indianization" and revival of island-bound traditions of veda mahaththaya employing traditional visha vedakama rooted in Buddhist teaching and practice as much as it does decolonization of Western influence—an effort that nationalist scientists regard as involving much the same thing.

Banu Subramaniam (2000, 71), an evolutionary biologist and feminist technoscience scholar, offers conceptual tools for approaching "Western" and "indigenous" sciences "without demonizing one with the other." Her concern is to "create, locate, and engage with a science that is also a political, social, and progressive institution," for example, by attending to the historical conditions that could give rise to a separation of "science" and "religion" in the first place (68). Subramaniam shows how the separation established the terrain for modern political, social, and intellectual discourse concerning their commensurabilities and incommensurabilities, over which stumbled generations of thinkers as they tried to sort faith from fact, truth from fiction. In India as well as in Sri Lanka, this debate became crucial to how nationalists and cosmopolitans would construct their identities and positions in the world. However, as Subramaniam notes, the Indian "right" was rather better at playing this game than the "left." For Hindu nationalists, "strategically employing elements of science and religion, orthodoxy and modernity . . . [would] . . . bring together a modern vision with an archaic vision"—what she calls "archaic modernity" (74). By this, Subramaniam meant how Hindu nationalism "warps" time by projecting modernist constructions of science and technology onto ancient India and the relevance of applying ancient Indian science and technology to modern problems. Appeals to evidence for Hinduism's scientific and Ayurveda's medical prowess as contained in the ancient texts exploited a desire for deep-rooted belonging and demonstrated, yet again, the poisonous danger of elements that did not fit the narrative (an example of what I have termed "when to look," in this case in the search for the origins of science).

Although claiming to be rooted in indigenous Sinhala Buddhist thought and practice, de Silva's constructive relativism and Jayasumana's elaborations of that philosophy are likewise better understood as a hybrid of many traditions. Running through their arguments are categorical separations between science and religion, culture and nature, mind and matter, soul and body, professional and lay, and sacred and profane—all of which reflect "modern" ontologies cast for re-traditionalizing purposes. De Silva's work thus also touches on many themes found in the critical science and technology studies (STS), most obviously, the social construction of what de Silva dismisses as "so-called" scientific knowledge and legacies of Euro-American colonialism in scientific ontology and epistemology. His approach, as well as those of his critics, reinforces a view of "Western Science" and "Our Science," the latter to be lauded or lampooned depending on one's position on the history of colonial and postcolonial sciences and their roles in processes of imperial subjugation and state formation.

Anthropologists and postcolonial science scholars have recently united around the need to "provincialize" theory and "think with" non-Western categories of thought (Chakrabarty 2000; da Col and Graeber 2011; Law and Lin 2017; Holbraad and Pedersen 2017). Given its political orientation, constructive relativism offers an especially interesting case study in that regard, risking an acceptance of "anything goes" relativism and the (at least tacit) approval of reactionary populisms and violent nationalisms (Latour 2004; Lynch 2017). Science scholars John Law and Wen Yuan Lin (2017) argue that caution is needed when embracing the "symmetry" of *all* claims to knowledge and truth (see also Bloor 1976; Callon 1986; Latour 2005). They call instead for a "variety of postcolonial symmetries" that can better handle the complexities of postcolonial science and environmentalisms in contexts where distinctions between the "villains" and the "heroes" of colonialism and anticolonialism are often unclear.

In this book, I do not try to resolve any of those debates. Rather, I approach them as part of the same landscape that makes up glyphosate regulation as a field of poisoncraft; that is to say, they were debates that interested my interlocuters and the problems they posed and the answers they gave would all contribute to the complex meanings and politics that glyphosate came to acquire in Sri Lanka. Along with a careful analysis of how those debates have emerged from and embody violent histories of colonialism, postcolonialism, and nationalism, I argue that understanding how constructive relativism's origins in a situated reading of Buddhist thought on matters of vision and knowledge itself blur into everyday epistemology deserves fuller exploration. De Silva's philosophy has popular appeal in Sinhala communities in Sri Lanka, I suggest, not simply because it complements nationalist sentiment but because it speaks to tacit understandings of how the world works. I thus take as my starting point science historian Jahnavi Phalkey's (2013, 330) call for a "departure from current historiographical preoccupations . . . to map and explain the lives, institutions, practices, and stories of science on the subcontinent as they connect with, and where they break away from, the world at large." One way ethnography can contribute to this effort is that it affords the opportunity to explore the contemporary forms, in thought and practice, of those ideas—in this case, in relation to how nonscientists also think about the nature and workings of knowledge.

As an example, I analyze a statement made by de Silva that provides a route into a "Sinhala Buddhist" mode of symmetrical thinking. In an article titled "Chemical Arsenics and Other Arsenics," in which he explained how his group had discovered the link between arsenic and CKDu, de Silva wrote, "It's simply like this. We can see professors. Professors cannot see Arsenic. We cannot see gods. Gods can see Arsenic. I like this because there is certain symmetry in it" (2011b). In this passage, de Silva was reflecting on the Buddhist theory of vision and ignorance that underpinned his methodology. Meant as a takedown of Sri Lankan scientists blinded by Western epistemology, he was also stating how fallible beings of this world (scientists) could not see the causal relationship between arsenic and CKDu that superior beings of the other world (gods) could see. Whether or not de Silva had used the term "symmetry" as an explicit reference to the STS concept I do not know. But if the STS concept of symmetry emerges from a commitment to valuing equally all knowledge forms, de Silva's commitment was instead to their hierarchical ordering. By "hierarchy," I mean two things. The first is in reference to what I have already described: de Silva's dismissal of Western science as a compromised form of knowledge. The second is in reference to hierarchies of knowledge that make up South Asian worlds, as I described in chapter 2.

De Silva's identification of "chemical arsenics," which are open to Western scientific investigation, and "other arsenics," which require divine investigation, relies on the presence or absence of *prathyaksha*, the "seeing eye" or "knowledge." The "availability" of prathyaksha itself reflects the structure of the Buddhist pantheon, which is in turn structured according to a hierarchy of spiritual purity and pollution, moral goodness and evil, and social and political corruptibility (Gombrich 1971; Obeyesekere 1979; Gombrich and Obeyesekere 1988; Kapferer 1988). Thus, the Buddha, the most exalted being, is wholly pure and good; he attained nirvana because he had acquired perfect "vision." Below him are the Bodhisattvas, beings on the path to nirvana, and the four guardian deities, including Natha Deviyo, each of whom is pure and "good," though fallible in some way. Their ability to "see" is more restricted than the Buddha's but still far superior to the sight of lesser beings, including humans. Thus, the ability of humans themselves to "see" depends, too, on their ability to understand and master Buddhist thought and practice.

Anthropologist Gananath Obeyesekere (1963) once suggested the Sri Lankan political pantheon reflects and was reflected in the Buddhist pantheon in terms of how people understand the structure of religious and political power, as well as their own agency to affect change in the world. Just as the Buddha, who having died and attained nirvana, is beyond reach, so the president does not respond to the requests of ordinary citizens. However, those beings lower on the scale, including deities and demons in the spiritual pantheon and parliamentarians, public servants, and local-level representatives and officers in the political pantheon, are open to appeal. This is also a reflection of, and reason for, their lesser purity and greater corruptibility. The practical significance is that other than the Buddha, no being is wholly good or wholly evil. All may be petitioned for help, though whether help is forthcoming depends on their relative position in the pantheon, their degree of self-interest or generosity, and their willingness to bend or break rules (Obeyesekere 1977, 1978).

Anthropologist Tharindi Udalagama (2018) has extended Obeyesekere's account in her description of how rural women in contemporary Sri Lanka gain agency over misfortune and suffering. Drawing from fieldwork in the north-central district, Udalagama shows how women distinguished between "seen" and "unseen" problems and appealed to help from worldly and otherworldly agents accordingly. For example, when confronted with problems that attracted the attention of other villagers or required a village-level response—problems that were public or "seen"—women tended to consult or be referred to this-worldly agents, including police, counselors, and the emissaries of otherworldly forces here on earth, Buddhist monks. Conversely, "unseen" problems such as suspected infidelity, the moral transgressions of significant others, and hidden physical and emotional violence and abuse were dealt with through consultation with a *maniyo* or her male equivalent, a *gurunanse*, who would communicate with deities or demons. Importantly, Udalagama shows how for the women she worked with, strategic engagement with the "seen" and the "unseen" provided opportunities for exerting agency over their lives.

Although Obeyesekere's model of religious and political power was based on a system of governance that has since changed, Udalagama's work demonstrates the continuing relevance of his central premise in contemporary Sri Lanka. I build on their ideas in the next chapter by showing how today political power resides partly in the ability of the president to master challenges emanating from the "unseen," which includes toxicological anxieties of CKDu and poisons within—a power that necessarily involves poisoncraft. Returning to the themes of this chapter, Obeyesekere's and Udalagama's contributions show how de Silva's consultation of the divine medic Mrs. Senanayake for help understanding a medical problem with unseen causes was entirely in keeping with popular Buddhist practice. However, while constructive relativism deploys distinctions between the seen and the unseen to build a nationalist toxicology, Udalagama shows how they give form to practices of everyday care. The point I want to stress is the wide appeal and application of Buddhist epistemology, which, in the hands of its human practitioners, becomes fallible. Yet as Subramaniam (2019, 8) reminds us, it is possible to be critical of nationalist articulations of science and religion without rejecting either while also embracing "their more progressive and imaginative possibilities."

THE POISONCRAFT OF GLYPHOSATE RESEARCH

As I have shown in this chapter, the hunt for Compound X became a project that extended far beyond clinical and environmental toxicology. The Rajarata-Kelaniya group promoted an anticolonial science that had a direct relationship with the meaning and organization of political authority in Sri Lanka. This relationship was core to the development of poisoncraft during this period of modern Sri Lankan history. As I argued in chapter 8, questions of where and when to look had brought into being an understanding of the shore-ringed nation that exists in the Buddhist nationalist imaginary. When Jayasumana and his colleagues had looked and found glyphosate, their toxicology provided further support and justification for the idea that insidious poisons represented a direct threat to the postwar nation. Their activities became an important part of poisoncraft during the 2010s, where the science and politics of CKDu coalesced to become an overriding concern of nation building. In the next chapter, I explore how this concern was taken up by successive presidents, whose office would itself become a bastion of poisoncraft.

10

The Presidents' Purificatory Work

"In thirty years we'll still be arguing about the cause of CKDu!" joked the past president and past prime minister of Sri Lanka, Mahinda Rajapaksa, to a mutual acquaintance in 2015—a joke made funnier because against all expectation he lost his presidency to a rival candidate earlier that year, in part due to his failure to ban glyphosate. In the previous chapter, I concluded with some brief reflections on the place and role of poisoncraft in Sri Lankan politics. In this chapter, I explore the theme in detail with specific reference to the changing relationship of presidential authority to the divine and the democratic and how the glyphosate controversy was both magnified by and has magnified that relationship. As I show, such matters preoccupied the three presidents who held office during the period of this study—Mahinda Rajapaksa (2005–15), Maithripala Sirisena (2015–19), and Gotabaya Rajapaksa (2019–22)—each grappling with his own efforts to introduce controls on pesticides. Failure to ban glyphosate helped speed the downfall of Mahinda Rajapaksa in 2015, while dithering over glyphosate became for his critics another example of Sirisena's political weakness. Sirisena's successor and Mahinda's brother, Gotabaya Rajapaksa, then staked his own reputation on banning all chemical pesticides and fertilizers, including glyphosate—a decision that led to his dramatic removal from office in 2022.

Exploring the unlikely entwined fates of pesticides and presidents, I describe how over the course of a decade of postwar development, during which the challenge of establishing and sealing a shore-ringed nation became paramount, a nationalist commitment to purification came to define the mission of the executive. The Sri Lankan presidency became in several key ways a project focused on poisoncraft. The three presidents' efforts were shaped by difficulties establishing scientific consensus on the relationship between glyphosate and CKDu. This coalesced with wider changes to the nature of the executive presidency itself, which, since 2009, had acquired considerable new powers while simultaneously coming to embody, in explicit terms, claims to a new kingly autochthony and divine authority. Meanwhile, a form of democratic authority premised on the functioning of modernist legal-rational institutions guided by a commitment to "evidence-based" policy making continued to govern key sectors of state. My aim in this chapter is thus to answer two questions: (1) How did an idea of, and drive toward, consensus building as an end in itself give expression to an idea of poison control as a key expression of presidential rule in Sri Lanka? (2) How did different models of authority invested in the presidency and state institutions shape the government's response to glyphosate?

PRESIDENTIAL POLITICS AND THE FATE OF A PESTICIDE

The Rajapaksa Ban

On March 12, 2014, just a few weeks after Jayasumana, Gunatilake, and Senanayake had published their glyphosate hypothesis, the government of President Mahinda Rajapaksa announced the herbicide would be banned. "An investigation carried out by medical specialists and scientists has revealed that kidney disease was mainly caused by glyphosate.... [The president] ... has ordered the immediate removal of glyphosate from the local market," Special Projects Minister S. M. Chandrasena told journalists (Chavkin 2014). Under normal circumstances, pesticide regulation would be the responsibility of the Pesticide Registrar and the Pesticide Technical Advisory Committee (PeTAC), a body that includes representatives from the health and agriculture ministries and other sector bodies, including the Tea Research Institute, the Paddy Research Institute, the Sugarcane Research Institute, and the Central Environmental Authority. These were far from normal circumstances, however, and neither the Pesticide Registrar nor the PeTAC had been involved in Mahinda Rajapaksa's decision to ban the molecule.

In the days following the announcement, the PeTAC requested a meeting with the president to share its concerns. According to media reports, the PeTAC was troubled by a decision that had been based on a hypothesis for which "there was no established scientific data to prove that this agro-chemical was the cause of kidney disease." Moreover, the PeTAC argued, "the country would face many difficulties if glyphosate is banned.... [I]t would have a major impact on the economy with both tea and paddy cultivations being affected" (Hettiarachchi 2014). Echoing those concerns, agriculture officials lobbied the executive to meet with the PeTAC. According to the director general of agriculture, Rohan Wijekoon, "around 60 per cent" of tea, paddy, rubber, maize, and vegetable cultivators relied on glyphosate for weed control (Wijewardena 2014a), and they would now struggle to find a suitable alternative. Issuing a stark warning, the agriculture minister, Mahinda Yapa Abeywardena, told reporters that the ban would be ruinous for the plantation sector, which was already facing a labor shortage and could not rely on manual weed control. "They depend heavily on the herbicide. . . . If there's a ban on its use . . . the entire sector could collapse within two or three months," he argued (Kirindi 2014).

Following those interventions, the government announced a halt on the ban pending further review of the scientific evidence. For the ban's supporters, however, the U-turn was evidence of international agroindustry interference in national policy making. Groups otherwise loyal to the Rajapaksa regime suspected elements "in the pocket of industry" that favored the health of the tea industry over the health of Rajarata paddy farmers were working against the executive. Meanwhile, Mahinda Rajapaksa's critics told me the pesticide companies had bribed the president to reverse the ban. United by their shared belief that glyphosate should be removed, the president's champions and detractors alike found reason to criticize Mahinda Rajapaksa for his stance on glyphosate. For his supporters, regulatory failure signaled a rare weakness in his ability to deal with the opposition within his own ranks. For his critics, the case provided further evidence of executive corruption—allegations of which had been mounting for some time.

It was indeed out of concern about waning influence over his large coalition and growing disquiet among his electoral base that led Mahinda Rajapaksa to call a presidential election two years ahead of schedule. On October 20, 2014, the government announced the election would take place on January 8, 2015. Taken by surprise, the opposition was disorganized and lacked a presidential candidate. The first month of the campaign was relatively quiet, and, despite the recent knocks to his popularity, few commentators seriously believed the incumbent Rajapaksa could be defeated. Just six weeks out from Election Day, the race changed dramatically when the health minister, Maithripala Sirisena, resigned from the government to join the new National Unity Party, a "popular opposition" of smaller parties, as its presidential candidate. Sirisena took with him several other parliamentarians, including the symbolically important Buddhist nationalist party, the Jatika Hela Urumaya (JHU; National Heritage Party), previously in coalition with Mahinda Rajapaksa. On December 19, Sirisena published his manifesto, *A Compassionate Maithri Governance—A Stable Country* (2014), which he framed as a direct response to the president's authoritarian and corrupt rule. Sirisena made combating CKDu through pesticide regulation a central election pledge. The manifesto, coauthored by Athuraliye Rathana Thero, a leading member of the JHU and key supporter of the glyphosate ban, stated that dependence on "foreign companies" selling agrochemicals to Sri Lanka "has created a number of serious problems" that Sirisena would commit to address.

> Not only does the country's money flow abroad, people are afflicted with serious illnesses due to the contamination of air, water and soil. Farmers, both men and women in Rajarata, the heartland of our rice economy, have been suffering from a fatal kidney

disease for the last two decades. Both Sri Lankan experts and the World Health Organization (WHO) have found the cause of this illness to be the mixing of brackish waters with sub-standard fertilizers and agrochemicals. (Sirisena 2014, 30–31)

The manifesto drew special attention to "a powerful invisible hand" that had "stopped the implementation of the recommendations" to ban glyphosate (30). Framed as a personal failing of Mahinda Rajapaksa himself, the president was quick to respond. Just five days after the publication of Sirisena's manifesto, on December 24, the president announced a targeted ban on glyphosate in those rural districts where CKDu was epidemic while allowing the chemical's continued use in the plantation sector. This would protect his crucial voter base in the Mahaweli while appeasing the business sector that feared the potential harm done by the loss of glyphosate to the tea industry. Nevertheless, and to almost everyone's surprise, Sirisena won the election of January 8, 2015, with 51.28 percent of the vote. Following a few hours of dangerous uncertainty during which it looked as if the defeated Rajapaksa might refuse to step down, Sirisena took office without resistance.

The Sirisena Ban

Five months after taking office, on May 22, President Sirisena formally announced a total ban on the import, sale, and use of glyphosate in all areas of Sri Lanka. The runup to this decision had been as fractious as Mahinda Rajapaksa's efforts a year before, with the sticking point being the unresolved question of what glyphosate restriction might mean for the plantation sector. Sirisena held a meeting with members of the PeTAC and representatives of the Presidential Task Force on CKDu, which Mahinda Rajapaksa had established a few years before, to discuss the issue. JHU parliamentarian Rathana Thero, now an adviser to the president working on projects related to the development of organic farming in the island, also attended.

According to a source at the meeting, Sirisena hesitated on the question of whether he should maintain his predecessor's targeted ban or introduce a complete ban. Evidence suggested the targeted ban had failed largely because glyphosate was readily available to purchase from districts that still permitted its use, fueling the growth of a black market in the chemical. One possible solution was to give the state-owned Ceylon Petroleum Company exclusive rights to import and sell glyphosate in the plantation sector, either in perpetuity or at least until remaining stocks in the country (amounting to about two years' worth) had run out—by which time a solution to the labor shortage could have been found. In what has now become an infamous incident, Rathana Thero reportedly became angry at what he perceived to be yet another attempt to backtrack on commitments to ban glyphosate. "He threw the election manifesto down on the table in front of the president and demanded that he ban glyphosate!" a source present at the meeting told me.

In the days after the May 22 announcement, the Peradeniya group wrote to President Sirisena asking that he reconsider the ban. The letter set out five objections, including the ban's lack of scientific grounding, its likely negative impact on agriculture and the livelihoods of people with CKDu the ban was purporting to help, and environmental damage caused by alternative methods of weed control that could increase soil erosion and water pollution. The letter called on the president to delay the ban until a full independent study of glyphosate's role in CKDu could be conducted. The Rajarata-Kelaniya group responded by calling into question its authors' motives. During the first week of June, Jayasumana and a representative of the Government Medical Officers' Association, Chinthaka Wijewardena, suggested that "three groups of academics co-ordinated by local agriculture scientists in Peradeniya, Colombo and overseas had been hired by multinational agrochemical companies to contribute articles in favour of a toxic agrochemical under attack around the world" (quoted in Waidyantha 2015). Replying to the allegations, Dr. Parakrama Waidyanatha, a toxicologist and member of the Peradeniya group, published an "open letter" to Jayasumana in which he defended the integrity of those calling into question Jayasumana's hypothesis.

> You cast totally unjustifiable and unsubstantiated aspersions that scientists who have been critical of the decision to ban glyphosate were "hired by multinational agrochemical companies" to do so. . . . As far as I am aware all of them are scientists of high integrity and honesty and well qualified in their fields of specialization, at least three of them being reputed senior professors of chemistry. You should cite specific evidence to prove that they are being hired by multinationals! Other than the few scientists in your group, no reputed scientist has hitherto said glyphosate is the cause of CKDU. (Waidyanatha 2015)

The National Academy of Sciences of Sri Lanka (NASSL), a nongovernmental but establishment body affiliated with the Peradeniya group, also weighed in. On June 8, the NASSL issued a statement questioning the ban and the risk it posed to further CKDu research. In particular, the NASSL argued, "We hope the ban on glyphosate would not make the authorities even more complacent on the funding and strengthening of quality scientific research which could help identify the true aetiology of CKDu" (NASSL 2015).

As debate raged in the media about the future of glyphosate, uncertainty continued to linger over the actual extent of the Sirisena ban. On May 25, the Pesticides Registrar issued a letter to pesticide companies stating the "**import and use of glyphosate of the herbicide Glyphosate is banned in Sri Lanka with immediate effect except** for a restricted amount to be used in plantation crop sector" (unpublished letter to pesticide importing companies; boldface in original). In early June, the finance minister, Ravi Karunanayake, also told reporters that the government had instructed customs officials to halt all glyphosate imports. However, the agriculture minister, Duminda Dissanayake, continued to suggest the government would permit the use of glyphosate in controlled amounts in the plantation sector, as the Pesticide Registrar's letter had also suggested. The Pesticides Registrar subsequently confirmed Dissanayake's position when he told reporters he had notified pesticide importers that glyphosate licensing had stopped except for use in tea estates. "We have not banned it totally," he said (Wijedasa and Surendraraj 2015). Finally, on June 10, the government issued a formal announcement that glyphosate would be subject to a full ban. The press release noted the concerns of the plantation sector but stated that the "Cabinet of Ministers . . . had discussed and decided to completely halt the import of Glyphosate" (News.lk: Government Official News Portal 2015).

Sirisena's glyphosate ban was the centerpiece of his election manifesto and Vasa Visa Nathi Ratak (Toxin-Free Nation) program, launched in early 2016. The overall aim of the program was to promote organic agriculture and halt foreign food imports, with the target of increasing organic food consumption by 25 percent within three years. Along with the glyphosate ban and regulations on some single-use plastics and asbestos, the Vasa Visa Nathi Ratak program helped raise Sirisena's profile as the "greenest" president in Sri Lanka's history. The program was also important for its explicit use of autochthonous imagery of soil and water and the threats to national sovereignty that pesticides represented.

> Over the past seventy years or so, our nation has been poisoned. We can feel it in our bodies and in the bodies of our children. We can sense it in our earth. We can taste it in our water. We can smell it in our air. Much that was once wholesome and beautiful is now lost but we . . . remember. It is time we, the people of Sri Lanka, took back our nation. It is time that we, collectively, work to rid our nation of the pesticides, the herbicides, the various murderous substances that are killing us all. We shall eat safe again and feel safe again. We shall be whole again. (President's Office 2015)

The government's call to become "whole again" slotted neatly into the discursive field of postwar purification that included processes of Sinhalization/Buddhification of the north and east, as well as autochthonous representations of the kind on display in the Victory Monument at Mullivaikal Lagoon. The Vasa Visa Nathi Ratak statement referred to the water and soil that is fundamental to Sinhala nationalist self-identification, from which springs forth the nation as a bounded "whole." Thus, the program became another expression of nationalist processes to achieve postcolonial islandness. If his defeat of the Tamil separatist threat and establishment of the shore-ringed nation defined Mahida Rajapaksa's presidency, purification of that new national space would define Sirisena's tenure.

The Ban Reversed

Sirisena came to power on a commitment to "good governance" and a promise to tackle the rampant corruption of the Rajapaksa years, but it was not long before his presidency began to sag under the weight of accusations of incompetence and inaction. At the same time, Mahinda Rajapaksa and his extensive network of supporters in the Parliament and the wider Sinhala community regrouped to plan their return to power. During the annual May Day rallies in Colombo in 2017, Mahinda Rajapaksa's procession dwarfed Sirisena's, a difference that was widely reported in the press and that political observers took as the first clear sign of his resurgent popularity. The following year, local elections saw Sirisena's National Unity Party suffer a massive defeat at the hands of Mahinda Rajapaksa's new political party, the Sri Lanka People's Front, which won 40 percent of the vote. Mahinda Rajapaksa himself was elected to Parliament as representative of the Kurunegala District.

With support draining away, Sirisena sought to shore up his power base in minority communities, whose votes had helped him win the presidency in 2015. This meant revisiting the glyphosate ban. A major factor in Mahinda Rajapaksa's failure to ban the chemical was the risk that it posed to the plantation sector, with ministers and industry spokespeople both claiming the loss of glyphosate would be ruinous. Tea and rubber exports represent significant foreign earnings for Sri Lanka, with plantations and subsidiary industries employing tens of thousands of people, mostly minority Tamils. Following Sirisena's ban, the Planters' Association of Ceylon had estimated a revenue loss of LKR 10–20 billion per year due to the increased cost of production arising from alternative weed control methods, putting jobs and livelihoods at risk (Lanka Business Online 2018). Crucially, lucrative export markets, including Germany and Japan, had announced restrictions on Sri Lankan tea after plantations started using the herbicide MCPA (2-methyl-4-chlorophenoxyacetic acid), a chemical banned in those countries, in place of glyphosate, which they permitted.

With the very future of the tea industry now in question, the ban was creating considerable uncertainty among a key constituency for Sirisena. The so-called Indian Tamils, the descendants of labor migrants imported to the island by the British during the nineteenth century to work on the plantations, continue to make up most sector workers today. Although ethnically and politically distinct from the Sri Lankan Tamil community that agitated for a separate state during the twentieth century, Indian Tamils have tended to vote with other minority communities against the Sinhala nationalist bloc. Districts with large populations of Indian Tamils voted for Sirisena and his party candidates in the 2015 and 2018 elections, but the danger now was that support could ebb away. During a postelection strategy review, Sirisena's team revisited the ban and concluded that lifting restrictions could help shore up wavering support in those communities. Coincidentally, Sirisena's team reached this decision just at the moment a government-sponsored review of the scientific evidence for the ban—which as far as I know was never made public—concluded there was no causal link between glyphosate and CKDu, opening the door to a policy reversal. Despite this development, Sirisena's cabinet remained divided on the issue, with the plantation and agriculture ministers both in support of lifting the ban and the health minister and JHU parliamentarian Rathana Thero opposed (Warakapitiya 2018). On July 11, 2018, Sirisena and his cabinet reached a compromise, agreeing to lift the ban for the plantation sector but maintaining it for all other uses (Jayawardana 2018)—exactly the position that Mahinda Rajapaksa had adopted four years earlier.

Sirisena's presidency would limp along for another twelve months. An attempt to appease the opposition by illegally deposing his prime minister and appointing Mahinda Rajapaksa to that role, swiftly followed by an attempt to end the parliamentary term and call fresh elections—a move the high court also ruled as illegal—only served to undermine his presidency further. However, it was the Islamist suicide attacks against churches and tourist hotels on Easter Sunday 2019 that inflicted the greatest damage to Sirisena's presidency. Six days after the attacks, Gotabaya Rajapaksa, Mahinda's brother and the former defense minister, announced his intention to run in the upcoming elections. Although the chances of Sirisena winning a second term had looked very unlikely for some time, and indeed he was open about not planning to run again, the events of Easter Sunday, coupled with the rise of Gotabaya Rajapaksa as a "strongman" politician and known sponsor of anti-Muslim Buddhist groups including the BBS, sealed Sirisena's fate.

The Ban Extended

Gotabaya Rajapaksa comfortably defeated his eventual opponent, Sajith Premadasa, the son of a former Sri Lankan president, and took office in November 2019. The COVID-19 pandemic, which struck a few months later, took up the first year of Gotabaya Rajapaksa's presidency, with the glyphosate question all but disappearing from political discussion. By early 2021, however, the issue of agrochemicals had returned with force. In April 2021, the president announced that all synthetic fertilizer imports would be halted and government support was given to the local production of organic fertilizer (Presidential Secretariat 2021). The policy was introduced as part of his national policy framework, "Vistas of Prosperity and Splendour," intended to create "a productive citizenry, a contented family, a disciplined and just society and a prosperous nation" (Ministry of Finance 2019). Soon thereafter, however, the policy spiraled to include a ban on all chemical pesticides—something not mentioned in the "Vistas" document. The new restrictions came into force on May 6, 2021.

Although the government maintained that the ban was a public health measure, the likelier reality was that it was trying to save foreign currency reserves. The 2019 terror attacks and the COVID-19 pandemic had each dealt significant blows to income from tourism. The country was struggling to meet international debt repayments that the Mahinda Rajapaksa government had amassed during the postwar boom years, and halting agrochemical imports was likely necessary to prevent a total economic collapse. Nevertheless, reactions to the ban were as acrimonious as they were swift. Debate in the media polarized on the question of whether any country had the capacity to feed its population using organic methods, let alone Sri Lanka, which was already struggling economically. The debate heightened when many farmers, faced with uncertainties over agrochemical supplies, simply stopped work. The food system collapsed, prices surged, and the government was forced to declare an economic emergency. To his detractors, however, Gotabaya Rajapaksa simply replied, "Lives are more valuable to me than a high yield" (Ramayanaka 2021). Although the president repeatedly stated the ban was irreversible, pesticides have had a habit of causing political havoc in Sri Lanka and banned chemicals of making a return—as Mahinda Rajapaksa and Sirisena both found to their cost. The president lifted the ban in November 2021 and in July 2022, following months of widespread protest, resigned his office and fled to Singapore. Former prime minister and longtime presidential hopeful, Ranil Wickramasinghe, was sworn in.

FROM EXECUTIVE PRESIDENTS TO PRESIDENT-KINGS

What role, if any, did Mahinda Rajapaksa's and Sirisena's failures regarding glyphosate lead to their defeat at the ballot box? The evidence suggests that the glyphosate controversy did influence the outcome of the 2015 and 2019 presidential campaigns, as well as the 2018 local elections. Glyphosate became an example of the incumbents' struggles to protect Sinhala Buddhist bodies and the body politic from a range of threats. Yet as Gotabaya Rajapaksa's complete agrochemical ban in 2021 attests, adopting a strong position on pesticides continued to be popular in Sri Lanka, apparently regardless of their obvious implications for food security. In this section, I turn my attention to how the relationship between glyphosate and presidential politics can be understood as involving more than matters of electoral expediency and reveals important changes to the nature of political power that the presidential office embodies.

Political sociologist Rajesh Venugopal (2015) has described the evolution of political power in postcolonial Sri Lanka as entailing shifts from the "masses" to the "elite," the legislature to the executive, and a kind of "fig leaf" nationalism to a committed Sinhala populism. From independence in 1948 until 1978, Sri Lanka was a parliamentary democracy with a presidential figurehead. Power lay in the hands of the electorate, who responded most favorably to policy commitments to infrastructure development, social welfare, and the advancement of the Sinhala majority. Elite interests, namely, those in pursuit of economic liberalization, were largely neglected. After 1978, the newly elected prime minister, J. R. Jayawardene, created the executive presidency as a means of redressing the balance from the masses to the elite while retaining a populist facade. The aim, Venugopal (2015, 686) argues, was "to forge a powerful centralised political structure that could push through market reforms that were otherwise electorally unfeasible," aided by symbolically powerful but largely empty commitments to Sinhala nationalism, "to lend legitimacy to some unpopular counter-populist agenda of state reform."

The election of Mahinda Rajapaksa to the presidency in 2005 marked the further expansion of executive powers that swiftly encompassed the economy. Through state takeovers of key businesses, the militarization of key sectors, and the brutal suppression of opposition voices in the south as well as the north, Mahinda Rajapaksa emerged as an oligarchic leader who deployed his vast financial wealth to gain and control political support across all levels of society (Widger 2016). After the war, the Rajapaksa brothers would define the new political reality of the shore-ringed nation in ways that differed significantly from previous decades. The electoral map a bounded Sri Lanka would represent necessarily reshaped the nature and extent of executive power. As I described in chapter 8, cartographic anxieties promulgated by calls for Tamil separatism gave way to toxicological anxieties promulgated by fears of poisons within. The mission of the executive switched from the resealing of the nation to the purification of its heartland soil and water as well as its shoreline. In other words, it would become a mission of poisoncraft.

This transition adds important detail to the history of presidential change outlined by Venugopal. Taking insight from David Graeber and Marshall Sahlins's (2017) discussion of kingly authority, I argue that a fuller account of political power in contemporary Sri Lanka requires reflection on the historical legacies of royal power and their persistence in democratic institutions. Questions of kingly authority rose to prominence in Sri Lankan political debate following the defeat of the LTTE in 2009, when jubilant Sinhalese celebrated M. Rajapaksa as a "warrior king" who had rescued the nation from calamity. The implied coronation was to be taken seriously by his supporters, indicating a new relationship between the executive presidency and autochthonous authority of a sovereign Sinhala state. While the office of president has always been associated with Buddhism and, like the kings of old, the president was charged with the protection of Buddhism (Evers 1972; Seneviratne 2000), after the war the relationship became more literal than figurative.

The Victory Monument at Mullivaikal Lagoon, as well as the rhetorical flourishes of Sirisena's Vasa Visa Nathi Ratak mission statement, precisely captured the autochthonous authority of the warrior-king. Like the first monarch of the world, Mahasammata, depicted at Mullivaikal, Mahinda Rajapaksa was "a jubilant soldier who appeared from the ground" to vanquish the Tamil threat. In official and popular discourse, the warrior-king was cast as a native soldier in a land that is only now "reclaiming" its history and destiny from European, Tamil, and Muslim "foreignness." While Mahinda Rajapaksa's successor, Maithripala Sirisena, argued that the "country needs a true human being, not a king" and rejected an explicit association between himself and the kings of past,[1] his program of national detoxification was deeply rooted in claims of island wholeness that shared considerable similarities with representations of the Mullivaikal monument. Meanwhile, Gotabaya Rajapaksa reclaimed the warrior-king mantle by cultivating the "strongman" identity enjoyed by his brother (Kandasamy 2019) and adopting a policy platform that was explicitly hostile to poisons like pesticides and Muslims.

The "islanded" (Sivasundaram 2013) roots of the president-king offer a significant revision of the classical Sinhala origin myth that had previously shaped the nationalist imaginary (Daniel 1996). That myth located Sinhala ancestry, and the ultimate source of kingly authority, in Vijaya, a North Indian prince (Strathern 2009). The model of authority attached to the warrior-king, on the other hand, abandoned the model of the "stranger-king" that Vijaya represented. The change is significant because, as Graeber and Sahlins (2017) have argued, kingly power in almost all premodern states derived from the fact that the king had conquered or been invited to rule over an autochthonous people. In modern states, the power of the warrior-king—who might otherwise be termed a president-king—derives from autochthonous sovereignty handed back via the ballot box. If autochthonous or popular sovereignty is just kingly sovereignty lent to the people in a democratic state (Graeber and Sahlins 2017), the president-king makes explicit the true origins, and limits, of popular sovereign power in kingly authority, to which it remains bound.[2]

By embodying both sources of authority, the president-king also transforms the relationship between Buddhist and political pantheons that I began to sketch in the previous chapter. In Obeyesekere's original formulation, the Buddha and the ceremonial president, positioned at the top of the Buddhist and political pantheons, were beyond the reach and cares of ordinary people. Real worldly power lay in the hands of the deities on the one side and ministers and public servants on the other. While the creation of the executive presidency bestowed the office with far-reaching power, authority remained wedded to the model of popular sovereignty; the president served at the pleasure of the electorate, so to speak. The president-king, however, reappropriates popular authority, drawing it to himself. One of the clearest articulations of this has been the incredible concentration of power in the hands of both Rajapaksa presidents, who, as many have argued, have

1. Although a rejection of kingly identity was important to Sirisena's efforts to distinguish himself from M. Rajapaksa, he nevertheless portrayed himself as a strong defender of Buddhist morality, famously calling for a medieval punishment of women concertgoers who had, apparently, thrown their underwear at a foreign pop singer.

2. As I worked on the final revisions of this text, US President Donald Trump would (literally) adopt a kingly mantle, sharing images of himself dressed up as a royal. Anti-Trump protesters seized on the image, denouncing it as a serious expression of his intent to dismantle democratic institutions and perhaps seek ways of staying in office beyond his second term. As a populist leader who appeals directly to nationalist autochthony, his kingly presentation perhaps signals a desire to become the United States's first president-king.

served at and for their own pleasure and the vast retinues across public and private sector organizations that their patronage created (Stone 2014). The result has been a realignment of Buddhist and political pantheons, with the president-king establishing a new equivalency with powerful deities who consciously control the fates of ordinary people.

THE PRESIDENTIAL TASK FORCE

Thus far, I have argued that following the civil war and the rise of CKDu, the power of the Sri Lankan presidency was expressed in and through poisoncraft. In this section, I discuss two presidential interventions in the glyphosate-CKDu debate that expressly illustrate this, a conference held in 2015 and an expert consultation held in 2016. The events had been organized under the auspices of the Presidential Task Force on CKDu, a special unit originally set up by Mahinda Rajapaksa but which by 2015–16 had come under Sirisena's leadership. The Task Force acted as a national coordinating body on scientific and humanitarian work related to CKDu, including fund-raising for CKDu patients and their families. The 2015 conference and the 2016 consultation had become flagship events for the Task Force and a physical manifestation of the emerging poisoncraft of presidential rule.

The 2015 Conference

In December 2015, Maithripala Sirisena's Presidential Task Force organized a national conference to review advances in scientific and medical understanding of CKDu. The intention was to run the meeting as a knowledge and policy exchange, leading to a set of recommendations that would "solve the 'u' in CKDu," as one organizer told me. Delegates would be broken into working groups that would reach consensus on specific scientific and medical challenges and present their findings to the president. When I attended a planning meeting of the Task Force in October, the management committee, made up of health and social welfare ministry officials, seemed excited by the prospect of having over a hundred dedicated experts in one room. There seemed to be a strong sense around the table that the "u" in CKDu was on the verge of resolution, with the offending poison announced during the meeting itself. I wrote in my field notes after the planning meeting, "It seems like the PTF [Task Force] expects to solve the CKDu question by the end of the year. Will the culprit be glyphosate or something else?" It did not turn out that way.

A week before the meeting someone leaked the program to the press, which questioned the credentials of those leading the working group sessions. CKDu pressure groups, many of them affiliated with the Rajarata-Kelaniya group, were dismayed to discover that the chairs of the final session on policy recommendations were none other than a past director and a board member of Sri Lanka's largest agribusiness. As the chairs were widely seen as individuals unable to participate objectively in a process that likely would have something negative to say about pesticides, pressure grew on the organizers to appoint different ones. On the morning of the meeting, a small group of environmental and agrarian rights campaigners staged a loud demonstration outside the venue and were successful in delaying the start by half an hour as delegates struggled to gain entry. Asela Iddawela, chair of the Task Force, agreed to meet the protesters and listen to their concerns, after which the group disbanded. Among their complaints was the high-profile involvement of agroindustry representatives and the choice of a high-end hotel to hold the meeting, the cost of which, protesters pointed out, could have been much better used helping CKDu patients. By 10 a.m., most delegates had no idea that the organizers had scrapped the original program days before and replaced it with a morning session of scientific talks and an afternoon session promoting the Task Force's community interventions.

In the end, the first half of the day was like the dozen other CKDu symposiums I had attended over the preceding years. Speakers and audience members alike, who overwhelmingly represented the Peradeniya and Colombo groups and affiliated scientific bodies and civil society organizations, jostled to promote their own theories and sometimes offered lively claims and counterclaims in support or denial of others they heard. Participants who left at lunchtime would have done so thinking the "u" in CKDu remained unknown. But when at 3 p.m. President Sirisena arrived with a flurry of TV crews, the tone changed. The president gave a speech during which he made the familiar argument that pesticides and fertilizers mixing with hard water lay behind CKDu. He offered banning glyphosate as a big step in the right direction but argued that the government should do more to reduce pesticide dependency among farmers. Via satellite link to a CKDu-affected village, the president declared the opening of a Task Force–sponsored reverse osmosis (RO) water purification plant, which could provide locals with a clean water supply. To launch a new fund-raising campaign, the organizers showed a music video featuring Sri Lanka's leading pop artists supported by a chorus of television and sports personalities. The video's visuals complemented the president's message. Shots of streams, rivers, and irrigation channels interspersed with images of farmers spraying their fields with pesticides left no question that the Task Force was certain agrochemicals caused the disease. The lyrics, too, reinforced this impression, containing reference to "harvested lands prepared by poisons" and "our heritage free of toxins and poisons." The optics of the meeting as it transpired—of scientific and medical uncertainties placed before, and in strong contrast to, a politics of certainty—illuminated the relationship between presidential and regulatory politics in Sri Lanka.

Dramatic moments of doubt had shaped the days and weeks leading up to the meeting. Nevertheless, the event climaxed with the president transcending those debates to make a very public statement about the role of agrochemicals in the unfolding disaster and offered the Task Force's public health projects and his Vasa Visa Nathi Ratak program as resolute answers to the crisis. Sirisena's presidential intervention communicated a commitment to purification—of both doubts from science and poisons from the environment—and one the satellite link to the water treatment plant in Polonnaruwa captured perfectly. The pomp and ceremony attached to the opening of the RO facility offered technical and metaphorical certainties where previously only contested hypotheses had existed, simultaneously offering up technological fixes for agrochemical environmental contamination *and* clearing murky scientific and political waters. They were also, of course, the pomp and ceremony of poisoncraft. In part 2, I reflected on the EU's monopolization of ignorance in the glyphosate debates taking place in European settings. In Sri Lanka, in contrast, ignorance would be swept away by the authority of the president-king. In the battle against CKDu, the president-king was not just a specialist in poison, but the island's most revered practitioner of the craft.

The 2016 Consultation

Just a few months after the tribulations of the 2015 Presidential Task Force conference, I began to hear rumors that a second knowledge exchange event was being organized. This time, however, the meeting was to take place behind closed doors, with invitations extended only to those with specific expertise. Moreover, most invited experts were to be international. After the last-minute changes to the 2015 conference and the general sense of dissatisfaction with what had been achieved, the decision to organize the 2016 consultation in this manner indicated a growing awareness within the Task Force that national efforts to building consensus were failing in the context of divisive politics.

The consultation took place over three days in April 2016, to "develop consensus on research priorities and cost-effective interventions for prevention and management" of CKDu (*Sunday Times* 2016). Taking part were over fifty clinicians, researchers, epidemiologists, toxicologists, agriculture scientists, social scientists, hydrologists, and delegates from India, the United Kingdom, Australia, Cuba, El Salvador, Finland, Sweden, Canada, and Costa Rica. In addition, a range of stakeholder organizations contributed, including the International Society of Nephrology and the Sri Lanka Society of Nephrology, as well as sponsors of past interventions, including the National Science Foundation, COSTI, and the WHO. Following the model initially proposed for the 2015 meeting, organizers divided participants into four groups and tasked them with reviewing evidence on a range of issues and agreeing on recommendations by consensus. Among the issues identified for discussion were priorities for research and intervention, including the role of pesticides, fluoride, and other occupational and environmental stressors. Oddly, the multifactorial hypothesis received no attention at all.

The WHO published the results of the consultation in a forty-eight-page report (WHO 2016) and presented it at a public meeting held in May at the Bandaranaike Memorial International Conference Hall in central Colombo. If any of those who participated in the event had hoped to see their preferred hypothesis vindicated, they would have left disappointed. The report dismissed the role of cadmium, arsenic, and fluoride in CKDu and found the evidence for glyphosate "inconclusive due to lack of consistency of the findings, lack of temporality where association was observed and limitations in the methods used for measuring exposures" (16). In conclusion, the report recommended further research on water safety, agrochemicals including glyphosate, infections that harm the kidney (specifically leptospirosis), and heat stress and dehydration.

Many in the audience did not respond well to the report's conclusions, and, like the 2015 workshop, the meeting quickly bifurcated into a debate riven by the uncertainties of science and a politics of certainty. During the question-and-answer session, chief advocates of the cadmium, arsenic, and fluoride hypotheses each challenged the conclusions reached. Even supporters of the glyphosate hypothesis, on which judgment had been delayed pending further research, criticized the consultation for failing to recognize what they argued should be obvious to all, accusing the consultation of perpetuating a coverup of the kind that had undermined the 2013 study. Rathana Thero, the Buddhist monk and JHU parliamentarian who championed the glyphosate ban, criticized scientists for their uncertainty. Referencing the insight of the president-king and his coterie of ministers, he asked derisively, "How can it be that our scientists still don't know the cause when our politicians do?" The problem, the Thero argued, was that scientists were endlessly debating what had become obvious to everyone else—namely, the role of glyphosate in CKDu. Professor Rizvi Sheriff, a leading Sri Lankan nephrologist who regularly chaired scientific meetings on CKDu, was the first panel member to reply to the Thero. Sherriff responded that the elimination of cadmium, arsenic, and fluoride as possible causal agents had helped narrow down the search for an ultimate cause of CKDu. To his mind, this development even prompted the need to change the name of the disease. "It is no longer accurate to say 'CKD of *unknown* origin,'" Sherriff argued. "We should now say 'CKD of *uncertain* origin.'"

The exchange between the Thero and the professor represented expressions of and conflicts between divine and democratic authority, in this context embodied proximally in the two men, who stood in for the president-king on the one side and the "rational" institutions of state on the other side. A tension running through all the interventions sponsored by the Presidential Task Force on CKDu was precisely how to manage those different resources of, and recourses to, power. When the Thero commended politicians for knowing the cause of CKDu and lambasted scientists for their uncertainty, he was, after Nalin de Silva, referencing the vision and knowledge of those on the true path and the blindness and ignorance of those on the false path (see chapter 9). The professor's reply, meanwhile, stressed the importance of incremental learning. For the Thero, intervention could and should be justified based on the divine authority of "seeing" politicians like

President Sirisena. Conversely, the professor saw *uncertainty* itself as grounds to act. As Sheriff told the audience:

> If we don't know then we can't do anything. But if we are only uncertain, we have the obligation to do something. We have all of these theories. At least one of them, or some of them combined, must be right. We can, say, take this idea of water pollution and then provide clean water. By doing that we might see a decrease in the number of cases. Then we can also try to get these farmers to drink more water in the fields [another theory is that CKDu is caused by growing heat stress among agricultural workers exposed to the effects of global warming].

The professor's call to action was premised on the notion that uncertainty was not, as might be supposed by the Thero, a barrier to action but rather an *opportunity* to act (see Samimian-Darash and Rabinow 2015). Other scientists in the audience agreed and offered up a raft of interventions that the Task Force could be doing, including the provision of clean drinking water and information campaigns to warn against chronic dehydration, alcohol and drug use, the consumption of sugary tea in the sun, and so on. On those points, at least, the Thero agreed, and the argument between professor and monk fizzled out.

THE POISONCRAFT OF PRESIDENTIAL RULE

My aim in this chapter has been to illustrate how presidential authority in Sri Lanka has transformed from democratic to kingly authority, shaping the politics of glyphosate in profound ways. As figureheads encompassing kingly and popular sovereignty, the presidents' interventions came with the authority of popular Buddhism. As I described in the previous chapter, Natha Deviyo, one of Lanka's four guardian deities, was instrumental in the development of the glyphosate hypothesis. His intervention in the CKDu story had significance for how the entwined fates of presidents and pesticides would play out. The presidents' power was not absolute, however, and all three presidents found themselves limited to evidence-based policy making. Although the 2016 consultation had been more successful than the 2015 conference, there remained the unsolved question of etiology. Eventually, too, the 2016 report's conclusions and recommendations came to little or nothing, with Sirisena's fall from office turning attention elsewhere. Nevertheless, the Task Force symbolized how the president's role was increasingly being defined, in explicit and certain terms, as ensuring the protection of the Sinhala nation from noxious poisons—as a commitment to poisoncraft, in other words.

Both interventions highlighted consensus building among their goals, and it is worth reflecting on this a little more. Consensus building around CKDu was always a matter of trying to build consensus over what consensus itself meant. For many members of the CKDu research community, if the search for consensus meant anything, it was pursuit of a justification to intervene to protect public health. The question was not *how* should people intervene—everyone from scientists to presidents to monks were unanimous in their belief that water was the problem—rather, the question was on what basis was an intervention around water deemed *just*. On what basis should scientists and policy makers consider the supporting evidence for an intervention sufficient to make such a decision? This was more than a matter of considering the "weight of evidence" but encompassed, too, those questions of divine and democratic authority that I have explored in this chapter. In the face of scientific uncertainty, the justness of CKDu interventions would come from the president-king's ability to see the truth in poison.

In the final chapter, I move on to consider how the pesticide industry responded to the glyphosate ban both locally and internationally.

11

Lions and Sharks

Agribusiness Resistance to the Glyphosate Ban

In November 2015, a Monsanto delegation that included Daniel Goldstein, MD, a senior toxicologist from the company, and Herman Autrup, a toxicologist from Aarhus University in Denmark, visited Sri Lanka to lobby against the glyphosate ban. With the trip arranged by CropLife Sri Lanka, a local branch of the international agroindustry body, the men gave three invitation-only talks to audiences from the agribusiness, academic, and policy worlds. They also held private meetings with the Pesticide Registrar and officials from the Ministries of Agriculture, Plantations, and Health. I attended each of the three talks, which included two half-day events (a meeting sponsored by the plantation industry and a panel session held as part of an academic conference) and a full-day session (organized by the Sri Lankan Toxicological Society). Across all three events, the message of Autrup's and Goldstein's talks varied little. Autrup focused on the science of hazard/risk management and why the IARC was wrong to classify glyphosate a probable carcinogen (even though this decision had nothing to do with Sri Lanka's efforts to ban glyphosate). Goldstein laid out criticisms of the glyphosate hypothesis itself and what he labeled "The Jayasumana Papers"—the collection of Rajarata-Kelaniya studies that had sought to demonstrate the relationship between glyphosate and CKDu. Both visitors' talks cast doubt on the veracity of claims being made against the safety of glyphosate and its possible relationship with CKDu.

Beyond this, their talks were finely pitched, appealing to their hosts' sense of hospitality and professional associations. Each man opened by paying gracious thanks to their local partners, praising the "hospitality" they had received in "this beautiful island." Goldstein also presented himself as an expert on CKDu around the world—"which I have followed for a number of years," he told audiences, without spelling out why he, a Monsanto toxicologist, had done so. Goldstein was also careful to reference his past collaborations with Sri Lankan toxicologists when he and Monsanto had assisted their work on paraquat suicides. Goldstein's interventions in the glyphosate debate were thus not to be taken as those of somebody with no familiarity or connection with Sri Lanka. They were carefully crafted to signal his long-standing and well-meaning contributions to public health in the island.

Despite such strategic positioning, their visit attracted public criticism from several constituencies, including members of all three research groups and wider environmental and political communities. Members of the Peradeniya group, who attended the first event hosted by the plantation industry, told me they had done so in good faith, thinking it was an academic meeting, and were angry when they realized it was "a lobbying event." A leading figure in the Rajarata-Kelaniya group attended the second session that had formed part of an academic meeting, during which he challenged Goldstein's rejection of the glyphosate hypothesis. In a comment dripping with sarcasm, he thanked Goldstein "for all the publicity [he was] giving to their work." The Toxicological Society's day-long session, held at the Bandaranaike Memorial International Conference Hall (BMICH), a state venue with strong associations of presidential patronage, suffered a blow when the health minister, billed as the chief guest, canceled at the last moment. The story I heard was that the minister's advisers suggested he stay away for fear of how it might play with voters. Finally, considerable criticism appeared in media outlets. Commentators attacked Goldstein and Autrup for staying in "luxury five-star hotels" while "innocent farmers suffered and died in the Rajarata." Some also questioned the motives of those who had invited them to speak, including the Sri Lankan Toxicological Society, which hosted the third session.

Of course, much of this was to be expected—par for the course for agribusiness figures touring a country where glyphosate had been at the top of the political agenda for several years. But there were other, more surprising ways in which the speakers fell afoul of local pesticide politics. Something that caught my eye during Autrup's three talks, titled "Living with Chemicals," was the way he had chosen to represent the difference between hazard and risk on his PowerPoint slides. During the first two sessions, Autrup had portrayed hazard and risk as uncaged and caged lions, respectively. By the third session, which took place several days later and after a set of closed talks with the national Pesticide Registrar, he had swapped images of lions for images of sharks.

Now, risk experts often use lions to represent hazard and risk in this way. Leaf through any textbook on the subject, and there is a good chance you will find images of caged and uncaged lions, illustrating the same message that EFSA happens to characterize with sharks (see figure 1). Autrup was perhaps only following convention in his talk. Nevertheless, the lion (*sinha*) has historical and political significance in Sri Lanka and is especially important within Sinhala nationalism. The mythical origin of the Sinhala community lies in human-lion relations ("Sinhala" means "of lions"). A representation of a lion clutching a ceremonial *kastane* sword features centrally in the national flag of Sri Lanka, while two vertical color bars represent the Tamil and Muslim communities. Critics of the design suggest the flag formalizes Sinhala dominance of the island, pointing to how the lion faces minority communities, bearing its sword, in a provocative stance. In any case, the notion that Sinhala people display the characteristics of the lion (*sinha* also means "brave") has featured centrally in the nationalist imaginary (Daniel 1996).

Despite the conventional use of lion images, Autrup's deployment of them still jarred when I saw them in a Sri Lankan setting. I have studied Sinhala nationalism long enough to know how certain uses of national and ethnic symbolism could trigger negative responses in audiences, and not just the ultra-nationalists among them. Over the twelve months before Autrup's visit, a few incidents involving foreign tourists' "disrespectful" display or engagement with Sinhala Buddhist imagery had caused scandal, resulting in their arrest and imprisonment. By the time of Monsanto's visit, questions of how Buddhism should be represented and by whom had become a national(ist) talking point, and I was sure that some objection would be raised to Autrup's presentation. Refracted through the nationalist prism, saffron-green groups, already suspicious of any attempt to challenge the glyphosate ban, could well read the caged lion as an effort on the part of international agents to exert control over the Sinhala people. Here not only was a foreign scientist arguing against Sri Lanka's sovereign right to prevent poisons from entering the nation, but he was using the lion, the very symbol of Sinhala identity, to do so. That for his final talk Autrup had swapped lions with sharks suggests someone had pointed this out.

In this final chapter of part 3, I explore forms of industry resistance to the glyphosate ban and Jayasumana's positive reception in international environmental and scientific circles. Monsanto's direct interventions in Sri Lankan politics, policy, and science was, of course, deeply antagonistic to an already thwart situation. None of this was made any easier by the history and composition of the Sri Lankan pesticide market. Companies with origins in British colonial enterprises, as well as companies owned by members of Sri Lanka's minority communities—Muslims, Tamils, and Christians—dominated the field. Moreover, no Sri Lankan company produced its own pesticides; agribusinesses imported from abroad, mostly from manufacturers based in India, China, and the Middle East.

All this provided easy fodder for Buddhist nationalist groups. They portrayed the cause of CKDu, the presence of glyphosate, and the plight of Sinhala farmers more generally as problems rooted in the history of colonialism, contemporary capitalism, and the ability of the island's minority to make money off the toil of the majority—the exact same resentments that led to the civil war, in other words. Yet at the same time, Sri Lanka's environmental activist community was also deeply international. Despite the conflation of saffron-green politics, some of the key actors were funded by "foreign" NGOs—ironically, the very organizations that Buddhist nationalists had long attacked for allegedly supporting Tamil separatists.

In a context where the government's poisoncraft had been directed to sealing the nation's borders, the cross-border traffic of pro- and anti-glyphosate movements shed further light on the nationalist mission of poison control. The first half of the chapter explores the history of Monsanto's involvement in Sri Lanka pesticide regulation, which predated the glyphosate ban. The second half explores Jayasumana's celebration by environmental groups in Europe and scientific groups in the United States.

TOXIC CONNECTIONS

Their friendly demeanor notwithstanding, it is difficult to imagine Monsanto ever thought Goldstein's and Autrup's tour would do anything other than antagonize an already difficult situation for the company—as indeed the possible gaffe over lions made clear. Certainly, at that point President Sirisena was unlikely to revisit the ban, and just a few months later he launched his Toxin-Free Nation program, further cementing his commitment to agricultural detoxification. On the other hand, the visit was a defiant display—a very public declaration that industry was not going to just give up and walk away. But to focus on Goldstein's and Autrup's critical reception in wider environmental and political circles is to miss the point. Autrup did not make any claim to previous involvement with Sri Lankan toxicology, but for Goldstein an earlier history of collaboration with Sri Lankan scientists on suicide prevention provided an important and valuable grounds for mutuality that he could exploit. What at first glance would appear to be two clearly defined opposing sides in fact turns out to be a more complex set of international relations among toxicologists with decades of professional and personal ties between them.

To understand the nature of Monsanto's interventions in Sri Lanka, I travel back a decade to a time when glyphosate's rival herbicide, paraquat, was the focus of regulatory concern. During the 2000s, glyphosate had come off patent and cheaper versions were becoming available in Sri Lanka. Nevertheless, farmers still preferred paraquat to glyphosate, and glyphosate vendors struggled to improve sales. Thus, when researchers started paying attention to paraquat's use in suicide, deaths from which were magnitudes higher due to its much greater acute toxicity, Monsanto spotted an opportunity. Realizing that farmers' attachment to paraquat represented a significant hurdle to increasing glyphosate's market share, Monsanto worked to have paraquat banned. The company set about this by contributing to suicide prevention research, including the work of the South Asian Clinical Toxicology Research Collaboration (SACTRC), some of whose members Goldstein already knew through professional toxicology circles. "Clinical toxicology is a small world," Goldstein told me over lunch after one of his talks in Colombo. "I've known several of those guys for a long time—from before I was with Monsanto."

Goldstein and his colleagues at Monsanto assisted SACTRC researchers by helping establish the acute toxicity of glyphosate formulations versus paraquat formulations when used as a suicide method. "We lent our labs for the toxicological work," Goldstein told me. When I asked Goldstein why Monsanto had gotten involved, he explained that their participation was as much a matter of ensuring glyphosate did not get caught up in any regulatory decision against paraquat as it was motivated by an interest in seeing the end of paraquat suicides. Indeed, their results had demonstrated a case fatality rate of glyphosate poisoning of just 3.2 percent, compared to paraquat's case fatality rate of 60 percent (Roberts et al. 2010), a key finding that would ensure paraquat's removal from sale in Sri Lanka and glyphosate's protection from regulation. Nevertheless, Goldstein was thoughtful about the wider implications of SACTRC's research. "Although some of their conclusions are uncomfortable for us [as an industry], it's good quality work and we have to take it seriously and listen to them," he told me.

The story of the Monsanto-SACTRC connection took a twist when in 2017 litigation against Monsanto in the United States forced the company to release hundreds of internal emails to the public. Referred to as the "Monsanto Papers," the database told a story of corporate interference in glyphosate science and regulation, in which Goldstein was a key participant. One email showed how Goldstein and his colleagues referred to their work as "Whack-a-Mole" (Baum Hedlund Aristei & Goldman PC 2019). What Goldstein meant is that they operated as a kind of rapid deployment unit tasked with quashing scientific studies and regulatory developments critical of glyphosate whenever and wherever they appeared around the world. In one exchange, Goldstein proposed he "beat the shit out of" an anti-GMO campaign group, Moms Across America, which had been calling for glyphosate to be banned. Other emails revealed Goldstein's and colleagues' involvement in ghostwriting and editing "independent" scientific studies arguing for glyphosate's safety, as well as coordinating pressure from sympathetic scientists and groups on journals to retract critical studies and promote glyphosate safety (Gillam 2021b).

Among those emails flagged by lawyers as evidence of ghostwriting included communications between Goldstein and SACTRC. Specifically, the emails referred to the very publication that emerged from their work assessing glyphosate's acute toxicity (Roberts et al. 2010). The emails included in the files did not suggest any obviously dubious influence by Monsanto on the research and writing process of that publication. Goldstein and his colleagues were listed as coauthors on the paper and their contributions to the research described. The email chain showed Monsanto's authors making corrections and revisions to some background information and interpretations of the results.

However, what I find interesting about the collaboration is how it points to the complex nature of professional relationships that comprise industry, academic, and regulatory toxicology as they span the world and Sri Lanka. Those relationships allowed Goldstein to position himself as something of a long-standing participant in Sri Lankan toxicology that helped give his visit to the island defending glyphosate a certain legitimacy. Highlighting the link not only allied Goldstein with members of the Colombo group who had been involved with that work, but also indirectly with members of the Rajarata-Kelaniya group who had themselves collaborated and published with international members of the SACTRC team.

Thanks to those connections, at the Toxicological Society event the chair introduced Goldstein to the audience as "one of us"—a positionality that Goldstein reaffirmed through reference to his professional and personal relations with esteemed members of the audience. Goldstein's manner during the event gave a sense that he was among friends, speaking at ease and with confidence about a matter of mutual concern. The existing friendliness between Goldstein and the Society was reinforced when at the end of the day the chair made a point of inviting Goldstein back to Sri Lanka to update the Society on advances in CKDu toxicology. In the meantime, he added, Goldstein should join COSTI's *CKDu and Sri Lanka* Basecamp forum. "Discussions can sometimes get . . . a little heated," the chair joked to laughter in the hall, "but your expertise will be very welcome!"

True to his word, Goldstein became a regular contributor to discussions on the forum. Always careful to disclose his employment with Monsanto but engaging on the site in a personal capacity, Goldstein commented on matters of toxicology and not only those that related to glyphosate. As during his visit to Sri Lanka, he came across as a compassionate observer wanting nothing more than to help relieve the suffering of CKDu-affected communities. Goldstein's presence on the forum did not pass without comment or criticism, of course. Some members challenged Goldstein on matters of science and the reliability of industry-sponsored studies that he might have cited. A few contributors protested the notion that COSTI had permitted a Monsanto employee to join the forum at all. One member demanded he explain why Monsanto, an American company, was so interested in the Sri Lankan glyphosate ban. "Sri Lanka is not a US colony!" he objected.

Goldstein's answer revealed something important about Monsanto's own engagement with and understanding of chemical-sovereignty movements around the world. "We're worried it could lead to a domino effect where larger markets follow suit," he wrote. I read Goldstein's surprisingly frank response as more provocation than justification. He pointed out that Sri Lanka was a small market that did not present any financial danger to Monsanto—a remark he underscored by emphasizing that most glyphosate sold in Sri Lanka was produced by generic manufacturers, not Monsanto. The real risk to the company was in how a successful ban in Sri Lanka might give momentum to campaigns in larger, more valuable markets, for example, where Roundup Ready crops were grown.

Monsanto's interventions in the glyphosate and CKDu debates highlighted the reach the company had into Sri Lankan scientific worlds. Prior professional and personal relationships had given legitimacy to Goldstein's new efforts to present himself as a *collaborator* in the effort to find the cause of CKDu, even if he was also transparent about his aim of acquitting glyphosate. Anthropologists have drawn attention to the double meaning at play in the word *collaboration* (Kenworthy et al. 2018; Sariola and Simpson 2019). On the one hand, "collaboration" refers to what Salla Sariola and Bob Simpson (2019, 4) have referred to as the "warm" themes of professional mutuality and egalitarian exchange that comprise joint efforts to solve scientific problems. Collaboration can also refer to the "cooler" themes, "to cooperate as a traitor, especially with an enemy occupying one's own country" (4).

While Goldstein was concerned to promote the "warm" themes of his collaboration on suicide prevention research in Sri Lanka, it was precisely the "cooler" themes that his critics highlighted. Goldstein's reception in Sri Lanka was similarly double-edged. He held a pharmakon-like presence, at once offering a cure for uncertainties about CKDu etiology and poisoning the debate by further antagonizing already bitter arguments between the Rajarata-Kelaniya, Peradeniya, and Colombo groups.

OPPOSITION RESEARCH

The Monsanto delegation's interventions in Sri Lanka formed only one aspect of the company's efforts to challenge the glyphosate ban. Jayasumana's leading role in research on glyphosate and CKDu more widely had turned him into something of a celebrity in international environmentalist circles. This also brought him to the attention of Monsanto and its supporters. Sri Lankan agribusinesses had started to coordinate their own investigations into Jayasumana and members of his group. A director of Sri Lanka's largest agribusiness regaled me with a list of what he called "shocking" revelations their investigations had found. This included an allegation that Jayasumana's interest in CKDu extended only so far as it provided a vehicle for his long-standing desire to enter politics. "Glyphosate was just a good cause to get behind," he told me. Likewise, he said, Presidents Mahinda Rajapaksa and Sirisena had only agreed to ban glyphosate as a personal favor to their friends in the Rajarata-Kelaniya group. A third source told me that even Jayasumana himself had admitted glyphosate was not the cause of CKDu and only made the claim to attract international attention.

I was then put in touch with Monsanto's sole local representative in Sri Lanka, Thiran. A man with the look of someone whose job had just become a lot more complicated, Thiran and I met for two hours in an upmarket Colombo coffee shop during which time he unburdened himself of the whole glyphosate saga as he saw it. Starting off with the business of Mrs. Senanayake's divine revelation and finishing with the twists and turns of Sirisena's complete ban of glyphosate, Thiran was incredulous it had all come to this: his star product taken off the shelves thanks to a weak hypothesis in a predatory pay-to-publish journal. He left me with a copy of a Monsanto-authored briefing paper that dissected and discredited, page by page, Jayasumana's claim that glyphosate was the mysterious "Compound X" responsible for CKDu. Monsanto had ensured that the paper was shared with decision makers across government, from the Pesticide Registrar to the president himself, I was told.

With efforts under way to discredit his work and reputation, Jayasumana traveled to The Hague in the Netherlands in October 2016 to give evidence to the International Monsanto Tribunal, an initiative organized by environmental groups and including the veteran campaigner Vandana Shiva. The tribunal took place over two days during which a panel of five "judges" heard testimony from a range of witnesses about Monsanto's crimes against human rights and the environment. During his own testimony, Jayasumana listed the numerous ways the pesticide industry had tried to undermine him.

> They initially attacked me and other members of the research team through social media, web sites, printed and electronic media. My reputation was severely damaged by false accusations. Industry published a full-page advertisement in all national newspapers demanding withdrawal of our findings within two weeks if not they will go the court. We just neglected their hyping but nothing has happened. Then they threat me in various ways. They directly influenced my university via then vice chancellor. I had to cancel my PhD registration at University of Kelaniya and reregistered at Rajarata University as a result of their weight. My family, my self, friends and PhD supervisors have undergone severe mental pressure during this period. (Jayasumana 2016)

As the tribunal was a civil society initiative with no formal governmental affiliation at the national or international level, Monsanto could easily dismiss its verdict that the company was guilty of "ecocide"—a pattern of corporate malpractice "causing serious damage or destroying the environment, so as to significantly and durably alter the global commons or ecosystem services upon which certain human groups rely" (International Monsanto Tribunal n.d.). When I asked Goldstein about the initiative, he unsurprisingly dismissed it as a stunt. "Most people do not realize this is a place and not an institution—the activists rent a hotel ballroom in 'The Hague' and put on a kangaroo court," he told me.

Jayasumana's experiences tally with many of those who have taken on the pesticide industry. In this case, however, Jayasumana also attracted the attention of the American Association for the Advancement of Science (AAAS), the world's largest scientific professional organization and publisher of the journal *Science*. In 2019, the AAAS awarded its prize for Scientific Freedom and Responsibility to Jayasumana and his coauthor Sarath Gunatilake (though not, pointedly, the "divine mystic," Mrs. Senanayake). The AAAS described Jayasumana and Gunatilake as "two public health researchers who battled powerful corporate interests to uncover the deadly effects of industrial herbicides, solving a medical mystery and protecting the health of farming communities across the world" (Cohen 2019).

The AAAS reported how both men had faced death threats because of their work, while Gunatilake's employer, California State University, had investigated him for scientific malpractice after "industry-funded" scientists complained about his glyphosate hypothesis (the university later dropped its investigation, having found no evidence of wrongdoing). Commenting on the award, AAAS's director of scientific responsibility, Jessica Wyndham, stated, "To right a wrong when significant financial interests are at stake and the power imbalance between industry and individual is at play takes the unique combination of scientific rigor, professional persistence and acceptance of personal risk demonstrated by the two scientists recognized by this year's award" (Cohen 2019).

As far as the AAAS's initial statement was concerned, Jayasumana and Gunatilake had proven a link between glyphosate and CKDu. However, a few days later the AAAS announced it was "taking steps to reassess" the award "after concerns were raised by members and scientists" (AAAS [@aaas] 2019). In what had all the hallmarks of an industry-organized attack, the AAAS received dozens of complaints about its decision, forcing its U-turn.

Among those speaking out against the award was Kevin Folta, a professor of horticultural sciences at the University of Florida. Folta wrote about the AAAS decision on his *Illumination* blog and included a feature on his popular weekly "Talking Biotech" podcast. Through those platforms Folta criticized the AAAS for "overstepping the data" supplied by Jayasumana and Gunatilake on the glyphosate-CKDu link by presenting an unproven hypothesis as fact. "C'mon AAAS," he wrote on his blog. "If this was Natural News, Green Med Info, The Food Babe,[1] or any other kooky khemistree [sic] website then I might understand. They've been searching to vilify ag chemistries for decades. But this is AAAS. I'm a member. I'm always in awe at the awardees for their much deserved recognition" (Folta 2019).

On his "Talking Biotech" podcast, Folta speculated further on the motivations that may have led to Jayasumana and Gunatilake's nomination, as well as the "unscientific" wording of the press release that referred to glyphosate as the "killer herbicide" and "culprit" behind the CKDu epidemic. He argued that the AAAS intervention "provided red meat to the activists . . . who would love the AAAS, an esteemed organization, saying glyphosate is 'kidney failure-agenic.'" Careful not to attack the motives or credentials of Jayasumana and Gunatilake themselves (who Folta agreed would deserve celebration should a link between glyphosate and CKDu be proven), Folta suggested nevertheless that the pair "maybe . . . deserve a little heat" for their probable involvement with, and potential backing of, "Big Organic." Referring to Jayasumana's appearance at the Monsanto Tribunal— dismissed by Folta as a "fake tribunal"—Folta concluded by arguing "anyone of scientific acumen would steer clear of it." On the veracity of the glyphosate

---

1. Anti-GM, anti-agrochemical, pro-organic, pro–"natural living" websites.

hypothesis itself, Folta simply argued, "Maybe true, maybe not, but, based on 40 years of data? Probably not."

Responding to pressure, the AAAS said it would "address those concerns through a peer review and subsequently evaluate the award status" (Handunnetti 2019). By November, however, the AAAS had reinstated the award to Jayasumana and Gunatilake. Although standing by its original decision, the AAAS's language in the accompanying press release had notably softened. Gone were references to industry threats and the scientists' "battle against corporate interests," to be replaced instead with mention only of their "[investigation of] a possible connection between glyphosate and chronic kidney disease under challenging circumstances" (AAAS 2019). The AAAS also noted that Jayasumana and Gunatilake had identified an "association" between glyphosate and CKDu, "but a causal connection is not conclusive to date" (AAAS 2019). Nevertheless, the organization's decision was a vindication for Jayasumana and Gunatilake. "Science has prevailed," Jayasumana said. "That's why, after certain groups opposed our selection and undermined our professional work, the research work has been upheld as credible" (Handunnetti 2019).

THE POISONCRAFT OF POSTWAR UNIFICATION

Although the controversies that arose around the glyphosate ban would not suggest it, Sri Lanka is unique in the world for its long history of strong pesticide regulation. From the 1970s, successive governments were quick to ban chemicals shown to be bad for the environment and/or public health. Public health researcher Melissa Pearson (2015) has called this a form of "policy making under the radar." Her research showed how a small group of civil servants based in and around the office of the Pesticide Registrar formed an "epistemic community" that acted within its own mandate to ban the most toxic pesticides, dramatically reducing the suicide rate (Pearson et al. 2010). Significantly, scientists working on suicide prevention in Sri Lanka have flagged the notable absence of agrochemical industry interference in the Pesticide Registrar's decision making during that time. Thus, when compared to past regulatory actions, attempts to ban glyphosate were firmly "on the radar"—of industry groups as well as nationalist politicians. As one leading CKDu expert, Saroj Jayasinghe, would note in his own writing on the matter, "Naming an environmentally-induced disease can be controversial. . . . [There is] a strong possibility that vested interests (particularly agrochemical manufacturers) will challenge [any conclusion that blames pesticides]" (2014, 73).

As regulatory and legal challenges against glyphosate gathered pace, Monsanto became increasingly interventionist in domestic politics around the world (Gillam 2017). Working in tandem with the US government, which threatened trade reprisals, the company managed to stop or delay glyphosate bans in Vietnam and Thailand in 2019 and Mexico in 2020 (Gillam 2021a). Although evidence has yet to emerge showing the US government similarly intervened in Sri Lanka, it seems highly unlikely that the US embassy in Colombo would have been unaware of Goldstein's visit, or that other efforts to pressure the government were not under way behind closed doors. Leading the charge against considerable foreign powers, Jayasumana, a man defending the Buddhist nation against foreign attack, saw his reputation rise further still. On the international stage, Jayasumana also attracted the acclaim not only of anti-glyphosate movements, but mainstream scientific bodies. The ways in which Jayasumana's research on glyphosate held significance and meaning in different local contexts show the transmutative travel of poisoncraft across locations. An expression of nationalist poisoncraft being put to work for the purification of the nation in one context was understood as a more straightforward "David and Goliath" battle of lone scientist versus powerful corporation in another context. Likewise, lions in one context could symbolize chemical danger and in another context the mythical origins of a community of people. To push the analogy further, lions could symbolize the resistance of Sinhala Buddhism; Monsanto, the sharks circling the nation.

SUMMARY OF PART III

The Poisonous Gas of Communal Identity

IN THE EPILOGUE OF HIS BOOK on the rise of Sinhala Buddhist nationalism, anthropologist Stanley Tambiah commented on emerging trends of anti-Muslim violence across the three Theravada Buddhist–dominated countries of South and Southeast Asia, Sri Lanka, Burma (Myanmar), and Thailand. His words are worth repeating here both for the sad prescience they displayed and for his use of language that has importance for my argument.

> These convergent attitudes . . . [of anti-Muslim animosity] . . . should warn us about the militant and chauvinistic resonances that have constituted the dark underside and the other terrifying face of Buddhism as a religio-political complex, which in its positive aspects has attained to great humanistic conceptions and civilizational triumphs. This other face presents itself in the twentieth century as a distorted "political Buddhism" emptied of its ethical content and inflated with the poison gas of communal identity. Under its banner populist leaders mobilize masses who are losing their traditional roots and their traditional Buddhist moral restraints, and whip them into heady collective identity and a fury of displaced and misplaced anger against the alien others, the minorities, who are seen as a challenge to their chauvinistic manhood. (Tambiah 1986, 139)

Tambiah was writing in the 1980s, just a short time after full hostilities had broken out between the Tamil Tigers and government forces and years before the further atrocities that would come. Yet his words portend the Age of Toxicity that I described in the introduction—our contemporary time when the poisons of populism, chauvinism, and ethnic and religious nationalism have coalesced into something even more dangerous. Tambiah's words invoke pharmakon thinking. The moral and ethical goods of Buddhism that could provide answers to the conflicts then arising had been overcome by the "poisonous gas" of communal identity. It's a vision and a lesson that resonates some forty years later, because the returning metaphor of poison that Tambiah deployed to describe that political constellation continues to resonate today.

Politics is a toxicological problem, involving the identification and control of poisons that threaten the integrity of sovereign bodies. During the decade following Sri Lanka's civil war, the Sri Lankan body politic, from the executive president to ordinary citizens, became obsessed with that problem. Thus, my aim throughout part 3 has been to show how glyphosate became a matter of and for politics precisely because it played so well within a wider toxicologization of postwar state (re)formation. Driven partly by the question of what was causing an epidemic of kidney disease among farmers but also partly by arising toxicological anxieties in other registers, most notably fear of Muslim bioterrorism, glyphosate emerged as a key vehicle for the expression of those coalescing concerns. Sealing the borders of the shore-ringed nation was a project of poisoncraft.

Efforts to make Sri Lanka "whole again" required a purification of the commons to make it safe for Sinhala Buddhist bodies. Would the Sri Lankan postwar period have taken the turns that it did if glyphosate did not exist? Maybe or maybe not. What we do know is that while the ethnic conflict would have persisted, the conflation with glyphosate helped reveal what I argue was already there: its strong toxicological character. As in the European case, this was no historical coincidence; it was made possible because of the poisoncraft that has for millennia been integral to social life in South Asia. Cleansing the commons and cleansing bodies of the postwar nation could *only* have been a project of poisoncraft.

Conclusion

The Cauldron of Poisoncraft

The regulatory structures, practices, and politics of glyphosate in the European Union and Sri Lanka are fundamentally entangled with broader projects of (re)defining and (re)asserting sovereign power. Whether ultimately successful or not, they had become during the 2010s parts of wider efforts to delineate and defend sovereign territorialities at the levels of the European supranational state and the postwar Sri Lankan nation-state. By tracing those entanglements, I have explored the historical and anthropological interconnections between the meanings of poisons, the regulation of pesticides, and the political logics of chemical sovereignty.

POISONCRAFT

At the heart of the book lies the practice of poisoncraft—the field of cultural ideas, methods, and techniques that spans the poison lore of folk traditions and the formalized epistemologies of professional toxicologies. In part 1, I drew on the social anthropology of the gift to develop a conceptual framework for understanding Eurasian poisoncraft as a project that encompasses value-making and power in the elucidation of the noxious and the good in and of social life. I introduced poison not as a timeless universal but as a *timeful* substance—one that draws its meanings from deep histories and resonates across temporal and spatial divides. Poison, I argued, is a *returning metaphor*, a concept that reasserts itself through time, laden with moral, political, and affective significance. Across cultures and throughout the ages, poison has been central to how people comprehend danger, exchange, and relationality, from the peril of the unreciprocated gift to the threats posed by intimacy and commensality.

Poisoncraft brings into view the mythos and logos of poison—the symbolic, ritual, and moral dimensions of toxicity in metaphorical and material registers and the scientific, diagnostic, and regulatory knowledges that have sought to govern them. Poisoncraft can be found in everything from ancient traditions of healing and harm to contemporary regimes of chemical classification and control. Poisoncraft is not only concerned with the substances that can kill or cure, but also the broader cosmologies, ontologies, and techniques through which human and more-than-human bodies become intelligible as sites of vulnerability, danger, and intervention. In this sense, poisoncraft is a comparative and relational practice that persists across societies, and thinking in terms of poisoncraft allows us to follow the ways poison is made meaningful across different cultural, historical, and political formations. It includes the lore of witches and the expertise of chemists, the fairy tale and the clinical trial, the sacred and the secular. Thinking in terms of poisoncraft allows us to see that toxicology is not the triumph of scientific rationality over superstition but the continuation, and transformation, of older traditions of discerning poisonous danger and maintaining order.

Crucially, then, as a practice poisoncraft illuminates how contemporary struggles over chemical regulation, environmental justice, and bodily autonomy are informed by long-standing cultural logics of danger, permeability, and protection. This encompasses Mary Douglas's classic formulation of purity and power but extends it from the classificatory domain of pollution to the relational expanse of poison. Everyone inhabiting a chemically saturated world is engaged with practices of poisoncraft. This holds whether they are formulating crop protection technologies, advocating for environmental justice, or simply navigating the plethora of poisons they encounter in everyday life, from the cosmetics they might apply to the dinner invitations they might accept. To live in the world is to live as a specialist in poisoncraft.

Likewise, poisoncraft is central to the very structure of sovereign rule, which defines itself through the protection of territorial and biological integrity. Neither territory nor body is ever preconstituted; both are continually made and remade through their engagements with poison and the practices of regulation, which is to say, in the cauldron of poisoncraft. In Europe and Sri Lanka, it was no coincidence that at a moment when profound questions were being asked about what kind of supranational or national bodies those territories were or wanted to be, poison provided a material and a metaphor for thinking critically and experimentally with new ways of configuring the borders and contours of the political body and the biological body. Whether encountered in the form of agricultural pesticides, industrial pollutants, or the metaphorical poisons of political discourse, the lore of natural toxins and synthetic toxicants animated a range of affective, ethical, and epistemic responses in polycrisis Europe and postwar Sri Lanka.

My analysis of glyphosate controversies in the EU and Sri Lanka demonstrates how local poisoncraft traditions shaped emergent debates about chemical sovereignty—the right of communities and states to control their exposure to industrial pollutants. In South Asia, Ayurvedic traditions offered a theory of the sovereign body as an open and relational ecology—one that is porous to the influences of others and constantly susceptible to toxic infiltration. The protection of the self, in this schema, requires not individual insulation but collective purification, for example, through food taboos, kinship regulations, caste boundaries, and ritual practices that secure the integrity of group life. In Europe, by contrast, the Paracelsian model emerging in the sixteenth century saw the hardening of biological and state boundaries that required defense against poisonous incursion. When applied in the twenty-first century, that poisoncraft found expression in the workings of the European agencies striving to harden the union's borders in defense of the four freedoms of movement (of people, services, capital, and goods like glyphosate).

By foregrounding poisoncraft, I thus sought to open a space for anthropological engagement with toxicity that resists both reductionism and fatalism. It is an invitation to think with poison; to trace its cultural forms, its historical echoes, its political consequences, and its enduring capacity to both wound and heal. Thinking through poisoncraft draws attention to the long-run meanings that poisons like pesticides carry and convey. It allows us to trace what Marshall Sahlins (1981) once called the "historical metaphors and mythical realities" of cultural stories, including those that lie at the root of poison's ontogenesis and from which poison's materiality and semiosis derive. An attention to poisoncraft provides the tools for exploring such material-semiotic forms—the multiple registers that poison takes in contemporary discourse, from the poisons of populism that make toxic debates over immigration, trans rights, and climate change to the popular poisons like glyphosate that intoxicate environmental politics, allowing a coalescence of democratic movements in the face of toxic uncertainty and regulatory inertia.

CHEMICAL SOVEREIGNTY

The cases of glyphosate regulation in the European Union and Sri Lanka reveal the deep structural and epistemic difficulties involved in asserting what I have called chemical sovereignty, that is, the capacity of a political community to define, delimit, and manage its chemical exposures. At first glance, banning or regulating a substance like glyphosate appears to be a straightforward expression of sovereign will. Yet, as both contexts illustrated, efforts to enact such bans became rapidly caught in webs of scientific controversy, complex global trade agreements, and contested political legitimacy, all of which exposed the fragile foundations of sovereign power in the toxic present.

In the EU, regulatory decisions were formally delegated to the European Food Safety Authority and the European Chemicals Agency, institutions ostensibly committed to risk-based scientific assessment. However, competing toxicological paradigms (such as hazard-based vs. risk-based approaches) and a growing distrust of regulatory science, including its relations with corporate science and bad actors like Monsanto, turned the glyphosate issue into a cauldron of broader political contestation. It became impossible to debate the molecule's regulatory fate without invoking the history and future of the European project, the many crises facing the union, and the solidarity deficit that undermined collective decision making on contentious issues. The EU's decision in 2023 to extend glyphosate's approval for another ten years illustrated how supranational governance structures could erode rather than reinforce chemical sovereignty.

In Sri Lanka, the three efforts to ban glyphosate, in 2014, 2015, and 2021, were for their champions an assertion of the island's chemical autonomy in the face of international agribusiness pressure. Each time, the move was framed by political leaders as a measure to combat chronic kidney disease. The first and second bans were also expressions of morphing presidential power; the third was in the context of a total import ban on agrochemicals. The bans were the kind of action that global environmental movements, perhaps unaware of the local chauvinistic politics caught up within them, celebrated as largely unproblematic examples of progressive policy making. Yet the bans were each short-lived. The underpinning work of the Rajarata-Kelaniya group was ridiculed by scientists with competing hypotheses and a strongly held belief that the evidence for the glyphosate-CKDu connection simply did not exist. It also, of course, provoked backlash from powerful agribusiness actors, as well as factions within the state concerned about threats to export-oriented agriculture, particularly tea. When the government reversed its bans, it exposed the state's inability to sustain chemical sovereignty under the pressure of economic dependencies, scientific contestation, and geopolitical influence.

What those cases showed was that chemical sovereignty is both necessary and perpetually undermined. The very substances that states seek to regulate—persistent, mobile, and globally produced—far exceed the territorial logics of twenty-first-century political power that is once again embracing the Westphalian nation-state as its ultimate horizon. As the Age of Optimism withered and the Age of Toxicity grew, globalization, once heralded by trendy academic theorists and Euro-American political leaders as natural and inevitable, disappeared as an ideology driving regulation. Efforts to restrict chemicals like glyphosate would become sites of friction as morphing political entities and territorialities would seek to reconcile competing demands and assessments of risk. Moreover, as glyphosate's contested regulatory history showed, the production of authoritative toxicological knowledge was itself deeply embedded in the political economy of scientific community and evidence making. Chemical sovereignty, then, cannot be understood simply as a matter of legal capacity or institutional strength. It must also contend with the material agency and capacities of poisons themselves, and with the ways in which toxic substances entangle the crafts of poison in everyday life.

THE SOVEREIGN POISON AND ITS FUTURES

Poisoncraft and chemical sovereignty offer conceptual tools for grappling with the paradoxes of life in toxic times. Poisoncraft illuminates the deep historical roots of how poison is known, named, and negotiated. Chemical sovereignty brings into focus the contemporary struggles of states and supranational bodies to assert control over those poisons—to name what is safe, to decide who is protected, and to draw boundaries around what is allowed to enter the social and biological body. The interplay between those two terms also reveals their mutual implications. The more technocratic and scientific the governance of poisons becomes, the more crucial it is that we understand from where ideas about the noxious and the good derive. And the more poisons proliferate across planetary systems, the less plausible it becomes that any single body—individual, political, or scientific—can hope to contain or command them. The glyphosate controversies in the EU and Sri Lanka demonstrated these realities in stark terms. In both cases, the assertion of chemical sovereignty, whether through national bans or regional regulatory decisions, was undermined by the very forces that poisoncraft helps us understand—divergent cultural traditions of bodily vulnerability, conflicting toxicological paradigms, the ghostly presence of older fears, and the unresolved legacies of colonial and capitalist exposure.

Those examples provide further insight into how we are living through a crisis of sovereignty. As political bodies attempt to purify and protect themselves, they increasingly rely on logics of exclusion, quarantine, and immunity. Those logics, themselves forms of poisoncraft, promise control but often reproduce harm. They promise security but generate new forms of precarity. They promise clarity but are built on deeply unstable foundations: contested science, unequal exposure, and global circuits of chemical commerce that no single sovereign can fully oversee. From this perspective, poisoncraft is not just a tradition from which we might draw to understand chemical poisons, but a field of practice that might allow us to navigate and make sense of conditions of poisonous decline, uncertainty, and fear. Poisoncraft offers a critical language for interpreting the world in an Age of Toxicity in which borders are being imagined as prophylactics, in which purity has become an ideological project, and in which exposure has become the form through which inequality is lived. To think with poisoncraft is to reckon with the impossibility of total separation and the necessity of coexistence. It is to understand that sovereignty—whether over bodies, territories, or chemicals—can never be absolute and that attempts to make it so often become noxious, often creating new poisons in the name of protection. It is also to recognize that within poison lies not only death and danger, but relation, transformation, and critique. Poisons injure, but they also reveal the hidden structures of meaning that give shape to value and power and the contested meanings of risk and responsibility.

The future of chemical sovereignty will not be written by science and policy alone. It will emerge from a world already saturated with cultural ideas of poison—ideas that shape how people imagine harm and demand protection. In such a world, attempts to assert chemical sovereignty, whether through bans, regulations, or standards, will increasingly confront the limits of technocratic authority. Regulatory bodies may define toxicity in parts per million, but people continue to read poison in symptoms, suspicions, and stories. Whether in Europe or in Sri Lanka, sovereignty over chemicals is always entangled with sovereignty over place, body, and the production of identity and meaning. It is shaped by histories of exposure, infrastructures of inequality, and the uneven trust placed in experts, states, and corporations. Rather than see cultural ideas of poison as obstacles to regulation, future models of chemical sovereignty must recognize poisoncraft as foundational—as a condition of it. This means accepting that poison is not only embedded in but also constitutive of the moral, political, and affective life of communities. The futures of chemical sovereignty, then, lie in forms of governance that can hold ambiguity, that respect vernacular knowledges of harm, and that are attuned to the symbolic and material weight of poison. They will be shaped by how well we attend to the meanings poison carries, the relations it threatens and reveals, and the historical metaphors through which it continues to act. They will be futures in which we must all recognize our own specialisms in poisoncraft.

ACKNOWLEDGMENTS

This book has been ten years in the making, over which time I have accrued more debts than I can possibly repay. My foremost thanks go to all those who gave generously of their time. They included, at the international, EU, and local levels, representatives of the pesticide industry, regulators, municipal workers, farmers, environmentalists, and academics. In Sri Lanka, I also spent considerable time with members of the research community investigating the island's epidemic chronic kidney failure. My research in Sri Lanka benefited enormously from the assistance and friendship of Sarah Kabir and Upul Wickramasinghe, without whom I would have been perfectly lost. The Department of Sociology at the University of Colombo hosted me during my research, for which I am extremely grateful.

As described in the preface, I owe inspiration and intellectual debts to Tharindi Udalagama, Bob Simpson, Michael Eddleston, Andrew Russell, and Upul Wickramasinghe. Bob, Andrew, and Michael also read drafts of the funding proposal that allowed the research to take place. Colleagues in the Department of Anthropology at Durham University provided valuable comments on drafts of the chapters comprising part 2. I thank, in alphabetical order, Hannah Brown, Liana Chase, Pauline Destree, Yulia Egorova, Elaine Forde, Paolo Fortis, Leo Hopkinson, Loretta Lou, Istvan Praet, and Felix Ringel. Drafts of the chapters in part 3 benefited from being shared at meetings of the International Sri Lanka Research Group, regularly attended by Vindhya Buthpitiya, Nipesh Narayan, Ben Hildred, and Bob Simpson. The group became a vital, supportive virtual space to discuss work and ideas during COVID-19 lockdowns and after. My research on CKDu has benefited from ongoing conversations with Ciara Kierans and Alex Nading. Jeanne Marecek has been a source of constant support and insight since my first tentative steps in Sri Lanka as a doctoral researcher in 2004. Journalist Nalaka Gunawardena and toxicologist Ravindra Fernando guided my entry into CKDu research communities.

Audiences at the following meetings, among others, provided valuable feedback: Annual Conference on South Asia, Madison; Association of Social Anthropologists, Durham; Sri Lanka Roundtable, Amsterdam; Toxic Expertise Workshop, Warwick; Cultures of Toxicity conference, Warwick; Northern European Conference on Emergency and Disaster Studies, Uppsala; Food Studies Seminar Series, SOAS, London; Chronic Living conference, Copenhagen; CKDu research conference, Colombo.

The final manuscript benefited from readings by three anonymous reviewers and an Editorial Committee member at the University of California Press. My deep thanks go to Kate Marshall, my editor, who patiently waited for my much-delayed, and over-length, first draft, and Natalie Gomez, Francisco Reinking, and Sheila Berg, who saw the final version through to production. All errors and omissions remain my own.

The bulk of the research was supported by a Society and Ethics Research Fellowship from the Wellcome Trust (104433/Z/14/Z). A further grant from the Wellcome Trust made an Open Access version of this book possible. A limited amount of material in part 3 was collected as part of a project on charity, philanthropy, and development in Colombo, funded by a grant from the Economic & Social Research Council and the Department for International Development (ES/1033890/1). Some writing in part 1 was supported by a Global Challenges Research Fund (GCRF) award granted to Durham University.

This book is for my parents, Alan and Yvonne, and my children, Alba and Jessica.

GLOSSARY

Active molecule	The molecule with biocidal properties in a pesticide product and the focus of regulatory and activist attention. Glyphosate is the active molecule (or active ingredient) in all glyphosate-based herbicides, the most well known of which is Monsanto/Bayer's Roundup.
BfR	Federal Institute for Risk Assessment, Germany. Responsible for leading the safety assessment of glyphosate in 2013 and 2015, on behalf of EFSA and the EU.
CKDu	Chronic kidney disease of unknown origin. An epidemic disease in agricultural areas of Sri Lanka (and elsewhere in the world) that came to public and political attention during Sri Lanka's postwar years. CKDu became the reason the Sri Lankan government tried, several times, to ban glyphosate.
ECHA	European Chemicals Agency, part of the European Commission, responsible for chemical hazards assessment. ECHA feeds into agrochemical approval processes in the EU, led by EFSA.
EFSA	European Food Safety Authority, part of the European Commission, responsible for overseeing risk assessment and the (re)approval of active molecules in the European Union. EFSA was at the center of the glyphosate debate in Europe.
Gift	A thing given freely without payment or other kind of return. A material-semiotic description of negative or positive value, depending on what one does with it. *See* poison.

Hazard and risk	A way of separating danger into two distinct ontological domains, one an intrinsic property and the other a relational quality. In modern health and safety theory, all things contain intrinsic hazards, but they are only manifest when encountered in specific ways, for example, above a threshold level of exposure. Thus, risks are always contingent on relations in the world.
IARC	International Agency for Research on Cancer, part of the World Health Organization. IARC classified glyphosate a "probable carcinogen," setting off the EU's reassessment of glyphosate safety in 2015.
PEST committee	The European Parliament's Special Committee on EU authorization procedures for pesticides, convened in the wake of the glyphosate controversy.
Poison	A thing that poses material or symbolic danger. A material-semiotic description of negative or positive value, depending on what one does with it. *See* gift.
Poisoncraft	The field of cultural ideas and practices spanning the poison lore of folk traditions and professional toxicologies found in, for example, Paracelsianism and Ayurveda—the mythos and logos of poison.
Toxicology	Poison theory and practice that would become part of specialized medical and scientific practice, in this book explored through Ayurvedic and Paracelsian traditions.

BIBLIOGRAPHY

Abraham, Itty. 1996. "Science and Power in the Postcolonial State." *Alternatives: Global, Local, Political* 21 (3): 321–39. https://www.jstor.org/stable/40644865.

Abraham, Itty. 2006. "The Contradictory Spaces of Postcolonial Techno-Science." *Economic and Political Weekly* 41 (3): 210–17. https://www.jstor.org/stable/4417699.

Adams, Vincanne. 2023. *Glyphosate and the Swirl: An Agroindustrial Chemical on the Move*. Duke University Press.

AFP Sri Lanka. 2019. "Sri Lankan Authorities Found the Muslim Surgeon Had Not Performed Any Sterilisations." May 5.

Ali, Ameer. 2013. "Political Buddhism, Islamic Orthodoxy and Open Economy: The Toxic Triad in Sinhalese-Muslim Relations in Sri Lanka." *Journal of Asian and African Studies* 49 (3): 298–314. https://doi.org/10.1177/0021909613485708.

Almaguer, Miguel, Raul Herrera, and Carlos M. Orantes. 2014. "Chronic Kidney Disease of Unknown Etiology in Agricultural Communities." *MEDICC Review* 16 (2): 9–15. https://doi.org/10.37757/mr2014.v16.n2.3.

Alwis, A. A. P. de, and P. V. S. Panawala. 2019. "A Review of the National Response to CKDu in Sri Lanka." *Sri Lanka Journal of Social Sciences* 42 (2): 83–100. https://doi.org/10.4038/SLJSS.V42I2.7966.

Alwis, Malathi de. 2012. "'Girl Still Burning Inside My Head': Reflections on Suicide in Sri Lanka." *Contributions to Indian Sociology* 46 (1–2): 29–51. https://doi.org/10.1177/006996671104600203.

American Association for the Advancement of Science (AAAS). 2019. "AAAS Statement on the 2019 Award for Scientific Freedom and Responsibility." https://www.aaas.org/sites/default/files/2019-11/AAAS Statement on the 2019 Scientific Freedom and Responsibility Award.pdf.

American Association for the Advancement of Science (AAAS [@aaas]). 2019. "This Year's Recipients of the AAAS Award for Scientific Freedom & Responsibility." Twitter. 2019. https://twitter.com/aaas/status/1092475973650563073?lang=en.

Appadurai, Arjun. 2006. *Fear of Small Numbers: An Essay on the Geography of Anger*. Duke University Press.

Arcuri, Alessandra, and Yogi Hale Hendlin. 2019. "The Chemical Anthropocene: Glyphosate as a Case Study of Pesticide Exposures." *King's Law Journal* 30 (2): 234–53. https://doi.org/10.1080/09615768.2019.1645436.

Arnold, David. 2016. *Toxic Histories: Poison and Pollution in Modern India*. Cambridge University Press.

Auyero, Javier, and Debora Alejandra Swistun. 2009. *Flammable: Environmental Suffering in an Argentine Shantytown*. Oxford University Press.

Aven, Terje. 2016. "Risk Assessment and Risk Management: Review of Recent Advances on Their Foundation." *European Journal of Operational Research* 253 (1): 1–13. https://doi.org/10.1016/j.ejor.2015.12.023.

Bailey, F. G. 1971. "Gifts and Poisons." In *Gifts and Poisons: The Politics of Reputation*, edited by F. G. Bailey, 1–25. Basil Blackwell.

Ball, Phillip. 2006. *The Devil's Doctor: Paracelsus and the World of Renaissance Magic and Science*. Random House.

Bandara, Hansani. 2012. "FAO Blamed for Spread of Chronic Kidney Disease." *Sunday Times*, October 21, 2012.

Bandara, Kelum. 2017. "Sinhalese Culture and Theravada Buddhism Have Inseparable Link." *Daily Mirror*, February 16, 2017.

Bandarage, Asoka. 1983. *Colonialism in Sri Lanka: The Political Economy of the Kandyan Highlands, 1833–1886*. Mouton.

Bandarage, Asoka. 2013. "Political Economy of Epidemic Kidney Disease in Sri Lanka." *SAGE Open* 3 (4): 1–13. https://doi.org/10.1177/2158244013511827.

Banerjee, Pompa. 2000. "Hard to Swallow: Women, Poison, and Hindu Widowburning, 1500–1700." *Continuity and Change* 15 (2): 187–207. https://doi.org/10.1017/S0268416099003513.

Bass, Daniel. 2003. "Susantha Goonatilake, *Anthropologizing Sri Lanka: A Eurocentric Misadventure*. Bloomington: Indiana University Press, 2001." *Comparative Studies in Society and History* 45 (2): 423–24. https://doi.org/10.1017/S001041750322020X.

Bastin, Rohan. 2002. "Sorcerous Technologies and Religious Innovation in Sri Lanka." *Social Analysis* 46 (3): 155–74. https://doi.org/10.3167/015597702782409275.

Bastin, Rohan, and Premakumara de Silva. 2018. "Military Tourism as a State-Effect in the Sri Lankan Civil War." In *Military Pilgrimage and Battlefield Tourism: Commemorating the Dead*, edited by John Eade and Mario Katić, 101–24. Routledge.

Baum Hedlund Aristei & Goldman PC. 2019. "Monsanto Has Been Playing Whack-a-Mole to Derail Science for Years." https://www.baumhedlundlaw.com/blog/2019/april/new-monsanto-papers-documents/.

Bear, Laura, and Nayanika Mathur. 2015. "Remaking the Public Good: A New Anthropology of Bureaucracy." *Cambridge Journal of Anthropology* 33 (1): 18–34. https://doi.org/10.3167/ca.2015.330103.

Beck, Ulrich. 1992. *Risk Society: Towards a New Modernity*. Sage Publications.

Bennett, Jane. 1997. "The Enchanted World of Modernity: Paracelsus, Kant, and Deleuze." *Journal for Cultural Research* 1 (1): 1–28. https://doi.org/10.1080/14797589709367132.

Bennett, Jane. 2004. "The Force of Things: Steps Toward an Ecology of Matter." *Political Theory* 32 (3): 347–72. https://www.jstor.org/stable/4148158.

Benson, Peter, and Stuart Kirsch. 2010a. "Capitalism and the Politics of Resignation." *Current Anthropology* 51 (4): 459–86. https://doi.org/10.1086/653091.

Benson, Peter, and Stuart Kirsch. 2010b. "Corporate Oxymorons." *Dialectical Anthropology* 34 (1): 45–48. https://doi.org/10.1007/s10624-009-9112-y.

Berkwitz, Stephen C. 2013. *Buddhist Poetry and Colonialism: Alagiyavanna and the Portuguese in Sri Lanka*. Oxford University Press.

Berndt, Christian, Marion Werner, Finn Mempel, Annie Shattuck, and Zackary Okun Dunivin. 2025. "The Generics Revolution and the New Economic Geography of the Global Pesticide Industry." *Journal of Agrarian Change* (March). https://doi.org/10.1111/joac.70007.

Bernhardt, Emily S., Emma J. Rosi, and Mark O. Gessner. 2017. "Synthetic Chemicals as Agents of Global Change." *Frontiers in Ecology and the Environment* 15 (2): 84–90.

Bernstein, Anya, and Elizabeth Mertz. 2011. "Bureaucracy: Ethnography of the State in Everyday Life." *PoLAR: Political and Legal Anthropology Review* 34 (1): 6–10. https://doi.org/10.1111/j.1555-2934.2011.01135.x.

Bhishagratna, Kaviraj Kunjalal, ed. 1911. *The Sushruta Samhita*. Vol. II: *Nidana-Sthana, Sarira-Sthana, Chikitsita-Sthana and Kalapa-Sthana*. Published by the author.

Billé, Franck, ed. 2020. *Voluminous States: Sovereignty, Materiality, and the Territorial Imagination*. Duke University Press.

Birn, Anne-Emanuelle. 2014. "Philanthrocapitalism, Past and Present: The Rockefeller Foundation, the Gates Foundation, and the Setting(s) of the International/Global Health Agenda." *Hypothesis* 12 (1): 1–27. https://doi.org/10.5779/hypothesis.v12i1.229.

Bloch, Maurice E. F. 1998. *How We Think They Think: Anthropological Approaches to Cognition, Memory, and Literacy*. Westview Press.

Bloch, Maurice. 1999. "Commensality and Poisoning." *Social Research* 66 (1): 133–49. https://www.jstor.org/stable/40971306.

Bloor, David. 1976. *Knowledge and Social Imagery*. University of Chicago Press.

Boholm, Åsa. 2003. "The Cultural Nature of Risk: Can There Be an Anthropology of Uncertainty?" *Ethnos* 68 (2): 159–78. https://doi.org/10.1080/0014184032000097722.

Bonilla, Yarimar. 2017. "Unsettling Sovereignty." *Cultural Anthropology* 32 (3): 330–39. https://doi.org/10.14506/ca32.3.02.

Boudia, Soraya, and Nathalie Jas, eds. 2016. *Powerless Science? Science and Politics in a Toxic World*. Berghahn.

Bowker, Geoffrey C., and Susan Leigh Star. 1999. *Sorting Things Out: Classification and Its Consequences*. MIT Press.

Brow, James. 1996. *Demons and Development: The Struggle for Community in a Sri Lankan Village*. University of Arizona Press.

Bryant, Rebecca, and Madeleine Reeves. 2021. "Toward an Anthropology of Sovereign Agency." In *The Everyday Lives of Sovereignty: Political Imagination Beyond the State*, edited by Rebecca Bryant and Madeleine Reeves, 1–18. Cornell University Press.

Bryson, Sasha Turner. 2013. "The Art of Power: Poison and Obeah Accusations and the Struggle for Dominance and Survival in Jamaica's Slave Society." *Caribbean Studies* 41 (2): 61–90. https://dx.doi.org/10.1353/crb.2013.0030.

Buell, Lawrence. 2003. *Writing for an Endangered World: Literature, Culture, and Environment in the U.S. and Beyond*. Harvard University Press.

Buonsante, Vito A., Hans Muilerman, Tatiana Santos, Claire Robinson, and Anthony C. Tweedale. 2014. "Risk Assessment's Insensitive Toxicity Testing May Cause It to

Fail." *Environmental Research* 135 (November):139–47. https://doi.org/10.1016/j.envres.2014.07.016.

Burney, Ian. 2006. *Poison, Detection, and the Victorian Imagination*. Manchester University Press.

Busch, Lawrence. 2000. "The Moral Economy of Grades and Standards." *Journal of Rural Studies* 16 (3): 273–83. https://doi.org/10.1016/S0743-0167(99)00061-3.

Callon, Michel. 1986. "Some Elements of a Sociology of Translation: Domestication of the Scallops and the Fishermen of Saint Brieuc Bay." In *Power, Action, and Belief: A New Sociology of Knowledge?*, edited by John Law, 196–233. Routledge & Keagan Paul.

Candea, Matei. 2019. *Comparison in Anthropology: The Impossible Method*. University of Cambridge Press.

Candea, Matei, and Thomas Yarrow. 2024. "Emergent Explanation." In *Beyond Description: Anthropologies of Explanation*, edited by Paolo Heywood and Matei Candea, 81–103. Cornell University Press.

Carey, Matthew. 2018. *Mistrust: An Ethnographic Theory*. Hau Books.

Chakrabarty, Dipesh. 2000. *Provincializing Europe: Postcolonial Thought and Historical Difference*. Princeton University Press.

Chandrajith, R., J. P. Padmasiri, C. B. Dissanayake, and K. M. Prematilaka. 2012. "Spatial Distribution of Fluoride in Groundwater of Sri Lanka." *Journal of the National Science Foundation of Sri Lanka* 40 (4): 303–9. https://doi.org/10.4038/jnsfsr.v40i4.5044.

Chapin, Bambi L. 2014. *Childhood in a Sri Lankan Village: Shaping Hierarchy and Desire*. Rutgers University Press.

Chavkin, Sasha. 2014. "Sri Lanka Bans Leading Monsanto Herbicide Citing Deadly Disease Fears." International Consortium of Investigative Journalists. 2014. https://www.icij.org/blog/2014/03/sri-lanka-bans-leading-monsanto-herbicide-citing-deadly-disease-fears/.

Chen, Mel Y. 2012. *Animacies: Biopolitics, Racial Mattering, and Queer Affect*. Duke University Press.

Choy, Timothy. 2011. *Ecologies of Comparison: An Ethnography of Endangerment in Hong Kong*. Duke University Press.

CNN. 2004. "Bhopal Hoax Sends Dow Stock Down." December 3, 2004.

Cohen, Adam D. 2019. "Global Fight Against Lethal Herbicides Earns 2019 AAAS Scientific Freedom and Responsibility Award." https://web.archive.org/web/20190204211020/https://www.aaas.org/news/global-fight-against-lethal-herbicides-earns-2019-aaas-scientific-freedom-and-responsibility.

Cole, Luke, and Sheila Foster. 2001. *From the Ground Up: Environmental Racism and the Rise of the Environmental Justice Movement*. New York University Press.

Colombo Telegraph. 2019. "Gota Frontliner Iterates Anti-Muslim Campaign Has Been Paused for Polls." November 6.

Copeman, Jacob. 2011. "The Gift and Its Forms of Life in Contemporary India." *Modern Asian Studies* 45 (5): 1051–94. https://www.jstor.org/stable/25835712.

Copley, Caroline. 2016. "German Beer Purity in Question After Environment Group Finds Weed-Killer Traces" *Reuters*, February 25. https://www.reuters.com/article/us-germany-beer-idUSKCN0VY222/.

Correspondent. 2012. "Notes on the Military Presence in Sri Lanka's Northern Province." *Economic and Political Weekly* 47 (28): 34–40. https://www.jstor.org/stable/i23251606.

Cram, Shannon. 2016. "Living in Dose: Nuclear Work and the Politics of Permissible Exposure." *Public Culture* 29 (3): 519–39. https://doi.org/10.1215/08992363-3511526.

da Col, Giovanni. 2012. "The Poisoner and the Parasite: Cosmoeconomics, Fear, and Hospitality among Dechen Tibetans." *Journal of the Royal Anthropological Institute* 18 (Suppl. 1): 175-95. https://doi.org/10.1111/j.1467-9655.2012.01771.x.

da Col, Giovanni, and David Graeber. 2011. "Foreword: The Return of Ethnographic Theory." *HAU: Journal of Ethnographic Theory* 1 (1): vi–xxxv. https://www.journals.uchicago.edu/doi/10.14318/hau1.1.001.

Daily Mirror. 2018. "'Glyphosate Linked to Kidney Disease'—Prof. Channa Jayasumana." March 29.

Daniel, E. Valentine. 1996. *Charred Lullabies: Chapters in an Anthropography of Violence*. Princeton University Press.

Das, Veena. 1995. *Critical Events: An Anthropological Perspective on Contemporary India*. Oxford University Press.

Davis, Frederick Rowe. 2014. *Banned: A History of Pesticides and the Science of Toxicology*. Yale University Press.

Debus, Allen G. 1977. *The Chemical Philosophy: Paracelsian Science and Medicine in the Sixteenth and Seventeenth Centuries*. David & Charles.

Debus, Allen G., and Michael T. Walton, eds. 1998. *Reading the Book of Nature: The Other Side of the Scientific Revolution*. Sixteenth Century Publishers.

Deichmann, W. B., D. Henschler, B. Holmstedt, and G. Keil. 1986. "What Is There That Is Not Poison? A Study of the *Third Defense* by Paracelsus." *Archives of Toxicology* 58 (4): 207-13. https://doi.org/10.1007/bf00297107.

Deleuze, Gilles, and Félix Guattari. 2004a. *Anti-Oedipus: Capitalism and Schizophrenia*. Translated by Robert Hurley, Mark Seem, and Helen R. Lane. Continuum.

Deleuze, Gilles, and Félix Guattari. 2004b. *A Thousand Plateaus: Capitalism and Schizophrenia*. Translated by Brian Massumi. Continuum.

De Silva, K. M. 1998. *Reaping the Whirlwind: Ethnic Conflict, Ethnic Politics in Sri Lanka*. Penguin Books.

De Silva, M. W. Amarasiri, Steven M. Albert, and J. M. K. B. Jayasekara. 2017. "Structural Violence and Chronic Kidney Disease of Unknown Etiology in Sri Lanka." *Social Science & Medicine* 178: 184-95. https://doi.org/10.1016/j.socscimed.2017.02.016.

De Silva, Nalin. 2006. "Constructive Realism." Kalaya. http://www.kalaya.org/npe051127.html.

De Silva, Nalin. 2011a. "Arsenic." Kalaya. http://www1.kalaya.org/search?q=trance.

De Silva, Nalin. 2011b. "Chemical Arsenics and Other Arsenics." *Sunday Divaina*, May 15.

De Silva, Nalin. 2011c. "Devivaru, Arsenic and Science." Kalaya. http://www1.kalaya.org/search?q=arsenic.

De Silva, Nalin. 2011d. "Get Ready for a Humanitarian Attack." Kalaya. http://www1.kalaya.org/2011/05/get-ready-for-humanitarian-attack.html.

De Silva, Nalin. 2013a. "Arsenic as the Cause of CKDU." Kalaya. http://www1.kalaya.org/2013/04/arsenic-as-cause-of-ckdu.html.

De Silva, Nalin. 2013b. "Arsenic as the Cause of CKDu." *The Island Online*, March 12.

De Silva, Nalinde. 2013c. "Arsenic as the Cause of CKDu –II." *The Island Online*, March 19.

Dharmagunawardhane, H. A., and C. Dissanayake. 1993. "Fluoride Problems in Sri Lanka." Edited by C. B. Dissanayak-*Environmental Management and Health* 4 (2): 9–16. https://doi.org/10.1108/09566169310033422.

Dharmawardana, Chandre. 2016. "Combating a New Form of Kidney Disease Ravaging the Rajarata." *Sri Lankan Scientist* 2, no. 2 (October–December).

Diamond, Norma. 1988. "Miao and Poison: Interactions on China's Southwest Frontier." *Ethnology* 27 (1): 1–25. https://doi.org/10.2307/3773558.

Dolan, Catherine, and Dinah Rajak. 2016. *The Anthropology of Corporate Social Responsibility*. Berghahn.

Douglas, Mary. 1966. *Purity and Danger: An Analysis of Concepts of Pollution and Taboo*. Routledge.

Douglas, Mary. 1970. *Natural Symbols: Explorations in Cosmology*. 2nd ed. Routledge.

Douglas, Mary. 1990. "Foreword: No Free Gifts." In *The Gift: The Form and Reason for Exchange in Archaic Societies*, vii–xxviii. Routledge.

Duclos, Vincent, Tomás Sánchez Criado, and Vinh Kim Nguyen. 2017. "Speed: An Introduction." *Cultural Anthropology* 32 (1): 1–11. https://doi.org/10.14506/ca32.1.01.

Dumit, Joseph. 2006. "Illnesses You Have to Fight to Get: Facts as Forces in Uncertain, Emergent Illnesses." *Social Science and Medicine* 62 (3): 577–90. https://doi.org/10.1016/j.socscimed.2005.06.018.

Dumont, Louis. 1970. *Homo Hierarchicus: The Caste System and Its Implications*. Translated by Mark Sainsbury. University of Chicago Press.

Dumont, Louis. [1980] 2013. "On Value." *HAU: Journal of Ethnographic Theory* 3 (1): 287–315. https://doi.org/10.14318/hau3.1.028.

Dunn, Elizabeth Cullen. 2012. "The Chaos of Humanitarian Aid: Adhocracy in the Republic of Georgia." *Humanity: An International Journal of Human Rights, Humanitarianism, and Development* 3 (1): 1–23. https://doi.org/10.1353/hum.2012.0005.

Durkheim, Émile. 1933. *The Division of Labour in Society*. Translated by George Simpson. Free Press.

Edelman, M., T. Weis, A. Baviskar, S. M. Borras Jr., E. Holt-Giménez, D. Kandiyoti, and W. Wolford. 2014. "Introduction: Critical Perspectives on Food Sovereignty." *Journal of Peasant Studies* 41 (6): 911–31. https://doi.org/10.1080/03066150.2014.963568.

Eriksen, Thomas Hylland. 2016. *Overheating: An Anthropology of Accelerated Change*. Pluto Press.

Esposito, Roberto. 2011. *Immunitas: The Protection and Negation of Life*. Polity Press.

European Chemicals Agency. 2011. "Guidance on Information Requirements and Chemical Safety Assessment." Helsinki. December. https://www.echa.europa.eu/guidance-documents/guidance-on-information-requirements-and-chemical-safety-assessment.

European Coal and Steel Community (ECSC), High Authority. 1951. "Treaty Establishing the European Coal and Steel Community." https://eur-lex.europa.eu/legal-content/EN/TXT/?uri=CELEX:11951K.

European Commission. 2017. "Communication from the Commission on the European Citizens' Initiative 'Ban Glyphosate and Protect People and the Environment from Toxic Pesticides.'" Strasbourg.

European Commission. Directorate-General for Communication and Jean-Claude Juncker. 2016. "State of the Union 2016." Publications Office of the European Union. https://data.europa.eu/doi/10.2775/968989.

European Commission. Directorate-General for Communication and Jean-Claude Juncker. 2018. "State of the Union 2018." Publications Office of the European Union. https:/commission.europa.eu/strategy-and-policy/strategic-planning/state-union-addresses/state-union-speeches/state-union-2018_en/.

European Commission. Group of Chief Scientific Advisors. 2016. "Explanatory Note on Scientific Advice for the Regulatory Assessment of Glyphosate in Plant Protection Products." Brussels. https://scientificadvice.eu/advice/glyphosate/.
European Food Safety Authority (EFSA). 2023. "Hazard vs. Risk." https://www.efsa.europa.eu/en/campaigns/hazard-vs-risk#:~:text=Risk%3A,of%20a%20hazard%20causing%20harm.
European Parliament. 2016. "EU's Pesticide Risk Assessment System: The Case of Glyphosate. Study for the ENVI Committee." Strasbourg.
European Parliament and Council of the European Union. 2009. "Regulation (EC) No 1107/2009 of the European Parliament and of the Council of 21 October 2009 Concerning the Placing of Plant Protection Products on the Market and Repealing Council Directives 79/117/EEC and 91/414/EEC." *Official Journal of the European Union.* https://eur-lex.europa.eu/eli/reg/2009/1107/oj.
Evans-Pritchard, E. E. 1976. *Witchcraft, Oracles, and Magic Among the Azande.* Abridged ed. Clarendon Press.
Evers, Hans-Dieter. 1972. *Monks, Priests, and Peasants: A Study of Buddhism and Social Structure in Central Ceylon.* Brill.
Falzon, Mark-Anthony. 2020. *Birds of Passage: Hunting and Conservation in Malta.* Berghahn.
Farmer, Jared. 2002. *Elderflora: A Modern History of Ancient Trees.* Picador.
Fernando, Manjula. 2011. "Key to Mystery Killer Disease Found." *Sunday Observer,* June 12.
Folta, Kevin. 2019. "What Am I Missing?" *Illumination 2.0.* https://kfolta.blogspot.com/2019/02/what-am-i-missing.html.
Fortun, Kim. 2001. *Advocacy After Bhopal: Environmentalism, Disaster, New Global Orders.* University of Chicago Press.
Fortun, Kim. 2010. "Essential2life." *Dialectical Anthropology* 34 (1): 77–86.
Fortun, Kim, and Mike Fortun. 2005. "Scientific Imaginaries and Ethical Plateaus in Contemporary U.S. Toxicology." *American Anthropologist* 107 (1): 43–54. https://doi.org/10.1525/aa.2005.107.1.043.
Foucault, Michel. 1979. "What Is an Author?" In *Textual Strategies,* edited by Josue V. Harari, 141–60. Cornell University Press.
Fox, Richard G. 2002. "The Study of Historical Transformation in American Anthropology." In *Anthropology, by Comparison,* edited by Andre Gingrich and Richard G. Fox, 187–202. Routledge.
Frank, Patricia, and M. Alice Ottoboni. 2011. *The Dose Makes the Poison: A Plain-Language Guide to Toxicology.* Wiley.
Galt, Ryan E. 2008. "Beyond the Circle of Poison: Significant Shifts in the Global Pesticide Complex, 1976–2008." *Global Environmental Change* 18 (4): 786–99. https://doi.org/10.1016/j.gloenvcha.2008.07.003.
German Federal Institute for Risk Assessment (BfR). 2015. "Final Addendum to the Renewal Assessment Report (Public Version)—Glyphosate." https://bartstaes.be/assets/data/files/Documents/CopyPasteStudy/Final_Addendum_to_the_Renewal_Assessment_Report_Public_Version.pdf.
Geschiere, Peter. 2009. *The Perils of Belonging: Autochthony, Citizenship, and Exclusion in Europe and Africa.* University of Chicago Press. https://doi.org/10.1353/anq.0.0059.

Geschiere, Peter. 2013. *Witchcraft, Intimacy, and Trust: Africa in Comparison*. University of Chicago Press.
Giddens, Anthony. 1999. *Runaway World: How Globalization Is Reshaping Our Lives*. Profile.
Gillam, Carey. 2017. *Whitewash: The Story of a Weed Killer, Cancer, and the Corruption of Science*. Island Press.
Gillam, Carey. 2021a. *The Monsanto Papers: Deadly Secrets, Corporate Corruption, and One Man's Search for Justice*. Island Press.
Gillam, Carey. 2021b. "Revealed: Monsanto Owner and US Officials Pressured Mexico to Drop Glyphosate Ban." *The Guardian*, February 16.
Gillin, J. 1934. "Crime and Punishment among the Barama River Carib of British Guiana." *American Anthropologist* 36 (3): 331–44. https://www.jstor.org/stable/662148.
Gingrich, Andre, and Richard G. Fox, eds. 2002. *Anthropology, by Comparison*. Routledge.
Goldstein, Donna M. 2014. "Toxic Uncertainties of a Nuclear Era: Anthropology, History, Memoir." *American Ethnologist* 41 (3): 579–84. https://doi.org/10.1111/amet.12087.
Gombrich, Richard F. 1971. *Buddhist Precept and Practice: Traditional Buddhism in the Rural Highlands of Ceylon*. Routledge.
Gombrich, Richard, and Gananath Obeyesekere. 1988. *Buddhism Transformed: Religious Change in Sri Lanka*. Princeton University Press.
Goody, Jack. 2010. *The Eurasian Miracle*. Polity Press.
Gooneratne, I. K., A. K. P. Ranaweera, N. P. Liyanarachchi, N. Gunawardane, and R. D. Lanerolle. 2008. "Epidemiology of Chronic Kidney Disease in a Sri Lankan Population." *International Journal of Diabetes in Developing Countries* 28 (2): 60. https://doi.org/10.4103/0973-3930.43101.
Gould-Martin, Katherine. 1978. "Hot Cold Clean Poison and Dirt: Chinese Folk Medical Categories." *Social Science and Medicine* 12 (C): 39–46. https://doi.org/10.1016/0160-7987(78)90006-6.
Graeber, David. 2011. *Debt: The First 5,000 Years*. Melville House.
Graeber, David. 2015. *The Utopia of Rules: On Technology, Stupidity, and the Secret Joys of Bureaucracy*. Melville House.
Graeber, David, and Marshall Sahlins. 2017. *On Kings*. Hau Books.
Grandjean, Philippe. 2016. "Paracelsus Revisited: The Dose Concept in a Complex World." *Basic & Clinical Pharmacology & Toxicology* 119 (2): 126–32. https://doi.org/10.1111/cpt.12622.
Green Party. 2016. "Green Party MEPs Peed Off with Glyphosate Test Results." May 13. https://www.greenparty.org.uk/news/2016/05/13/green-party-meps-peed-off-with-glyphosate-test-results/.
Gregory, Christopher A. 1992. "The Poison in Raheja's Gift: A Review Article." *Social Analysis* 32 (December): 95–110. https://www.jstor.org/stable/23164554.
Gunawardene, Nalaka. 2012a. "Science and Politics of Mass Kidney Failure in Sri Lanka." Groundviews. 2012. https://groundviews.org/2012/08/19/science-and-politics-of-mass-kidney-failure-in-sri-lanka/.
Gunawardene, Nalaka. 2012b. "Watch Out! Everybody Lives Downstream." When Worlds Collide. https://collidecolumn.wordpress.com/2012/08/26/when-worlds-collide-30-watch-out-everybody-lives-downstream/.
Guneratne, Arjun. 2004. "Slash and Burn: A Swidden Critique of Sri Lankan Anthropology, *Anthropologizing Sri Lanka: A Eurocentric Misadventure*, by Susantha Goonatilake.

Bloomington: Indiana University Press, 2001. 306 Pp." *Current Anthropology* 45 (5): 718–20. https://doi.org/10.1086/425640.

Gupta, Akhil. 2012. *Red Tape: Bureaucracy, Structural Violence, and Poverty in India*. Duke University Press.

Haas, Peter M. 1992. "Introduction: Epistemic Communities and International Policy Coordination." *International Organization* 46 (1): 1–35.

Hacking, Ian. 1995. "The Looping Effects of Human Kinds." In *Causal Cognition: A Multi-Disciplinary Debate*, edited by Dan Sperber, David Premack, and Ann James Premack, 351–83. Harvard University Press.

Hacking, Ian. 2002. *Historical Ontology*. Harvard University Press.

Hacking, Ian. 2015. "Biopower and the Avalanche of Printed Numbers." In *Biopower: Foucault and Beyond*, edited by Vernon W. Cisney and Nicolae Morar, 65–80. University of Chicago Press.

Hamdy, Sherine F. 2008. "When the State and Your Kidneys Fail: Political Etiologies in an Egyptian Dialysis Ward." *American Ethnologist* 35 (4): 553–69. https://doi.org/10.1111/j.1548-1425.2008.00098.x.

Handunnetti, Dilrukshi. 2019. "'Science Prevails' as Suspension of Award for Herbicide Research Is Reversed." Mongabay. https://news.mongabay.com/2019/11/science-prevails-as-suspension-of-award-for-herbicide-research-is-reversed/.

Hansen, Thomas Blom, and Finn Stepputat. 2006. "Sovereignty Revisited." *Annual Review of Anthropology* 35 (1): 295–315. https://doi.org/10.1146/annurev.anthro.35.081705.123317.

Harding, Sandra. 2009. "Postcolonial and Feminist Philosophies of Science and Technology: Convergences and Dissonances." *Postcolonial Studies* 12 (4): 401–21. https://doi.org/10.1080/13688790903350658.

Hardt, Michael, and Antonio Negri. 2000. *Empire*. Harvard University Press.

Harman, Graham. 2005. *Guerrilla Metaphysics: Phenomenology and the Carpentry of Things*. Open Court.

Harman, Graham. 2018. *Object-Oriented Ontology: A New Theory of Everything*. Pelican.

Harrell-Bond, B. E. 1978. "The Fear of Poisoning and the Management of Urban Social Relations Among the Professional Group in Freetown, Sierra Leone." *Urban Anthropology* 7 (3): 229–51. https://www.jstor.org/stable/40552826.

Harris, Jonathan Gil. 1998. *Foreign Bodies and the Body Politic: Discourses of Social Pathology in Early Modern England*. Cambridge University Press.

Hawkes, Jacquetta. 1967. "God in the Machine." *Antiquity* 41 (163): 174–80.

Heatherington, Tracey. 2010. *Wild Sardinia: Indigeneity and the Global Dreamtimes of Environmentalism*. University of Washington Press.

Helfield, Randa. 1995. "Poisonous Plots: Women Sensation Novelists and the Murderesses of the Victorian Period." *Victorian Review* 21 (2): 161–88. https://www.jstor.org/stable/27794809.

Hepler-Smith, Evan. 2019. "Molecular Bureaucracy: Toxicological Information and Environmental Protection." *Environmental History* 24 (3): 534–60.

Hettiarachchi, Kumudini. 2014. "Expert Body Seeks Meeting with President on Proposed Glyphosate Ban." *Sunday Times*, March 16.

Hickel, Jason, and Naomi Haynes, eds. 2018. *Hierarchy and Value: Comparative Perspectives on Moral Order*. Berghahn.

Holbraad, Martin, and Morten Axel Pedersen. 2017. *The Ontological Turn: An Anthropological Exposition.* Cambridge University Press.

Holt, John Clifford, ed. 2016. *Buddhist Extremists and Muslim Minorities: Religious Conflict in Contemporary Sri Lanka.* Oxford University Press.

Hopkinson, Leo. 2022. "Only One Mayweather: A Critique of Hope from the Hopeful." *Journal of the Royal Anthropological Institute* 28 (3): 725–45. https://doi.org/10.1111/1467-9655.13762.

Horst, Maja, and Alan Irwin. 2010. "Nations at Ease with Radical Knowledge: On Consensus, Consensusing and False Consensusness." *Social Studies of Science* 40 (1): 105–26. https://doi.org/10.1177/0306312709341500.

Hull, Matthew S. 2012. "Documents and Bureaucracy." *Annual Review of Anthropology* 41 (1): 251–67. https://doi.org/10.1146/annurev.anthro.012809.104953.

Human Rights Watch. 2018. "'Why Can't We Go Home?': Military Occupation of Land in Sri Lanka." https://www.hrw.org/report/2018/10/09/why-cant-we-go-home/military-occupation-land-sri-lanka.

Hyndman, Jennifer, and Amarnath Amarasingam. 2014. "Touring 'Terrorism': Landscapes of Memory in Post-War Sri Lanka." *Geography Compass* 8 (8): 560–75. https://doi.org/10.1111/gec3.12149.

Ibrahim, F. 2014. "Intimate Gifts and 'Bad' Deaths: Reflections on Organ Transplants, State and Society in Gujarat." *Contributions to Indian Sociology* 48 (2): 165–90. https://doi.org/10.1177/0069966714525161.

Ileperuma, Oliver A. 2011. "Chronic Renal Failure in NCP and Arsenic: Science Versus Myth." *Sunday Times*, July.

Im, Eun-Soon, Jeremy S. Pal, and Elfatih A. B. Eltahir. 2017. "Deadly Heat Waves Projected in the Densely Populated Agricultural Regions of South Asia." *Science Advances* 3 (8): e1603322. https://doi.org/10.1126/sciadv.1603322.

Imtiyaz, A. R. M., and Amjad Mohamed-Saleem. 2015. "Muslims in Post-War Sri Lanka: Understanding Sinhala-Buddhist Mobilization Against Them." *Asian Ethnicity* 16 (2): 186–202. https://doi.org/10.1080/14631369.2015.1003691.

Indika, Suresh, Yuansong Wei, Titus Cooray, Tharindu Ritigala, K. B. S. N. Jinadasa, Sujithra K. Weragoda, and Rohan Weerasooriya. 2022. "Groundwater-Based Drinking Water Supply in Sri Lanka: Status and Perspectives." *Water* 14 (9): 1428. https://doi.org/10.3390/w14091428.

International Agency for Research on Cancer (IARC). 2015. "IARC Monographs Volume 112: Evaluation of Five Organophosphate Insecticides and Herbicides." March. https://publications.iarc.who.int/549

International Agency for Research on Cancer (IARC). 2019. "IARC Monographs on the Identification of Carcinogenic Hazards to Humans: Questions and Answers." https://monographs.iarc.who.int/wp-content/uploads/2018/07/IARCMonographs-QA.pdf.

International Monsanto Tribunal. n.d. "'Tribunal.'" Accessed July 28, 2021. https://www.monsanto-tribunal.org/How.

Jasanoff, Sheila. 1995. "Procedural Choices in Regulatory Science." *Technology in Society* 17 (3): 279–93. https://doi.org/10.1016/0160-791X(95)00011-F.

Jasanoff, Sheila. 2005. *Designs on Nature: Science and Democracy in Europe and the United States.* Princeton University Press.

Jasanoff, Sheila, and Hilton R. Simmet. 2017. "No Funeral Bells: Public Reason in a 'Post-Truth' Age." *Social Studies of Science* 47 (5): 751–70. https://doi.org/10.1177/0306312717731936.

Jaspers, Karl. 1953. *The Origin and Goal of History*. Translated by Michael Bullock. Yale University Press.

Jaworski, Katrina. 2014. *The Gender of Suicide: Knowledge Production, Theory and Suicidology*. Routledge.

Jayasinghe, Saroj. 2011. "Conceptualising Population Health: From Mechanistic Thinking to Complexity Science." *Emerging Themes in Epidemiology* 8 (2): 1–7. https://doi.org/10.1186/1742-7622-8-2.

Jayasinghe, Saroj. 2014. "Chronic Kidney Disease of Unknown Etiology Should Be Renamed Chronic Agrochemical Nephropathy." *MEDICC Review* 16 (2): 72–74. https://doi.org/10.37757/mr2014.v16.n2.12.

Jayasinghe, Saroj, and Chula Herath. 2018. "Keep Glyphosate Ban: Use Precautionary Principle." *The Island Online*, March 28. http://www.island.lk/index.php?page_cat=article-details&page=article-details&code_title=182253.

Jayasinghe, Saroj, Lars Lind, Samira Salihovic, Anders Larsson, and P. Monica Lind. 2019. "DDT and Its Metabolites Could Contribute to the Aetiology of Chronic Kidney Disease of Unknown Aetiology (CKDu) and More Studies Are a Priority." *Science of the Total Environment* 649: 1638–39. https://doi.org/10.1016/j.scitotenv.2018.09.116.

Jayasinghe, Saroj, and Yong-Guan Zhu. 2020. "Chronic Kidney Disease of Unknown Etiology (CKDu): Using a System Dynamics Model to Conceptualize the Multiple Environmental Causative Pathways of the Epidemic." *Science of the Total Environment* 705: 135766. https://doi.org/10.1016/j.scitotenv.2019.135766.

Jayasumana, Channa. 2014. "Glyphosate and Its Defenders—A Reply." *The Island Online*, June 25.

Jayasumana, Channa. 2016. "Memo N°3: Channa Jayasumana Health Expert, Sri Lanka La Haye, October 15th–16th, 2016." Monsanto Tribunal. https://en.monsantotribunal.org/upload/asset_cache/1053455779.pdf?rnd=0O0Yls.

Jayasumana, Channa, Sarath Gunatilake, and Priyantha Senanayake. 2014. "Glyphosate, Hard Water and Nephrotoxic Metals: Are They the Culprits Behind the Epidemic of Chronic Kidney Disease of Unknown Etiology in Sri Lanka?" *International Journal of Environmental Research and Public Health* 11 (2): 2125–47. https://doi.org/10.3390/ijerph110202125.

Jayawardana, Sandun. 2018. "Glyphosate Ban Lifted." *Sunday Times*, July 15.

Jazeel, Tariq. 2013. *Sacred Modernity: Nature, Environment, and the Postcolonial Geographies of Sri Lankan Nationhood*. Social Scientists' Association.

Jeffery, Roger, and Patricia Jeffery. 1997. *Population, Gender and Politics: Demographic Change in Rural North India*. Cambridge University Press.

Jeganathan, Pradeep, and Qadri M. Ismail, eds. 1995. *Unmaking the Nation: The Politics of Identity and History in Modern Sri Lanka*. Social Scientists' Association.

Juncker, Jean-Claude. 2016. "Speech by President Jean-Claude Juncker at the Annual General Meeting of the Hellenic Federation of Enterprises (SEV)." European Commission. June 21. https://ec.europa.eu/commission/presscorner/detail/de/SPEECH_16_2293.

Kandasamy, Niro. 2019. "Sri Lanka Election: Will the Country See a Return to Strongman Politics?" The Conversation. 2019. https://theconversation.com/sri-lanka-election-will-the-country-see-a-return-to-strongman-politics-125806.

Kapferer, Bruce. 1988. *Legends of People, Myths of State*. Smithsonian Institution Press.
Kapferer, Bruce. 2005a. "Introduction: Oligarchic Corporations and New State Formations." *Social Analysis* 49 (1): 163–76. https://www.jstor.org/stable/23175299.
Kapferer, Bruce. 2005b. "New Formations of Power, the Oligarchic-Corporate State, and Anthropological Ideological Discourse." *Anthropological Theory* 5 (3): 285–99. https://doi.org/10.1177/1463499605055961.
Kase, Robert, Muris Korkaric, Inge Werner, and Marlene Ågerstrand. 2016. "Criteria for Reporting and Evaluating Ecotoxicity Data (CRED): Comparison and Perception of the Klimisch and CRED Methods for Evaluating Reliability and Relevance of Ecotoxicity Studies." *Environmental Sciences Europe* 28 (1): 1–14. https://doi.org/10.1186/s12302-016-0073-x.
Katsanidou, Alexia, Ann-Kathrin Reinl, and Christina Eder. 2022. "Together We Stand? Transnational Solidarity in the EU in Times of Crises." *European Union Politics* 23 (1): 66–78. https://doi.org/10.1177/14651165211035663.
Kaufman, David B. 1932. "Poisons and Poisoning Among the Romans." *Classical Philology* 27 (2): 156–67.
Keane, Helen. 2002. *What's Wrong with Addiction?* University of Melbourne Press.
Kelly, Ann H., Frederic Keck, and Christos Lynteris. 2019. *The Anthropology of Epidemics*. Routledge.
Kemper, Steven. 1991. *The Presence of the Past: Chronicles, Politics, and Culture in Sinhala Life*. Cornell University Press.
Kenworthy, Nora, Lynn M. Thomas, and Johanna Crane. 2018. "Introduction: Critical Perspectives on US Global Health Partnerships in Africa and Beyond." *Medicine Anthropology Theory* 5 (2). https://doi.org/10.17157/mat.5.1.613.
Kierans, Ciara. 2020. *Chronic Failures: Kidneys, Regimes of Care, and the Mexican State*. Rutgers University Press.
Kierans, Ciara, and Cesar Padilla-Altamira. 2021. "Describing Chronic Kidney Disease of Unknown Origin: Anthropological Noticing and the 'Residual' Category." *Qualitative Research* 21 (3): 360–75. https://doi.org/10.1177/1468794120972605.
Kirindi, Chandani. 2014. "Dangerous Weedicide: No Total Ban." *Sunday Times*, March.
Klimisch, H.-J., M. Andreae, and U. Tillmann. 1997. "A Systematic Approach for Evaluating the Quality of Experimental Toxicological and Ecotoxicological Data." *Regulatory Toxicology and Pharmacology* 25 (1): 1–5. https://doi.org/10.1006/rtph.1996.1076.
Konrad, Monica. 2005. *Nameless Relations: Anonymity, Melanesia and Reproductive Gift Exchange Between British Ova Donors and Recipients*. Berghahn.
Krishna, Sankaran. 1994. "Cartographic Anxiety: Mapping the Body Politic in India." *Alternatives: Global, Local, Political* 19 (4): 507–21. https://www.jstor.org/stable/40644820.
Krishna, Sankaran. 1999. *Postcolonial Insecurities: India, Sri Lanka, and the Question of Nationhood*. University of Minnesota Press.
Kularatne, S. A. M. 2015. "CKD in Rajarata Surfaced in Early 90s: Unpublished Personal Experience." *The Island Online*, June 19.
Lahusen, Christian, and Maria Grasso. 2018. "Solidarity in Europe—European Solidarity: An Introduction." In *Solidarity in Europe*, edited by Christian Lahusen and Maria Grasso, 1–18. Palgrave Macmillan.
Lane, Richard W., and Joseph F. Borzelleca. 2008. "Harming and Helping Through Time: The History of Toxicology." In *The Principles and Methods of Toxicology*, 5th ed., edited by A. Wallace Hayes, 3–44. CRC Press.

Langston, Nancy. 2010. *Toxic Bodies: Hormone Disruptors and the Legacy of DES*. Yale University Press.
Lanka Business Online. 2018. "Planters' Association Hails Decision to Lift Ban on Glyphosate." May 2.
Lanka News Web. 2019. "Personal Grudge Between Safi and Channa Jayasumana!" https://www.lankanewsweb.net/66-special-news/44612-Personal-grudge-between-Safi-and-Channa-Jayasumana-.
Latour, Bruno. 1990. "Postmodern? No, Simply Amodern! Steps Towards an Anthropology of Science." *Studies in History and Philosophy of Science Part A* 21 (1): 145–71. https://doi.org/10.1016/0039-3681(90)90018-4.
Latour, Bruno. 2004. "Why Has Critique Run out of Steam? From Matters of Fact to Matters of Concern." *Critical Inquiry* 30 (2): 225–48. https://doi.org/10.1086/421123.
Latour, Bruno. 2005. *Reassembling the Social: An Introduction to Actor-Network-Theory*. Oxford University Press.
Latour, Bruno, and Paolo Fabbri. 2000. "The Rhetoric of Science: Authority and Duty in an Article from the Exact Sciences." *Technostyle* 16 (1): 115–34. https://doi.org/10.31468/cjsdwr.449.
Latour, Bruno, and Steve Woolgar. 1986. *Laboratory Life: The Construction of Scientific Facts*. Princeton University Press.
Law, John, and Wen Yuan Lin. 2017. "Provincializing STS: Postcoloniality, Symmetry, and Method." *East Asian Science, Technology and Society* 11 (2): 211–27. https://doi.org/10.1215/18752160-3823859.
Leach, Edmund. 1968. *A Runaway World?* British Broadcasting Corporation.
Lefort, Claude. 1986. *The Political Forms of Modern Society: Bureaucracy, Democracy, Totalitarianism*. Edited by John B. Thompson. MIT Press.
Levey, Martin. 1963. "Ibn Al-Wahshiya's 'Book of Poisons,' 'Kitab al-Sumum': Studies in the History of Arabic Pharmacology II." *Journal of the History of Medicine and Allied Sciences* 18 (4): 370–77. https://doi.org/10.1093/jhmas/xviii.4.370.
Levey, Martin. 1966. "Medieval Arabic Toxicology: The Book on Poisons of Ibn Wahshiya and Its Relation to Early Indian and Greek Texts." *Transactions of the American Philosophical Society* 56 (7): 1–110.
Li, Hwei. 1960. "On Parasites, Poison and Witchcraft in Ancient China and the Modern Southwest." *Bulletin of the Institute of Ethnology, Academia Sinica*, no. 9: 271–84.
Liboiron, Max. 2017. "Toxins or Toxicants? Why the Difference Matters." Discard Studies: Social Studies of Waste, Pollution & Externalities. https://discardstudies.com/2017/09/11/toxins-or-toxicants-why-the-difference-matters/.
Liu, ChiChing, Alan T. Linde, and I. Selwyn Sacks. 2009. "Slow Earthquakes Triggered by Typhoons." *Nature* 459 (7248): 833–36. https://doi.org/10.1038/nature08042.
Lynch, Caitrin. 2002. "Anthropologizing Sri Lanka: A Eurocentric Misadventure." *American Anthropologist* 104 (4): 1240–41. https://doi.org/10.1525/aa.2002.104.4.1240.2.
Lynch, Michael. 2017. "STS, Symmetry and Post-Truth." *Social Studies of Science* 47 (4): 593–99.
Madduma Bandara, C. M. 1985. "The Mahaweli Strategy of Sri Lanka—Great Expectation of a Small Nation." In *Strategies for River Basin Management*, edited by J. Lundqvist, U. Lohm, and M. Falkenmark, 265–77. Springer.
Malinowski, Bronisław. 1922. *Argonauts of the Western Pacific: An Account of Native Enterprise and Adventure in the Archipelagos of Melanesian New Guinea*. Routledge and Kegan Paul.

Malkan, Stacy. 2003. "Chemical Trespass: The Chemical Body Burden and the Threat to Public Health." *Multinational Monitor* 24 (4): 9–13.

Manderson, Lenore. 1981. "Traditional Food Beliefs and Critical Life Events in Peninsular Malaysia." *Social Science Information* 20 (6): 947–75. https://doi.org/10.1177/053901848102000606.

Maskiell, Michelle, and Adrienne Mayor. 2001a. "Killer Khilats, Part 1: Legends of Poisoned 'Robes of Honour' in India." *Folklore* 112 (1): 23–45. https://doi.org/10.1080/00155870120037920.

Maskiell, Michelle, and Adrienne Mayor. 2001b. "Killer Khilats, Part 2: Imperial Collecting of Poison Dress Legends in India." *Folklore* 112 (2): 163–82. https://doi.org/10.1080/00155870120082218.

Mauss, Marcel. [1925] 1990. *The Gift: Forms and Functions of Exchange in Archaic Societies*. Translated by W. D. Hall. Routledge.

McDonough, P., and E. Tsourdi. 2012. "The 'Other' Greek Crisis: Asylum and EU Solidarity." *Refugee Survey Quarterly* 31 (4): 67–100. https://www.jstor.org/stable/45054948.

McGilvray, Dennis B. 2008. *Crucible of Conflict: Tamil and Muslim Society on the East Coast of Sri Lanka*. Duke University Press.

McGoey, Linsey. 2007. "On the Will to Ignorance in Bureaucracy." *Economy and Society* 36 (2): 212–35. https://doi.org/10.1080/03085140701254282.

McMahan, David L. 2002. *Empty Vision: Metaphor and Visionary Imagery in Mahayana Buddhism*. RoutledgeCurzon.

Ministry of Finance. 2019. "National Policy Framework Vistas of Prosperity and Splendour." Colombo.

Mintz, Sidney W. 1985. *Sweetness and Power: The Place of Sugar in Modern History*. Penguin Books.

Mintz, Sidney W., and Christine M. Du Bois. 2002. "The Anthropology of Food and Eating." *Annual Review of Anthropology* 31 (1): 99–119. https://doi.org/10.1146/annurev.anthro.32.032702.131011.

Moore, Mick. 1993. "Thoroughly Modern Revolutionaries: The JVP in Sri Lanka." *Modern Asian Studies* 27 (3): 593–642. https://doi.org/10.1017/S0026749X00010908.

Mori, Shoko, Eve J. Lowenstein, and Charles Steffen. 2018. "The Largest Mass Poisoning in History: Arsenic Contamination of Well Water in Bangladesh." *Skinmed*. http://europepmc.org/abstract/MED/30207531.

Morrison, B. M., M. P. Moore, and M. U. Ishak Lebbe. 1979. *The Disintegrating Village: Social Change in Rural Sri Lanka*. Lake House Investments.

Muggah, Robert. 2008. *Relocation Failures in Sri Lanka: A Short History of Internal Displacement and Resettlement*. Zed Books.

Mukharji, Projit Bihari. 2016. "Parachemistries: Colonial Chemopolitics in a Zone of Contest." *History of Science* 54 (4): 362–82. https://doi.org/10.1177/0073275316681803.

Munn, Nancy D. 1986. *The Fame of Gawa: A Symbolic Study of Value Transformation in a Massim (Papua New Guinea) Society*. Duke University Press.

Murphy, Michelle. 2006. *Sick Building Syndrome and the Problem of Uncertainty: Environmental Politics, Technoscience, and Women Workers*. Duke University Press.

Murphy, Michelle. 2013. "Studying Unformed Objects: Deviation." *Cultural Anthropology* website. https://culanth.org/fieldsights/364-studying-unformed-objects-deviation.

Murphy, Michelle. 2017. "Alterlife and Decolonial Chemical Relations." *Cultural Anthropology* 32 (4): 494–503. https://doi.org/10.14506/ca32.4.02.

Nanda, Meera. 2001. "We Are All Hybrids Now: The Dangerous Epistemology of Post-Colonial Populism." *Journal of Peasant Studies* 28 (2): 162–86. https://doi.org/10.1080/03066150108438770.

Nanda, Meera. 2003. *Prophets Facing Backward: Postmodern Critiques of Science and Hindu Nationalism in India*. Rutgers University Press.

Napoli, Ester di, and Deborah Russo. 2018. "Solidarity in the European Union in Times of Crisis: Towards 'European Solidarity'?" In *Solidarity as a Public Virtue? Law and Public Policies in the European Union*, edited by Veronica Federico and Christian Lahusen, 193–248. Nomos Verlagsgesellschaft.

National Academy of Sciences of Sri Lanka (NASSL). 2015. "NASSL Statement on the Banning of Glyphosate." Press Release.

Neslen, Arthur. 2017. "EU Report on Weedkiller Safety Copied Text from Monsanto Study." *The Guardian*, September 15. https://www.theguardian.com/environment/2017/sep/15/eu-report-on-weedkiller-safety-copied-text-from-monsanto-study.

News.lk: The Government Official News Portal. 2015. "Govt. Issues Gazette Notification Banning Glyphosate." https://www.news.lk/news/political-current-affairs/item/8198-govt-issues-gazette-notification-banning-glyphosate.

Nguyen, Vinh-Kim. 2019. "Of What Are Epidemics the Symptom? Speed, Interlinkage, and Infrastructure in Molecular Anthropology." In *The Anthropology of Epidemics*, edited by Ann H. Kelly, Frederic Keck, and Christos Lynteris, 154–77. Routledge.

Nicholls, Clara Ines, and Miguel A. Altieri. 1997. "Conventional Agricultural Development Models and the Persistence of the Pesticide Treadmill in Latin America." *International Journal of Sustainable Development & World Ecology* 4 (2): 93–111. https://doi.org/10.1080/13504509709469946.

Noys, Benjamin. 2014. *Malign Velocities: Accelerationism & Capitalism*. Zero Books.

Obeyesekere, Gananath. 1963. "The Great Tradition and the Little in the Perspective of Sinhalese Buddhism." *Journal of Asian Studies* 22 (2): 139–53. https://doi.org/10.2307/2050008.

Obeyesekere, Gananath. 1977. "Social Change and the Deities: Rise of the Kataragama Cult in Modern Sri Lanka." *Man* 12 (3–4): 377. https://www.jstor.org/stable/2800544.

Obeyesekere, Gananath. 1978. "The Fire-Walkers of Kataragama: The Rise of Bhakti Religiosity in Buddhist Sri Lanka." *Journal of Asian Studies* 37 (3): 457–76. https://doi.org/10.2307/2053572.

Obeyesekere, Gananath. 1979. "Religion and Polity in Theravada Buddhism: Continuity and Change in a Great Tradition. A Review Article." *Comparative Studies in Society and History* 21 (4): 626. https://doi.org/10.1017/S0010417500013220.

Obeyesekere, Gananath. 1981. *Medusa's Hair: An Essay on Personal Symbols and Religious Experience*. University of Chicago Press.

Obeyesekere, Gananath. 1984. *Origins and the Institutionalization of Political Violence*. Edited by James Manor. St. Martin's Press.

Ondaatje, Michael. *Anil's Ghost*. Vintage Books, 2001.

Ong, Aihwa. 2006. *Neoliberalism as Exception: Mutations in Citizenship and Sovereignty*. Duke University Press.

Oreskes, Naomi, and Erik M. Conway. 2010. *Merchants of Doubt: How a Handful of Scientists Obscured the Truth on Issues from Tobacco Smoke to Global Warming*. Bloomsbury Press.

Ortner, Sherry B. 2016. "Dark Anthropology and Its Others: Theory Since the Eighties." *HAU: Journal of Ethnographic Theory* 6 (1): 47–73. https://doi.org/10.14318/hau6.1.004.

Osella, Filippo, and Caroline Osella. 1996. "Articulation of Physical and Social Bodies in Kerala." *Contributions to Indian Sociology* 30 (1): 37–68. https://doi.org/10.1177/006996679603000102.

Ostling, Michael. 2013. "'Poison and Enchantment Rule Ruthenia': Witchcraft, Superstition, and Ethnicity in the Polish-Lithuanian Commonwealth." *Russian History* 40 (3–4): 488–507. https://doi.org/10.1163/18763316-04004013.

Parry, Jonathan. 1986. "The Gift, the Indian Gift and the 'Indian Gift.'" *Man* 21 (3): 453–73. https://doi.org/10.2307/2803096.

Parry, Jonathan P. 1994. *Death in Banares*. Cambridge University Press.

Pearson, Melissa, Zwi B. Anthony, and Nicholas A. Buckley. 2010. "Prospective Policy Analysis: How an Epistemic Community Informed Policymaking on Intentional Self Poisoning in Sri Lanka." *Health Research Policy and Systems / BioMed Central* 8: 19. https://doi.org/10.1186/1478-4505-8-19.

Pearson, Melissa, Anthony B. Zwi, Nicholas A. Buckley, Gamini Manuweera, Ravindra Fernando, Andrew H. Dawson, and Duncan McDuie-Ra. 2015. "Policymaking 'Under the Radar': A Case Study of Pesticide Regulation to Prevent Intentional Poisoning in Sri Lanka." *Health Policy and Planning* 30 (1): 56–67. https://doi.org/10.1093/heapol/czt096.

Peebles, Patrick. 1990. "Colonization and Ethnic Conflict in the Dry Zone of Sri Lanka." *Journal of Asian Studies* 49 (1): 30–55. https://doi.org/10.2307/2058432.

Perera, Jayantha. 1992. "Political Development and Ethnic Conflict in Sri Lanka." *Journal of Refugee Studies* 5 (2): 136–48.

Perera, Sasanka. 2016. *Warzone Tourism in Sri Lanka: Tales from Darker Places in Paradise*. Sage Publications.

PEST Committee. 2018a. *Documentation Relating to the Committee's Work from February to December 2018*. European Parliament.

PEST Committee. 2018b. *Report on the Union's Authorisation Procedure for Pesticides*. European Parliament.

PEST Committee. 2018c. *Verbatim Reports of the Six Hearings Held by the Committee*. European Parliament.

Pesticide Action Network (PAN). 2013. *Pesticides in Your Daily Bread: A Consumer Guide to Pesticides in Bread 2014*. https://www.pan-uk.org/site/wp-content/uploads/Pesticides-in-Your-Daily-Bread-2014.pdf.

Pethe, Vasant P. 1973. "Hindus, Muslims and the Demographic Balance in India." *Economic and Political Weekly* 8 (2): 75–78.

Petryna, Adriana. 2002. *Life Exposed: Biological Citizens After Chernobyl*. Princeton University Press.

Phalkey, Jahnavi. 2013. "Focus: Science, History, and Modern India." *Isis* 104 (2): 330–36. https://doi.org/10.1086/670950.

Pieris, Kamalika. 2016. "Chronic Kidney Disease and Eelam Pt 1." LankaWeb. http://www.lankaweb.com/news/items/2016/12/10/chronic-kidney-disease-and-eelam-pt-1/.

Pollock, Sheldon. 2006. *The Language of the Gods in the World of Men: Sanskrit, Culture, and Power in Premodern India*. University of California Press.
Portier, Christopher J. 2020. "A Comprehensive Analysis of the Animal Carcinogenicity Data for Glyphosate from Chronic Exposure: Rodent Carcinogenicity Studies." *Environmental Health* 19 (1): 18. https://doi.org/10.1186/s12940-020-00574-1.
Portier, Christopher J., Bruce K. Armstrong, Bruce C. Baguley, Xaver Baur, Igor Belyaev, Robert Bellé, Fiorella Belpoggi et al. 2016. "Differences in the Carcinogenic Evaluation of Glyphosate Between the International Agency for Research on Cancer (IARC) and the European Food Safety Authority (EFSA)." *Journal of Epidemiology and Community Health* 70 (8): 741–45. https://doi.org/10.1136/jech-2015-207005.
Portier, Christopher J., and Peter Clausing. 2018. "Update to 'Re: Tarazona et al. (2017): Glyphosate Toxicity and Carcinogenicity: A Review of the Scientific Basis of the European Union Assessment and Its Differences with IARC. DOI: https://doi.org/10.1007/S00204-017-1962-5.'" *Archives of Toxicology* 92 (3): 1341. https://doi.org/10.1007/s00204-017-2138-z.
Presidential Secretariat. 2021. "Importation of Chemical Fertilizers Will Be Stopped Completely …" https://www.presidentsoffice.gov.lk/index.php/2021/04/22/importation-of-chemical-fertilizers-will-be-stopped-completely/.
President's Office [Sri Lanka]. 2016. "A Toxin Free Nation: Three Year Plan." Strategic Management Enterprise Agency.
Proctor, Robert N. 1995. *The Cancer Wars: How Politics Shapes What We Know and Don't Know About Cancer*. Basic Books.
Radicati, Alessandra. 2019. "Island Journeys: Fisher Itineraries and National Imaginaries in Colombo." *Contemporary South Asia* 27 (3): 330–41. https://doi.org/10.1080/09584935.2019.1620685.
Raheja, Gloria Goodwin. 1988. *The Poison in the Gift: Ritual, Prestation, and the Dominant Caste in a North Indian Village*. University of Chicago Press.
Rakopoulos, Theodoros. 2016. "Solidarity: The Egalitarian Tensions of a Bridge-Concept." *Social Anthropology* 24 (2): 142–51. https://doi.org/10.1111/1469-8676.12298.
Ramachandran, S. 1994. "Renal Diseases: Sri Lankan and Global Spectrum." *Journal of the Ceylon College of Physicians* 27: 27–35.
Ramayanaka, Wasantha. 2021. "Experts Warn Outright Ban on Fertilisers Would Cripple Farmers and Harvest." *Sunday Times*, May 9.
Ramsay, Georgina. 2016. "Avoiding Poison: Congolese Refugees Seeking Cosmological Continuity in Urban Asylum." *Social Analysis* 60 (3): 112–28. https://doi.org/10.3167/sa.2016.600307.
Rao, M. S. 1968. "The History of Medicine in India and Burma." *Medical History* 12 (1): 52–61. https://doi.org/10.1017/s002572730001276x.
Redfield, Sarah E. 1984. "Chemical Trespass?—An Overview of Statutory and Regulatory Efforts to Control Pesticide Drift." *Kentucky Law Journal* 73: 856–918. https://uknowledge.uky.edu/klj/vol73/iss3/8.
Robbins, Joel, Nicolas Langlitz, Emir Mahieddin, Erica Weiss, Corinna Howland, Bruce Knauft, and Cheryl Mattingly. 2023. "Anthropology Bright and Dark: Relativism, Value Pluralism, and the Comparative Study of the Good." *Social Analysis* 67 (4): 43–100. https://doi.org/10.3167/sa.2023.670403.

Roberts, Darren M., Nick A. Buckley, Fahim Mohamed, Michael Eddleston, Daniel A. Goldstein, Akbar Mehrsheikh, Marian S. Bleeke, and Andrew H. Dawson. 2010. "A Prospective Observational Study of the Clinical Toxicology of Glyphosate-Containing Herbicides in Adults with Acute Self-Poisoning." *Clinical Toxicology* 48 (2): 129–36. https://doi.org/10.3109/15563650903476491.

Rosa, Hartmut. 2013. *Social Acceleration: A New Theory of Modernity*. Translated by Jonathan Trejo-Mathys. Columbia University Press.

Rotarians Colombo West. 2012. "Kidney Dialysis Project." Unpublished report.

Rozakou, Katerina. 2017. "Solidarity #Humanitarianism: The Blurred Boundaries of Humanitarianism in Greece." *Etnofoor* 29 (2): 99–104. https://www.jstor.org/stable/26296172.

Russell, Andrew, and Tom Widger. 2018. "Ambivalent Objects in Global Health: Editors' Introduction." *Journal of Material Culture* 23 (4): 391–95. https://doi.org/10.1177/1359183518804841.

Sahlins, Marshall D. 1981. *Historical Metaphors and Mythical Realities: Structure in the Early History of the Sandwich Islands Kingdom*. University of Michigan Press.

Salgado, Nirmala S. 1997. "Sickness, Healing, and Religious Vocation: Alternative Choices at a Theravāda Buddhist Nunnery." *Ethnology* 36 (3): 213–26. https://www.jstor.org/stable/3773986.

Samimian-Darash, Limor, and Paul Rabinow. 2015. *Modes of Uncertainty: Anthropological Cases*. University of Chicago Press.

Sangiovanni, A. 2013. "Solidarity in the European Union." *Oxford Journal of Legal Studies* 33 (2): 213–41. https://www.jstor.org/stable/24562774.

Sariola, Salla, and Bob Simpson. 2019. *Research as Development: Biomedical Research, Ethics, and Collaboration in Sri Lanka*. Cornell University Press.

Sarkar, N. K., and S. J. Tambiah. 1979. *The Disintegrating Village: Report of a Socioeconomic Survey Conducted by the University of Ceylon*. University of Sri Lanka, Colombo Campus.

Schulke, Daniel A. 2017. *Veneficium: Magic, Witchcraft, and the Poison Path*. 2nd ed. Three Hands Press.

Senanayake, Nari. 2019. "Searching for CKDu: Mystery Kidney Disease, Differentiated (in)Visibility, and Contingent Geographies of Care in Dry Zone Sri Lanka." *Geoforum*, July. https://doi.org/10.1016/j.geoforum.2019.07.001.

Senanayake, Nari. 2020. "Tasting Toxicity: Bodies, Perplexity, and the Fraught Witnessing of Environmental Risk in Sri Lanka's Dry Zone." *Gender, Place & Culture* 27 (11): 1555–79. https://doi.org/10.1080/0966369X.2019.1693345.

Seneviratne, H. L. 2000. *The Work of Kings: The New Buddhism in Sri Lanka*. University of Chicago Press.

Seoighe, Rachel. 2017. *War, Denial and Nation-Building in Sri Lanka: After the End*. Springer International.

Sfiligoj, Eric. 2019. "What's Next With Glyphosate? Top Ag Retailers Weigh in on Roundup." CropLife. December 18. https://www.croplife.com/croplife-top-100/whats-next-with-glyphosate-top-ag-retailers-weigh-in-on-roundup/.

Shanmugaratnam, Nadarajah. 2020. "Editorial: Environment and Society in Sri Lanka." *Polity* 8 (1): 2–3.

Shapin, Steven, and Simon Schaffer. 1985. *Leviathan and the Air-Pump: Hobbes, Boyle, and the Experimental Life*. Princeton University Press.

Shapiro, Nicholas, and Eben Kirksey. 2017. "Chemo-Ethnography: An Introduction." *Cultural Anthropology* 32 (4): 481–93. https://doi.org/10.14506/ca32.4.01.
Shaviro, Steven. 2015. *No Speed Limit: Three Essays on Accelerationism*. University of Minnesota Press.
Shore, Cris. 2013. *Building Europe: The Cultural Politics of European Integration*. Routledge.
Shotwell, Alexis. 2016. *Against Purity: Living Ethically in Compromised Times*. University of Minnesota Press.
Sigerist, Henry E. 1961. *A History of Medicine*. Vol. 2: *Early Greek, Hindu, and Persian Medicine*. Oxford University Press.
Silva, Vera, Luca Montanarella, Arwyn Jones, Oihane Fernández-Ugalde, Hans G. J. Mol, Coen J. Ritsema, and Violette Geissen. 2018. "Distribution of Glyphosate and Aminomethylphosphonic Acid (AMPA) in Agricultural Topsoils of the European Union." *Science of the Total Environment* 621 (October): 1352–59. https://doi.org/10.1016/j.scitotenv.2017.10.093.
Simpson, Bob. 2004. "Localising a Brave New World: New Reproductive Technologies and the Politics of Infertility in Sri Lanka." In *Reproductive Agency, Medicine, and the State: Cultural Transformations in Childbearing*, edited by Maya Unnithan-Kumar, 43–58. Berghahn Books.
Simpson, Bob. 2006. "'You Don't Do Fieldwork, Fieldwork Does You': Between Subjectivation and Objectivation in Anthropological Fieldwork." In *The SAGE Handbook of Fieldwork*, edited by Dick Hobbs and Richard Wright, 126–37. Sage Publications.
Simpson, Bob. 2020. *Peripheral Visions: Anthropological Perspectives on Bioethics, Biomedicine, and Biotechnologies in Sri Lanka*. Social Scientists' Association.
Simpson, Bob, and Salla Sariola. 2012. "Blinding Authority: Randomized Clinical Trials and the Production of Global Scientific Knowledge in Contemporary Sri Lanka." *Science, Technology & Human Values* 37 (5): 555–75. https://www.jstor.org/stable/23474407.
Singer, Merrill, and Hans Baer, eds. 2009. *Killer Commodities: Public Health and the Corporate Production of Harm*. AltaMira Press.
Sirisena, Maithripala. 2014. "A Compassionate Maithri Governance—A Stable Country." New Democratic Front.
Sivasundaram, Siva. 2013. *Islanded: Britain, Sri Lanka, and the Bounds of an Indian Ocean Colony*. Oxford University Press.
Smart, B. 1999. *Facing Modernity: Ambivalence, Reflexivity and Morality*. Sage Publications.
Smith, Sara H. 2009. "The Domestication of Geopolitics: Buddhist-Muslim Conflict and the Policing of Marriage and the Body in Ladakh, India." *Geopolitics* 14 (2): 197–218. https://doi.org/10.1080/14650040802693382.
Snodgrass, Jeffrey G. 2001. "Beware of Charitable Souls: Contagion, Roguish Ghosts and the Poison(s) of Hindu Alms." *Journal of the Royal Anthropological Institute* 7 (4): 687–703. https://doi.org/10.1111/1467-9655.00084.
Spencer, Jonathan. 1990. "Writing Within: Anthropology, Nationalism, and Culture in Sri Lanka [and Comments and Reply]." *Current Anthropology* 31 (3): 283–300. https://www.jstor.org/stable/2743630.
Spencer, Jonathan. 2002. *Sri Lanka: History and the Roots of Conflict*. Routledge.

Spencer, Jonathan. 2003. "A Nation 'Living in Different Places': Notes on the Impossible Work of Purification in Postcolonial Sri Lanka." *Contributions to Indian Sociology* 37 (1–2): 1–23. https://doi.org/10.1177/006996670303700102.

Spencer, Jonathan. 2014. "Anthropology, Politics, and Place in Sri Lanka: South Asian Reflections from an Island Adrift." *South Asia Multidisciplinary Academic Journal*, no. 10 (December). https://doi.org/10.4000/samaj.3812.

Sri Lanka Army. 2009. "Puthukkudiyiruppu Victory Monument Unveiled." https://www.army.lk/news/puthukkudiyiruppu-victory-monument-unveiled.

Sri Lanka Association for the Advancement of Science (SLAAS). 2011. "SLAAS Refutes Arsenic Claims." *Daily News*, July 11.

Star, Susan Leigh, and James R. Griesemer. 1989. "Institutional Ecology, 'Translations' and Boundary Objects: Amateurs and Professionals in Berkeley's Museum of Vertebrate Zoology, 1907–39." *Social Studies of Science* 19 (3): 387–420. https://doi.org/10.1177/030631289019003001.

Steffen, Will, Wendy Broadgate, Lisa Deutsch, Owen Gaffney, and Cornelia Ludwig. 2015. "The Trajectory of the Anthropocene: The Great Acceleration." *Anthropocene Review* 2 (1): 81–98. https://doi.org/10.1177/2053019614564785.

Sternbach, Ludwik. 1974. *A History of Indian Literature: Subhasita, Gnomic and Didactic Literature*. Edited by Jan Gonda. Otto Harrassowitz.

Stevens, Alta Mae. 2000. "Poison and Nurturance: Changing Food and Community Symbolism Among Haitians in Oldtown, a New England City." *Journal of Haitian Studies* 5–6 (1999–2000): 20–28.

Stewart, James John. 2014. "Muslim-Buddhist Conflict in Contemporary Sri Lanka." *South Asia Research* 34 (3): 241–60. https://doi.org/10.1177/0262728014549134.

Stoler, Ann Laura. 2013. "'The Rot Remains': From Ruins to Ruination." In *Imperial Debris: On Ruins and Ruination*, edited by Ann Laura Stoler, 1–35. Duke University Press.

Stone, Jason G. 2014. "Sri Lanka's Postwar Descent." *Journal of Democracy* 25 (2): 146–57. https://dx.doi.org/10.1353/jod.2014.0024.

Strathern, Alan. 2009. "The Vijaya Origin Myth of Sri Lanka and the Strangeness of Kingship." *Past & Present* 203: 3–28.

Strathern, Marilyn, ed. 2000. *Audit Cultures: Anthropological Studies in Accountability, Ethics and the Academy*. Routledge.

Strathern, Marilyn. 2020. *Relations: An Anthropological Account*. Duke University Press.

Subramaniam, Banu. 2000. "Archaic Modernities: Science, Secularism, and Religion in Modern India." *Social Text* 18 (3): 67–86. https://muse.jhu.edu/article/31881.

Subramaniam, Banu. 2019. *Holy Science: The Biopolitics of Hindu Nationalism*. University of Washington Press.

Sunday Times. 2016. "Fresh Effort to Solve the 'Unknown' Aspect of CKDu." May 15.

Tambiah, Stanley S. J. 1986. *Sri Lanka: Ethnic Fratricide and the Dismantling of Democracy*. I. B. Tauris and University of Chicago Press.

Thabrew de, W. Vivian. 2011. *Subhashitaya (Good Sayings): Sinhala Paraphrase and English Translation*. Suhada Press.

Theodossopoulos, Dimitrios. 2016. "Philanthropy or Solidarity? Ethical Dilemmas About Humanitarianism in Crisis-Afflicted Greece." *Social Anthropology* 24 (2): 167–84. https://doi.org/10.1111/1469-8676.12304.

Tiruchelvam, Neelum. 2000. "The Politics of Federalism and Diversity in Sri Lanka." In *Autonomy and Ethnicity: Negotiating Competing Claims in Multi-Ethnic States*, edited by Y. Ghai, 197–218. Cambridge University Press.

Tousignant, Noémi. 2018. *Edges of Exposure: Toxicology and the Problem of Capacity in Postcolonial Senegal*. Duke University Press.

Tropp, Jacob. 2002. "Dogs, Poison and the Meaning of Colonial Intervention in the Transkei, South Africa." *Journal of African History* 43 (3): 451–72. https://www.jstor.org/stable/4100603.

Tsing, Anna Lowenhaupt. 2015. *The Mushroom at the End of the World: On the Possibility of Life in Capitalist Ruins*. Princeton University Press.

Udalagama, Tharindi Dayara. 2018. "Beautiful Mistakes: An Ethnographic Study of Women's Lives After Marriage in a Rural Sinhala Village." PhD dissertation, Durham University. http://etheses.dur.ac.uk/12788/.

Ulmer, Alexandra, and Omar Rajarathnam. 2019. "Unsubstantiated Claims Muslim Doctor Sterilized Women Raise Tensions in Sri Lanka." Reuters, June 6.

Venugopal, Rajesh. 2015. "Democracy, Development and the Executive Presidency in Sri Lanka." *Third World Quarterly* 36 (4): 670–90. https://doi.org/10.1080/01436597.2015.1024400.

Vogel, David. 2012. *The Politics of Precaution: Regulating Health, Safety, and Environmental Risks in Europe and the United States*. Princeton University Press.

Vogel, Sarah A. 2008. "From 'the Dose Makes the Poison' to 'the Timing Makes the Poison': Conceptualizing Risk in the Synthetic Age." *Environmental History* 13 (4): 667–73. https://www.jstor.org/stable/25473294.

Waidyanatha, Parakrama. 2018. "Lift Glyphosate Ban Fully." *Daily News*, June 18.

Wamanan, Arthur, and Dinidu de Alwis. 2011. "Furor over Arsenic Shakes Agri Sector." *The Nation*, June 19.

Wanigasuriya, K. 2012. "Aetiological Factors of Chronic Kidney Disease in the North Central Province of Sri Lanka: A Review of Evidence to-Date." *Journal of the College of Community Physicians of Sri Lanka* 17 (1): 15–20. https://doi.org/10.4038/jccpsl.v17i1.4931.

Warakapitiya, Kasun. 2018. "Cabinet Divided over Glyphosate Ban." *Sunday Times*, March 25.

Weaver, Virginia M., Jeffrey J. Fadrowski, and Bernard G. Jaar. 2015. "Global Dimensions of Chronic Kidney Disease of Unknown Etiology (CKDu): A Modern Era Environmental and/or Occupational Nephropathy?" *BMC Nephrology* 16 (1): 145. https://doi.org/10.1186/s12882-015-0105-6.

Weber, Stefan, and Helmut Burtscher-Schaden. 2019. "Detailed Expert Report on Plagiarism and Superordinated Copy Paste in the Renewal Assessment Report (RAR) on Glyphosate." https://left.eu/content/uploads/2019/01/Expertise-RAR-Glyphosat-2018-01-11-1.pdf.

Webster, Charles. 2002. "Paracelsus, Paracelsianism, and the Secularization of the Worldview." *Science in Context* 15 (1): 9–27. https://doi.org/10.1017/s0269889702000340.

Weeks, Andrew. 1997. *Paracelsus: Speculative Theory and the Crisis of the Early Reformation*. State University of New York Press.

Weeraratne, Stanley, and Sunil J. Wimalawansa. 2015. "A Major Irrigation Project (Accelerated Mahaweli Programme) and the Chronic Kidney Disease of Multifactorial Origin in Sri Lanka." *International Journal of Environmental & Agriculture Research* 1 (6): 16–27.

Weerasekera, Akila. 2008. "Bio-Terrorism the Cause of Chronic Kidney Disease?" *The Island Online*. http://www.island.lk/2008/09/27/features2.html.

Weeratunge, Nireka. 2000. "Nature, Harmony, and the Kaliyugaya: Global/Local Discourses on the Human-Environment Relationship." *Current Anthropology* 41 (2): 249–68. https://doi.org/10.1086/300127.

Wenger, Etienne. 1998. *Communities of Practice*. Cambridge University Press. https://doi.org/10.1017/CBO9780511803932.

Werner, Marion, Christian Berndt, and Becky Mansfield. 2022. "The Glyphosate Assemblage: Herbicides, Uneven Development, and Chemical Geographies of Ubiquity." *Annals of the American Association of Geographers* 112 (1): 19–35. https://doi.org/10.1080/24694452.2021.1898322.

Weston, Kath. 2013. "Lifeblood, Liquidity, and Cash Transfusions: Beyond Metaphor in the Cultural Study of Finance." In *Blood Will Out: Essays on Liquid Transfers and Flows*, 24–41. https://doi.org/10.1002/9781118656235.ch1.

White, Daniel. 2017. "Affect: An Introduction." *Cultural Anthropology* 32 (2): 175–80. https://doi.org/10.14506/ca32.2.01.

Wickramasinghe, Nira. 2007. "Multiculturalism: A View from Sri Lanka." OpenDemocracy. https://www.opendemocracy.net/colonial_multiculturalism.jsp.

Wickramasinghe, Upul Kumara. 2023a. "Philanthropic Science: An Ethnographic Study of Chronic Kidney Disease Uncertain Etiology (CKDu) and Health Philanthropy in Sri Lanka." PhD dissertation, University of Durham.

Wickramasinghe, Upul Kumara. 2023b. "Screening Charity Recipients: Health Philanthropy, Medical Diagnosis, and Kidney Disease Prevention in Sri Lanka." *Medicine Anthropology Theory* 10 (3): 1–29. https://doi.org/10.17157/mat.10.3.7764.

Widger, Tom. 2012. "Suffering, Frustration, and Anger: Class, Gender and History in Sri Lankan Suicide Stories." *Culture, Medicine, and Psychiatry* 36 (2): 225–44. https://doi.org/10.1007/s11013-012-9250-6.

Widger, Tom. 2014. "Pesticides and Global Health: 'Ambivalent Objects' in Anthropological Perspective." Somatosphere. http://somatosphere.net/?p=8770.

Widger, Tom. 2015a. "Learning Suicide and the Limits of Agency: Children's 'Suicide Play' in Sri Lanka." In *Suicide and Agency: Anthropological Perspectives on Self-Destruction, Personhood, and Power*, edited by Ludek Broz and Daniel Münster, 165–82. Ashgate.

Widger, Tom. 2015b. "Suicide and the 'Poison Complex': Toxic Relationalities, Child Development, and the Sri Lankan Self-Harm Epidemic." *Medical Anthropology: Cross Cultural Studies in Health and Illness* 34 (6): 501–16. https://doi.org/10.1080/01459740.2015.1012616.

Widger, Tom. 2015c. *Suicide in Sri Lanka: The Anthropology of an Epidemic*. Routledge.

Widger, Tom. 2016. "Philanthronationalism: Junctures at the Business/Charity Nexus in Post-War Sri Lanka." *Development and Change* 47 (1): 29–50. https://doi.org/10.1111/dech.12185.

Widger, Tom. 2018. "Suicides, Poisons, and the Materially Possible: The Positive Ambivalence of Means Restriction and Critical-Critical Global Health." *Journal of Material Culture*. https://doi.org/10.1177/1359183518799525.

Widger, Tom, and Upul Wickramasinghe. 2020. "Monsoon Uncertainties, Hydro-Chemical Infrastructures, and Ecological Time in Sri Lanka." In *The Time of Anthropology: Studies of Contemporary Chronopolitics*, edited by Elisabeth Kirtsoglou and Bob Simpson, 123–41. Routledge.

Wijedasa, Namini, and Joshua Surendraraj. 2015. "Glyphosate Ban Mired in Confusion." *Sunday Times*, June 7.

Wijesekara, Anura. 2011. "The Arsenic Upheaval: Truth and Fiction." *The Island Online*, June 17.

Wijewardena, Don Asoka. 2014a. "Ban on Glyphosate: President's Order Put on Hold." *The Island Online*, March 25.

Wijewardena, Don Asoka. 2014b. "Docs to Urge Govt. to Claim Damages from Agro Chemical Companies." *The Island Online*, February 2.

Wijewardena, Don Asoka. 2014c. "President Wants to Make SL Free of Agrochemicals by 2020." *The Island Online*, June 8.

Wijewardena, Don Asoka. 2015. "Fight over Glyphosate Gets Brutal. (An Open Letter to Channa Jayasumana.)" *The Island Online*, June 3.

Wimalawansa, Shehani A., and Sunil J. Wimalawansa. 2015. "Protection of Watersheds, and Control and Responsible Use of Fertiliser to Prevent Phosphate Eutrophication of Reservoirs." *International Journal of Research in Environmental Science (IJRES)* 1 (2): 1–18.

Wimalawansa, Sunil J. 2014. "Should Glyphosate Be Banned Without Scientific Evidence? Chronic Kidney Disease of Multi-Factorial Origin (CKD-Mfo)." *The Island Online*, March 24.

Wimalawansa, Sunil J. 2016. "The Role of Ions, Heavy Metals, Fluoride, and Agrochemicals: Critical Evaluation of Potential Aetiological Factors of Chronic Kidney Disease of Multifactorial Origin (CKDmfo/CKDu) and Recommendations for Its Eradication." *Environmental Geochemistry and Health* 38 (3): 639–78. https://doi.org/10.1007/s10653-015-9768-y.

Wimalawansa, Sunil J. 2018. "There Is No Evidence That Organochlorine Pesticides, Such as DDT, Cause Chronic Kidney Disease of Unknown Etiology." *Science of the Total Environment* 649 (September): 1636–37. https://doi.org/10.1016/j.scitotenv.2018.09.117.

Woost, Mike. 1999. "From Shifting Cultivation to Shifting Development in Rural Sri Lanka." *Anthropology of Work Review* 19 (3): 23–27. https://doi.org/10.1525/awr.1999.19.3.23.

World Health Organization (WHO). 2016. "International Expert Consultation on Chronic Kidney Disease of Unknown Etiology, Colombo, Sri Lanka, 27–29 April 2016." Colombo.

Wujastyk, Dominik. 2001. *The Roots of Ayurveda: Selections from Sanskrit Medical Writings*. Penguin.

Zuhair, Ayesha. 2016. *Dynamics of Sinhala Buddhist Ethno-Nationalism in Post-War Sri Lanka*. Centre for Policy Alternatives. https://www.cpalanka.org/wp-content/uploads/2016/04/Dynamics-of-Sinhala-Buddhist-Ethno-Nationalism-in-Post-War-Sri-Lanka.pdf.

INDEX

2,4-D, 118
2-methyl-4-chlorophenoxyacetic acid (MCPA), 176

Abeysekera, Tilak, 122, 124
Age of Optimism, 5–7, 204
Age of Toxicity, 6, 111, 199, 204–5
agrochemicals, 2, 4, 149, 162, 172, 177–78, 182, 204; regulation of, 54
alchemy, 38–39, 53
American Association for the Advancement of Science (AAAS), 194; Folta and, 195–96; Jayasumana/Gunatilake, award for, 194–96
Andrieu, Eric, 65, 98, 101, 103–4. *See also* European Union, solidarity and; PEST Committee
Andriukaitis, Vytenis Povilas, 106–7. *See also* European Union, solidarity and
Anthropocene, 22; Great Acceleration of, 22; toxic acceleration and, 22. *See also* Chemical Anthropocene
Anuradhapura, 133*fig.*, 146, 150–51
arsenic, 153; CKDu and, 125–27, 156, 158–63, 184; de Silva, CKDu and, 159, 167; hard water and, 158–60; Jayasumana, CKDu and, 158–59, 162–63; Rajarata-Kelaniya group and, 159–62; rice, claims of contamination, 159–61; Senanayake, CKDu and, 159–60, 162–63. *See also* pesticides
Asclepius, 28

Autrup, Herman, 187–90; hazard *vs.* risk and, 187–88
Axial Age, 14, 26–28, 34
Ayurveda, 46–47, 49–50, 163, 165; Hindu nationalism, association with, 165; as the "Science of Life," 46. *See also* body, biological; body politic
Ayuso, Pilar, 106

Bandaranaike Memorial International Conference Hall, 187, 188
Bangladesh, 153
BASF, 57, 84
Bayer, 8, 57
Bhopal disaster (1984), 10–11, 23, 57
Blair, Tony, 6
blood, 1, 4, 29, 42, 47, 51
Bodu Bala Sena (BBS; Buddhist Power Force), 144, 177
body, biological: Ayurveda and, 47, 49; body politic, relationship with, 9–11, 42–43, 50, 130–31, 138; immunity and, 42; poison and, 8, 18, 24, 29, 33, 37, 42, 44, 70; poisoncraft and, 77; sovereignty/boundaries and, 7, 10–11, 15, 39, 49–51
body, European, 15–16, 18, 61–62; Paracelsian idea of, 67, 203; poisoncraft and, 61, 63, 71–77, 99; sovereignty and, 93. *See also* European Union, solidarity and; glyphosate, Europe and

body, Sri Lankan, 116; body politic and biological body, Sinhala nationalism and, 138, 142, 200; Tamil Eelam, threat to, 138, 140, 142, 144, 150; toxic/poisonous threats to, 130–31, 142, 150–53, 155, 175, 185, 200
body politic, 8–11, 15, 18, 33; Ayurveda and, 203; immunity and, 42; openness and, 50; poison and, 11, 42–43; poisoncraft and, 79; sovereignty/boundaries and, 50–51, 200. *See also* body, biological
Brexit, xii, 6, 59
Buddhism, 44–45, 50, 117; Buddha Prathyaksha and, 157, 167; Catholic missionaries and, 45; hierarchy and, 167; morals/ethics and, 199–200; sovereignty and, 45–46; vision/seeing eye and, 157, 166–68, 184
Buddhism, Sinhala, 36, 45, 49, 127, 134, 138, 142, 150, 155, 197, 199; agricultural development and, 117, 131; autochthony and, 140, 144, 148, 179; Buddhist indigenous science, as alternative to Western science, 157, 160, 163, 165–67; Cultural Triangle, 131, 133*fig.*, 151; hierarchy and, 49; imagery and, 188–89; indigenous culture and, 156; nationalist teleology and, 152; perceived threats to, 131, 156, 162, 197; postcolonial era and, 157; rice farming, links with, 131, 149; water, association with, 149. *See also* Buddhist nationalism; Sri Lanka presidency
Buddhism, Theravada, 134, 134n1, 157, 199
Buddhist nationalism, 3, 13, 17, 116–17, 123, 127–28, 189, 199; anthropology and, 127–28; Buddhist fertility, threats to, 144–46; chemical poisons and, 146; Christian community and, 117; CKDu and, 134, 139; decolonization of Sri Lankan science, 123–24, 155, 164; Muslims, as perceived threat, 116, 124, 130, 139, 142, 144–46, 153, 180, 199; nationalist groups, 144; pesticides and, 116; right to rule and, 117; Tamil community and, 117, 189. *See also* Rajarata-Kelaniya group; Sri Lanka, postwar
bureaucracy, 77–79, 95; adhocracy and, 95–96; bureaucratic documents, 81; bureaucratic will to ignorance, 88; molecular bureaucracy, 15, 68–69; order *vs.* chaos, 78–79, 95; regulatory bureaucracy, 66; satisficing and, 95–96; solidarity and, 107–8; as specialists in poisoncraft, 79; toxicity and, 79; trust and, 87
Burtscher-Schaden, Helmut, 86, 94, 103–4

capitalism, 5, 13, 22–23, 29, 119, 164, 189; pesticide capitalism, 57

Capri, Ettore, 73, 75
Centre for Education, Research, and Training in Kidney Diseases (CERTKiD), 124
Chemical Anthropocene, 4, 120, 153
chemical sovereignty, 3, 7–8, 203–6; European Union and, 203–4, 206; poisoncraft and, 3; Sri Lanka and, 16, 204, 206
Chernobyl disaster (1986), 10–11, 23
China, 6, 8, 27, 125; generic chemicals, production of, 8; Sri Lankan sovereignty, threat to, 139
chronic kidney disease of multifactorial origin (CKD-mfo), 125
chronic kidney disease of unknown etiology (CKDu), 2, 16, 115–17, 119–29, 146–49, 164, 170–74, 181, 189–93, 200, 209; Accelerated Mahaweli and, 120–22, 126, 135*fig.*, 147–52; cadmium and, 184; *CKDu and Sri Lanka Basecamp* forum, 115, 122, 146, 192; consensus and, 115–16, 127, 171, 181, 185–86; contested space and, 134; critical cartography and, 134; Cultural Triangle and, 131, 132*fig.*, 151; cyanobacteria theory, 151, 153; diagnosis, 119–20; etiology, 115, 120, 122–25, 128–29, 147, 150, 152, 155, 162, 182, 185, 193; first cases, suggested dating of, 146–48; fluoride and, 124–26, 136*fig.*, 151, 153, 183–84; glyphosate and, 2, 115–17, 121, 123–29, 140, 145–46, 155, 162–63, 169–71, 174, 176, 181–82, 184, 187, 193–96, 204; groundwater and, 134, 136*fig.*, 151–52, 173; hard water and, 124, 158–60, 162–63, 182; herbal remedies, 158; international epidemiology of, 120; LTTE bioterrorism and Eelam boundary, 123, 128, 140, 141*fig.*, 142, 146; mechanistic/single-factorial approaches to, 16, 126–27; mortality, 121–22; multifactorial approaches to, 16, 125–27, 183; Muslim bioterrorism, false attribution to, 128, 200; North Central Province (NCP) and, 131, 134; poisoncraft and, 121, 123–26, 131; Rajarata/Mahaweli colonies, association with, 151–52; reverse osmosis (RO) water purification and, 182–83; Sri Lankan epidemiology of, 131–32, 132*fig.*, 135*fig.*, 139–40; toxic acceleration and, 121–22. *See also* arsenic; Buddhist nationalism; chronic kidney disease of multifactorial origin (CKD-mfo); Colombo group; Jayasumana, Channa; Peradeniya group; Presidential Task Force on CKDu (Sri Lanka); Rajapaksa, Mahinda; Rajarata-Kelaniya group; Ramachandran, S.; Sirisena, Maithripala

climate change, 4, 22, 203
Clinton, Bill, 6
Colombo group, 125–27, 134, 140, 152, 155, 182, 193; complex adaptive systems (CAS) approach, 125–27; Goldstein and, 192; Jayasinghe and, 116, 125–27; multiple poisons, as etiology for CKDu, 125–26; Sunil/Shehani Wimalawansa and, 125–26, 152; Weeraratne and, 152
colonialism, 4, 6, 11–12, 37, 157, 189, 205; science, impact on, 155, 165–66. *See also* Mukaveti, Alagiyavanna; Sri Lanka
Committee on the Environment, Climate and Food Safety (ENVI), 72
Coordinating Secretariat for Science, Technology, and Innovation (COSTI, Sri Lanka), 115, 183, 192

DDT, 125
de Silva, Nalin, 123, 156, 165–66, 184; Buddha Prathyaksha and, 157, 167; constructive relativism, theory of, 156–58, 160, 164–66, 168; criticism of, 160; indigenous medical practices and, 163–64; Sinhala Buddhist science and, 157, 166–67; Western science, criticism of, 156, 160, 163, 166–67. *See also* arsenic; Jayasumana, Channa; Senanayake, Priyantha
Diderich, Bob, 85–86
Dissanayake, Duminda, 174–75
Dow Chemical, 57
Durkheim, Émile, 112

elderflora, 34–35
El Salvador, 163
European Chemicals Agency (ECHA), 69, 82, 107–8, 203–4, 209
European Coal and Steel Community (ECSC), 62
European Commission, 2, 59, 63–64; glyphosate approvals and, 2; regulatory fitness and performance (REFIT) review, 64; Scientific Advice Mechanism (SAM), 64
European Communities (EC), 62
European Crop Protection Authority (ECPA), 73–75
European Economic Community (EEC), 62
European Food Safety Authority (EFSA), 2, 16, 63, 65, 69, 74, 76, 80, 82, 85, 89, 97, 107, 204, 209; hazard *vs.* risk, 71–73, 73*fig.*, 74, 188, 204; IARC, contrast with, 71, 75, 80–82; industry studies and, 71, 94; molecule *vs.* formulation, 71, 75–78; open science and,

102–3; regulatory division of labor, 76. *See also* glyphosate, Europe and
European Glyphosate Taskforce (GTF), 83, 90; BfR, relationship with, 90–95; guideline/non-guideline studies and, 93
European Green Party, 1
European Parliament, 1, 58–59, 63–65, 69, 72, 82–83, 98, 100–101, 108; Committee on Environment, Public Health, and Food Safety (ENVI committee), 64; Green MEPS, 60
European Union (EU), xii, 1, 6, 9–10, 16; decision making and, 60, 65, 104–6, 111, 204; early history, 62; ethno-nationalisms in, 3, 59–60, 111; EU foreign minister position and, 62; euro and, 60, 62; four freedoms and, 62, 67, 102, 203; glyphosate, threat to, 15–16, 59, 100; Member States, 67, 15, 59–60, 62, 65, 67, 69, 76–77, 88, 106; poisoncraft and, 60–61, 65–66, 68–70, 88–89, 96, 99, 108, 111–12; REACH regulation, 83, 90; regulatory science, right to, 61; Schengen Area, 69, 100; single market, 15, 62, 67–70; sovereignty debates in, 11; structural functionalism and, 112; sui generis metaphor and, 61, 100; supranational state, idea of, xii, 9–10, 15, 18, 62, 69–70, 88, 201–2, 204; threats to, 59. *See also* European Union, solidarity and
European Union, solidarity and, 15–16, 60, 99–100, 107–9, 111–12, 204; Andrieu and, 101–2, 106–8; Andriukaitis and, 108; democracy and, 101–2, 105–8; Hansen and, 108; Juncker and, 99, 108; Omarjee and, 108; poisoncraft and, 111–12; science and, 102–8, 111; sui generis, concept of, 100; treaties and acts, 99. *See also* PEST Committee

Federal Institute for Risk Assessment (Germany, BfR), 83, 89–92, 97, 209; glyphosate safety studies and, 90–94; non-guideline studies and, 94; plagiarism scandal and, 93–95, 103. *See also* European Glyphosate Taskforce (GTF)
fertilizers, 117–18, 148, 170, 173, 182. *See also* Rajapaksa, Gotabaya
Folta, Kevin, 195–96. *See also* American Association for the Advancement of Science (AAAS)
Foucault, Michel, 78, 88, 96

gifts, 28–31, 201, 209; *dan* (Hindu religious gift), 29; inequality and, 30; poisons and, 29–31, 53; value and, 30–31, 201

238   INDEX

Global 2000, 86, 94, 103
globalization, 5, 11, 22, 204; national identity, impact on, 153
Global North, 5; pesticide production in, 7; regulatory agencies, concentration of in, 8
Global South, 5, 29; circle of poison and, 7–8; pesticide imports, 7
glyphosate, xi, 4, 12–14, 166; as boundary object, 9–10, 15, 60–61; chemical formula for, 5; glyphosate-metal complexes and, 2; as Group 2A carcinogen, designation of (IARC/WHO), xi, 1–2, 16, 57–58, 63–64, 71, 73, 75, 80–81, 94–95, 102, 187; residues in tissue/soil and, 1; Roundup, commercial name for, 1, 8, 15, 60, 118–19; safety studies and, 89–92; toxicity of, 3, 91–92, 96, 191. *See also* chronic kidney disease of unknown etiology (CKDu); Federal Institute for Risk Assessment (Germany, BfR)
glyphosate, Europe and, xi, 1–2, 9–12, 15–17, 58–59, 62–64, 69–70, 72, 81, 112, 201, 203, 205; active molecules *vs.* product formulations, 75, 209; approval extensions of, 63, 204; attempted ban of, 4, 11; chemical sovereignty and, 2–3; EFSA assessments, 63, 65–66, 71, 75–76, 80–83; EFSA reassessments, 82–83, 103; European body, importance for, 63; European identity, importance for, 63, 65; European solidarity, threat to, 59–61; European sovereignty and, 65, 82, 111–12; ignorance and, 89, 96, 183; individual country bans, 77; intrinsic *vs.* relational properties/risk, 75; open internal borders/free movement and, 70–71; regulatory renewal (2013), 63. *See also* European Glyphosate Taskforce (GTF); Federal Institute for Risk Assessment (Germany, BfR); glyphosate Renewal Assessment Report (RAR)
glyphosate, Sri Lanka and, xii, 2, 9–12, 15–17, 154, 201, 203–5; ban, revocation of (2021), 2, 178, 204; ban of (2015), 2, 4, 16, 119, 123, 155, 171–77, 184, 187–90, 193, 196; chemical sovereignty and, 2–3; initial approvals, 118; national unity and, 2. *See also* chronic kidney disease of unknown etiology (CKDu); Coordinating Secretariat for Science, Technology, and Innovation (COSTI, Sri Lanka)
glyphosate Renewal Assessment Report (RAR), 16, 82, 89–90; guidelines, 83–87; IARC, response to, 83; industry studies and, 82, 85, 94, 104, 109; plagiarism scandal and, 93–95; Rapporteur Member State (RMS) and, 83; rigor/objectivity and, 83; sovereign exception and, 97. *See also* European Glyphosate Taskforce (GTF); Good Laboratory Practice (GLP); Klimisch score
Goldstein, Daniel, 187–88, 190–92, 194, 197. *See also* Colombo group; paraquat; Rajarata-Kelaniya group
Good Laboratory Practice (GLP), 82–86, 89–90; academic (non-guideline) studies and, 84–87; criticism of, 85–87; industry and, 85–86
Government Medical Officers' Association (GMOA, Sri Lanka), 161
Gunatilake, Sarath, 123, 162, 171. *See also* American Association for the Advancement of Science (AAAS); Jayasumana, Channa
Guteland, Jytte, 94

Hansen, Bjorn, 107. *See also* European Union, solidarity and
Hensel, Andreas, 90, 94, 103–4
hierarchy, 36–37; South Asia and, 37, 167; value and, 35–36. *See also* Buddhism; Buddhism, Sinhala; poison
Hinduism, 29, 37, 46, 143, 146, 158; nationalism and, 153, 164–65. *See also* Ayurveda
Hohenheim, Philippus von. *See* Paracelsus

Ibn al-Washiya, 28
ignorance, 82, 87–89; government regulation and, 87–88; guideline studies and, 87, 93; knowledge and, 87–90; non-guideline studies and, 93; sovereign ignorance, 82, 89; will to ignorance, 88. *See also* bureaucracy; glyphosate, Europe and; Sri Lanka presidency
Ileperuma, Oliver, 124
imperialism, cultural, 155, 163
India, 10–11, 26, 28, 46, 49, 153, 164; cartographic anxiety, 153; as postcolonial nation, 10; Sri Lanka, relationship with, 134, 150, 152; Tamil community and, 117, 138–39, 142, 150, 152
Industrial Revolution, 4, 22
International Agency for Research on Cancer (IARC), xi, 65, 70, 210; hazard *vs.* risk, 71–74; molecule *vs.* formulation, 75; public safety studies and, 71. *See also* European Food Safety Authority (EFSA); glyphosate; glyphosate Renewal Assessment Report (RAR)
International Monetary Fund, 11

INDEX   239

International Monsanto Tribunal, 194–95
International Society of Nephrology, 183

Jathika Hela Urumaya (JHU; National Heritage Party), 123, 172, 177, 184
Jayasinghe, Saroj, 116, 125, 196. *See also* Colombo group
Jayasumana, Channa, 2, 16, 163–64, 174, 193, 197; attempts to discredit, 193–94; CKDu/glyphosate/Compound X and, 162–63, 168–69, 171, 193–95; de Silva and, 163, 165; LTTE bioterrorism theory and, 123, 140; Mohamed Shafi and, 145–46; Natha Deviyo, revelations from, 162–63; positive international reception of, 189–90, 194–97. *See also* American Association for the Advancement of Science (AAAS); arsenic; Rajarata-Kelaniya group
Jayawardene, J. R., 117–18, 178
Juncker, Jean-Claude, 2, 58–59, 62, 108; nationalism as poison, view of, 59–60, 62–63. *See also* European Union, solidarity and

kasippu (illicit liquor), x. *See also* pesticides
Klimisch score, 82, 84, 89–90, 94; academic studies and, 84

Liberation Tigers of Tamil Eelam (LTTE), 117, 122, 128, 134, 138–39, 142–44, 179, 199; Sea Tigers and, 142; Southern India and, 142, 152. *See also* chronic kidney disease of unknown etiology (CKDu)

Macron, Emmanuel, 77
magic, 21, 24, 31, 53
Mahaweli Development and Irrigation Project, 117–21, 135*fig.*, 150–51; Accelerated Mahaweli Development Project (AMDP), 117–22, 126 135*fig.*, 147–50; agricultural modernization and, 117–19, 148; background and aims, 117; cascade irrigation system, 149; glyphosate and, 119, 121; hybrid crops/chemicals and, 118; Mahaweli Master Plan (MMP), 117–18; North Central Province (NCP), 131, 134; as postcolonial project, 117, 150; societal impact, 119; Tamil separatism and, 117; toxic acceleration and, 121–22. *See also* chronic kidney disease of unknown etiology (CKDu)
Mauss, Marcel, 28–30
mistrust, 87, 89
modernity, 22–23, 33, 50, 153; archaic modernity and, 164–65; chemical modernity, 147; medical modernity and, 41

Monsanto, 1, 8, 13, 16, 57–58, 60, 81, 89–90, 187–94; glyphosate patent, 119; regulatory/political interference and, 191, 196–97, 204; Roundup Ready seeds, 118, 192. *See also* European Glyphosate Taskforce (GTF); International Monsanto Tribunal; pesticide regulation, Sri Lanka and
Monsanto Papers, 82, 191
Movement for Land and Agricultural Reform (MONLAR), 147–48
Mukaveti, Alagiyavanna, xii, 36, 47, 49–50; metaphor and, 47–49, 51; morality and, 44–45; poison and, 44–46, 48–49; Portuguese colonialism and, 44–45; *rasayana* and, 49; Sinhala Buddhism and, 44–45, 49; *Subhāṣitaya* and, xii, 43–45, 48; sui generis metaphor and, 47
Mulleriyawa, Ranjit, 124

Natha Deviyo, 158, 160, 162–63, 167, 185. *See also* Jayasumana, Channa; Senanayake, Priyantha
National Academy of Sciences of Sri Lanka (NASSL), 174
Nietzsche, Friedrich, 88
Noichl, Maria, 105

Organisation for Economic Co-operation and Development (OECD), 8, 84–86

Paracelsus, xi, 37–43, 49–50; biblical story of Creation and, 39; "the dose makes the poison," concept of, 40, 79; Martin Luther and, 40–41; medical toxicology of, 40, 42–43, 50, 67–68; poisoncraft and, 39, 41–43, 50, 60, 66, 68, 70–71, 73–77, 112; poison, theories on, 40–41; political thought, influence on, 42–43; *The Third Defense* and, 39–40; thought of, 38–39. *See also* pesticide regulation, European Union and; Spinoza, Baruch
paraquat, x, xii, 118–19; Goldstein/suicide prevention and, 188, 190–91, 193; Sri Lankan ban (2007), 119
Peradeniya group, 124–27, 134, 140, 155, 163, 174, 182, 188, 193; fluoride, as etiology for CKDu, 124; geologic poisons, as etiology for CKDu, 124; hard water, as etiology for CKDu, 124; mechanistic approach, 126–27; Sirisena glyphosate ban and, 174. *See also* Centre for Education, Research, and Training in Kidney Diseases (CERTKiD)
Peradeniya University, 123–25

240   INDEX

PEST Committee, 64–65, 72–76, 82, 85–86, 90, 94, 103, 210; affect and, 107–8; democracy, definition and meaning of, 105–7, 109; mandate of, 65, 98, 100; science, definition and meaning of, 102–9; science, relationship with politics and, 108–9; solidarian bureaucracy and, 108

Pesticide Registrar (Sri Lanka), 161, 171, 174–75, 187, 194, 196; decision making and, 196

pesticide regulation, European Union and, 61–62, 64, 76; active molecules vs. product formulations, 68–70, 75–77; carcinogenicity and, 70; chemical industry and, 68; EU responsibility and sovereign power, 76–78; European Council Directive 91/414/EEC, 69–70; "Fortress Europe," idea of, 67; hazard vs. risk, 68–76; historical background to, 67–68; industry studies, 81–82; key principles, 69–70; Member States' responsibility, 76–77; molecular bureaucracy and, 15–16, 68–69; open internal borders/free movement and, 76; Paracelsian poisoncraft and, 68–69, 74–76; procedural reviews (2016–2018), 64–65, 72, 81; Regulation (EC) No. 1107/2009, 69–70, 77; social/political angles of, 68; US vs. EU regulatory environments, 58, 87–88, 95; zonal system, 76. See also European Chemicals Agency (ECHA); European Food Safety Authority (EFSA); International Agency for Research on Cancer (IARC); PEST Committee

pesticide regulation, Sri Lanka and, 116, 172, 178, 188, 196; arsenic-based pesticides, ban of, 158; chemical pesticides ban (2021), 177; Monsanto's involvement in, 190–93; pesticide market and, 189. See also glyphosate, Sri Lanka and; Rajapaksa, Gotabaya; Rajapaksa, Mahinda; Sirisena, Maithripala

pesticides, ix–xi, 12, 182; arsenic and, 158–59; chemistry, 57; *kasippu* (illicit liquor) and, x; markets for, 54; paradox of, xi; production of, 7; suicide and, 118, 158; *thelbehet* (lit., "medicine oil," Sinhala term), x, 119; toxicity, 57

Pesticide Technical Advisory Committee (PeTAC, Sri Lanka), 171, 173

Peterle, Alojz, 72, 103–4

pharmakon, xi, 26, 28, 30, 34, 193, 199

poison, x–xii, 3–4, 8, 14–16, 18, 31, 53–54, 111–12, 201–6, 210; anxieties and, 32–34; commensality and, 21, 32–34, 201; cosmogenesis and, 46–47; *duk* (poison), 31; ethnographic record on, 24; femininity and, 25, 31–33, 51; healers and, 26; hierarchy and, 49–50; immobile poisons and, 46; kinship and, 32; knowledge and, 3, 9, 14, 25, 30; meaning and definitions of, 23–25; meta-materiality, 51; mobile poisons and, 27–28, 30, 46; natural poisons and, 46; risk and, 72; self-poisoning and, ix, 32; sovereignty and, xii, 3, 10–12, 53–54, 202; synthetic poisons and, 46; timefulness and, 34–35. See also Bhopal disaster (1984); Chernobyl disaster (1986); gifts; witchcraft

poison control, 3–4, 11, 106, 112, 171, 189; moleculeism and, 68; thresholds, as boundary markers, 11

poisoncraft, xii, 3–4, 8, 10, 14–15, 18, 21, 24, 53–54, 99, 155–56, 200–203, 205–6, 210; allopathic poisoncraft and, 54; Ayurvedic poisoncraft and, 50–51, 54, 203; definition of, 21–22, 35, 53; early modern political thought and, 42–43, 78–79; immunity and, 42, 112, 205; moral concerns/principles and, 27–28; origins of, 24–25; sovereign governance and, 12, 46–47, 49. See also body, biological; body, European; body politic; bureaucracy; chemical sovereignty; chronic kidney disease of unknown etiology (CKDu); European Union (EU); European Union, solidarity and; Paracelsus; pesticide regulation, European Union and; Sri Lanka; Sri Lanka, postwar; Sri Lanka presidency; toxicology

Polonnaruwa, 133*fig.*, 150–52

populism, 6, 164, 166, 178, 199, 203

Portier, Christopher, 80, 83, 86, 93, 95–96

Premadasa, Sajith, 177

Presidential Task Force on CKDu (Sri Lanka), 173, 181, 184–85; 2015 conference on CKDu, 181–85; 2016 consultation on CKDu, 183–85

Rajapaksa, Gotabaya, 145, 156, 161, 170, 177; election of (2019), 177; synthetic fertilizer import ban (2021), 177–78; as warrior king, 180

Rajapaksa, Mahinda, 170–71, 173, 175–79, 181, 193; autochthony and, 179–80; glyphosate ban and, 171–73, 177–78, 193; oligarchy and, 179; as warrior king, 179

Rajapaksa dynasty, 130, 172; concentration of power in, 180–81; corruption and, 175; oligarchy and, 179

Rajarata-Kelaniya group, 123–29, 134, 140, 155–56, 157–63, 181, 187–88, 193, 204; Buddhist nationalism and, 127–28, 168; conspiracy and, 160; Goldstein and, 192; Jayasumana and, 123–24, 145–46, 155–56, 162, 169, 187; mechanistic approach, 126–27; philosophy/politics, 156–58; single poison, as etiology for

INDEX 241

CKDu, 123; Sirisena glyphosate ban and, 174; *veda mahaththaya* (village physicians), CKDu treatments and, 164–65; *visha vedakama* (poison healing), CKDu treatments and, 164–65. *See also* arsenic; de Silva, Nalin; Senanayake, Priyantha
Rajarata University, 2, 123
Ramachandran, S., 146
Rathana, Ven. Athuraliye, 123, 172–73, 177, 184–85
regulatory review, 80–95, 111; harmonization *vs.* standardization, 85, 87–88; ideology and, 106; plagiarism and, 93–95; pro-glyphosate groups and, 105. *See also* Good Laboratory Practice (GLP); Klimisch score
regulatory science (European Union), 12, 16, 61, 79, 81–87, 94; European sovereign power and, 111–12; industry, influence on, 88–89, 94, 96, 102–4, 109; shared European values and, 105; trust and, 89, 204. *See also* Good Laboratory Practice (GLP); Klimisch score; science writing
regulatory science (Sri Lanka), 118, 172
Rice Research and Development Institute (RRDI, Sri Lanka), 161
risk assessment, 69, 72, 83, 85, 90, 95–96, 109, 111, 210; intrinsic hazard *vs.* relational (extrinsic) risk, 74–75; risk = hazard + exposure (concept), 72, 74. *See also* European Food Safety Authority (EFSA); International Agency for Research on Cancer (IARC)
risk management, 58, 61, 71–72, 74, 77, 187; intrinsic hazard/extrinsic risk, 74. *See also* European Food Safety Authority (EFSA); International Agency for Research on Cancer (IARC)
Rivasi, Michèle, 106
Rotterdam Convention, 8

science and technology studies (STS), 165–67
science writing, 18, 79, 81–82, 94, 96, 111
Scientific Revolution, 38
Senanayake, Priyantha, 158–60, 162, 171; de Silva, consultations with, 159, 168; Natha Deviyo, revelations from, 158, 160, 163, 193. *See also* arsenic; Jayasumana, Channa
Senegal, 11
Sheriff, Rizvi, 184–85
Shiva, Vandana, 194
Sinhala (People of the Lion), 143
Sinhala Ravaya (Sinhalese Roar), 144
Sinha Le (Lion's Blood), 144
Siribaddana, Sisira, 123
Sirisena, Maithripala, 2, 170–71, 175–81, 185, 193; autochthony and, 175; CKDu and, 171, 182;

election victory (2015), 173; glyphosate ban, 173–78, 182, 190, 193; Indian Tamils and, 176; Vasa Visa Nathi Ratak (Toxin-Free Nation) program and, 2, 175, 179–80, 183, 190
sociality, 3, 14, 24, 32–33, 81
South Asian Clinical Toxicology Research Collaboration (SACTRC), 190–92
sovereignty, 6–9; crisis of, 205; dynamic nature of, 7; food sovereignty and, 7; graduated/voluminous concepts of, 6; post-ontological sovereignty and, 6; Westphalian concepts of, 6, 9, 127, 204. *See also* body, biological; body, European; body politic; Buddhism; chemical sovereignty; China; European Union (EU); glyphosate, Europe and; glyphosate, Sri Lanka and; poison; Sri Lanka; Sri Lanka, postwar; Sri Lanka presidency
Spinoza, Baruch, 41–42, 60; biblical story of Adam, 42
Sri Lanka, ix, 9–10, 16; agricultural crisis in (2021), 178; British colonialism and, 134, 138–39, 148; cartographic anxieties, 153, 179; chronic kidney disease in, ix–x; civil war in, ix, xii, 6, 134, 137*fig.*, 138, 147, 150, 152, 179, 181, 189, 199–200; Dry Zone and, 117, 147, 150; Easter Sunday suicide bombing (2019), 145, 177; Green Revolution and, 2, 148; islanding and, 134, 138, 140, 142, 175, 180; lion symbolism, importance of, 188–90, 197; migration and, 139; North Central Province (NCP), 122–23, 131, 134, 143; organic agriculture in, 149, 173, 175, 177–78; pesticides in, ix–x, 149, 175, 182; poisoncraft and, 116, 155, 166–70, 190; Portuguese colonialism and, 44–45, 50, 139; postcolonial period and, 18, 131, 134, 138, 140, 142, 147, 150–54, 164, 166, 175; Rajarata ruins, 150–51; saffron-green politics and, 123, 189; science and religion in, 164–65; Sinhala nationalism and, 138–39, 142–43, 145, 150, 153, 156, 164–65, 175, 178–79, 188–89; Sinhala/Tamil communities and, 134, 138, 142–43; Sinhala/Tamil languages and, 134, 138; "sons of the soil" (*bhumiputra*) and, 143; sovereignty and, 11, 175, 189, 201–2; suicide rate in, ix–x, 128, 190, 196; Tamil Muslims and, 139; Tamil nationalism and, 138–39; tea industry in, 139, 171–73, 176, 204; Western Province, 123. *See also* Buddhism, Sinhala; Buddhist nationalism; chronic kidney disease of unknown etiology (CKDu); Liberation Tigers of Tamil Eelam (LTTE); paraquat; Tamil Eelam

Sri Lanka, postwar, 9–10, 18, 131, 181, 200; autochthonous imagery, 144, 148, 153, 175, 179; glyphosate and, 16, 115, 126; island/shore-ringed nation, imaginary of, 130, 139–40, 142–44, 146, 150, 169–70, 175, 179, 200; poisoncraft and, 131, 139, 144, 154, 179, 197, 200; poisonous threats and, 116, 130–31, 139, 144, 169, 180, 182; policy making and, 171–72, 185, 196, 204; purification and, 170, 175, 179–80, 183, 197, 200; Sinhalization/Buddhification of Muslim/LTTE areas, 143, 175; sovereignty and, 139, 144; toxicological anxieties and, 152–54, 179, 200; (re)unification and, 116, 139, 200; Victory Monument (Mullivaikal) and, 143–44, 175, 179–80; water politics and, 142–44. *See also* Buddhism, Sinhala; Rajapaksa, Gotabaya; Rajapaksa, Mahinda; Sirisena, Maithripala; Sri Lanka presidency

Sri Lankan National Science Foundation, 2, 125, 183

Sri Lankan Toxicological Society, 187–88, 192

Sri Lanka presidency, 170, 182, 185, 204; autochthony and, 171, 175, 179–80; Buddhism and, 179–81, 185; divine authority and, 171, 184; executive presidency and, 178–80, 200; ignorance and, 183; impact of glyphosate on election campaigns, 178; poisoncraft and, 170–71, 181, 183; popular sovereignty and, 180, 185; postcolonial development of, 178–79; president-king, idea of, 180, 180n2, 181, 183–86; royal power and, 179–80, 180n1; Sinhala origin myth and, 180. *See also* Rajapaksa, Gotabaya; Rajapaksa, Mahinda; Sirisena, Maithripala

Sri Lanka Society of Nephrology, 183

Stockholm Convention, 8

subhā-ṣitaya (codes for ethical life), 43, 45–46. *See also* Mukaveti, Alagiyavanna; *Suśruta-saṃhitā*

Suśruta, 28, 46–47; Creation and, 46; toxicology and, 46–47, 49. See also *Suśruta-saṃhitā*

Suśruta-saṃhitā, 28, 44, 46–47; *Kalpasthāna* (Section on Procedures) and, 46; poison and, 46

Syngenta, x, 57

Tamil Eelam, 138, 150. *See also* body, Sri Lankan; Liberation Tigers of Tamil Eelam (LTTE)

toxicants, 22–23, 33, 127, 202

toxicity, 14–15, 21, 26, 203; "toxic," emergence of and meanings of term, 22–23; toxic acceleration and, 22–23; uncertainty and, 23. *See also* Age of Toxicity; bureaucracy; glyphosate; pesticides; poison

toxicology, xi–xiii, 3, 10–14, 25, 35, 54, 156, 190–92, 202, 205, 210; allopathic traditions of, 15, 26, 53; ancient world and, 33; Ayurvedic traditions of, xi, 15, 46, 50, 53; Indian toxicology and, 28; mechanistic/complexity frames, 127; medical toxicology and, 25, 36; modern toxicology and, 25–26, 28; nationalism and, 10–12; origins of, 24–26; poisoncraft and, 35; public health and, 33; regulatory toxicology, 67, 78, 192; sovereign governance and, 46–47. *See also* Paracelsus; Sri Lanka, postwar; Suśruta

Udalagama, Tharindi, ix–xi
Ukraine, 10–11
UN Food and Agriculture Organization (FAO), 160
United Kingdom, xii, 6
United Nations Environment Programme (UNEP), 8
University College Colombo (UCC), 125
University of Colombo, ix
Url, Bernhard, 86, 107

Waidyanatha, Parakrama, 174
Weber, Max, 78–79
Weber, Stefan, 94
Wickramasinghe, Ranil, 178
Wickramasinghe, Upul, xii, 122
Wijewardena, Chinthaka, 174
Wimalawansa, Shehani, 125
Wimalawansa, Sunil, 122, 125, 152
witchcraft, 3, 13, 21, 23, 31–33, 53, 202
World Bank, 11, 144, 148
World Health Organization (WHO), xi, 120, 125, 162, 173, 183

Founded in 1893,
UNIVERSITY OF CALIFORNIA PRESS
publishes bold, progressive books and journals
on topics in the arts, humanities, social sciences,
and natural sciences—with a focus on social
justice issues—that inspire thought and action
among readers worldwide.

The UC PRESS FOUNDATION
raises funds to uphold the press's vital role
as an independent, nonprofit publisher, and
receives philanthropic support from a wide
range of individuals and institutions—and from
committed readers like you. To learn more, visit
ucpress.edu/supportus.

www.ingramcontent.com/pod-product-compliance
Lightning Source LLC
Chambersburg PA
CBHW020535030426
42337CB00013B/864